ANTHROPOLOGICAL FILMMAKING

VISUAL ANTHROPOLOGY
A series of books edited by Jay Ruby, The Center for Visual
Communication, Mifflintown, Pennsylvania

Volume 1   ANTHROPOLOGICAL FILMMAKING
           Anthropological Perspectives on the Production
           of Film and Video for General Public Audiences
           Edited by Jack R. Rollwagen

Volume 2   MIDDLETOWN
           The Making of a Documentary Film Series
           Dwight W. Hoover

Additional volume in preparation

Volume 3   THE FILMS OF JOHN MARSHALL
           Edited by Jay Ruby

ANTHROPOLOGICAL FILMMAKING

Anthropological Perspectives on the Production of Film and Video for General Public Audiences

Edited by

Jack R. Rollwagen
State University of New York, Brockport

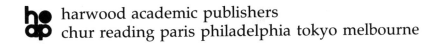
harwood academic publishers
chur reading paris philadelphia tokyo melbourne

Copyright © 1988 by Harwood Academic Publishers GmbH, Poststrasse 22, 7000 Chur, Switzerland. All rights reserved.

Published 1988
Third Printing 1992

Harwood Academic Publishers

Post Office Box 90
Reading, Berkshire RG1 8JL
United Kingdom

58, rue Lhomond
75005 Paris
France

5301 Tacony Street, Drawer 330
Philadelphia, Pennsylvania 19137
United States of America

3-14-9, Okubo
Shinjuku-ku, Tokyo 169
Japan

Private Bag 8
Camberwell, Victoria 3124
Australia

Library of Congress Cataloging-in-Publication Data
Anthropological filmmaking.
  (Visual anthropology, ISSN 0897-1463; v. 1)
  Includes index.
  1. Motion pictures in ethnology.   2. Ethnology—
Methodology   I. Rollwagen, Jack R.   II. Series.
GN347.A58   1988   306'.0208   88-6834
ISBN 3-7186-0478-7

Cover photo reproduced courtesy of Asen Balikci.

CONTENTS

INTRODUCTION TO THE SERIES

VISUAL ANTHROPOLOGY is a book series devoted to the illumination of the human condition through a systematic examination of all that is made to be seen. It is our intention to demonstrate the value of an anthropological approach to the study of the visual and pictorial world. We intend to present ethnographic studies of the cultural complexities of pictorial media production, analyses of the visible world of non-verbal communication from micro-studies of body movement to macro-views of the built environment, and unique attempts to communicate an anthropological understanding through pictorial means. The result will be a deepening of our knowledge of how visual and pictorial communication functions in our quest to make meaning.

Jay Ruby

Introduction

Jack R. Rollwagen
Department of Anthropology
SUNY College at Brockport

The anthropological filmmaker, just like the ethnographer, must be content to present something about a dynamic process at a particular moment in time regardless of the fact that all of the variables are constantly in flux. Tribal peoples are vanishing. Anthropological interests and perspectives have changed greatly during the century of the evolution of the discipline. The 16mm equipment that made ethnographic film a reality in the period following World War II is now sharing the technological arena with new advances in technology (video camcorders and microcomputers for editing, for example) which allow many more filmmakers to explore the possibilities of preparing visual documents which reflect their own interests and perspectives.[1]

The purpose of this work is to make available a collection of articles by individuals who are both anthropologists and filmmakers. Most of the earlier works available to readers interested in anthropological filmmaking are either books or articles authored by a single individual (which results in only one individual's perspective) or collections of articles in which a large proportion of the authors are not anthropologists (which is not particularly helpful to one who wishes to understand how anthropologists make films). It is my belief, and it was that belief which led me to the editing of this book, that the understandings which anthropologists have who wish to make films are quite different from the understandings of non-anthropologists who wish to make films. It was my conclusion that much of the material that is available to guide the anthropologist who wishes to begin an exploration of filmmaking is of little value simply because the conceptual framework which non-anthropologists bring to filmmaking is not sophisticated in those areas which anthropologists guide anthropological filmmaking. I hasten to add that this does not imply that non-anthropologist filmmakers are not sophisticated in their own frameworks. But simply that the anthropological framework (which is what makes what anthropologists do "anthropological" film) makes different demands on the anthropologist, demands that may not be considered "important" or even "relevant" to non-anthropologists. The preceding statement, complicated as it may be, is not intended to suggest that anthropologists who make films will all make films alike or out of a common conceptual framework. The very works in this edited volume will attest to that. Anthropology, like any academic discipline, has its own diversity, its own opposing points of view, and an evolutionary process which constantly introduces new conceptual tools and positions. Thus, the perspectives, conceptual tools, theories, arguments, and practices of earlier anthropology exist as a set of ancestors for the guidance of contemporary anthropologists. And, like any other practice, anthropologists draw upon the perspectives, conceptual tools, theories, arguments, and practices of non-anthropologists and in adopting them adapt them to make them their own.

In most contemporary discussions of anthropological filmmaking, the assumption is that the "filmmaking" is for research purposes or that the audience for the film will be classroom audiences (particularly classrooms in which anthropologists will be present to "interpret" the film). By contrast, the specific purpose of soliciting the articles in this edited book was to bring together a collection of articles on anthropological filmmaking in which the authors discuss the processes and problems in making anthropological films for general public audiences, whatever the ultimate mechanism of distribution. Thus, one theme which is explored in this book is the problem of communication. In this case, the "communication" problem is (1) how to present the conclusions that a particular anthropologist has arrived at in the course of many months of fieldwork to an audience which has not had the benefit of the same amount of time in the field; and (2) how to present something about the nature of the cultural systems of the subjects of the film to that audience. In the first instance, the focus is upon the "anthropologist as interpreter"; in the second stance, the focus is upon the people who are the subjects of the anthropological film. This problem of "conceptualization, translation, and communication" lies at the center of "anthropological" filmmaking, since it demands that the person who does the anthropological filmmaking understand the nature of the distortion that he/she as "filter" is.

A second theme that runs through this book is the concern with the audiences who are the "consumers" of the final product. Because of the expense of making 16mm film (the cost of equipment and film stock, of mounting expeditions into often remote areas of the world, post-production expenses, release time to edit, distribution of the final product and other concerns too numerous to mention) the number of "films" by anthropologist/filmmakers in the past that eventually reached general audiences of any kind were relatively small in proportion even to those kind of documentaries which most general audiences would conclude were "anthropological" in nature. Thus, when most people watch programs on television about the last of the world's tribal peoples or about field studies of primates or about small farmers in Latin America they are not particularly concerned with the credentials of the filmmaker. Rather, they are concerned with how interesting the program is, how "valuable" it is to them, and whether it increases their insight into the lives and concerns of other human beings. "Good" films have a depth of understanding and a way of presentation which allows individuals of varying levels of sophistication to appreciate them all at the same time.

A third theme in this book is diversity; diversity of subject matter, diversity of approach, and diversity of experience. Anthropologists only rarely conduct research on the very same people that other anthropologists have studied. Anthropologists exploring the same conceptual subject matter approach it differently and may choose to examine contrastive populations than other anthropologists have studied precisely because it allows comparisons. Anthropologists who wish to make films may do so for a variety of reasons, may experience quite different filmmaking experiences, and may have a variety of conclusions about their experiences. The articles in this book explore not only a wide variety of geographically diverse populations, but also a variety of quite diverse experiences and conclusions about the process of filmmaking.

A fourth theme is the concern that anthropologists as participants in a filmmaking endeavor have is the degree of control that they exercise over the final product. Frequently, because of the nature of production and distribution, anthropologists have less control over the process than they might wish. Anthropologists are sometimes employed by production companies before any footage is shot, during the shooting, or even in the post-production period to work on the narrative. In other cases, anthropologists may be one of a "team" in which the other member of the "team" is the "filmmaker." In yet other cases, anthropologists who have had complete control over the production of their film frequently encounter events in the post-production and distribution process which introduce non-anthropological concerns into the final product. This may result in films which present subjects, events, and processes in ways other than that which the anthropologist might wish. Conversely, because of the increasing sophistication of the subjects themselves, anthropologists increasingly find that they may be required to conceptualize the film from the point of view of their subjects, a process that has its own problems.

A fifth theme represented in the book is the context in which anthropological filmmaking proceeds. Massive social forces, some of long duration (like the transformation of the world by capitalism since the 1500s) and some of more recent venue (such as the impact of the feminism of the 1970s on anthropology), are reflected in the subject matters of the films produced by anthropologists and in the writings about those films. In earlier years, anthropologists were very concerned with what is sometimes called "salvage ethnography," the recording of film footage about almost any aspect of the way of life of the remaining tribal peoples, or other peoples whose stable cultural patterns were disappearing. More recently, anthropologists have turned to the examination of the very changes that represented the departure from the stable cultural systems which they had hoped to record in earlier times. Ethnographic studies, the major intent of which is to record "actuality," and ethnological studies, the major intent of which is to explain and interpret, exist side by side. The impact of political economic perspectives on anthropology in recent years has led to the presentation of cultural systems in ways that might seem unfamiliar to earlier anthropologists. Similarly, to those who were accustomed to an anthropology dominated by a male gender bias, the feminist perspectives evolved in the 1970s, particularly the radical feminist perspectives, represent a major departure from previous studies. Yet each of these perspectives in anthropology and in anthropological filmmaking reflect processes and context much larger than anthropology itself.

A sixth theme is that of the experiences of the anthropologist as he/she sets about filmmaking. This edited book contains a variety of experiences by 20 anthropologists in places both exotic and ordinary, remote and nearby. The problems that these anthropologists encountered in conducting fieldwork and in the filmmaking process serve to suggest how different the anthropological filmmaker's concerns are than those of other filmmakers. It is not unusual in the accounts contained herein for the fieldwork on which a film is based to take two or more years. The insights from such an involvement prove very enlightening, shattering those first impressions that investigators with shorter stays in the field might have. For anthropologists, any fieldwork is enlightening, but the introduction of a camera into a fieldwork situation often brings up issues that would not arise otherwise. Film is a more public media than books, both in the making and in the "telling." Films are often made in a public arena, while written ethnography frequently occurs in a more private space. Films are mostly seen by audiences collectively while books are mostly read by individuals independently. What might not be objectionable if written is frequently a cause for distress to those filmed when it becomes available on film. Conversely, with the increasing availability of both programming and inexpensive recording equipment, the sophistication of those who are the focus of anthropological attention has risen dramatically in recent years. Increasingly, anthropologists find themselves in the midst of a veritable gaggle of "native" filmmakers each of whom is intent upon his or her own recording of the same event that is the concern of the anthropologist. In such a context, the anthropological filmmaker becomes a somewhat different kind of beast, a fellow photographer with whom one can discuss technical problems and solutions. As in many other cases, anthropologists often find that the understandings of the "natives" are valuable and insightful.

One of the current controversies within anthropology serves to bring to the fore a seventh theme for the book. In the past, anthropologists perceived themselves as writing about and recording on film something that seemed to many of them as "objective reality" (although no one would be comfortable in actually saying that). In recent years, under the impact of the symbolic anthropologist and others, anthropologists are more likely to assume that there are at least three interpretations going on in any communication: the interpretation of the individual participant in a cultural system being studied, the interpretation of the anthropologist, and the interpretation of the reader of the written work or the viewer of the anthropological film. In that sense, cameras (and the films produced by them) are but the tools of the filmmaker who uses them. Thus, in a most important sense, films represent what the filmmaker thinks more than they represent "reality" or "actuality." What cultural actuality is and how one goes about making an anthropologically "sophisticated" film is central to the discussion of a number of authors in this work.

NOTE

1 "Film" in this introduction and in the book as a whole, refers to works produced either on "film" or on video tape. Similarly, "filmmaking" refers to the process in which either medium is used. This understanding is conventional (see Rabiger 1987:3)

REFERENCE CITED

Rabiger, Michael (1987). Directing the Documentary. Boston: Focal Press.

Collaboration In Ethnographic Filmmaking: A Personal View

Timothy Asch
Center for Visual Anthropology
University of Southern California

ABSTRACT: In summary, collaboration depends for its success on common goals. Ethnographic film can only become a productive tool for anthropologists if they can influence the creation of a film at every stage from planning to filming to editing. If anthropologists come to consider ethnographic film as data, as valid texts for research, rather than (or at least as well as) simply entertainment, then their commitment will be greater than it has been in the past, and they will seek better conditions for collaboration on a project involving film.

A unified effort is necessary to protect the rights of anthropologists and of people filmed, rights guaranteeing access to footage and determining in large part the content of that footage. But this effort will only be forthcoming when anthropologists recognize the value of ethnographic film. Recognition depends on publishing integrated film and written materials that prove valuable for instruction and research. The problem is at the moment, a circular one.

This paper is divided into two sections: a discussion of what collaboration entails if one's primary interest is the use of film in ethnographic research or the production of films for anthropological instruction; and a shorter section on collaboration between anthropologists and television producers.[1]

A. Anthropologists and Filmmakers

1. Film as a Research Tool:

Film making is both arduous and expensive. Each year thousands of dollars are spent making what is called ethnographic film, much of which

1

has little or no ethnographic value. Generally speaking, anthropologists have shown little interest in the potential use of ethnographic film. The indifference of the profession is a reflection of the lack of scholarly resources in which film has been integrated with written materials and of the lack of projects in which film has been used as a research tool. I suggest this is because an appropriate methodology for using film in research has not been developed. At the heart of any such methodology must be effective strategies for collaboration between anthropologists and filmmakers, strategies that increase the depth and quality of anthropological research.

The data on which the field of anthropology relies come from ethnographic recording. At first, data were recorded in writing. When tape recorders and still cameras became available some anthropologists used them as additional recording tools. With 16mm and super-8mm cameras and portable video-tape equipment, more options are now available. Of central consideration in choosing among techniques is the type of data required and how best to get them. Audio-visual technology is most effective when applied in research that is facilitated by repeated viewing of unique events. It can also be used to present research findings and to elicit new information from informants.

For social anthropologists ethnographic films are analogous to linguists' field recordings. Just as linguistic "texts" are often transcriptions of recordings, so we might think of sound-synchronous films (plus transcriptions and annotations of recorded speech and images) as comprising anthropological texts derived from ethnographic film records. Such texts are renditions of recorded events filtered through an observer or analyst. By considering ethnographic film as texts I emphasize this feature, as well as the fact that film, like all texts, can be shared with others. Implicit is the notion that a text, whatever its content, is selected in relation to a research objective, is suitable for analysis and is as accurate a rendition of an utterance or action as the analyst can make. This may seem obvious, but most ethnographic film has been and still is being taken to tell a scripted story; it is not taken to create a text. I want to emphasize this point because it has a serious bearing on the nature of appropriate ethnographic film collaboration.

Current technology permits the production of excellent research material with small-format, audio-visual equipment: video-tape or super-8mm film. Both these methods require only one operator (but can be used more effectively if two people collaborate, one recording sound, the other picture). The quality of such recordings is adequate for seminars, but 16mm remains the preferred standard for projection and therefore for films, intended for commercial distribution. The resolution is much higher and permits larger-screen projection and finer analysis of images for research; and the industry is geared for 16mm production. With rare exceptions, at least two people are required for 16mm filming: one to operate the camera and one the tape recorder.[2] For all these reasons I shall concentrate primarily on 16mm filming in discussing collaboration.

The most common collaboration is between a filmmaker, who photographs, and an anthropologist, who records sound. Since effective use of a 16mm camera requires more experience than does adequate sound recording,[3] and since filming restricts one's view of an event more than sound recording does, I shall refer to the filmmaker as photographer and the anthropologist as sound recordist. However, most of my remarks are valid if the roles are reversed.

Ordinarily an ethnographic filmmaker is so concerned with making film form and film sense out of the images seen through the viewfinder that it is very difficult to see the larger field of social interaction that may be affecting the subjects being filmed. Whenever possible, it is the anthropologist's job to try to provide a broader context for the filmmaker. When filming behaviour, continuity cannot be maintained unless the filmmaker can predict what is going to happen next--not necessarily the content of an interaction, but the direction in which people will move and who is likely to interact with whom. The anthropologist, if he or she has been in the field for months or years, speaks the language and knows the individuals who are being filmed, is in a better position to predict behaviour than is the filmmaker. Furthermore, it is the anthropologist who should be able to identify significant events or interactions and draw the filmmaker's attention to them.

In theory, events have beginnings, consist of sequential progressions, and have endings which are determined by the participants. In filming, however, it is not always possible to determine when an event begins or when it ends, nor is it possible to decide precisely when the camera should be turned on. While the continuity of social interaction can be more or less maintained with film, the filmmaker must still consider carefully the problems of "bounding" inherent in describing any social event. Observer and subjects may differ greatly in their perceptions of when an event or interaction begins and ends and whom it includes.

Selecting when and what to film is a subjective decision.[4] But, once having begun, the people being filmed are likely to convey more about themselves if each shot is held as long as possible and follows their interactions. Continuity, as an aim in ethnographic filming, ideally means continuous filming of a subject-bounded event. In order to follow action continuously the filmmaker must have as clear an idea as possible of what people are going to do. Guidance by the anthropologist is invaluable.

2. Collaboration:

It is important to distinguish between two types of collaboration: a collaboration among equals, that is, between people who share equal responsibility for the outcome of the project; and a collaboration between people who are not equal, that is, in which one party is being hired to perform a specific function, such as when an anthropologist serves as an ethnographic consultant for a filmmaker or when a filmmaker serves as a technician for an anthropologist. In either case, parties should be clear about which type of collaboration they are undertaking. I shall focus on collaboration between equals because I feel it is the one most likely to produce valuable results.

A starting point in any film collaboration is the question: Why use film? If it is to create a research text, then the goals are very different from those of a television programme and the responsibilities of the participants will differ. However, during filming the respective goals need not dictate very different strategies: a method of filming that permits flexible use of the resulting footage can be employed. Such a method places emphasis on obtaining research footage.

By focusing on the actions of a few people engaged in activities relevant to the research of the anthropologist, and by leaving the camera running for long uninterrupted periods, the resulting footage is likely to be valuable for research. With the addition of a few distant location shots and some cut-aways,[5] as well as a few rolls of film related to a script, the footage should be equally valuable as a resource for editing film for instruction or for television. In other words, films with different purposes can be made from the same footage, if that footage is taken with research needs in mind.

Whether one is interested in film for research or for instruction, I suggest that a collaborative project should be considered first and foremost as an ethnographic investigation. Those involved must discuss at each step what technique best facilitates this investigation. At times it might be more appropriate to make stereo-sound recordings or a slide-tape[6] than to film.

When I was working with Douglas Lewis and Patsy Asch on Flores, in eastern Indonesia, we were fortunate to have a variety of audio-visual equipment. We had thought it might be possible to video-tape certain events while we were filming in order to get immediate participant feedback related to our footage; but we soon found that whenever we used 16mm sound-synchronous film in such a mountainous area the logistics demanded all our energy. However, I discovered that many of the interactions Lewis wanted to film were fairly static conversations or ritual chanting that could be recorded as slide-tapes. The action seemed highly repetitive, small details were significant, and the viewer might learn more about Lewis's research by concentrating on a few still images than on moving film. Moreover, since these exchanges were often very long, filming would have been extremely expensive (slide-tapes are approximately 1/30th of the cost of 16mm film). As our fieldwork progressed we continually discussed what we should record and how best to do it in order to produce the best research document. Sometimes it seemed advisable to use the video-tape recorder, particularly if subjects were poorly lit and it was awkward to use lights (our video camera required minimal lighting),[7] or if Lewis felt that by careful examination of video-tape with participants he would learn more than by waiting to analyze film after leaving the field. At other times, recording myths for example, it seemed wisest to concentrate on getting uninterrupted stereo-sound recordings. Certainly the experience of studying both our video and our stereo tapes helped prepare us to film other events with greater sensitivity.

Whether three people should collaborate at all is a difficult decision that depends on circumstances. Each person added to a team further disturbs the delicate social relationships that are being observed and filmed. One person can live unobtrusively almost anywhere; people usually accept an outsider and make allowances for ignorance, and they are usually as interested in studying the foreigner as the foreigner is in studying them. After living in a community and learning the local language, a fieldworker can invite in a second person as a guest, a friend. But three people are often too many to feed and take care of. And three can be a difficult number in other respects as well: two may unite, or appear to, against the third. At different times I have been part of collaborative teams of two and of three members, often in the same geographic area. These experiences have convinced me that where possible the team should be limited to two, with the anthropologist taking sound as well as guiding the filmmaker. If the focus of a project is a dramatic event that absorbs the attention of the participants, and if the work is too exhausting for two, then a team of three or more may be justified.

An excellent example was when three of us--Lewis (anthropologist), Patsy Asch (sound recordist) and I (filmmaker)--filmed a lengthy ceremony on Flores. Lewis, during two years of previous fieldwork, had never observed this type of inter-clan ceremony because it had not been performed for twenty years. Since people were either reluctant or unable to describe, before the event, what would happen, Lewis needed to concentrate on trying to make sense of what we observed in order to guide our filming and later to analyze the data.[8] During periods of intense action, when filming was almost continuous, Lewis occasionally had to record sound, relieving Patsy Asch so that she could reload magazines, label film and sound rolls, and keep track of equipment. At night Lewis was also required to operate the lights and batteries so that we could move around the large forest clearing in which the rituals were being performed. In this situation we certainly needed three people; and to hundreds of people participating in a dramatic event, whether there were two foreigners or three made little difference.

In contrast, when I worked among the Yanomamo Indians of Venezuela with a team of only two I felt it was easier than when I worked with three, although Yanomamo villages seemed to absorb three people as easily as two. The Yanomamo live in circular villages. The rear walls of their houses form a continuous stockade; there are no internal walls dividing nuclear families one from another, and the covered circular living space is open to a large central clearing. Our hammocks were added to the chain of over 200 that circled the village. The difficulties we met were largely of our own making. As three of us tried to adjust to each other and to a highly challenging situation, tensions arose.

The first time Linda Connor and I filmed a Balinese traditional healer, a spirit medium who lived in an isolated hamlet, three people would have been awkward. We were filming interactions between a few people in cramped settings, we were dependent on the hospitality of the healer, and I was a stranger. Connor recorded sound while I filmed, loaded magazines and handled lights. Two years later, when we returned to record people's reaction to our earlier footage, Patsy Asch accompanied us as sound recordist. On that occasion a team of three was not awkward. The major difference was that I was no longer a stranger and that by holding public showings of our footage of the hamlet's collective cremation ceremonies the purpose of our being there was made clear to everyone. When we filmed a healing session Connor again recorded sound because, although less experienced, she could follow and participate in the Balinese discussion; she became one of the subjects of the film as well as sound recordist. Linguistic competence is a great asset when recording conversation is of prime importance, even though it may mean sacrificing some sound quality for comprehension of speech.

In making decisions about the size and composition of a team it is important to consider the compatibility of all prospective members during all phases of production, including fieldwork. Availability of financing may also be a factor, as well as the types of interactions to be filmed. One must take into account the number of participants, the predictability of events, reactions of people to being filmed, and possible restrictions on who may be present. Gender is often an issue in fieldwork, not least in filming. In Afghanistan, Patsy Asch and Pam Hunte were able to film women's domestic activities long before I was; but, because she was a woman, Patsy was prohibited from attending one of the rituals in Flores. In choosing a team, therefore, the purpose of filming must be taken into account. One must also be aware that one cannot negate one's gender. A team of two men filming the Yanomamo, for example, are bound to make films that reflect a male perspective. To overcome male bias in ethnographic film (as prevalent there as in written ethnography) we need to train more female anthropologists and filmmakers, not to pretend such bias does not exist. Relationships with people being filmed are often easier if a team includes at least one woman and one man.

Chance can play an important part in collaboration. Funding, personnel and opportunity have to come together at the same time. My involvement in the Yanomamo film project is a case in point. A human geneticist, James V. Neel, wanted a record of his fieldwork techniques; the anthropologist Napoleon Chagnon phoned Asen Balikci in Montreal to ask if he could recommend a filmmaker. Balikci suggested Chagnon telephone me. In describing Yanomamo feasting to me, Chagnon referred to Mauss's THE GIFT, a book I had been discussing with my students at Brandeis University. I was convinced that it would be worth any hardship to demonstrate that film of social interaction could be used to illustrate an important anthropological concept, so I agreed to collaborate on the project as an opportunity to persuade the university to buy the camera he wanted. The concurrence of these events transformed a plan to make a simple 2000-ft record using a small Bolex camera into a major 12,000-foot ethnographic film project using a professional, sound-synchronous Arriflex camera.

The participants in any successful film collaboration must have appropriate training and experience. The anthropologist must have done enough fieldwork to identify a need for the use of film, and must understand the local language and know members of the community well enough to impose upon them the added burden of the filmmaker and his equipment. Before commencing a project it is essential to talk with the people one wants to film and to obtain their permission. In most cases the anthropologist is responsible for the logistics of working and living within the community, being in a position to arrange for housing and supplies and probably more experienced in applying for visas, travel and work permits. The anthropologist may provide ethnographic and linguistic training for the filmmaker and perhaps make available field notes and relevant publications.[9]

The filmmaker has to be experienced enough to select, handle and maintain the appropriate equipment.[10] All equipment which is to be used together must be tested together. Before leaving for Flores we had our Nagra tape recorder, a machine we had used on several expeditions, cleaned and checked. We tested it with our omnidirectional microphone before leaving Australia, but it was not until we reached Flores that we discovered that the technician in Canberra had altered the input for the directional microphone and it was consequently not receiving enough power. Fortunately I was able to rewire the recorder. In a remote village in Afghanistan we lost a couple of days trying to get a wooden case made for my camera so that it could be carried safely by camel, protected from the penetrating dust and yet immediately available for use. The case provided for the camera, an Eclair which I had never used before, made it necessary to take the camera apart each time it was packed or unpacked.

3. Preparation for Fieldwork:

Before leaving for the field the filmmaker and the anthropologist should shoot several short sequences in varied conditions that simulate the expected field situation. This experience is important for the acquisition of technical skill: the anthropologist must learn to handle the tape recorder effectively and efficiently, to monitor sound, and to learn what recording quality is satisfactory. Simulated lighting and sound conditions will help the filmmaker test the compatibility and appropriateness of all the equipment. Even if not intending to record sound, the anthropologist should take part in such tests and learn to handle the tape recorder in case of emergency. Trial filming is

also the best way for collaborators to learn to communicate with one another in filming situations. By working in a setting in which there is minimal stress, where a scene can be repeated or filming can stop for discussion
about options, people are free to experiment, to begin to learn about one
another, and to respect differences in perspective. For example, filming often conflicts with sound recording: a distant, wide-angle view means action
is placed in a broader context, but the closer the microphone the greater the
clarity of sound; lighting may be best from one angle, sound from another;
and respect for the desires of the people being filmed may dictate the choice
of a third location. An introduction to these problems and potential conflicts
should come well before a critical moment in filming.

It is only by synchronizing sound and picture and trying to edit short
sequences of interaction on film (such as a child being left by its father at a
day-care centre, members of a family co-ordinating their actions so that they
come together at the dinner table, or a game of pool at a pub) that one can
judge the effectiveness of one's technique. The anthropologist, in particular,
learns something about the nature of filmmaking and gets a more realistic
idea of the technical limitations, possibilities and time involved in working
with film. Making these sequences is a brief course in social relations as
well as in the acquisition of the necessary skills, and is well worth the cost.

Time spent, before going into the field, in discussing exactly what kind
of film you want and for what purpose is never wasted. People intending to
collaborate would benefit from looking together at a variety of films (not
necessarily finished products) and discussing the range of options.

When we first collaborated, Chagnon had a latent idea about the kind of
film he wanted to make, whereas I knew exactly what kind of film I wanted
to make. I had seen several filmmakers come back from the field with up to
60,000 feet of film and then edit a 2000-foot film. The waste of the
remaining footage seemed to me to be a tremendous loss. I had been influenced by the models for research film of Richard Sorenson and Carlton Gajdusek, and by John Marshall's ideas about filming events in detail with sequences of social interaction. I was excited about exploring a methodology
based on sequence filming, the creation of research films and then of
instructional films with synchronous sound and subtitles. I had been strug-
gling to use existing films for teaching and wanted materials in which
theoretical and ethnographic writings could be integrated with film.

As we worked together it became clear that Chagnon wanted to make
self-contained, didactic films. It was as though he were writing a lecture on
film. The differences between his goals and mine were not apparent in the
field. If events are filmed in detail one can make highly scripted film or sequences of interactions; the argument only arises in the editing room.

When we were filming Yanomamo it seemed appropriate to have
Chagnon select the focus, choosing both events and individuals he felt
would best illustrate aspects of Yanomamo society that interested him. We
had agreed, even before we met, that our first film would be about

Yanomamo feasting (the illustration of Mauss's THE GIFT). On our second trip we continued to focus on events of interest to Chagnon but I thought it important to get additional coverage, particularly of women's and children's activities. I was influenced by remarks such as Margaret Mead's: "If Yanomamo are so fierce, it is important to know how individuals get to be that way." We had lots of footage of Yanomamo displaying fierce behaviour, but I thought we should also show gentler domestic interactions. I have found that film images often lead to generalizations. If people only see film of violent behaviour then many assume that violence is the only behaviour typical of Yanomamo. We did film domestic sequences (see A MAN AND HIS WIFE WEAVE A HAMMOCK, A FATHER WASHES HIS CHILDREN, DEDEHEIWA WEEDS HIS GARDEN), but on some occasions Chagnon was bitter because he felt I was wasting our film. Since we had not reached agreement, he did not document all the interactions I filmed. In SAND PLAY, for example, we do not know what fantasies children are acting out: capturing women? holding feasts? destroying villages? simply sand play? Many anthropologists have been fascinated by this detailed footage but they are frustrated by the lack of accompanying information.[11] A filmmaker working with an anthropologist must be prepared to concentrate on the particular research of that anthropologist and accept, to some degree, the anthropologist's judgement about priorities; yet decisions must be mutual or they will be only partially executed. Compromise is always required. When Chagnon and I edited films together we compromised, which usually meant alternating (editing a film one of us wanted, then a film the other wanted) a principle we extended to alternating the sequence of our names on the credits.

4. A Contract

It may be advisable to write a contract, not so much to have a legally binding agreement (because it is the spirit and not the letter of a contract that will produce useful results) but because in writing a contract, in trying to reach agreement and plan for all contingencies, many problems become evident and some can be avoided. This can be a first step towards discovering whether a partnership is feasible.

In several cases where I have not had a contract I have been disappointed in aspects of a collaboration; things I thought had been agreed upon, things I perhaps took for granted, were not important to the other person. For instance, I feel it is very important to be in the field for a minimum of three months and was shocked when it turned out that one of my colleagues only intended to stay two weeks. Again, I have always felt that instructional films should be accompanied by written materials, but when it actually came to writing study guides for films a number of my colleagues have not co-operated, nor have they welcomed the idea of my doing the writing.

The following are some of the points that should be considered in writing a contract:

(a) a definition of the aims and goals of the project;

(b) an outline of the type of footage to be collected and its intended use;

(c) an outline of the responsibilities and duties of each member of the team during all phases of the project, including a commitment to complete all agreed-upon materials;

(d) agreement on how much time each party will spend on each phase of the project: preparation, fieldwork, production;

(e) clarification of ownership, copyright and credits;

(f) clarification of financial responsibilities;

(g) a clause outlining procedures for amending the contract or ending the collaboration.

In writing grant proposals many of the same issues are considered. However, since proposals are usually written by one of the parties only, and since they are written with the requirements of the granting agency in mind, they do not necessarily reflect the full intentions of those collaborating. A proposal does not take the place of a contract, although in the past I have naively assumed it did.

5. Recurring Problems:

There are a number of recurring problems that are perhaps inherent in ethnographic film collaboration.

1. The goals of the participants may differ radically, whether they are aware of this or not.

2. An anthropologist who knows a language and society well, who had been adopted by a group, often resents it when the filmmaker comes along and wants to be given hard-earned knowledge and contacts. Likewise, an experienced filmmaker may feel resentment when the anthropologist, with neither training nor experience, sees himself as an instant film producer.

3. Fieldwork isolates people from their own culture and places them in an unknown or unfamiliar setting. The anthropologist is likely to be concerned about what the filmmaker may do and faces potential embarrassment for everyone should the filmmaker's behaviour be socially inappropriate. Any newcomer (particularly one who has to do a conspicuous job such as filming) is likely to transgress, and even subtle mistakes can create problems. The greater the pressure to film immediately on arrival the greater the likelihood of mistakes. During my first trip to Roti I made several. Perhaps my

greatest error was trying to climb a lontar palm in order to prepare to film lontar tapping. I have climbed trees frequently in order to film and felt perfectly confident, but the Rotinese did not share my confidence. One night, after being caught practising at dusk, I was told that unless I promised never to climb again I would have to leave because they could not accept responsibility for my safety. We sealed the agreement with several glasses of lontar gin.

The tensions created by attempting to adopt new behaviour patterns so as not to offend people can put strain on more familiar, taken-for-granted relationships such as that between anthropologist and filmmaker.

4. During filming the anthropologist may feel he or she has no influence because there is no way of knowing exactly what the filmmaker is seeing through his lens. Filming is a selective process: the framing, duration and focus of each image is controlled by the filmmaker, and in the end the anthropologist's role can only be an advisory one or one of interference. This is why mutual trust and an understanding of the anthropologists's research goals must be established early in a collaboration.

5. A perennial problem for a filmmaker without experience in the community being studied is that of language. Not knowing the language of the local community can create frustration, both for the filmmaker desperate to understand and for the anthropologist exhausted from interpreting in both directions.

6. Since people's habits and inclinations, as well as their job requirements, may well differ, living arrangements in the field must reflect these differences.

7. Periods of inaction, particularly for the filmmaker, interspersed with intense filming, often at the expense of sleep, can make any one of us edgy. Anger in a field situation (as Jean Briggs illustrates so clearly in her book, NEVER IN ANGER) can be damaging when the anger of foreigners is felt to be frightening. Even the Yanomamo, infamous as "the fierce people," were extremely upset when Craig Johnson and I argued. One of the headmen came up to me and took my hand, begging me not to speak any more. Certainly there is no place for anger during filming. Let me give an illustration from Flores.

We were in the midst of filming a large, confusing ceremony and had been working for over a week with little respite. It was the final night, there would be no sleep, and we had to be ready to film continuously. As dusk came on, each of the groups representing different houses in the valley decorated their animals and prepared for their grand entrance into the ritual grove. Each group came in separately, dancing and screaming out of the blackness and into our lights; huge pigs and goats swayed above the heads of their bearers, who paraded them around the central altar. As we could not afford to film every group, we wanted to wait for those groups we knew best. As it grew darker it became difficult to identify people, so I asked Lewis to go out and see which group was coming next. He came back shortly saying there was no way he could tell who was who among the hundreds milling around in the darkness and we would just have to sit and wait. I was furious, because I knew I could only film an entrance properly if I were prepared. I thought I had made a simple and necessary request and that Lewis was being unco-operative. But he had even more difficulty seeing under those conditions than I did; he could not recognize people. He felt very uncomfortable, as we all do when we find we cannot rely fully on our senses. I stormed out to get the information myself but, although I did find the people I wanted, my anger interfered with filming and as a consequence I missed their entrance. The next day I realized I had put Lewis in an impossible situation. What I perceived as the needs of filming interfered with our normal respect for one another and my emotional reaction became a real obstacle

8. Issues of dominance often emerge, particularly when men work together. Since the filmmaker and anthropologist need one another to create something that is valuable their roles ought to be recognized simply as different, not dominant/submissive.
9. A product creates additional tension over issues such as credits (whose name comes first?), ownership, distribution arrangements, royalties (if there are any), public showings, etc.

The list of problems could be endless. But if care and time are taken to establish a relationship, to define roles and agree on the product desired, if all parties agree to discuss their problems, and if a realistic schedule allotting sufficient time to each step of the project is planned at the beginning, most of these problems can be dealt with.

6. Transcriptions:

The importance of transcription merits special mention. Few ethnographic filmmakers worry about getting transcriptions but rely on the anthropologist to translate, directly from the sound track, only those conversations included in a final film. But if film is thought of as a text with research value, then transcribing conversation becomes vitally important. Many anthropologists feel capable of doing the transcriptions themselves, and certainly they have to be responsible for the final form, but transcribing is extremely arduous and time consuming. It is often possible to hire local people to transcribe sound-tapes, and this helps to ensure accuracy and the most efficient use of time in the field. In Indonesia we tried several different methods.

On Flores we hired an extremely capable young woman from the community who had recently left school. She was able to identify (far better than Lewis) every speaker and could catch comments mumbled in the background as well as those clearly recorded. With little instruction she was able to produce excellent transcriptions. However, there were some problems: the job was too lengthy for one person and, being a young woman, she did not know the ritual language of male chanters as well as she knew everyday language. Moreover, because of ritual prohibitions she was not allowed to hear tapes of certain rituals.

On Bali we used many people as transcribers, mindful of material that might be personal. A high-school teacher from the neighbouring town over-corrected people's utterances and left out repetitions and incomplete or over-lapping sentences that we felt were essential. The wife of a local official was accurate but too busy to give much time to the task. In the end most of the material was sent to a man in Singaraja who made his living doing transcriptions and copying documents.

We had no tapes transcribed while we were on Roti, but after our return a Rotinese came to Australia to live with us for three months and he transcribed all conversation.

In every case such transcriptions are only a first step; the anthropologist must spend additional time making corrections. An advantage of completing transcriptions in the field is that they are easily checked with native speakers and particular points can be clarified with informants prior to beginning the translations.[12] I strongly recommend that in planning ethnographic film projects both money and time for completing transcription be included. Translation is another extremely difficult problem; it is generally left for the anthropologist to do after fieldwork is completed.

7. Collaboration After Fieldwork is Completed:

The period following fieldwork is by far the most difficult part of a project and, oddly enough, is usually the least well planned. Frequently money (at least money for salaries) has only been raised for fieldwork, and anthropologists often think they can squeeze film production in with their other commitments. Actual filming takes only a fraction of the time it takes to prepare a film text or edit even a simple film, let alone analyze film texts.[13]

Before editing begins it is essential to know exactly what kind of product you want. Even something as basic as synchronizing sound and picture can be done in at least three different ways, each suitable for a different end: a narrated commercial film; a text for one's own research; or a text for an archive. The important thing is to decide on options and agree on each person's commitments and on an appropriate time schedule. For example, in making a research film the anthropologist must complete his analysis of the footage before the filmmaker can edit it. The anthropologist must be able to work with the complete, uncut film in which events still occur in their chronological sequence. The analysis of the footage will in turn be invaluable in producing a final film, whether it be purely a research document or a film for general distribution.[14]

If several films on different topics are planned from one corpus, one way to handle the material is to annotate carefully only the footage relevant to one topic and have the anthropologist concentrate on that analysis and those translations rather than trying to complete an archival version of all the film. However, it is wise to record on tape brief annotations of all footage as it is looked at for the first time, even if that tape is never transcribed. These comments, identifying people, places, events and objects, are a minimum requirement in case some rolls are never analyzed.

The degree to which emphasis is placed on research depends on how and why footage was collected in the first place. Frequently I have been asked to make a film to illustrate someone's published research. Since the anthropologist does not expect to derive new insights from the footage and any accompanying written materials are likely to be a rehash of previous publications, he or she is less likely to find the time or enthusiasm to participate as fully as would, say, a graduate student who is immersed in new data and who wants to use film for research.

There is a current debate about whether ethnographic films should be self-contained or whether they should be integrated with written materials. Anthropologists rightly point to the limitations of film. While film is an effective means of capturing the visual and conversational details of a particular social interaction, the same film cannot convey the background information required because the subjects leave so much unexpressed. Yet this background information is crucial to enable the audience to make sense of the images and conversation recorded by film. When filmmakers try to provide extensive background through narration they obscure what film can do; that is, they tend to obliterate what is being conveyed by the subjects' actions and speech. The additional information required to understand the fleeting messages recorded on film can best be provided in supplementary written material. Only in this way can sufficient information be assembled to establish the film as a document of anthropological value. On the other hand, film-school graduates, who have been trained to expect film to stand on its own, view any need for supplementary written material as an admission of failure. So, too, do many anthropologists who have shown films in lieu of lectures as self-contained documents that are not integrated with the other materials of their courses.

As I see it, if a film has little or no narration it offers greater potential for teaching by obliging students to interpret what they are seeing in relation to their own experiences, reading and lectures, and in discussion with one another. This requires, however, accompanying written material that

provides the background necessary for students to explore their interpretations and to answer some of their questions. This works most effectively if
video-cassette recordings of films, accompanied by written materials, are
available in libraries for independent study. In this way film is entering
universities through fields such as literary criticism and history rather than
through anthropology or psychology. I think this is largely because ethnographic films have not been integrated with scholarly research and used as a
basis for scholarly publications. This brings me back to the nature of who
has been collaborating with whom and why, and the need for anthropologists to play a more significant role in instigating filmmaking.

Just before I left for Indonesia in 1978 my camera had to be repaired and
consequently it needed to be tested when I arrived there. James Fox, who
was to join me in Indonesia, was delayed, waiting for his visa. I had met
Connor only once, but Fox and a number of colleagues had spoken highly
of her fieldwork so I went to visit her in Central Bali. Rather than testing
my camera by filming random shots, I thought we could film something
which related to her research. Connor suggested filming a trance seance.

Since this film was directly relevant to Connor's research, she was able
to use the seance I filmed as a case-study in her thesis. The transcriptions,
translations and analysis she needed for her thesis made it easier to edit a
useful instructional film and Connor was prepared to write a monograph to
accompany the film. Our goals meshed: I had been seeking just this type of
collaboration in which the film contributed directly to the research of the
participating anthropologist, and Connor was delighted to have the footage
for analysis and to have a film that would illustrate her research. Likewise,
the monograph provided me with a model of what a collaborative ethnographic film project can produce.

As I had to wait in Bali for an extra two months, Connor and I took
additional film of the medium and of a collective cremation in the medium's
hamlet, footage focusing on how people from an economically poor hamlet
co-operate to perform a major ritual. We have subsequently produced three
more films on the same healer (see references) and are currently editing a
cremation film that will include film and recorded dialogue of participants as
they watched the cremation footage on video cassette. Working on this
footage has renewed Connor's interest in Balinese cremations and she has
applied for funding for further fieldwork in order to complete a monograph
on hamlet cremations.

Connor, Patsy Asch and I have not produced a research film according
to the Sorenson-Gajdusek model (1963, 1966; Sorenson 1967) in which all
footage shot is placed in the order recorded, with a separate synchronized
sound track, an annotation track and a translation track. Instead we have experimented with instructional films and written documentation. We have
produced four films that contain most of our footage of a Balinese healer,
and we are writing a monograph that contains careful ethnographic annotations, translations and analysis. We feel that the resulting materials are

more thorough and certainly more accessible for research than are most of the research films we have seen, and their preparation has directly facilitated Connor's own work.

Moreover, Lewis, Patsy Asch and I are currently experimenting with a research film that will include not only all our footage but also the recorded reactions of the participants on seeing the footage, and which will have careful annotations, transcriptions and translations.

Throughout this section I have emphasized the key role which the anthropologist must play in directing the focus of a project whenever footage is intended either as data for research or to illustrate research findings. The following section suggests ways to enhance the value to anthropologists of footage taken by television crews working in collaboration with ethnographers.

B. Television Producers and Anthropologists

In the collaboration between a television producer and an anthropologist the latter has usually been hired as a consultant, primarily to introduce the television crew to the people to be filmed and to facilitate filming by acting as interpreter and culture-broker. In most instances the reward has been a salary and, during editing, a few courtesy screenings in which advice is sought and occasionally followed. Some directors have filmed the anthropologist as a narrative device, a way of saying to their audiences: "These people may seem weird, but to this handsome all-American/French/Australian/Japanese scholar they are friends." The anthropologist may feel that through these interviews he or she has some control over the programme, but this is often illusory because a skillful editor can take statements out of context and present an interpretation very different from that intended by the anthropologist. Of course, there have been sensitive television directors who have tried to make their films reflect the views of the anthropologist with whom they collaborated, but this is not a necessary consequence of the structural relationship between them. Since television directors come to a collaboration with certain strengths (well-trained technicians, money, equipment and an audience), I doubt that the nature of the relationship between anthropologist and television producer will change radically in the immediate future unless anthropologists act concertedly.

1. Examples of Anthropological TV Series:

During the last decade or so there have been a number of television series devoted to ethnographic film. The most successful series to date, by anthropological standards, was DISAPPEARING WORLD, produced by Brian Moser at Granada Television. Between 1970 and 1978 Moser produced twenty-three ethnographic films, each focusing on a particular people: THE

MURSI, THE RENDILLI, THE LAST OF THE CUIVA, MASAI WOMEN, etc. As television documentaries, these films were of high standard, but I know of no case in which they had value for research, and their use in teaching anthropology was limited, except in cases such as ONKA'S BIG MOKA or the SHILLUK OF SOUTHERN SUDAN in which the films illustrated aspects of pre-existing ethnographies (Strathern 1971; Evans-Pritchard 1948).

In a series entitled FACE VALUES, the British Broadcasting Corporation drew on footage taken in five societies to produce a series of programmes that focused on themes such as "ourselves and others," "men and women" and "social space." Such ideas work well in the tradition of Jacob Bronowski or Kenneth Clarke, where a single scholar presents his view of a subject. But a generalized vision such as FACE VALUES offers does not convey anyone's passion and tends to misrepresent the ethnographic data in order to make general points.

The most prolific television series is Japanese, produced by Junichi Ushiama. The Japanese have divided the world into seven regions, each with its own producer and director, and sent out film teams to make didactic films. It is my impression that they do not rely on anthropologists but work as journalists, a few of whom have some anthropological training.

Michael Ambrosino, in his 1980 and 1981 U.S. Public Broadcasting series ODYSSEY, tried a fourth approach. This was a series of programmes drawn from different sources with different styles, representing prehistory, archaeology, biographies of famous anthropologists and ethnography. The quality varied, but Ambrosino was one of the few producers to accept some programmes from independent filmmakers, such as John Marshall (N!AI, THE STORY OF A !KUNG WOMAN), thereby creating a potential market for programmes derived from the collaboration of anthropologists and filmmakers (see THE THREE WORLDS OF BALI by Abrams and Lansing).

Ethical Questions:

We know that television now affects the lives of millions of people. This effect is no longer confined to people in Western industrialized nations. I was in Trinidad when the President, Eric Williams, initiated a programme to build community centres throughout the country. Each was to receive a sewing machine and a television set. Television, Williams explained, was intended to foster an educational programme that would unite the entire population. In theory this could well have happened, but in 1966 all he could afford to produce was twenty minutes a day devoted to issues such as health measures: how to brush teeth properly, etc. To extend the viewing time Trinidad had to purchase inexpensive foreign programmes, which are a vehicle for the expansion of Western cultural imperialism (see YAP...HOW DID YOU KNOW WE'D LIKE TV? by Dennis O'Rourke).

Throughout the non-industrialized world the pattern has been repeated. One night in Java I went to visit one of the royal families in Yogyakarta. They hardly interrupted their television viewing to welcome me. I was invited to join them and, to my utter astonishment, saw KOJAK in English. The sound track was occasionally interrupted by a hasty summary in Indonesian. My hosts were unable to tell me either what the story was about or why it interested them.

I have digressed to make the point that television programmes produced in industrialized countries, particularly English-speaking countries, are often exported to non-industrialized countries. I have no evidence that ethnographic films have been among these exports, but they could well be. For this reason, in collaborating in the production of television programmes, anthropologists should be aware that they may have distribution wider than the country in which they are produced. One consideration in making ethnographic film in foreign countries is the use the governments of those countries might make of them. Government officials can insist on being supplied with copies of all films and may feel they can use them in any way they wish. Some anthropologists may decide not to film because they are opposed to providing the government with copies of their footage on the grounds that the rights of privacy of the people filmed must be protected: people are often unwilling to have film of themselves shown locally, but are content to have it seen abroad (see Wiseman's HIGH SCHOOL and many films of Australian Aborigines). Anthropologists know that very often the rights of isolated people, sometimes the very people filmed, are threatened by their own regional and national governments. Ethnographic film can be used by governments to reinforce the urban or majority view that these people are backward and must be forced to "modernize": put on clothes, give up pagan rites, move into villages.

Issues such as these must be considered. Participation in making ethnographic film, even more so than writing ethnography, raises moral questions about the relationship of the anthropologist to the people studied. The commercial value of the product adds immeasurably to the problem. In most communities there are people who believe that someone will be making a fortune out of recordings of their music or film of their ceremonies. Certainly, few ethnographic films ever make much money; but if there are royalties these can be shared with those filmed. Frequently the anthropologist, who has spent the longest period of time in the community, is in the best position to decide how such royalties should be distributed, in what amounts and into whose hands.

Many of the points that I have made about collaboration between anthropologist and filmmaker can be generalized to include a collaborative relationship with a community, but here the anthropologist has additional problems because many people are not in a position to protect or even identify their own interests in relation to film.

When a television crew (which usually has no training in anthropology and little experience of working in a foreign society) is involved, the interests of the community may be ignored because the film crew's need to get a particular shot or record a particular scene can override social constraints. The good will of the people who trust "their" anthropologist has often led to outrageous demands being made upon them, justified as necessary when filming. I have been tempted to transgress knowingly in order to get what to me was a crucial shot. In some cases people ignored my transgressions (for example, when I raised my head above the medium's while filming the trance seance in Bali). In other cases I have been chastised. In no case have I persisted when people have asked me to stop filming, though I almost turned off the camera while filming THE AX FIGHT. A man held up his hand to get me to stop filming. I moved my eye from the camera to smile at him; he smiled back, lowered his outstretched hand, and I continued filming. This interaction can be seen in the film. The camera and filmmaker are often seen as an impersonal machine; from time to time one needs to confirm one's humanity.

Tension over whether to film or not frequently arises during interactions of particular interest to anthropologists. While we were filming a cremation in Bali a woman went into a trance. Trance behaviour was a focus of Connor's research and we had no footage of spontaneous trance, only footage of a professional medium at a trance seance. Connor, prompted by several Balinese, told me to stop filming, but her expression revealed the regret she felt. I assumed the interdiction was to avoid harming the woman (soul-loss, for example) or to avoid embarrassment, but I was later told that it was for my own protection. As the violence of possession eased, I was permitted to film her return to normal consciousness. At times people cannot explain why one should not film and this is perhaps the most difficult thing for us to accept, coming as we do from a verbalizing, rationalizing society.

These problems extend to ethical questions related to the use of footage. Chagnon took a 2 1/2 minute sequence of a Yanomamo man beating his wife over the head with a piece of firewood. We looked at it together with James V. Neel and his wife, thinking we might include it in our film on genetics (1971). We three men agreed it was too disturbing to show. Mrs. Neel saw this as a typically protective male view and argued that the beating was no worse than the experiences of many wives in America. We agree; but we still decided not to use the footage.

2.   Guidelines for Anthropologists who are Collaborating with TV Producers:

Although I have cited many problems of working with television personnel, I do recommend anthropologists continue to collaborate with responsible directors and producers, but they must realize that the work is time consuming and can be troublesome. Anthropologists should call on their professional organizations to provide guidance in designing contracts to help broaden the value of such projects and to protect the rights of the people filmed. It is, after all, only because an anthropologist has strong personal ties with a community that a film crew is able to get sensitive material; but this puts the onus on the anthropologist to secure the right of final approval before the film is shown publicly.

Ownership of ethnographic film involves special problems. The person or organization providing the money should not necessarily have sole ownership of the footage. In a world that is rapidly moving toward cultural homogeneity, ethnographic footage (particularly of non-Western people) becomes part of a common heritage, invaluable for all humanity, regardless of how any particular code of law views its ownership. And, of course, it has special historical value for the people filmed and for their descendants.

I recommend that we foster the concept of usufruct. If a television company sponsors an ethnographic film then it should be allowed exclusive rights to the edited product and might be guaranteed all television rights for a specified period of years (say a maximum of five). However, most ethnographic film teams return with twenty to thirty hours of footage from which they produce a one-hour documentary. The anthropologist should be guaranteed access to the unused footage for research purposes.

A scandalous example of waste occurred when the BBC made FACE VALUES. To promote this series the BBC education department asked the Royal Anthropological Institute to collaborate and, through the RAI, it managed to interest Prince Charles in introducing the series. With this enhanced prestige, the producers obtained a huge budget. Several scholars who had spent years doing research in the areas to be filmed were hired as consultants, both in the field and later in the cutting room. The RAI drew up a contract to try to protect the anthropologists and ensure them a salary that would, among other things, enable them to command respect from the production team. The anthropologists believed the BBC would take their consultations seriously and were led to believe that the BBC would donate the unused footage to the RAI, or to the anthropologists directly involved, for use in research and instruction. In many instances culturally-revealing events were recorded in detail for FACE VALUES, but commitment to thematic comparison encouraged the use of snippets which then had to be held together by narration. The 3 per cent that was shown amounted to little more than a trailer for the footage as a whole. When the programme was broadcast, the consultant anthropologists found that in the final editing some of the material had been distorted to present a programme that the BBC producers felt would interest their viewers. In one case, for example, stock footage shot at different times and in different places was combined with current footage to represent a single dramatic ritual performance, thereby rendering the sequence ethnographically spurious. But the saddest aspect of the collaboration emerged when the anthropologists discovered the RAI would not be able to recover any of the footage; the BBC was not legally empowered to give or sell footage produced with public funds. Indeed, the RAI was informed that it would take an Act of Parliament to change the existing laws to permit this donation.

Having seen in the cutting room excellent detailed coverage of events that they might never see again, and would certainly never have the resources to film themselves, anthropologists bemoaned the lost opportunity of being able to use that footage in their own research and teaching. It seems clear that this material should belong to the public (in the form of texts available in an archive for research use) and to the scholars through whose efforts it was assembled and with whose knowledge it can be presented most accurately. Obtaining unused footage has always been a problem in working with commercial networks, but here is a case where a government-supported public agency (the BBC) had an opportunity to give invaluable material to a national agency eminently qualified to receive it (the RAI). As is so often the case with corporate self-interest, the waste here is monumental and the consideration for scholarship negligible.[15] One could cite many other examples. For instance, Jane Goodall claimed in the mid-sixties that she was not permitted to use for her own research any of the NATIONAL GEOGRAPHIC footage of chimpanzees taken at Gombe.

If a professional body of anthropologists drew up guidelines for use when negotiating with television companies, we could begin to effect a change. I recommend that contracts specify that after a designated number of years all unused footage (original and workprint) be donated to an archive where it can be properly stored to ensure preservation and where it can be used for research. Several archives could be chosen, perhaps from FIAFC (Federation Internationale des Archives du Film). The consultant anthropologist should be permitted to use all workprint for research and should be permitted to edit a film using original footage including that used in commercial film.[16] Whenever appropriate, anthropologists should be encouraged to return and show the film to the people filmed; they too have a legitimate right to the footage and their reactions to it will generate new research data. Ultimately, the participants and their descendants should be permitted to use the remaining workprint, and to copy the original for their own research, teaching or entertainment. I recommend that in the meantime an archive hold the film in trust or the people filmed; it should be given to them when they can demonstrate that their country has adequate facilities to preserve the footage (FIAFC has set standards).

If anthropologists, acting as a professional group, establish guidelines for collaboration, television companies will be forced to accept their conditions. An individual can rarely assert his rights against a corporation, but television companies would feel more obliged to honour contracts if, for example, a body such as the American Anthropological Association threatened to publicize condemnation of them.

A by-product of allowing anthropologists access to unused footage is that they would encourage the filming of events of interest to their research;

more films for instruction that reflect the interests of contemporary anthropology would be made. In time, the quality of television programmes might improve. Certainly contracts would encourage greater participation by anthropologists in providing intellectual guidance throughout production. If an anthropologist were paid a retainer, regardless of hours spent at the studio, it would encourage the producer to include the anthropologist at every stage. The anthropologist's financial incentive might be reduced but, provided the retainer was a reasonable sum to begin with, a desire to protect his or her own reputation and the integrity of the people filmed would be a compensatory incentive.

Summary

In summary, collaboration depends for its success on common goals. Ethnographic film can only become a productive tool for anthropologists if they can influence the creation of a film at every stage from planning to filming to editing. If anthropologists come to consider ethnographic film as data, as valid texts for research, rather than (or at least as well as) simply entertainment, then their commitment will be greater than it has been in the past, and they will seek better conditions for collaboration on a project involving film.

A unified effort is necessary to protect the rights of anthropologists and of people filmed, rights guaranteeing access to footage and determining in large part the content of that footage. But this effort will only be forthcoming when anthropologists recognize the value of ethnographic film. Recognition depends on publishing integrated film and written materials that prove valuable for instruction and research. The problem is at the moment, a circular one.

ACKNOWLEDGEMENTS

This article was first published as "Collaboration in Ethnographic Film Making: A Personal View," CANBERRA ANTHROPOLOGY, volume 5, No. 1, April 1982, pp. 8-36. It is reprinted in this volume with the permission of CANBERRA ANTHROPOLOGY. I have made minor changes for this publication.

I would like to acknowledge the help that Patsy Asch has given in clarifying and contributing ideas to this paper. I wish to thank the institutions that have sponsored my work: Documentary Educational Resources; The Australian National University; Brandeis University; Harvard University; The National Science Foundation; The Wenner-Gren Foundation for Anthropological Research; the Rock Foundation; the Institute Venezuelana de Investigaciones Cientificas; and Lembaga Ilmu Pengetahuan Indonesia. Many of my current ideas about ethnographic film stem from my long collaboration with John

Marshall, with whom I co-founded Documentary Educational Resources.

I hope my colleagues will forgive me when I draw on our experiences to illustrate certain points in this paper. The anecdotes inevitably do injustice to the complexity of the situations and may sometimes make us look even more foolish than we are.

NOTES

1 I have collaborated in nine ethnographic filming expeditions:

Team Members	People Filmed	Field-Work	Duration of Project
Elizabeth Marshall Thomas (writer)	Dodoth (Uganda)	1961	1961-1962
Karl Reisman	Trinidad	1966	1966-1967
Napoleon Chagnon (anthropologist), James V. Neel (geneticist), and colleagues	Yanomamo (Venezuela)	1968	1968-1971
Napoleon Chagnon (anthropologist), Craig Johnson (sound)	Yanomamo	1971	1971-1975
Asen Balikci (anthropologist), Bayazid Hatsak (interpreter), Patsy Asch (sound)	Pashtoon	1975	1975-1976
James J. Fox (anthropologist)	Roti (Eastern Indonesia)	1977	1977-
James J. Fox	Roti	1978	1978-
Linda H. Connor (anthropologist)	Balinese (Indonesia)	1978	1978-
Linda H. Connor (anthropologist), Patsy Asch (sound)	Balinese	1980	1980-
E. Douglas Lewis (anthropologist)	Ata Tana Ai (Eastern Indonesia)	1980	1980

2 Outstanding exceptions are Napoleon Chagnon's MAGICAL DEATH (Yanomamo Indians, Venezuela) and William Geddes' THE LAND DAYAKS OF BORNEO and RITUALS OF THE FIELD (Malaysia), and MIAO YEAR (Thailand).

3 However, professional sound recording may well require as much training and experience as professional filming.

4 These ideas are expanded in a paper I am writing entitled "Motion Picture Film in Ethnographic Research." I am indebted to E. Douglas Lewis for discussions on this subject.

5 "Cut-away" is filmmaker's jargon for shots that are not properly part of the action (such as a close-up of someone's face, a shot of a bird or flower taken at a different time) but inserted to make action appear continuous or smooth or to bridge a passage of time.

6 A slide-tape is a sequence of slides synchronized with sound. There are a number of tape recorders on the market today that permit one to put a pulse on one of the stereo tracks. When connected to a projector, this pulse will change the slides automatically. Slide tapes can be produced with sound recordings made while photographing or dubbed with related sounds, including narration. This is the least expensive and least obtrusive way to record an event visually.

7 A video camera with a low-light vidicon tube can add six extra stops to a normal video or film camera, permitting one to film wherever the human eye can see clearly.

8 Lewis's analysis will take into account additional data collected when we returned to Flores in 1982 to show the footage to participants and to record their reactions.

9 On the way to our field site in Afghanistan, Balikci gave a series of evening seminars on aspects of Pashtoon life, emphasizing the problems facing nomads as more and more agriculturalists settled in their migration path north of the Hindu Kush. Because Balikci's remarks pertained specifically to the group we were to film, this was more valuable than any of our preparatory reading.

10 One irksome problem is that different items of equipment are not always compatible. Not only do plugs have different types of connectors, not all professional microphones work with all professional tape recorders; nor are two tape recorders necessarily compatible for duplicating tapes, a requirement for transcriptions. Cameras and tape recorders must be specially equipped to record synchronized sound.

11 We have not finished SAND PLAY, but a trial version is available from Documentary Educational Resources.

12 In Afghanistan we were accompanied by a Pashtoon-speaking Afghan linguist, Bayatsid Hatsak, who taught at the University of Kabul. He was interpreter, guide and friend. Whatever success we had in communicating with people we owe to his skill. Unfortunately he was not asked to transcribe our tapes, but Richard Sorenson brought him to the Smithsonian to record a running translation on tape synchronized with the film and original sound. Although this helps the viewer follow dialogue, it is not adequate for research because it is unclear exactly which English phrase

translates which Pashtoon phrase, nor is it clear whether such things as repetition or aborted sentences are Hatsak's hesitation as he searches for an English equivalent or correspond exactly to the Pashtoon speaker's utterances. The key to all decisions related to filming is to be able to identify the purpose of collecting and interpreting data in order to decide what technique is most appropriate.

13 A Harvard undergraduate student, Seth Reichlin, spent months analyzing the eight-minute version of THE AX FIGHT, one of our Yanomamo films, in order to write his thesis for Harvard College; he received first class honours.

14 A list follows of some of the options available during final production and who is likely to be responsible for them (F = filmmaker, A = anthropologist; a capital letter refers to major responsibility, lower case to secondary responsibility where involvement is desirable):

Basic

Transfer of sound to 16mm magnetic tape	F
Synchronize sound and picture	F
Organize footage either chronologically or topically	F
Evaluate all footage	A,F

Research Film

Annotate each shot	A,f
Transcription, morphemic gloss, brief grammar (if not available), translation	A
Analysis (optional, depending on the purpose of the research film)	A

Feedback

(optional) recording of participant reactions to the film
A,f

Editing of film(s) for distribution

Editing	F,a
Narration (optional)	A,f
Subtitles	A,f
Trial testing (perhaps on video) and evaluation	A,f

Final Production   F

Monograph, written to accompany film(s)
A,f

---

15 Since writing this paper I have heard that the BBC has made a few addi-

tional films from the material assembled for FACE VALUES. It is only recently that some television companies have gone to the expense of maintaining storage facilities to enable them to do this. But much time has elapsed since the material was shot and the BBC has not consulted anthropologists about what they have done with the footage, with the result that the new films remain distortions of actual events. Several years after this article was originally written I have now been told that Jonathan Benthal (Director of the R.A.I.) has managed to get all the unused film delivered by truck to the R.A.I. offices in London; finally there is a happy ending to this grim story.

16 Many universities have 16mm editing facilities and television studios staffed by people qualified to assist anthropologists who want to use footage for research or who want to edit instructional films or video tapes. Transferring footage to U-matic cassette is often the simplest and cheapest way for scholars to work with it.

REFERENCES CITED

Briggs, J. (1970). Never In Anger. Cambridge, MA: Harvard University Press.
Chagnon, Napoleon (1974). Studying the Yanomamo. New York: Holt, Rinehart and Winston.
Chagnon, Napoleon (1977). Yanomamo: The Fierce People. Second edition. New York: Holt, Rinehart and Winston.
Connor, Linda, Patty Asch, and Tim Asch (1984). Jero Tapakan: A Balinese Healer. Ethnographic Film Monograph No. 1. Watertown, MA Documentary Educational Resources.
Evans-Pritchard, E.E. (1948). The Divine Kingship of the Shilluk of the Nilotic Sudan. Cambridge: Cambridge University Press.
Mauss, Marcel. The Gift. London: Cohen and West.
Sorenson, E.R. (1967). A Research Film Program in the Study of Changing Man. Current Anthropology 8: 433-469.
Sorenson, E.R., and C. Gajdusek (1963). Research Films for the Study of Child Growth and Development and Disease Patterns in Primitive Cultures. A Catalogue of Research Films in Ethnopediatrics. Bethesda: National Institutes of Health, National Institute of Neurology, Disease and Blindness.
Sorenson, E.R., and C. Gajdusek (1966). The Study of Child Behavior and Development in Primitive Cultures. Pediatrics 32(1):2.
Strathern, A. (1971). The Rope of Moka: Big-Men and Ceremonial Exchange in Mount Hagen, New Guinea. Cambridge: Cambridge University Press.
Strathern, A. (1979). Ongka: A Self-Account by a New Guinea Big-Man. New York: St. Martin's Press.

FILMS CITED

A BALINESE TRANCE SEANCE (1979). A film by Tim Asch, Linda Connor, and Patsy Asch. 30 minutes, color, sound. Distributor: Documentary

Educational Resources, Watertown, Massachusetts.

A CURING CERMONY (1958). A film by John Marshall. 8 minutes, color, sound. Distributor: Documentary Educational Resources, Watertown, Massachusetts.

A FATHER WASHES HIS CHILDREN (1974). A film by Tim Asch and Napoleon Chagnon. 15 minutes, color, sound. Distributor: Documentary Educational Resources, Watertown, Massachusetts.

A JOKING RELATIONSHIP (1958). A film by John Marshall. 13 minutes, color, sound. Distributor: Documentary Educational Resources, Watertown, Massachusetts.

A MAN AND HIS WIFE WEAVE A HAMMOCK (1974). A film by Tim Asch and Napoleon Chagnon. 12 minutes, color, sound. Distributor: Documentary Educational Resources, Watertown, Massachusetts.

AN ARGUMENT ABOUT A MARRIAGE (1958). A film by John Marshall. 18 minutes, color, sound. Distributor: Documentary Educational Resources, Watertown, Massachusetts..

THE AXE FIGHT (1974). A film by Tim Asch and Napoleon Chagnon. 30 minutes, color, sound. Distributor: Documentary Educational Resources, Watertown, Massachusetts.

DEBE'S TANTRUM (1958). A film by John Marshall. 9 minutes, color, sound. Distributor: Documentary Educational Resources, Watertown, Massachusetts.

THE FEAST (1969). A film by Tim Asch and Napoleon Chagnon. 29 minutes, color, sound. Distributor: Documentary Educational Resources, Watertown, Massachusetts.

HIGH SCHOOL (1968). A film by Frederick Wiseman. 74 minutes, black and white, sound. Distributor: Zipporah Films.

JERO ON JERO: A BALINESE TRANCE SEANCE OBSERVED (1980). A film by Tim Asch, Linda Connor, and Patsy Asch. 17 minutes, color, sound. Distributor: Documentary Educational Resources, Watertown, Massachusetts.

JERO TAPAKAN: STORIES FROM THE LIFE OF A BALINESE HEALER (1983). A film by Tim Asch, Linda Connor, and Patsy Asch. 25 minutes, color, sound. Distributor: Documentary Educational Resources, Watertown, Massachusetts.

THE KAWELKA: ONGKA'S BIG MOKA (1977). A film by C. Nairn, A. Strathern, and M. Strathern. 52 minutes Distributor: Granada Television.

LAND DAYAKS OF BORNEO (1966). A film by W. Geddes. 38 minutes, color, sound. Distributor: New York University and Pennsylvania State University.

THE LAST OF THE CUIVA (1971). A film by Brian Moser and Bernard Arcand. 65 minutes, color, sound. Distributor: Granada Television.

MAGICAL DEATH (1973). A film by Napoleon Chagnon. 29 minutes, color, sound. Documentary Educational Resources, Watertown, Massachusetts.

A MAN CALLED "BEE" (1975). A film by Napoleon Chagnon and Tim Asch. 40 minutes, color, sound. Distributor: Documentary Educational Resources, Watertown, Massachusetts.

MASAI WOMEN (1874). A film by Chris Curling and M. Llewelyn-Davis. 52

minutes, color, sound. Distributor: Granada Television.
THE MEDIUM IS THE MASSEUSE: A BALINESE MASSAGE (1983). A film
    by Tim Asch, Linda Connor, and Patsy Asch. 35 minutes, color,
    sound. Distributor: Documentary Educational Resources, Watertown,
    Massachusetts.
MIAO YEAR (1968). A film by W. Geddes. 62 minutes, color, sound.
    Distributor: University of California Extension Media Center.
THE MURSI (1974). A film by L. Woodhead and D. Turton. 52 minutes,
    color, sound. Distributor: Granada Television.
N!AI: THE STORY OF A !KUNG WOMAN (1980). A film by John Marshall.
    59 minutes, color, sound. Distributor: Documentary Educational Re-
    sources, Watertown, Massachusetts.
THE RENDILLE OF NORTHERN KENYA (1977). A film by Chris Curling and
    A. Grum. 52 minutes, color, sound. Distributor: Granada Television.
RITUALS OF THE FIELD (1980). A film by W. Geddes. 90 minutes, color,
    sound. Distributor: Department of Anthropology, University of Syd-
    ney.
SAND PLAY (1971). A film by Tim Asch and Napoleon Chagnon. 19 1/2
    minutes, color, sound. Distributor: Documentary Educational Re-
    sources, Watertown, Massachusetts.
THE THREE WORLDS OF BALI (1981). A film by Ira Abrams and S. Lansing.
    59 minutes, color, sound. Produced in conjunction with Odyssey.
    Distributor: Documentary Educational Resources, Watertown, Mas-
    sachusetts.
WEEDING THE GARDEN (1974). A film by Tim Asch and Napoleon
    Chagnon. 14 minutes, color, sound. Distributor: Documentary
    Educational Resources, Watertown, Massachusetts.
YANOMAMO: A MULTIDISCIPLINARY STUDY (1971). A film by Tim Asch,
    J.V. Neel, and Napoleon Chagnon. 45 minutes, color, sound. Dis-
    tributor: Documentary Educational Resources, Watertown, Mas-
    sachusetts.
YAP...HOW DID YOU KNOW WE'D LIKE TV? (1979). A film by Dennis
    O'Rouke. 54 minutes, color, sound. Distributor: Ronin Films, Can-
    berra.

REVIEWS OF SOME OF THE FILMS OF TIMOTHY ASCH

Almquist, Eric (1975). Review of MAGICAL DEATH. American Anthropolo-
    gist 77(1): 179.
Baker, Paul T. (1972). Review of YANOMAMO: A MULTIDISCIPLINARY
    STUDY. American Anthropologist 74(1-2): 195.
Blaustein, Richard (1979). Review of THE AXE FIGHT; THE YANOMAMO
    MYTH OF NARO AS TOLD BY KEOBAWA; THE YANOMAMO
    MYTH OF NARO AS TOLD BY DEDEHEIWA; MAGICAL DEATH;
    CHILDREN'S MAGICAL DEATH. Journal of American Folklore
    92(364): 252-254.
Geertz, H. (1984). Review of A BALINESE TRANCE SEANCE; JERO ON
    JERO: A BALINESE TRANCE SEANE OBSERVED; THE MEDIUM IS

THE MASSEUSE: A BALINESE MASSAGE; JERO TAPAKAN: STO-
RIES FROM THE LIFE OF A BALINESE HEALER. American Anthropologist 86(3): 809-811.

Kessinger, Kenneth M. (1971). Review of THE FEAST. American Anthropologist 73 (2): 500-502.

Klein, Patricia A. and John F. Klein (1977). Review of THE AXE FIGHT.
American Anthropologist 79 (3): 747.

O'Connor, John (1976). Review of A MAN CALLED "BEE." New York Times,
July.

O'Connor, John (1976). Review of THE AXE FIGHT. New York Times, July.

O'Connor, John (1976). Review of MAGICAL DEATH. New York Times, July.

Seronde, Antoine (1975). Review of OCAMO IS MY TOWN. American Anthropologist 77 (1): 195-198.

Tavakolian, Bahram (1984). Review of THE SONS OF HAJI OMAR. American
Anthropologist 86(3): 806-807.

Weiler, A.H. (1976). Review of A MAN CALLED "BEE." New York Times,
March 5.

Weiler, A.H. (1976). Review of THE AXE FIGHT. New York Times, March 5.

Weiler, A.H. (1976). Review of MYTH OF NARO AS TOLD BY KAOBAWA.
New York Times, March 5.

Wolf, Eric (1972). Review of MAGICAL DEATH. American Anthropologist
74 (1-2): 196-198.

Anthropologists And Ethnographic Filmmaking

Asen Balikci
Department of Anthropology
Université de Montréal

ABSTRACT: This article deals with two related topics, the strategies utilized in the production of ethnographic films and the pedagogical value of visual texts assembled under the supervision of anthropologists. Following an enumeration of the attributes of ethnographic film, an effort is made to summarize the various patterns of collaboration between anthropologists and filmmakers at several levels of production. While ideally the anthropologist should be his own cameraman, it is concluded that a collaborative project has obvious advantages leading to better products for wider distribution. It is further assumed that one of the aims of ethnographic film is the diffusion of the anthropological message connected with holism and cultural relativism. In this respect, the author describes the classroom use of the Netsilik Eskimo film project and associated MACOS curriculum program. The impact of these materials was strong enough to provoke a national controversy in the U.S. during the early 1970s. The controversy is related to the contradiction between the idealized Eskimo stereotype held by the public and the ethnographer's version of Eskimo culture and personality.

Introduction

Margaret Mead made one of her last public appearances at the 1977 Ethnographic Film Festival at the American Museum of Natural History. I was in the audience and she sent instructions that I was to meet her in a room behind the podium. I found her sitting in an armchair, obviously very feeble and her face showing the signs of pain and sickness. She inquired about ongoing ethnographic film projects, whether the visual records obtained in particular field locations were sufficiently detailed or what could be done to encourage a young colleague to continue filming. She appeared worried. She knew that the end was near, the end of numerous traditional and isolated cultures some of which she had studied and seen change and some others that had remained unknown to the outside world and were in

31

danger of losing their distinctive originality. It is that fear of loss, of irre-
trievable loss of something original, a unique cultural expression of a long
historical growth that motivated her teacher, Franz Boas, to study the Eskimos and West Coast Indians and to accumulate thousands of pages describing native customs and texts which today are the main vestiges of these
now vanished cultures. The example of Franz Boas and Margaret Mead motivated several generations of anthropologists to study small, isolated and
traditional communities and establish written records of their life ways.
These studies had a double objective. First, to provide records for the suc-
ceeding generations in the local community to be able to recognize the cultural continuity linking them to their forefathers. Second, to allow scientists and general readers to discover the intrinsic originality and specific
functioning of the local culture. In this presentation, I shall defend the point
of view that these two objectives of Franz Boas and Margaret Mead can be
better served with the intensive utilization of modern audio-visual techniques leading both to a higher degree of recording accuracy and at the same
time immensely widening the audience interested in learning about the
moral and philosophical significance of other, primarily exotic cultures. I
say all of this with the clear understanding that audio-visual records (that is,
ethnographic film) are not a substitute for written descriptions and analyses
but a supplement and an important one. In other words, ethnographic film
(considered as fully part of anthropology) can help answer the famous question formulated by the 18th century French philosopher Montesquieu:
"coment peut-on être persan?" ("how can one be Persian?").

Ethnographic film refers to a large and amorphous category of audio-
visual productions. It is characteristically difficult to define precisely or in a
bounded manner. Definition criteria may refer to production personnel,
style, shooting strategy, content, structure, audience, utilization, and so
forth. Analyses of ethnographic film productions with reference to these parameters point to a considerable variability. Styles may be observational,
reflexive, dydactic-expositional, analytical, documentary, and so forth. Content may vary ad infinitum, from simple recordings of primitive technology
to elaborate treatment of urban patterns. The setting may be literally everywhere: the Kalahari desert or the Arctic coast, village India or urban America. In reference to structure, the range of variability is truly astounding,
from a simple sequence of one person doing something in real time to
highly structured feature length productions. Concerning utilization, ethnographic film comprises such diverse categories as research footage, educational films, and television productions. In a sense, ethnographic film
translates the variability of style and application of anthropology itself with
the fundamental difference that ethnographic film is characteristically descriptive to the point of largely excluding analysis (Jarvie 1983).

After recognition of the unbounded nature of our film genre it is possible to point to a few elements which can make some films more ethno-

graphic than others.

First and foremost is a direct shooting strategy, in vivo, excluding sce-narization, scripting, prearranged settings and professional actors. Preference is given usually to long takes from a "normal" social distance with lengthy coverage of spontaneous interactions, from beginning to end with illustra-tion of full bodies. This recording strategy distinguishes our genre from the documentary style which is more structured, accepts readily playing with angles and visual effects and forces the recorder to constantly think of the editor's scissors. In a sense the ethnographic filmer is almost entirely preoccupied with content while the documentarian is obliged to additionally think about form, this I consider a basic difference.

Second is the participation of the anthropologist at one or several levels of production. This is an important criterion making for the automatic in-clusion of the film in the ethnographic category (Heider 1976).

Third is the preference given to non-Western societies, particularly ex-otic cultures. This tendency lies at the core of the ethnographic film tradi-tion, although in recent times a preoccupation with western rural-folklore and urban subjects has become prevalent.

The fourth criterion concerns utilization. There is the professional as-sumption that good ethnographic footage can be used for research purposes and good ethnographic film can be shown in the classroom. In this sense often it is classroom utilization that defines the ethnographic nature of a film with the corollary that TV productions somewhat lack in ethnographic purity.

Fifth is the relation of our productions to published data mostly in monograph format. This is a basic criterion obviously increasing the peda-gogical significance of the audio-visual product. To this there is no easy parallel in the documentary tradition.

There is finally another definitional criterion for ethnographic film and a highly important one. It concerns ethnographic truth. This is a complex and hotly debated issue. Obviously, all filming involves selectivity and consequently all films are constructions, ethnographic documentaries being constructions of a higher order than monothematic productions. This ele-ment of artifice is sometimes difficult to comprehend by the public which is fascinated by the realism of the color pictures and the vividness of the syn-chronous sound. It appears all real, yet it is not. In reference to this issue, the responsibility of the field ethnographer is great. It is his task to care-fully select the elements of culture-specific behavior to be filmed and to in-tegrate them in a manner which is close to the simple descriptive model that he/she, as ethnographer, has built of the local culture for filmic purposes. Obviously, film is not an appropriate medium for sophisticated anthropo-logical analysis. The ethnographer, however, can select and put together the visual elements of a culture with the final aim of constructing a wider and more comprehensive composition. Both in the single sequence and the global composition the ethnographer has the moral responsibility to record and interpret local life ways with a maximum of empirical fidelity and as closely as possible to his descriptive film model. That is what we call "truth" in ethnographic film.

These six criteria can help define what is ethnographic in a film and simultaneously draw a flexible boundary between the documentary and the ethnographic genres. In order to better explain the nature of ethnographic film, the following paper will thus discuss two aspects of the production and utilization of ethnographic film: (1) the personnel involved in the production of ethnographic film; and (2) the role of ethnographic film in the diffusion of the anthropological message.

The Personnel Involved in the Production of Ethnographic Film

One of the fundamental issues in the production of ethnographic films is whether the field anthropologist should operate the camera and shoot his/her own films, or is it better for him/her to be accompanied by a crew responsible for the technical task of audio-visual recording and possibly film direction? Does the participation of a professional director-cameraman in the film project reduce the ethnographicness of the final product? In my opinion this is an issue of central importance for our genre with a direct and determining influence on style, format and utilization of final product. Further, it is a heated issue with diametrically opposed positions expressed with vigor and conviction. The views of Jean Rouch are well known; he admits that the ethnologist is best qualified, even the only one qualified to infiltrate an indigenous environment and record exotica. The ethnologist at the camera brings forth "the irreplaceable quality of real contact between the person filming and those being filmed" (Rouch 1975:92). In case of failure the ethnologist-cameraman should be the only one to blame for any "impurity" (Rouch 1975:92). This is not the place to discuss the notions of purity and impurity and their relevance in the structuring of the ethnographer's perceptions and the ethnographic reality. The creeping danger of impurity however allows Rouch to write: "the films of Asen Balikci on the Netsilik Eskimo or the recent series of films by Ian Dunlop on the Baruga of New Guinea are for me good examples of what must not happen again" (1975:91). The opposite view is discussed by M. Godelier (1982) and defended by Tim Asch among others with Asch publishing recently a full catalogue on the collaboration modalities between anthropologists and filmmakers (Asch 1982). Here I shall join company with Asch and try to briefly expose the virtues of such collaboration without of course proclaiming disdain for the practice of the solitary ethnologist-cameraman capable of achieving excellence. I should add that in the course of private conversations in several countries many anthropologists and director-cameramen expressed dissatisfaction about joint film ventures summing their statements with a simple:

"it doesn't work." Why is it so?

Completed ethnographic films in the broadest sense as distinguished from research footage have been produced by three kinds of field personnel. First, anthropologists alone acting as director-cameramen, second, filmmakers alone, third, collaborative teams comprising an anthropologist and a cameraman with or without directorial duties. In the first category we can include those of Jean Rouch's films for which he has conducted previous field work as evidenced in publications (Rouch 1981), N. Chagnon filming shamanistic performances in MAGICAL DEATH, G. Klima's film work on East African pastoralists, W. Geddes on the Land Dayaks of Borneo and further contributions in Malaysia and Thailand, Juillerat's remarkable film on slash and burn farming in New Guinea (UN JARDIN A LAFAR), Ivo Strecker's survey of Hamar rituals, etc. These are apparently the productions excluding impurities and consequently most highly regarded by Jean Rouch.

Second is the vast category of films produced by filmmakers without anthropological expertise. These films are generally considered more or less ethnographic by virtue of their exotic subject matter, their use of a candid camera strategy or their inclusion in a classroom curriculum or anthropological film festival. The list could be extremely long, suffice it to mention NANOOK OF THE NORTH; GRASS, Preloran's films on Argentinian communities together with some Film Board productions such as Gosselin's CESAR ET SON CANOT; and more recently McDougall's films on East African pastoralists. Further, apparently whole television series are sometimes considered as ethnographic such as the Japanese MAN series by Y. Ushiyama are produced without the collaboration of anthropologists. It is clear that ethnographic film is not the exclusive domain of ethnographers. It is natural that documentarians would like to explore cultural diversity. However, it is the anthropologist's duty to submit these documentaries to evaluation and criticism from a vigorously anthropological perspective before their inclusion in our genre.

Let us examine briefly the large and extremely varied category of films involving the collaboration of anthropologists, mostly field anthropologists and cameramen acting usually as director-cameramen. Here can be included our "classics," the films which in a recent survey of visual anthropology in Canada clearly appeared as most widely used in the classroom. These are the Bushmen, Yanomamo and Netsilik series together with DEAD BIRDS. The profession's preference for these productions is easy enough to understand: it concerns serial presentation allowing for deeper and continuous student involvement, relevance of ethnographic detail, sobriety of expositional style and relatedness to the literature. With the exception of the Netsilik series these productions have one characteristic in common, they were shot and directed by anthropologically trained filmmakers: Robert Gardner, John Marshall and Timothy Asch. As for the Netsilik series, it was an anthropologist who was fully in charge of content with the filmmakers responsible for form. The Netsilik series however appears as more rigidly structured and more "fabricated" in the documentary style and in this sense, lacking the ethnographic spontaneity and directness of the other serial productions. It is my assumption that the emergence of a class of anthropologically trained filmmakers is a crucial development with productions perceived as establishing ethnographic standards for further work. It is important to note that these efforts took place with no consideration of television imperatives.

Similar developments have taken place in France with Jean Rouch and Jean Arlaud acting as anthropologically trained filmmakers, Jean Rouch in the Sigui series with Germaine Dieterlen and Jean Arlaud among the Nyangatom and later the Guajiro with Michel Perrin. For the rest, French production exhibits a variety similar to that found in the US: filmmakers alone working in the ethnographic tradition such as Jean-Dominique Lajour's outstanding contributions on French folklore, and professional cameramen accompanying anthropologists in the field. French production is substantial, often experimental, well sheltered in CNRS-SERDDAV, a remarkable institution where anthropologists and filmmakers can meet and establish joint projects. It should be noted that ethnographic films in France (as in the rest of Europe) have practically no classroom distribution. The inclusion of ethnographic films in the curricula remains essentially a North American practice.

Collaboration between anthropologists and filmmakers has resulted in the production of some outstanding television series. The British have led the way in this field with Granada's "Disappearing World" series (Loisos 1980) and more recently with the "Worlds Apart" program at the BBC directed by Chris Curling. I believe it is correct to state that this form of collaboration was established by Granada's producer Brian Moser as an original and basic feature of the series. The highly acclaimed "Disappearing World" series has set the pattern for several other television serials: Gordingley's "Face Values" and Attenborough's "The Tribal Eye" in Britain, and in the United States, M. Ambrosino's "Odyssey" as well as the important Canadian series on the Montagnais Indians of Quebec produced by Arthur Lamothe with the collaboration of anthropologist Remi Savard. It should be noted that in the case of television series the role of the producer as initiator of individual projects and selector of production personnel including the anthropologist is greatly determinant. This situation is different from the prevalent practice in the US and France where it is the anthropologist or the anthropologically trained filmmaker who initially formulates the project. Further it seems that in Britain there are no ethnographic film endeavors outside the television format. In this case Britain stands in sharp contrast with the US and France.

This brief survey clearly indicates that collaboration between anthropologists and filmmakers is a well established practice in several countries resulting in important and successful productions of various formats. It is impossible to fully summarize the various forms and levels at which such collaborations have taken place. They may concern several of the following practices.

First in reference to the anthropologist's input:

1. The anthropologist after prolonged field work contributes to the definition, articulation and conceptualization of the project; this task he may share or not with the filmmaker, at the initial stages at least.
2. The field anthropologist has an understanding of the culture as a whole and the ways its constituent parts are interconnected. With this knowledge he has the responsibility to select a film theme representing a vital element of social life or culture. It is the anthropologist's task to invite visual treatment of the theme in an intelligible and intellectually satisfying manner which can never be a "full" description and analysis of the subject. He has to select and tie the different threads together. He has to translate his perceptions to the filmmaker. It is obvious that an anthropologically trained filmmaker is well equipped to share his knowledge. It is in this way that we should probably understand the ethnographic quality of THE FEAST, THE HUNTERS and DEAD BIRDS.
3. In the field the anthropologist can be a good helper: he can introduce the crew to a totally alien situation, look after accommodation, help select actors, smooth conflictual situations in case he is not part of them, act as interpreter, even take sound, etc.
4. Back from the field the anthropologist can help annotate the footage, translate the dialogue (as Ivo Strecker has done for RIVERS OF SAND) and participate in the editing.

Now, from the point of view of the filmmaker, all these points are of the highest value. The filmmaker finds in the anthropologist a competent informant and collaborator and finally sees hope to go beyond the usual journalistic style of most documentaries. He can get an inside view of the workings of the indigenous community and build a story line with the elements provided by the anthropologist. He can impose structure on a material to which he cannot obtain access easily by himself. Clearly the collaborative project leads to finer detail, greater ethnographic integrity and higher visual quality. All this makes for wider distribution circuits. Much of the evidence indicates that such partnerships have led to significant and highly successful productions. Why then the repeated dissatisfactions and criticisms?

First, there are the obvious personality, ideological and temperamental differences that can oppose two individuals thrown together in an utterly strange environment and this for a prolonged period. There are indeed many cases of famous quarrels opposing anthropologist to filmmaker in the field. Further, the anthropologist who has succeeded in establishing warm relationships with trusted informants and feels deep empathy for the community may find the specific and often rigid demands of the film crew overbearing. In case of tensions and misunderstandings with the community he may feel his mediating position as endangering his network and may strongly resent the ambiguity of his new position. This will reflect on his collaboration with the filmmaker. The latter may object to the slow pace of proceedings and highly unpredictable nature of events and blame the anthropologist. In the field a variety of factors can put a strain on the partnership.

Yet there seems to be deeper factors contributing to the misunderstanding: first in reference to training, second, at the level of expectations. Often the anthropologist entering a film project is quite ignorant of film techniques and strategies. On my first shooting trip to the Netsilik Eskimos I thought I should apply the lessons learned at Margaret Mead's seminar on field methods and techniques and proceeded to instruct my partner, a first class documentarian, in the virtues of filming whole bodies, whole people in whole acts. I thought this to be both good ethnography and good filming. The documentarian decided otherwise; he considered me as a kind of compulsive illuminatus and did everything to have me removed from the project. I stayed and with much humility had to learn painfully about the nitty-gritty of documentary filmmaking. It is my feeling that similar situations must have occurred elsewhere.

The anthropologist's ignorance of film technique is paralleled by the documentarian's ignorance of anthropology considered usually by him a purely academic and inaccessible discipline. There are very few documentarians who make efforts to acquire some anthropological knowledge. Thus, in the field, while the documentarian makes full use of his craft and talent, the anthropologist applies but a fragment of his, a frustrating situation usually resented as such by both partners. Clearly an anthropologically trained filmmaker is in a much better position to understand and creatively use his partner's knowledge. In case, however, that the partnership involves a documentarian, I will suggest for the anthropologist to train himself in the medium and move in the direction of film and not vice versa.

The greatest disappointments and frustrations by anthropologists concern scholarly expectations. Generally, the anthropologist approaches the film project with the primary intention of accumulating visual ethnographic data and the more the better. The temptation to play Boas is real, in the sense of aiming at a full, "complete" record, or drawing a rounded picture of a whole culture or preserving on color film for posterity a highly original culture in imminent danger of total disintegration and final oblivion. Now these temptations are most often expressed by American anthropologists; they are very rarely heard of in Britain or France where encyclopedic, archival or anthropo-missionary efforts are looked upon with suspicion. Needless to say, the anthropologist who enters the film project with such expectations is bound to be disappointed. The obsession with completeness is even more strongly apparent at the other end of the film project. Here it is the British social anthropologists who lead the chorus. Loizos has well described British frustrations in regard to ethnographic film. More recently Richard Tapper commenting on a film shot mainly by Tim Asch on Pashtoon nomadism regrets the absence of the following themes: "the complexity of ethnic relations in the region, the tribal structure of the Pakhtuns, the social organization of nomadic camps, the basis of social rivalry, the ecological, economic and demographic problems inherent in pastoral nomadism in the area and in particular Islam..." (Woodburn 1982:677). Clearly what Tapper would have preferred is to comment on a monograph translated into film. Criticisms of this sort are frequently expressed in Britain where ethnographic film does not seem to enjoy great prestige among academics. As a British social anthropologist put it in the course of a convention: "the main virtue of ethnographic film is to show that the people we write books about do exist in reality."

Analysis is the second level at which anthropological frustrations are concentrated. Modern anthropology is synthesis and analysis and there is a good chance that the anthropologist entering a film contract has done exactly this in previous writing. He will try to pass some of his analytical perceptions to the filmmaker with the hope that they will find their way to the screen. The film medium, however, is essentially descriptive and particularly unsuited for the translations of analytical discourse. Jarvie has reached the conclusion that since no analysis is possible on film it is a bad tool for anthropologists (1983). Starting from the obvious this is a hasty conclusion indeed. While it stresses what film cannot do it fails to appreciate its real potentialities. Meanwhile, both in the field and later at the editing table, the anthropologist may feel failure at his inability to proceed with analysis and may project this feeling on to his relationship with the filmmaker.

Let us consider now the position of the filmmaker with no anthropological training. Many among the most talented of documentarians avoid altogether entering a field partnership with an anthropologist. To my knowledge not one of the director-cameramen at the National Film Board of Canada has ever agreed to collaborate with an anthropologist in the field. It is true that Michel Brault worked with Jean Rouch but this was Jean Rouch the filmmaker, not the anthropologist. The reason is that the documentarian sees himself as an artist, a creator who wants to make "un film d'auteur, une oeuvre d'art." Anthropological input becomes a constraint, artistic genius does not need science. Years ago I invited Michel Brault to participate on the Netsilik Eskimo project. He answered "I am not interested in just loading the camera and shooting, I want to make film." Now this posture has a bearing on the partnership with the anthropologist. In most projects the documentarian is in a position of authority, he makes the film, he is responsible to the producer and if the anthropologist participates too much he can be excluded from the editing table. This happened to me with a National Film Board project.

I have presented my comments in a pessimistic mood. This need not be the case (as many successful partnerships testify). Probably I have projected here my own frustrations as an anthropologist. In conclusion I would like to express caution in regard to partnerships with documentarians while warmly recommending the participation of anthropologically trained film-makers.

Ethnographic Film and the Diffusion of the Anthropological Message

What is the anthropological message? And what is the role of ethno-graphic film in the diffusion of the anthropological message? There is, of course, great divergence among anthropologists on this issue. But going back to the Boasian tradition, one can propose that the anthropological message consists basically in a certain perception of culture, and more specifically, of other cultures, particularly exotic cultures. It is assumed that cultures can be understood on their own terms, that they can be studied as original wholes, and that they are the end result of unique, local, historical developments. Each culture is endowed with distinct moral and ideological characteristics. Cultures can be described from within and possibly configu-rations integrating their different parts established. One study method that fits this conception of culture well is the descriptive, stressing the elements of culture content presented in enumerative fashion to the detriment of so-cial form and to the exclusion of comparative, causal or developmental strategies. Stressing the original and unique in a culture, it is assumed im-possible to consider a given culture morally superior or somewhat better than another. There are certainly simple and complex cultures. On a scale of complexity we can place the Shoshone or Bushmen hunters at the lower end of the scale and American or Japanese cultures at the upper end. This, how-ever, does not imply that Americans are morally superior to he Eskimos. This is the position of cultural relativism. In Boasian terms, the anthropo-logical message consists of a descriptive approach to culture together with the basic postulate of cultural relativism. I assume that ethnographic film, properly understood, is particularly suited to accomplish this dual task. In a historical perspective it is within the framework of the Boasian tradition that ethnographic film has no place in European academe where different methodological traditions prevail, while it is very much part of the Ameri-can anthropological tradition. On the other side, ethnographic films are reg-ularly used in American classrooms. This brings us to the central issue concerning the utilization and impact of ethnographic films and more pre-cisely the manner in which true ethnographic film as distinguished from the spurious category promote the notion of cultural relativism. This with the understanding that the contribution of ethnographic film to descriptive detail is obvious. Film has the capacity to condense and synthesize with economy an enormous amount of visual information, and thus acts successfully as a supplement to written analysis without ever replacing it. This illustrative function of ethnographic film is widely accepted in American classrooms and does not need comment. It is rather the deeper impact on the viewer resulting from a prolonged exposure to a given set of ethnographic films that concerns us here.

For several years I had the opportunity to use segments of the Netsilik Eskimo film series describing the traditional life style of a remote land of arctic hunters. These films describe the annual migration cycle of the group prior to the introduction of rifles in the area. Each of the nine film units has a central theme - a seasonal subsistence activity taking place at particular camp sites. Various family and community activities taking place simultaneously are also described. There is no English narration or subtitles. Although an effort has been made to render the visual text intelligible for elementary school children, obscure points do remain, and this is natural and inevitable in the case of exotic culture. Further, throughout the films we have concentrated on the daily activities of a principal family consisting of a father, a mother and a five year old boy. I have used these films together with accompanying published materials mostly in undergraduate courses on introductory anthropology, cultural ecology or culture area studies.

The first reaction of the students reveals a strong empathy and curiosity for the principal actors right from the beginning of the screening procedure. The questions asked: "Is Itimangnerk suffering in the cold? How did Itimangnerk obtain Kinguk as wife? They seem to get along very well, do they quarrel occasionally?" and so forth. With the continuation of screenings and readings the questions reflect a widening of understanding: "Why are winter camps larger than summer camps? Is it strictly because of the necessity of collective hunting or are there additional, purely social reasons? Shamanistic activities have not been included in the film but surely at the time shamans must have officiated and what were their functions? Are these functions different in winter and summer? Why is there less sharing in summer? Why is it that kinship does not succeed in integrating camp society?" Clearly the questions become more abstract, revealing a better grasp of the material. Throughout the process the students remain astonished: "Itimangnerk and Kinguk seem to act in an intelligible and predictable way (like us) yet at the same time they live in an extreme environment and are totally different from us. How come?" That is exactly the pedagogical aim of ethnographic film properly conceived: to bring the extremely strange closer to us, to make the highly exotic intelligible, and in a sense, almost trivial. Let us summarize the film-based pedagogical process: the learner feels empathy for the actors, his ethnographic curiosity is awakened by the visualization of the strange culture and the obscure moments in the film. Then, with the help of the teacher and progress in reading, relations between different categories of data are perceived and explored with the help of general anthropological notions such as adaptation, ecological pressure, flexibility, bilateral filiation, etc. The exposure to ethnographic film acts as a substitute for actual field work, the viewer has the illusion of actually being there and observing, discovering the people. The visual ethnography allows him/her to perceive global cultural patterns he/she can further analyze with the help of printed material. Ethnographic film demystifies exotic forms and allows the viewer to perceive a strangely foreign culture from inside and to decode it (so to speak) in its own terms with the help of printed texts. The final effect of the visual experience is to facilitate in the viewer perception of an original cultural whole.

Strangely enough, a similar result can be produced to a limited degree by screening a single episode. In this process, ethnographic film resembles structural analysis. Levi-Strauss points to the necessity for the field observer to obsessively concentrate on extreme detail because often such a detail can reveal a structural form. In reference to such an episode David Mac-Dougall has written:

> Among the Netsilik Eskimo films there is a scene in which a small child snares a seagull, slowly and inexpertly stones it to death and brings it triumphantly to his mother, who cuts off the feet for him to play with. For a long time, he makes the feet run over the ground, holding one in each hand. The cameraman has the good sense to follow this sequence of events, and in its totality it reveals something of another way of life with extraordinary conciseness. It tells more about the socialization of children, or their attitudes toward life or suffering or their relationships to their mothers. By some intuitive means it better prepares us to understand other aspects of the culture--its mobility, its ecology, its beliefs (MacDougall 1976:149).

It is in this sense then that ethnographic film contributes to the diffusion of the anthropological message: it invites the audience to perceive an exotic culture as a distinct and original whole to be studied in its own terms. This, however, is the privilege of true ethnographic film produced with the active collaboration of a field anthropologist. With films of the other, spurious category, different results can be obtained.

At this point I should briefly mention a curious and important controversy that followed the initial distribution of the Netsilik Eskimo films in 1973 and the associated elementary (fifth and sixth grade) curriculum unit called MACOS. Soon after the introduction of the Netsilik films in the U.S., numerous parent groups protested publicly against both course and film. Public rallies were held, newspaper articles published, televised commentaries presented. Gradually the public uproar intensified, the controversy became a national issue and led to discussions in front of the entire House of Representatives. It was Representative Conlan from Arizona who voiced the most explicit criticisms (on May 11, 1976). After unmasking the relativistic morality of the course (Embedded in the MACOS material is an "anything goes" philosophy which subtly unteaches morality, patriotism,

American values, Judeo-Christian ethics and beliefs, so that children will be more accepting of a world view rather than an American view.), Conlan criticized the Netsilik Eskimo films. "The exaggeration of the media has always been modulated by the use of black and white and by narrated interpretations, both of which remove the viewer from actuality and offer a point of view. The new films are in vivid color and are silent...Every day it is violence and death." Now this statement has important implications: it admits the powerful impact of ethnographic film, it clearly states that ethnographic film is closer to actuality (the social reality depicted) and in this sense different from the usual documentaries and, in the context of the discussion it assumes that ethnographic film is well suited to carry over the relativistic message. The criticisms expressed by Conlan are valid, they underline with strength the obvious relativistic philosophy of course and films. They are exaggerated, however, in the sense that the teaching materials in reference to the Netsilik Eskimos who do not involve contempt or rejection of American values, they simply invite students to adopt a rational attitude towards Eskimo life styles. It is my conviction that Conlan's brutal and emotional rejection of the Netsilik Eskimo films hides deeper truths. Basically, Conlan objects to the observational style of the Netsilik films describing the Eskimos as truthfully as possible the way they are in actuality. Conlan clearly points to certain dangers in showing the Eskimos as they are. What are these dangers? I believe that these dangers are the contradictions between the perception American school children have of the Eskimos (that is the American STEREOTYPE of the Eskimos) and elements of ethnographic truth contained in the Netsilik Eskimo films.

What is the stereotype of the Eskimos among school children on this continent? To answer this question, my students conducted a survey in five elementary classrooms (grades 2 and 3) in the Montreal area and northern Vermont. Children were invited to make drawings of the Eskimos and to explain the personality characteristics of the Eskimos. In two classes the children had already had some instruction on the Eskimos, in the other three, none. The stereotype comprises the following characteristics: The Eskimos live in a vast, white and cold country, they are clad in warm furs, live in igloos and have dog sledges. Their main sustenance is fish and occasionally whale. The Eskimos are happy people, in all of the drawings the Eskimo are smiling, they are clean because there is plenty of water around where they can wash, and their igloos are as white and clean inside as they are outside, the Eskimos are extremely active people and share their food generously, they have no chiefs, are very peaceful and are very much our friends. Further, they are free. One boy in Vermont added: "They are as free as we Americans!" This is an extremely positive stereotype. Children contrast the Eskimos to the Indians, who are considered as fighters and cruel. They are our enemies! Now many of these moral characteristics of the Eskimos are similar to the virtues of Protestants: hard work, egalitarianism, a peaceful disposition, freedom. Basically, the children in our sample consider

the Eskimos as a kind of primitive Protestant; upon the Eskimos are projected middle class American values; the white arctic is like the symbolic
playground of middle America.

How did this stereotype arise? This is an extremely difficult question.
What is obvious is that the Eskimos have become part of American
elementary classroom culture. In Victorian times, already many family
magazine articles written by arctic explorers and their admirers had popular-
ized the Eskimos. It is my conviction, however, that the release of
NANOOK contributed substantially to the elaboration and diffusion of the
stereotype. In a fascinating recent study, the British film critic, Paul Rotha,
gives substantial evidence of a veritable nanookmania following the release
of the film! Igloos were built in front of the theaters, dogs were harnessed to
sledges on street corners, Eskimo pies sold, special music composed, and so
forth. According to publicity of the times, the marvel and drama of the fear-
less, lovable happy-go-lucky Eskimos! Real life, love, struggle, laughter
and drama of the Arctic! Are the Eskimos human? See Nanook, the star
hero, and Nyla, his help and heart mate, as they go through life's drama
amid the snow and ice of the bleak Arctic! Pa Eskimo, Ma Eskimo, all the
Eskimo kids, Eskimo dogs, Eskimo hunting, Eskimo life, love, action and
thrills, etc., etc. The impact of Nanook must have been considerable. It is
my belief that it is in nanookmania that we have to search for the roots of
the present day Eskimo stereotype. In later years Hollywood also made substantial use of the Eskimos. The National Geographic magazine exploited
the theme skillfully and with the help of television commercials and newspaper cartoons the caricature of the Eskimo penetrated our daily lives and
reached the classrooms.

The ethnographic films on the Netsilik Eskimos and associated written
materials carry a different message and obviously they contradict the stereotype of the Eskimo as a primitive Protestant. It is in this sense that,
according to Representative Conlan's wording, they illustrate violence and
death, every day. Clearly, we are in the presence of two kinds of ethnographic film. The first genre is the filmmaker's ethnographic documentary
of wide popular appeal. In some cases it may strengthen existing stereotypes. The other kind is the true ethnographic film produced with the
participation of field anthropologists. It can be used in conjunction with
published literature. Its impact is of a different sort altogether. It is ethnographic film devoted to the description of truth that is best suited for the
diffusion of the anthropological message.

This brief survey points to an astonishing variety of accomplishments,
various projects have employed different production strategies influenced by
distinct and mostly hidden ideologies with highly divergent utilizations.
These are accomplishments by western anthropologists and filmmakers
working in the field in the 1960s and 1970s. Recently there has been a substantial weakening of production efforts and very few major films have been
completed. Exhaustion of the older and the absence of a new generation of

anthropological filmmakers is only a partial explanation of the downturn movement of which the documentary is a part. We hope filmmakers from the Third World will be able to take the lead and initiate production projects in their own countries. We also hope that their efforts will be equally beneficial to both East and West.

ACKNOWLEDGEMENTS

This article is a condensation of two different papers. The first was presented at the Visual Anthropology Conference XIth International Congress of Anthropological and Ethnological Sciences, Vancouver, B.C., August 1983. The second was read at a seminar in March 1984 at the Department of Anthropology, University of Vermont, Burlington. I would like to thank Jack Rollwagen for his generous help in the preparation of this article.

REFERENCES CITED

Asch, Timothy (1982). Collaboration in Ethnographic Film Making: A Personal View. Canberra Anthropology 5 (1):8-36. (See the revised version by Asch in this volume.)

Godelier, Maurice (1981). Reflexions sur l'usage des moyens audio-visuels en anthropologie. IN Anthropologie Visuel en France, Paris.

Heider, Karl (1976). Ethnographic Film. Austin: University of Texas Press.

Jarvie, I.E. (1983). The Problem of the Ethnographic Real. Current Anthropology 24(3):313-325.

Loisos, Peter (1980). Granada Television's Disappearing World Series: An Appraisal. American Anthropologist 83(3):573-594.

MacDougall, David (1976). Prospects of the Ethnographic Film. IN Movies and Methods, B. Nichols (ed.), Berkeley: University of California Press.

Mead, Margaret (1975). Visual Anthropology in a Discipline of Words. IN Principles of Visual Anthropology, Paul Hockings, (ed.) The Hague, Mouton, pp. 3-12.

Rouch, Jean (1981). Une retrospective. Paris: CNRS-SERDDAV.

Rouch, Jean (1975). The Camera and Man. IN Principles of Visual Anthropology, Paul Hockings (ed.). The Hague: Mouton, pp. 83-102

Woodburn, James (ed.) (1982). The Royal Anthropological Institute Film Library Catalogue. London: The Royal Anthropological Institute.

Against Reductionism And Idealist Self-Reflexivity: The Ilparakuyo Maasai Film Project[1]

Peter Biella
Department of Anthropology
Temple University

ABSTRACT: The literature on anthropological film is dominated by reductive materialist and idealist epistemologies. For this reason, films which use the shooting styles recommended in the literature perpetuate errors specific to each epistemology and fail to express ideas which are crucial to anthropology. The long-take, observational style recommended by the reductive materialist school cannot present theory, whereas the exclusive discussion of methodology recommended by the advocates of idealist self-reflexivity leaves no time for ethnography. Marx' emergent materialist critique of reductionism and idealism is important for an adequate filmmaking epistemology. This is exemplified in the author's films of the Ilparakuyo Maasai of Tanzania. The praxis of filmmaking is described and shown to raise issues too complex to be handled by reductionism or idealism. Epistemological errors, metaphorically perpetuated in reductive and idealist filmmaking styles, effectively resist verbal refutation but can be critiqued visually with a style based on the work of Brecht. In the Ilparakuyo films, sequences of still photographs, cinemascope and double-images visually reveal the errors and futility of arguments for the observational and self-reflexive styles.

I. Introduction

This paper is part of a larger study of the relevance of emergent historical materialism to ethnographic film (Biella 1984). With the concept of the growth of knowledge through praxis, I first critique the philosophical foundations of two recent anthropological film theories and contrast them with the more adequate epistemology of emergent materialism. The second section of this paper gives examples from my filming among Tanzania's Ilparakuyo Maasai to show the inadequacies of the two dominant theoretical trends, reductive materialism and idealist self-reflexivity. I argue that film-

47

maker ignorance, the praxis of the people who are filmed, and the social disruptions caused by filmmaking can only be explained with a philosophy that recognizes emergence as a major factor. Reductive and idealist theories of anthropological film fail to recognize any type of social innovation or praxis. Such theories therefore recommend styles of filming which radically inhibit innovations and praxis in cinematic expression. Because of the great extent of inhibition in most anthropological cinema, the stylistic experiments made in the Ilparakuyo films, which I discuss at the end of this paper, suggest needed alternatives.

II. Three Epistemologies in Anthropological Film

a. *Reductive Materialism:* The majority of writings on ethnographic film theory come from the philosophical perspective of reductive materialism. This theoretical work is materialist because it assumes the pre-existence of the material world, properties of which man can discover and put on film. But the dominant theory is also reductive, and therefore inadequate, because it cannot theorize or explain change and man's transformation of himself and the world. For the reductive materialist, science merely reflects what is: it cannot create something new. Reductive theory, therefore, inadequately theorizes how the ethnographic filmmaker affects and is affected by the world in his practice of science.

The most vigorous spokesman for the reductive materialist position in ethnographic film is Karl Heider (1976). Heider's position is an extreme form of reductive materialism called physicalism. The essence of Heider's physicalist theory is that it equates "truth" and knowledge of "reality" solely with man's "natural" perception (1976:77). Knowledge of the world, Heider says, is possible because our perception allows us to *reflect* the world's properties. It is certainly true that our perception does give us useful information about the world. However, Heider takes this truth to unjustifiable lengths. His recommended techniques for recording ethnographic "truth" on film require the filmmaker to maximize the so-called "attributes of ethnographicness" (Heider 1976:3-15, 46-117). Because, for Heider, these attributes supposedly allow film to reproduce human perception with little "distortion" (1976:50, et passim), it can likewise reproduce truth.

The "attributes of ethnographicness" require the ethnographic filmmaker to use a very limited style and repertoire of filmmaking techniques. Briefly, these techniques are the exclusive use of long-takes, synchronous sound, wide-view ("whole bodies") compositions, and the shooting of "whole acts," i.e., whole cultural events without any significant omissions. Heider's film style therefore is designed to maximize what might be called the original spatio-temporal continuities of the ethnographic situation which was filmed (cf. Burch 1973:3-16). Long-takes, for Heider, are ethnographic "truth": selecting which of these continuity-"truths" to film is "theory" (Heider

1976:50, 83, 114).

In my view, these definitions of "truth" and "theory" are completely indefensible. Heider's concern to maximize "attributes of ethnographicness," to preserve spatio-temporal continuities as much as filmically possible, derives from an epistemology which is actively hostile to any theory. By limiting the permissible repertoire of filmmaking techniques to the would-be reproduction of spatio-temporal continuities, Heider rules out almost all stylistic means of articulating theoretical ideas. Although such ruled-out techniques as non-sync sound and editing juxtapositions are extremely useful in the development of ideas in film, they do not reproduce Heider's idea of "natural" perception. For him, techniques which do not reproduce continuities are less than scientifically true.

Heider's insistence upon "attributes of ethnographicness" eliminates from his definition of good anthropology any films in which the theoretical perspective does not principally require continuous spatio-temporal data. Heider therefore eliminates all important theoretical perspectives from his definition of anthropology.

For Heider, ethnographic material which is filmed correctly is said to replicate "natural" perception; because it replicates perception, it is said to naturally exude order and meaning. This physicalist reflection theory is the most naive form of reductive materialism. A second, contradictory view exists within the reductive tradition of anthropological film theory, however, that of Humian induction. The major proponent of this alternative view is E. Richard Sorenson (1967, 1975a, 1975b; cf. Collier 1967). According to him, filmed ethnographic material is also said to replicate perception closely: yet, precisely because film *is* like "natural" perception, this view says that it is chaotic and meaningless without subsequent scientific analysis.

Sorenson is far more cautious than Heider in admitting a reduction of "reality" and "truth" to the visual. Indeed, Sorenson frequently argues that film does not replicate "reality," but only provides "data" about a part of "non-recurrent phenomena" (Sorenson and Gajdusek 1963:112; Sorenson and Jablonko 1975:152; Sorenson 1975a:446; 1975b:3). However, these disclaimers must be regarded skeptically: unless Sorenson assumes a reductive epistemology, it is impossible to find consistency in his grandiose claims about the utility of his films for future research or to discover any motive behind his recommendations for filmmaking style.

The first of Sorenson's recommendations is that the researchers undertake "programmed sampling" (Sorenson and Jablonko 1975:153) in which the topic of ethnographic interest is to be filmed with the same style that maximizes Heider's "attributes of ethnographicness." That is, the filmmaker should use long-takes, sync-sound, and film whole bodies and whole acts. Unlike Heider, Sorenson describes a second major task of contemporary anthropological film. It is the preservation of ethnographic data for future research. Sorenson specifies that in this future research, both the data require-

ments and the theoretical purpose are entirely unknown at the time of filming (Sorenson and Gajdusek 1963:112; Sorenson 1967:445, 1975a:446).
Sorenson therefore recommends "digressive searching" with film: this is
shooting which is unplanned, undirected and unmotivated. When "digressive
searching" is combined with programmed and opportunistic filming, Sorenson says that the ideal ethnographic film strategy is reached (Sorenson and
Jablonko 1975). Under such a filming strategy, data are "maximally preserved" and supposedly will reward "almost endless scientific and historical
inquiry" (Sorenson 1967:446).

Such a position is theoretically reductive and scientifically unsound. In
Sorenson as in Heider, the infinity of all possible data is reduced to a small
collection of continuous spatio-temporal perceptions emitted from the
movie screen. Sorenson calls these cultural "samples" (Sorenson and
Jablonko 1975). Contrary to this view, however, it is impossible that all
important facets of a culture could be "sampled" in the twenty or thirty
hours of film that Sorenson has to expend, or that each facet might be
recorded frequently enough to achieve an adequate sample size. Behind
Sorenson's vocabulary of natural science lies the fact that, for *most*
"scientific and historical inquiry," his sample data are necessarily inappropriate and statistically insignificant. At best, they are suggestive and interesting.

b. *Idealism:* The most extensive published critique of reductive materialism in ethnographic film theory is by Jay Ruby (1975, 1976, 1977,
1980). Unfortunately, Ruby's objections are based on idealist epistemology.
Because of this, his own recommendations for "reflexive," scientific film
technique have no valid epistemological support.

Following Worth and Gross (1974), Ruby states that meaning is produced by the active application of an "interpretive strategy" (Ruby 1976:5-6,
1980:157). Such a strategy allows the ethnographic film viewer to infer
what the filmmaker has implied. For Ruby, a series of filmmaking techniques which he calls "reflexive" are required in ethnographic films. Reflexive techniques are supposed to give the audience insight into the methodology and production of a film. Such techniques, Ruby (1975, 1976) asserts,
can provide scientific implications and thus stimulate scientific inferences
from the audience. Without reflexive implications about the producer, process and product of filmmaking, a film cannot be considered anthropological
or scientific. Ruby (1980:165) writes, "Being reflexive is virtually synonymous with being scientific."

Because Ruby is committed to an epistemological position in which
meaning is produced by man, he rejects

> the positivist position that meaning resides in the world
> (1980:155).

Thus, Ruby rejects a position which is roughly that of Heider, since, for him, meaning is the perception of the world. Ruby's rejection of reductive materialism is consistent with the premises of praxis theory and emergent materialism: it is true that many things come to have meaning for man, but meaning does not reside in the world independent of him. Rather, meaning is a production of human consciousness in relation to the world.

As Ruby continues the statement quoted above, however, he makes assertions the validity of which is denied by emergent materialism. In rejecting positivism, Ruby also rejects the idea

> that human beings should strive to discover the inherent, immutable and objectively true reality. We are beginning to assume that human beings construct and impose meaning on the world. We create order. We don't discover it (1980:155; cf. Ruby 1977:5).

Here, Ruby makes an idealist argument with his epistemological unification of "meaning" and "order." Praxis theory makes a contrary interpretation: whereas "meaning" could not exist independently of man, "order" certainly does (cf. Lenin 1972 [1908]:135-6, 176). Yet Ruby asserts that "order" in the world is not discovered. Clearly within the tradition of idealist philosophy, Ruby argues that thought alone is responsible for the order of the world. (However, Ruby's idealism is inconsistent: see, for example, 1975:107, 1980:173 n.2.)

By arguing that a reflexive film is virtually synonymous with one that is scientific, Ruby confuses two distinct scientific practices. The first is the historic process whereby a community of scientists reflects on a work, tests its assumptions and conclusions, and finally judges it. The second practice is performed by one anthropologist in the production of reflexive comments about his or her ethnography or ethnographic film. The first reflexive practice, by the community of scientists, demonstrates truth in Ruby's argument that reflexivity is scientific. But the second practice, an individual anthropologist's reflexive remarks, certainly cannot make a work scientific, however appropriate such remarks may sometimes be. Ruby treats the practice of the scientific community as if it did not exist and concentrates entirely on the individual. The ideologies of idealism and individualism apparent in this move ignore the historical development of science. Further, they illegitimately bestow the credibility of collective scientific practice on a particular individual's work.

Because of his idealist assumptions, which have apparently led to his excessive concern with "reflexivity" and "inference," Ruby fails to make reasonable suggestions for the production of ethnographic film. His major recommendation, to be "reflexive," is both shallow in perspective and impossible of accomplishment. Ruby writes:

> A filmic ethnographic work must include a scientific jus-
> tification for the multitude of decisions that one makes in
> the process of producing a film--the framing and length of
> each shot, selection of subject matter, technological deci-
> sions (such as the choice of film stock, lens, etc.), type of
> field sound collected, use of studio sound, editing deci-
> sions, etc. (1975:10).

If these recommendations were followed literally, there would never be time for ethnographic study: each reflexive "scientific justification" would become the source of an infinity of reflecting justifications, and anthropology would be reduced to methodology. Although Ruby has elsewhere stated that it is possible to be too reflexive (1980:160), he has not shown how a filmmaker may follow his strictures and yet avoid excess. I believe that no solution is possible within the parameters defined by his idealist conception of science.

Ruby's "reflexivity" lapses into an idealistically conceived world of the anthropologist's inner musings. The material world, and praxis within it, have no entry into film. For this reason, Ruby's idealism prevents him from adequately theorizing two valid points which are made by reductive-materialist ethnographic film theory: first, that a large portion of the world exists independently of human meanings; second, that a large portion of the world has inherent order. Like the reductivists, however, Ruby lacks an adequate theory of emergence and the relationship between theory and practice.

c. *Emergent Materialism:* This philosophical position assumes the material pre-existence of the world: it therefore shares the major premise of all types of materialism. It is also concerned with man's ability to understand the world, to introduce change in it, and be changed by it: it is, therefore, a theory of emergence that includes important insights from the idealist tradition. A discussion of the epistemological errors of reductive materialism and idealism will serve to outline emergent materialism and its importance for an adequate theory of anthropological film.

Heider makes a fundamental epistemological error which separates his physicalism from all other forms of materialism, reductive and emergent: it is the idea that to perceive is to understand. All *other* philosophical materialisms concur that appearances can be deceiving. For example, Marx writes:

> Science would be superflous if there were no difference
> between the appearance of things and their essence (cited
> in Godelier 1970:341).

Lenin, too, renounces Heider's premise that "reality" is the perceptual image of things:

> Verification of (perceptual) images, differentiation be-
> tween true and false images, is given by practice (1972
> [1908]:119).

Lenin therefore sees "practice" as allowing man to differentiate between ignorant perception and more exact knowledge. We must, he writes,

> not regard our knowledge as ready-made and unalterable,
> but must determine how knowledge *emerges* from igno-
> rance, how incomplete, inexact knowledge becomes more
> and more exact (1972 [1908]:111; italics omitted and
> supplied).

Practice, in the sense of experimentation, can permit the emergence of more
exact knowledge and more adequate theory. This is a fundamental premise of
emergent materialism. Reductive materialism has a place for neither emergence nor theory.

In an important sense, Ruby's idealist argument is an advance over
those of Heider and Sorenson. Ruby argues that the practice of creating
meaning can create order. Although Ruby wrongly sees the production of
meaning as the only source of order, it is nonetheless true that meaning is
one source. Marx acknowledges the importance of the discovery of this fact
by idealist philosophers: unlike reductive materialists, idealists recognize
"the active side," man's theoretical and ideational creativity (Marx 1972
[1845]:107). Idealism correctly identifies a second type of practice, independent from experimentation, in which the mental goals of man shape the
world in their own image (cf. Colletti 1972). In Lenin's words:

> The idea of the transformation of the ideal into the real is
> *profound*. Very important for history. But also in the per-
> sonal life of man it is evident that there is much truth to
> this. Against vulgar (reductive) materialism (1961
> [1914]:114; original italics).

Lenin's teleological praxis is materialist, the evolutionary emergence of
man's power to create an order independent of himself and the order of the
pre-existent world. Ruby, on the other hand, understands this creativity in
idealist terms: man's creation can never contribute an order independent of
thought.

The two epistemological theories discussed above, reductive materialism and subjective idealism, have a long history in the political struggle of
ideas. Marx, Engels and Lenin wrote extensive critiques against both (Marx
1972 [1845], 1977 [1843]; Marx and Engels 1974 [1845-6]; Engels 1954
[1876-8]; Lenin 1961 [1914], 1972 [1908]). These thinkers did this not because philosophy and epistemology were concerns which they believed to be

most crucial; on the contrary, they did it because reasonable epistemology is the only viable philosophical support for their crucial *social scientific* theories. The philosophies which they critiqued so mangled and distorted reasonable epistemology that the air had to be cleared.

Yet the fact that reductive materialist and idealist arguments, which have been favorites of the bourgeoisie for two hundred years, are still being invented, or repeated without citation, is ample proof that refutation does not allow the air to remain clear for long. Reductive materialism and idealism re-emerge in adaptation to the latest technological media for the discovery and dissemination of social scientific ideas. The materialist reduction of theory to spatio-temporal continuity, like the idealist reduction of science to self-indulgence, equally repress crucial truths of social science. Unquestionably, radical social science has a profound role to play in social change, and for this very reason, it is suppressed.[2] Further, it is through the medium of film that social scientific ideas, such as they are, reach the vast majority of their audience. Thus, ethnographic film, and an emergent materialist ethnographic film theory, have strategic importance in the ideological class struggle (Althusser 1971).

III. The Practice of Filmmaking Among the Ilparakuyo

A domain in which the theoretical struggle must be fought is the recognition of the means by which filmmaking practice influences film theory. Although a theoretical refutation of reductive materialism and idealism provides the foundation for an adequate epistemology, practical experience also lays the groundwork for theory. The discovery of knowledge and the creation of new ideas through interactive practice are crucial elements in my films about the Ilparakuyo Maasai.[3] Scenes from these films and experiences of filming give insight into both praxis and innovation with an evocative power absent in theory. Some specific experiences of filming in an Ilparakuyo (singular: Olparakuoni) Maasai homestead bring to light several levels of praxis in ethnographic film production.

a. *Ignorance and Anthropological Filmmaking:* Any theory of the emergence of knowledge must contend with the practical realities of ignorance. At the time of filming, I was not a specialist in Ilparakuyo ethnography. Some of the problems of ignorance which I encountered could have been avoided or lessened. Others, however, are simply part of the territory of anthropological filmmaking and cannot be prevented by pre-production preparation. For example, in the sense that a high shooting ratio permits the filmmaker to gather footage about many specific contextual factors, the limited supply of both film-stock and time which many ethnographic filmmakers face has important implications. Shortages prevent some people who are met in the field from becoming potential "characters" in the film.

Limited stock and time require filmmakers to become increasingly committed to certain "characters" and "story-lines" and thus to remain ignorant of others. Both the audience and the filmmaker necessarily remain ignorant of many facets of the filmed society because narrative conventions of the "story-line" and the requirements of structured knowledge must be maintained to some extent. One experience among the Ilparakuyo is very revealing in this regard.

I can speak neither Kiswahili nor Maa.[4] I was very dependent on nonverbal material and on frequent (but usually somewhat delayed) translations. The language problem was quite significant for my filmmaking decisions. At one point, I was given a bad translation which epitomizes how filmmaking decisions can be influenced by error and ignorance. One of my translators had been told that a woman was in a great deal of trouble because she had taken snuff. The translator did not realize that the right to use snuff must be purchased by an Olparakuoni wife from her husband, and that this woman had not purchased the right. In an effort to explain why the woman was in so much trouble, he erroneously interpreted the statement about snuff-taking as a metaphor. He told me that the wife was to be punished because she had been promiscuous. I was thus led to believe that she and her father-in-law, the Olparakuoni elder named Koisengé, were involved in a major dispute over her sexual activities. In pursuit of my misunderstanding, I wasted almost an hour of film and quarter-inch tape, a large investment of resources, filming the two whenever they were together. Further, I was constantly confused because neither of the supposed disputants showed much anger. From other translations, I knew that their sometimes peevish discussions never turned to the topic of sexuality. Because of their reticence to discuss the argument openly, I made a somewhat desperate hypothesis: I guessed that dispute settlement among the Ilparakuyo is very indirect. Later, of course, I learned that the indirectness about the topic of sexuality resulted from he fact that there *was* no dispute over sexuality! However, my commitment of film to his particular non-existent indirectness sensitized me: I later found that many Ilparakuyo disputes actually do take an indirect form (Biella and Cross 1981). My knowledge was emergent.

Ignorance plays a crucial role in the praxis of ethnographic film production. The fact that the filmmaker makes errors of interpretation and can also correct them cannot be explained by reductive materialism. Contrary to it, seeing is not understanding unless seeing has an adequate theoretical foundation: thus, errors about what is seen often occur. On the other hand, errors can be corrected, not because some new material has been seen, but because theoretical principles are learned.[5] Nor can idealism, which does have some concern with theory, adequately explain the episode concerning snuff. Idealism can only consistently explain error as a tautological contradiction *inside* the head of the inquiring subject. My errors resulted from ignorance of policies and traditions which were entirely *outside*: if I had created their "order," I would never have needed to throw away any footage! Praxis theory is thus necessary to explain the possibility of ignorance as well as the means to overcome it.

b. *Heisenberg's Principle and the Praxis of the People Filmed:* Praxis is also important for an adequate theory of ethnographic film because of the emphasis which it places on man's creative potential: man not only reflects the world, but can also manipulate it and change it to his own ends. Neither reductive materialism nor idealism can contend with the fact that the people about whom ethnographic films are made have the capacity for praxis. Several situations which we filmed were transformed because of the filmmaking. In one case, Koisengé was annoyed that his young son had stolen a little money and bought a drug with it from nearby, ethnically-distinct Wakwere farmers. Petty theft by herdboys is not serious or unusual, but indulgence in pleasures specific to the farming people was a breach of Ilparakuyo tradition which Koisengé did not want to encourage. Koisengé thus shamed his son with a stroke of visual poetic justice. Since the boy's offense was to ignore tradition, Koisengé demanded that we begin filming, and he led his son to the boy's traditional place in the homestead, the cattle byre. Positioning the boy before a large steer, Koisengé cried to us, "Ho-kay! This is the herd boy and this is the steer. So! Take a picture!" (See Plate 1.)

In this example, Koisengé both invents the theory and engages in the practice of a media event. By having us film his son in his traditional place, the cattle byre, we reified the boy's shame on film, and gave him a visual moral tale, with himself as the protagonist. Obviously, the reflection theory of reductive materialism is powerless even to admit the premises of this story. The presence of our cameras created the possibility for Koisengé's filmmaking practice. The cameras, with the help of a brilliantly intuitive Olparakuoni director, *created* the situation which film is supposed by Heider only to *reflect*. Koisengé's praxis molded a new element, the camera, into a unique utterance about traditional values: his visual poem reflects tradition and changes the world in the same moment.[6]

Ethnographic film theory must account for the praxis which results from interaction between filmmaker and people filmed. In the literature, discussion of this phenomenon is rare, perhaps because of the fear that it would unleash criticism of ethnographic film based on analogies with the Heisenberg Uncertainty Principle. This Principle states that to know the position of an atomic particle it is necessarily to remain ignorant of its momentum, and vice versa. This is true because the act of observing either the position or momentum changes the other and thus renders knowledge of it uncertain (Heisenberg 1971; Jammer 1974). By analogy, the act of observing ethnographic encounters renders knowledge of them uncertain as well. However, the episode described here, of Koisengé and his son, like others which occurred during my filming, shows that the analogy is misleading; in physics, the Principle states that to observe is to change; but it also states that to observe is necessarily to remain ignorant of the change. I

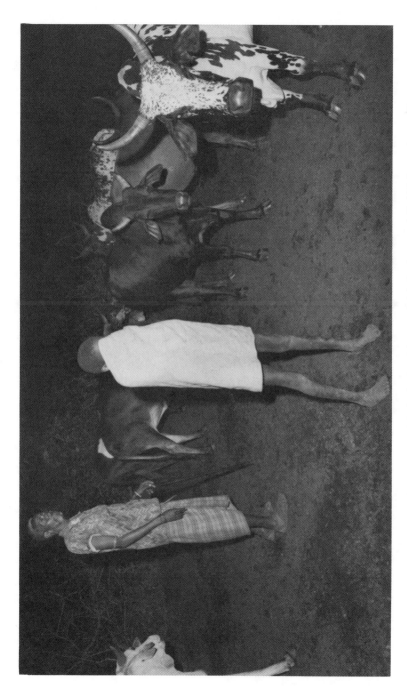

PLATE 1: *Koisengé*: "Ho-kay! This is the herd boy and this is the steer! So! Take a picture!" (Photo: Richard Cross, © 1984, Contemporary Historians)

found that although filming often initiated innovation and praxis, the result was often a *heightened* form of activity which was comprehensible because it emphasized traditional values. If we had not been there, Koisengé might not have dramatically led his son to the cattle byre: however, the byre remains a focus of traditional values among the Ilparakuyo, regardless of our filmmaking.

Idealist philosophy is incapable of explaining Koisengé's praxis. Idealism attributes creativity to only one "subject," in this case, the ethnographic filmmaker. Accordingly, the "object" of films is merely an idea in a world whose order is created by the "subject." Because these "ideas" actually have the creative and emergent properties attributed only to the "subject," the dichotomy of subject and object in idealism cannot stand.

c. *Disruptions Caused by Filmmaking:* The third aspect of praxis in ethnographic film is exposed in the disruptions which our filmmaking made among the Ilparakuyo. Although it led to amusement, it also caused embarrassment and even fear. Ilparakuyo elders frequently asked me to play back tape recordings for them: mundane statements that had been taped took on humorous nuances with playback; jokes that were told became riotously funny. On one occasion, however, I realized that the tape which I randomly chose to play back did not give pleasure. I later learned that an Olparakuoni elder, for whom this conversation was replayed and who was not present when it was recorded, had been discussed on the section of the tape which he heard. The conversants civilly but firmly agreed not to leave aside a particularly large share of meat for this man. Although they were perfectly within their rights and discussed the policy which justified their decision, the playback of the tape created an entirely unprecedented situation: people appeared to be rude only because of the recording technology. Elders never asked me to play back tapes after this occurred.

The next day, an Olparakuoni wife was told the story of the playback. A few minutes later, while I was taping her, she suddenly stopped speaking. With fear in her eyes, she had someone tell me in English that I must not allow her husband to hear the recording I had just made. She had been taped explaining her reason for leaving the homestead that afternoon: she said that because her husband was drinking heavily, she feared he might beat her. If he learned from the tape that this was her reason for leaving, he would be furious.[7] (After this, I resolved not to play back *any* tapes in which I did not understand the content.)

Our filmmaking created a unique practical danger: for the Olparakuoni wife, it also added a dimension to the epistemological status of speech and knowledge in general. Without recording technology (that is, in the present normal state of Ilparakuyo society) the spoken word is rapid-fading. It can therefore be entrusted to the discretion of the listener. With books, tape recordings and playback, the repetition of a complex idea no longer depends solely on a willful act by a speaker. Among the Ilparakuyo, discretion and trust therefore have an epistemological status which they do not have in literate societies: they are the only necessary prerequisites for attaining and bestowing many kinds of knowledge.

Praxis theory understands knowledge as a dialectic of the world and ideas. This episode demonstrates that through the co-transformation of the two, basic assumptions about the nature of knowledge itself can be changed in praxis.[8] The Olparakuoni wife realized that a danger was implicit in the new medium of film, particularly when combined with my ignorance. She therefore sought to prevent the danger by making a traditional appeal to my discretion.

In this account, and in the story of Koisengé and his son, the interaction between traditional ideas, a new technology and filmmakers resulted in completely unprecedented situations which the Ilparakuyo could successfully manipulate. The dominant theories of ethnographic film fail to account for the praxis which is related here. If, as Heider strongly implies, an Olparakuoni elder and wife are no more than objects of data to be reflected in long-shot, they could not transform the future of the film by directing or censoring it: their successful praxis refutes reductive materialism. Similarly the decisive manipulation of our filming by the Ilparakuyo reveals that the ability to impose meaning on the world is not the monopoly of the "self-reflexive subject": this refutes idealism.

IV. Style as Critique in the Ilparakuyo Films

The struggle against reductive and idealist theories in anthropological film must also be waged on the level of cinematic style. Following Bertolt Brecht (1964), a number of theoreticians outside the domain of anthropology present cogent arguments for a more adequate ethnographic and documentary film style (Eaton 1983; Kuhn 1978; MacBean 1983; MacCabe 1974; Nichols 1981, 1983; Solanas and Gettino 1976; Wollen 1982). Like Brecht, these authors argue that stylistic innovation is a crucial element in the presentation of scientific ideas. My own work finds, within the anthropological problematic, innovative models in Jean Rouch (Eaton 1979) and the MacDougalls (MacDougall 1978).

Unlike written film theory, film style (as relatively independent of film content) communicates on a subliminal, metaphorical level. Because this level of communication is subliminal, it has a propagandistic value which cannot be negated with words. Stylistic metaphors, like Heider's "long-takes equal truth," or Ruby's "self-reflexive style equals science," are a kind of non-verbal swindle. They do not argue for the validity of the metaphor on screen. Rather, they merely perpetuate an invalid verbal argument through visual means. Whereas the verbal arguments make statements of fact, and are therefore refutable, visual film styles only reflect factual claims metaphorically. Like other metaphors, therefore, they "cannot be corrected by reference to proper usage nor by the way things turn out" (McClosky 1964:216). In order to counteract the communicational value of stylistic metaphors, I fight fire with fire: my Ilparakuyo films employ a number of stylistic counter-metaphors. In this, I follow Brecht's lead.

a. *The Historically-Transient Power of Style:* Brecht identifies a metaphor in the realist style of Aristotelian theater. There, the audience is encouraged to equate the events depicted on the tragic stage with the real events of the world. Since the appropriate response to theatrical tragedy is audience passivity, Brecht (1964:189) argues that theatrical realism has an ideological consequence. If an audience is led to believe in the metaphor that "All the world's a stage," it will be inclined to respond to social tragedies with the same passivity appropriate to the theater: it will not take an active role against preventable tragedies, such as those brought about by capitalist exploitation. Brecht transforms the metaphor. Rather than encouraging social passivity, he encourages his theatrical audience to be active, to challenge plots and the judgments of characters. Brecht's alienation effects remake the metaphor between world and stage by encouraging criticism of the theater and social relations in the world.

In order to apply Brechtian techniques to anthropological filmmaking, it is important to realize that Brecht has been strategically misinterpreted by non-Marxist theorists. Typically, his alienation effects have been assumed to do no more than provide an amusing, "self-reflexive" alternative to the illusion of the theater. In fact, this interpretation ignores the historical specificity of Brecht's work. In the period of time when he worked, the illusion of the theater was a major means for the dissemination of ideology: not only social passivity but also the specific ideologies of theatrical characters were reinforced by this illusion. Now, with the advent of alienation effects in mainstream Hollywood films, such as those by Mel Brooks and Woody Allen, the reflexive shattering of the illusion of the theater has little innovative political effect. If Brecht were alive today, his stylistic strategy would be as varied as that of Godard (Biella and Shumar 1983).

Neither Brecht's self-reflexivity nor any other style can be depended on to communicate in the same way throughout history. Brecht uses many styles because he is aware of the emergent properties of the class struggle. Similarly, ethnographic filmmakers must contend with the fact that the interests of anthropology and of all science transform historically. Ethnographic film style must therefore link itself to historical concerns and must change with them. Otherwise, it becomes rigid and ineffective.

b. *The Strategy of Stylistic Metaphors in the Ilparakuyo Films:* The style of the Ilparakuyo films, like that of Brecht's work, addresses historically specific issues. Its major concern is to critique the dominant metaphors of reductive materialism and idealist reflexivity in anthropological film. The first means by which I critique the dominant style is through the fact that the Ilparakuyo films are made entirely from hundreds of still photographs. Instead of shooting motion pictures, cameraman Richard Cross shot long sequences of stills from each camera position while I simultaneously recorded sound on a Nagra. In post-production, the stills will be printed and copied with an animation camera onto 16mm film. This film, in turn, will be linked with the simultaneously-recorded sound for the final release prints.

Because the sequences of stills in my films are shot with one lens from one camera position, they break the traditional cinema taboo against jump-cuts. Further, because jump-cuts are the stereotypic means to emphasize breaks in spatio-temporal continuity, those in my films challenge a fundamental stylistic metaphor in much contemporary anthropological film, the long-take. Without doubt, the long-take is the dominant attribute of the basic "attributes of film ethnographicness." An inescapable need for long-takes is acknowledged by Heider (1976:82-6, 108), Sorenson (1975a:468-9; Sorenson and Jablonko 1975:154) and many other advocates of the reductive and dominant style of anthropological filming called observational cinema (e.g., Asch 1971; Asch, Marshall and Spier 1973; Bergum 1974; Hancock 1975; Lomax 1971, 1973; Peterson 1973; Sandall 1975). Because the cinematic long-take is supposed to duplicate "natural" perception by preserving basic spatio-temporal coordinates, reductive theory assumes that it also preserves "truth." The sequences of stills in the Ilparakuyo films present hundreds of jump-cuts and thus actively deny the preservation of temporal continuity. Yet the fact that these sequences also provide a viable basis for insight into ethnographic relations proves that "truth" transcends continuity and the long-take. The relationship between "truth" and the cinematic image can only be one of signification and not ontology. Signification can take on many emergent transformations. The jump-cuts and sequences of stills in the Ilparakuyo films thus are analogous to Brecht's alienation effects.

A second way that I critique observational cinema's stylistic metaphor is with a panorama camera. Roughly one-third of the film is shot with a Widelux, a still camera that gives a field-of-vision like cinemascope. Since the observational cinema school demands that whole-bodies be shown in wide-angle context, the panoramic images of my films give nearly seventy-five per cent more context than the aspect-ratio of normal 16mm films. The metaphorical irony of the panoramic images is that they cannot give more "truth" or holism than can any other type of vision. They are thus a visual *reductio ad absurdum* of the observational style. (See Plate 2.)

Some sections of the Ilparakuyo films intercut panoramic images with those of the normal 16mm aspect ratio. This makes the audience aware both of the inescapability of the frame-line and of the fact that all formats, no matter how wide, must delimit vision. The subliminal message of this is that criteria other than the wide-angle lens must be used to judge the value of an anthropological film (de Heusch 1962).

PLATE 2: In addition to providing about 75 percent more visual data than the normal 16mm aspect ratio, the panoramic images of the Ilparakuyo films reveal the interpenetration of ethnographic context and filmmaker self-reflexivity. (Photo: Richard Cross. ©1984, Contemporary Historians)

c. *The Stylistic Interpenetration of Reductionism and Self-Reflexivity:*
The panoramic images of my films have a special implication for the
opposition between the two major theories of ethnographic film. Just as the
epistemology of emergent materialism shows that these two theories are
incomplete but mutually fulfilling, so too my panoramic images show that
the more completely is the spatio-temporal context shown on the screen,
the greater is the likelihood that the filmmakers will also appear. Naturally,
a part of the spatio-temporal context of film production is the filmmakers
themselves. This particular part is of exclusive interest to the self-reflexive
school of filmmaking, but it is virtually ignored by the observational
group. By taking the latter's demand for context to an extreme, I show that
the two theories of film merge. As the context increases, observational cinema becomes its opposite! The search for a full context leads logically to
reflexivity, just as the desire to be reflexive about fieldwork demands ac-
knowledgement of an independent physical world.

Related to the observational cinema metaphor that long-takes equal
truth is the claim that the observational cinema camera is equivalent to the
viewer's own eye (Asch, Marshall and Spier 1963:184; Prost 1973:3; Sandall 1972:193, 1975:129; Young 1975:70). In an important critique of film
ideology, Baudry (1974) suggests that this ideological metaphor is reinforced by the renaissance perspective created by motion picture camera
lenses. Baudry argues that many other means of depiction, such as Greek
frescoes, do not have a single point of visual origin. Insofar as
anthropological films use single-lens cameras, they reinforce a potentially
ideological impression that the viewer of the film knows as much about the
context of the shooting as he would had he been there.

Several scenes in the Ilparakuyo films play with the idea of multiple-
lens cameras. In one scene, shot at a well, Richard and I photographed with
two still cameras spaced twenty feet apart and aimed at 90 degrees to one
another. Like the metaphorical message of the panoramic images in other
scenes, the well double-take presents a greater visual context than is available from the normal 16mm format. It also demonstrates that a viewer can
be given too much spatio-temporal context. The unusual double-images of
this scene do not duplicate normal vision, although they do take the demand
for the "attribute of ethnographicness" called *whole-bodies* to a logical extreme. The extension of this logic results in its collapse. The scene shot at
the well provides such an excess of visual data that the audience is over-
whelmed. This proves that the reductionist, one-to-one metaphor of visual
context with holistic understanding is false.

Just as the excessively detailed double-images of the well show the
dangers of too much context, the final scene that I will discuss shows the
dangers of excessive reflexivity. During the first ten days of filming, I encouraged the Ilparakuyo to acknowledge the cameras and interact with us as
we filmed. On the eleventh day, however, I was bored with this and decided
to shoot a parody of the fly-on-the-wall, invisible-cameraman, observational

style. Unfortunately for my plan, on that morning two elders visited the homestead from several miles away and wanted to be brought up-to-date. This naturally required an extensive description of ourselves, the filmmakers whose peculiarities played a large part in the recent news. As an animated and reflexive discussion of our filmmaking took place (see Biella 1984:282-290), I grew more and more annoyed.

After about thirty minutes, I called to a man who often translated for us while we were in the field, Mr. Jonas Reuben Wanga. As the following excerpt from the transcript shows, when he came, I let out a burst of my frustration:

Peter [in English]:

> Jonas, I would like you to explain to these people that if all they ever talk about when I turn the tape recorder on is the tape recorder, when I go to America they're going to think that the Maasai always talk about tape recorders! And I'm trying to make a film about life here as it is. That's what I would like you to say. There is more to life than my tape recorder and I would like them to talk about their own lives rather than my life.

Jonas:

> Humm! (Laughs.) [In English] You mean that they are talking about your--

Peter [in English]:

> All they have talked about for the last twenty minutes is me. I want to make a film about them! Not me!

My exclamations, although rather insensitive, indicate one danger of including too much reflexivity in anthropological film. The fear is justified that excessive concern with self-reflexive methodology prevents the audience from attaining other kinds of insight. Yet, contrary to Heider, methodological discussions cannot reasonably be removed from all anthropological film. The transcript continues:

Jonas:

> (laughs) [in Maa to the others] He hears you talking and all you're talking about is the tape recorder and him. And you don't tell--

Mother of Toreto:

> Does he understand what we're saying?

Jonas:

> Yes. He understands. He knows some.

Mother of Toreto:

> Then, do we stop talking about...? Shouldn't we talk about these things that are unfamiliar?.....We talk about these things because these are the things that we don't know. So we look at these things and we ask, "How do these things work?" This is the one that takes words. Those take pictures, and the pictures come out.

This segment shows that some reflexivity can be both reasonable and unavoidable. However, no self-reflexive discussion can be limited only to pure method. The ethnographic context inevitably creeps into such discussions. Thus, the purist and idealist conception of reflexivity, per Ruby, has no viability. Earlier in this scene, a section of the conversation demonstrates that method cannot practically be distinguished from the indigenous context and value systems.

Historically, the Ilparakuyo Maasai have had a joking disdain for an unusual branch of the Maa-speaking people, the Ildorrobo, who are unlike all other branches of the Maasai in that they gain subsistence through hunting and gathering (cf. Galaty 1979). Further, the Ilparakuyo have historically expressed considerable hostility to their Bantu-speaking, farming neighbors (cf. Beidelman 1960, 1961, 1964). For example, Ilparakuyo refer to all farmers with the non-flattering term "*ilmek*."

In this scene, the methodology of our filmmaking is reflexively described in a way that is only meaningful when understood in the historical context of these hostilities. In explaining our filmmaking to the Olparakuoni elder, Mother of Toreto asserts that Richard and I avoid filming the Wakwere farmers because we do not like them. The elder, whom we had never met before and who knew nothing of our particular likes or dislikes, jokingly explains our methodology. Following is the relevant portion of the transcript:

Mother of Toreto:

> They don't like to photograph the *ilmek* more than our people.

Mahungo:

They don't like *ilmek?*

Mother of Toreto:

No, they don't.

Second Elder:

They despise the *ilmek* because they're just like *Ildorrobo!* (Laughs.) They don't like *ilmek* at all?

Mother of Toreto:

No.

Second Elder:

Ilmek have no meaning anyway.

I do not know whether, with this last line, the Second Elder is continuing the joke which he began in his previous statement. If he is serious, his reflexive remark about filmmaking methodology has suddenly transcended filmmaking and become an important ethnographic document in its own right. Yet, even as a joke it reveals the historical strain in relations between the pastoral Ilparakuyo and the Wakwere farmers. The fact that Mother of Toreto and the Second Elder identify hostility as the basis of our filmmaking method indicates less about our motives than about the social relations between the two groups. Thus, even a conversation which appears on the surface to be purely self-reflexive contains important clues about the values, history and material relations of the speakers.

V. Conclusion

Contemporary proponents of observational and self-reflexive cinema, while otherwise different, have all argued that the film styles which they recommend must dominate anthropological filmmaking because they alone are purely scientific. Such arguments for stylistic hegemony are futile because they all depend on a naive conception of science. The quest for purity logically leads these styles to merge into one another because the epistemologies on which they are based ignore the major contribution of emergent materialism, praxis. The film styles downplay the praxis of the filmmakers, the scientific community and the people who are filmed.

Unfortunately, arguments for the observational style dominate the literature of anthropological film, and the most visible alternative is the invalid self-reflexivity. This situation represses the creativity of other filmmakers by denying the fact that new possibilities in anthropological film expression have scientific value. The style of the Ilparakuyo films serves a scientific task in that it presents a corrective to a problem in the science of anthropology, reductive and idealist approaches to filmmaking. The Ilparakuyo films' style is valid insofar as it addresses its subject. However, it is not meant to inaugurate a new sytlistic hegemony. It is only one of many approaches to filmmaking which must emerge in response to emerging struggles in anthropology.

NOTES

1 An earlier draft of this paper was presented at the 1983 Annual Meetings of the American Anthropological Association in Chicago.

2 Lukács describes the intellectual climate: "The situation is least favourable in the social sciences. Here the power of apologetic traditions is at its strongest, and the ideological sensitivity of the bourgeoisie greatest. Here, accordingly, any penetrating mental grasp of the contradictions of real life leads almost unavoidably to a rapid and radical break with the (bourgeois) class. Any honest and genuinely scientific work in the field of social science that goes beyond that mere collection and arrangement of new data must inevitably come rapidly up against these barriers" (1980 [1938]:135).

3 Three films, still in progress, were shot in 1980. The fieldwork was led by anthropologist Peter Rigby, adoptive son of the Olparakuoni elder Koisengé who figures prominently in the films. Rigby's interest in ethnographic film began in the late 1960s, when he was ethnographic advisor to David and Judith MacDougall's films about the pastoral Jie of Uganda. He has published a great deal on questions of pastoral social formations from the perspective of emergent historical materialism (Rigby 1984). My cameraman was still-photographer Richard Cross. Because the style of the project demanded animating stills, Cross' technical skill and aesthetic sense were invaluable. He began his anthropological work in an ethnographic and visual study of the Colombian coastal community of Palenque (Friedemann and Cross 1979). Subsequently, his photographs with the Sandinistas on the front lines of the Nicaraguan civil war appeared widely in the world press (Cardinal and Cross 1982). Cross was killed in 1983, reportedly by a land mine, while on photojournalistic assignment in Honduras: he was attempting to penetrate the news-blackout of the CIA-backed, Nicaraguan *contras*. The political praxis of photography was his life's work.

4 Ignorance of local languages is endemic to anthropological filmmakers: they must regularly depend on the assistance of translators. The reason for this is primarily economic. Unlike academic anthropologists, most ethnographic filmmakers do not receive institutional support for

becoming specialists on the people they film. If they are to survive pro-
fessionally, they must move from culture to culture, as required by the
availability of production monies. Further, market conditions rarely permit an anthropological filmmaker to spend sufficient time in any one
ethnographic area so that language mastery becomes feasible. For example, Rigby and I failed in our plea to Granada Films for funding and distribution of our work because, we were told, they "already have a Maasai
film." (In film, novelty of the people to be filmed and not the anthropologist's theoretical interest largely determines funding.) The recently
opened anthropological film program at the University of Southern California makes the best of the very difficult language problem of ethnographic filmmaking. The program links Ph.D. candidates in cultural anthropology with Masters candidates in visual anthropology. The former
students have the time, resources and commitment necessary to work out
the mammoth problem of sound-track translations. The latter have the
skill necessary to film anthropological material satisfactorily.

5 I am grateful to my friend Melkiori S. Matwi, an anthropologist employed by the Tanzanian government, for explaining the Ilparakuyo
principles of snuff-taking among wives and thus correcting my error. After I returned to the United States, Mr. Matwi joined me and spent six
weeks preparing excellent translations of the Ilparakuyo tapes. Because
he is an Olparakuoni himself and knows everyone in the films, his
translations and subsequent explanation of those translations were invaluable.

6 Emergence and praxis are attributes of all people, but the Ilparakuyo are
unusually free from hindrances to their creativity. Peter Rigby has written extensively on the issue of unalienated praxis among pastoral peoples. He attributes it to the relative autonomy from capitalist relations of
production which is made possible by the Ilparakuyo age-set organization, among other factors (Rigby 1979a, 1979b, 1980). Also relevant to
the causes of unalienated praxis is the fact that cattle, as a major means
of production, are far more difficult to alienate than farm land in certain
geographical areas: as a result, pastoral groups in East Africa have historically been able to resist colonial and post-colonial exploitation with
singular success (Biella 1983).

7 John Collier (1967:42-5) relates an experience with a moral very similar
to mine: he suggests that the ethnographer may freely distribute "public"
photographs, such as baby pictures, but he is well advised to keep
"private" photographs to himself.

8 Interesting analyses of the transformation of epistemology and knowledge due to the invention of the printing press and the popularization of
books may be found in Goody (1968), Davis (1965) and Zukin (1977).

REFERENCES CITED

Althusser, Louis (1971). Ideology and Ideological State Apparatuses (Notes
    Towards an Investigation). IN Lenin and Philosophy and Other Es-
    says, Ben Brewster, trans. New York and London: Monthly Review,

pp. 127-186.
Asch, Timothy (1971). Making Ethnographic Film for Teaching and Research. PIEF Newsletter 3 (2):6-10.
Asch, Timothy, John Marshall and Peter Spier (1973). Ethnographic Film: Structure and Function. Annual Review of Anthropology 2:179:87.
Baudry, Jean-Louis (1974). Ideological Effects of the Basic Cinematic Apparatus. Film Quarterly 28 (2):39-47.
Beidelman, Thomas O. (1960). The Baraguyu. Tanganyika Notes and Records 55:244-278.
Beidelman, Thomas O. (1961). Beer Drinking and Cattle Theft in Ukaguru. American Anthropologist 63 (3):534-549.
Beidelman, Thomas O. (1964). Intertribal Insult and Opprobrium in an East African Chiefdom (Ukaguru). Anthropological Quarterly 37 (2):33-52.
Bergum, Clinton (1974). Defining Interpretive Film Practice. Paper presented at the Conference on Visual Anthropology, Philadelphia.
Biella, Peter (1983). Colonial and Post-Colonial Intervention in the Economic Base of East African Pastoral Societies. Paper presented at the African Studies Association meetings, Boston.
Biella, Peter (1984). Theory and Practice in Ethnographic Film: Implications of the Ilparakuyo Maasai Film Project. Ph.D. dissertation, Department of Anthropology, Temple University.
Biella, Peter and Richard Cross (1981). Maasai Solutions: A Film about East African Dispute Settlement. Philadelphia: Contemporary Historians. Limited edition.
Biella, Peter and Wesley Shumar (1983). One More Weekend: Reductionism in Henderson's "Towards A Non-Bourgeois Camera Style." Paper presented at the Conference on Culture and Communication, Philadelphia.
Brecht, Bertolt (1964). Brecht on Theater: The Development of an Aesthetic. John Willett, trans. New York: Hill and Wang.
Burch, Noel (1973). Theory of Film Practice. Helen R. Lane, trans. New York and Washington: Praeger.
Cardinal, Ernesto and Richard Cross (1982). Nicaragua: La Guerra de Liberacion. West Germany: Nicaraguan Ministry of Culture.
Colletti, Lucio (1972). Berstein and the Marxism of the Second International. IN From Rousseau to Lenin: Studies in Ideology and Society. John Merrington and Judith White, trans. New York and London: Monthly Review, pp. 45-108.
Collier, John Jr. (1967). Visual Anthropology: Photography as a Research Method. New York: Holt, Rinehart and Winston.
Davis, Natalie Zemon (1965). Printing and the People. IN Society and Culture in Early Modern France. Stanford: Stanford University Press, pp. 189-226.
de Heusch, Luc (1962). The Cinema and the Social Sciences: A Survey of Ethnographic and Sociological Films. Paris: UNESCO Reports and Papers in the Social Sciences, No. 16.
Eaton, Mick (1983). Another Angle on Anthropological Film: Review of "Two Laws." Screen 24 (2):55-59.
Eaton, Mick (ed.) (1979). Anthropology - Reality - Cinema: The Films of

Jean Rouch. Colchester and London: Spottiswoode Ballantyne, Ltd.

Engels, Frederick (1954). Anti-Dühring: Herr Eugen Dühring's Revolution in Science. Moscow: Foreign Language Press.

Friedemann, Nina and Richard Cross (1979). Ma Ngombe: Guerreros y Ganaderos en Palenque. Bogota: Editorial Carlos Valencia.

Galaty, John (1979). Pollution and Anti-praxis: Issues of Maasai Inequality. American Ethnologist 6 (4):803-16.

Godelier, Maurice (1970). System, Structure and Contradiction in DAS KAPITAL. IN Introduction to Structuralism, Michael Lane, ed. New York: Basic Books, pp. 340-58.

Goldschmidt, Walter (1972). Ethnographic Film: Definition and Exegesis. PIEF Newsletter 3 (2):1-3.

Goody, Jack (ed.) (1968). Literacy in Traditional Societies. Cambridge: Cambridge University Press.

Hancock, David (1975). Disappearing World: Anthropology on Television. Sight and Sound 44 (2):103-7.

Heider, Karl (1976). Ethnographic Film. Austin: University of Texas Press.

Heisenberg, Werner (1971). Physics and Beyond. New York: Harper and Row.

Jammer, Max (1974). The Philosophy of Quantum Mechanics. New York: John Wiley and Sons.

Kuhn, Annette (1978). The Camera I: Observations on Documentary. Screen 19 (2):71-83.

Lenin, V. I. (1961). Philosophic Notebooks. Collected Works, v. 38. Moscow: Progress Publishers.

Lenin, V.I. (1972). Materialism and Empirio-Criticism. Peking: Foreign Language Press.

Lomax, Alan (1971). Choreometrics and Ethnographic Filmmaking. Filmmaker's Newsletter 4 (4)::22-30.

Lomax, Alan (1973). Urgent Anthropology: Cinema, Science and Cultural Renewal. Current Anthropology 14 (4):474-480.

Lukács, Georg (1980). Marx and the Problem of Ideological Decay. IN Essays on Realism, David Fernbach, trans. Cambridge, Mass.: MIT Press, pp. 114-66.

MacBean, James Roy (1983). Two Laws from Australia: One White, One Black. Film Quarterly 36 (3):30-43.

MacCabe, Colin (1974). Realism and the Cinema: Notes on Some Brechtian Theses. Screen 15 (2):7-27.

MacDougall, David (1978). Ethnographic Film: Failure and Promise. Annual Review of Anthropology 7:405-25.

Marx, Karl (1972). Theses on Feuerbach. IN The Marx-Engels Reader, Robert C. Tucker, ed. New York: Norton, pp. 107-9.

Marx, Karl (1977). Critique of Hegel's "Philosophy of Right," Joseph O'Malley, ed. Cambridge and London: Cambridge University Press.

Marx, Karl and Frederick Engels (1974). The German Ideology, C.J. Arthur, ed. New York: International Publishers.

Maysles, Albert (1964). Thoughts on Cinéma Vérité and a Discussion with the Maysles Brothers. Interview by James Blue. Film Comment 2 (4):22-30.

McClosky, Mary (1964). Metaphors. Mind 73 (290):215-33.

Nichols, Bill (1981). Ideology and the Image: Social Representation in the

Cinema and Other Media. Bloomington: Indiana University Press.
Nichols, Bill (1983). The Voice of Documentary. Film Quarterly 36 (3):17-29.
Peterson, A. Y. (1973). Methods of Ethnographic Filming. Proceedings of the IXth International Congress of Anthropological and Ethnological Sciences, pp. 1-8 (reprint).
Prost, J. H. (1973). Filming Body Behavior. Proceedings of the IXth International Congress of Anthropological and Ethnological Sciences, pp. 1-53 (reprint).
Rigby, Peter (1979a). Olpul and Enteroj: The Economy of Sharing among the Pastoral Baraguyo of Tanzania. IN Pastoral Production and Society, Equipé écologie et anthropologie, eds. Cambridge: Cambridge University Press, pp. 329-47.
Rigby, Peter (1979b). Pastors and Pastoralists: The Differential Penetration of Christianity among East African Cattle Herders. Comparative Studies in Society and History 23 (1):96-129.
Rigby, Peter (1980). Pastoral Production and Socialist Transformation In Tanzania. Jipemoyo 2:32-84.
Rigby, Peter (1984). Persistent Pastoralists: Nomadic Societies In Transition. London: Zed Press.
Ruby, Jay (1975). Is Ethnographic Film a Filmic Ethnography? Studies in the Anthropology of Visual Communication 2 (2):104-111.
Ruby, Jay (1976). In a Pic's Eye: Interpretive Strategies for Deriving Significance and Meaning from Photographs. Afterimage 3 (9):5-7.
Ruby, Jay (1977). The Image Mirrored: Reflexivity and the Documentary Film. Journal of the University Film Association 29 (1):3-11.
Ruby, Jay (1980). Exposing Yourself: Reflexivity, Anthropology and Film. Semiotica 30 (1-2):153-179.
Sandall, Roger (1972). Observation and Identity. Sight and Sound 41 (4):192-6.
Sandall, Roger (1975). Ethnographic Film Documents. IN Principles of Visual Anthropology, Paul Hockings, ed. The Hague: Mouton, pp. 125-31.
Solanas, Fernando and Octavio Gettino (1976). Towards a Third Cinema. IN Movies and Methods: An Anthology, Bill Nichols, ed. Berkeley: University of California Press, pp. 44-64.
Sorenson, E. Richard (1967). A Research Film Program in the Study of Changing Man: Research Filmed Materials as a Foundation for Continued Study of Non-Recurring Human Events. Current Anthropology 8 (5):443-450.
Sorenson, E. Richard (1975a). Visual Records, Human Knowledge, and the Future. IN Principles of Visual Anthropology, Paul Hockings, ed. Hague: Mouton, pp. 463-76.
Sorenson, E. Richard (1975b). Visual Evidence: An Emerging Force in Visual Anthropology. Occasional Papers, National Anthropological Film Center 1:1-10.
Sorenson, E. Richard and Allison Jablonko (1975). Research Filming of Naturally Occurring Phenomena: Basic Strategies. IN Principles of Visual Anthropology, Paul Hockings, ed. The Hague: Mouton, pp. 151-63.

Sorenson, E. Richard and D. C. Gajdusek (1963). Investigation of Non-Recurring Phenomena: The Research Cinema Film. Nature 200:112-4.

Wollen, Peter (1982). Godard and Counter-Cinema: Vent d'Est. IN Readings and Writings: Semiotic Counter-Strategies. London: Verso, pp. 79-91.

Worth, Sol and Larry Gross (1974). Symbolic Strategies. Journal of Communication 24:27-39.

Young, Colin (1975). Observational Cinema. IN Principles of Visual Anthropology, Paul Hockings, ed. The Hague: Mouton, pp. 65-80.

Zukin, Barbara (1977). Mimesis in the Origins of Bourgeois Culture. Theory and Society 4 (3):333:358.

Visual Anthropology And The Future Of Ethnographic Film

John Collier, Jr.
San Francisco Art Institute

ABSTRACT: A major conflict between the photographic evidence and the hard science disciplines of anthropology threatens the future of ethnographic film. Despite eighty years of photography in social science, many ethnographers continue to distrust photographic evidence. The very presence of the photographer-filmmaker produces distortion in the visual record, dubbed reflexivity, but surely a similar distortion affects all ethnographic records. Visual anthropology has developed disciplines to correct this fault and to extend the scope of reliable field recording.

Several symposia at the 1978 meeting of the American Anthropological Association dealt with the distortive reflexivity of research and ethnographic film. At the same meetings Hubert Smith screened LIVING MAYA, that exploited reflexivity by making Smith and his crew visually part of the film experience, recording the empathetic fieldworkers participating directly in the action of native life. This human bridge-building unquestionably goes on all the time in field anthropology. LIVING MAYA was a popular television show, for audiences could bridge to Mayan life directly through Smith's interaction.

The projection of value judgments, or reflectivity, casts doubts on the data integrity of much ethnographic film. A case discussed is Gardner's DEAD BIRDS, which expresses a personal viewpoint on the actions and ethos of war among the Dani of West Irian. Though reflectivity runs all through the ethnographic record, we are conditioned to find written words more creditable than film records. Chagnon's ethnography, THE FIERCE PEOPLE, stresses a barbaric Yanomamo personality. Other authentic records clearly support his accounts of violent behavior, but Asch's films, made with Chagnon, show another side of Yanomamo personality, one of human warmth, humor, and gentleness. Here we experience the value of film as ethnographic record, for the films carried the behavioral record beyond description of fact and showed qualified behavior otherwise missing from the disciplined writings.

Most ethnographic films are outside-in. How can this flow be

73

reversed? Pretesting camera visualization through using photographs as probes in interviewing, is one approach. A more revolutionary way is to place the cameras in the hands and intelligence of native peoples, as Adair and Worth did with seven Navajo men and women -- producing a film series from the inside out, revealing how Navajos really observe time, space, and their world.

Visual anthropology can help bring clarity to the meaning of ethnographic film and help control the bias and reflectivity that now shadow its integrity. Finally, anthropologists as filmmakers should first of all retain their roles as ethnographers and not surrender their films to the manipulation of popular film media.

A major conflict has developed between visual comprehension and verbal communications in the behavioral sciences, that affects the future of anthropological film. Underlying this confrontation is a distrust of visual data in favor of verbally recorded evidence. My paper explores why this distrust has developed and how it has affected the style and authenticity of ethnographic film. First I review the historical uses of photography in ethnography.

In the late 1980s, members of the Stanley McCormick Hopi Expedition made the first expansive photographic ethnography, covering in detail the nine day Snake Dance. Yet, except for a research peak in the 1930s when Margaret Mead and Gregory Bateson studied child development with the camera (1942), photography's potential contribution to anthropology has not generally been exploited. This neglect, associated with an anxiety over the photographic fact, this raises questions about the nature of anthropology, for pragmatic scientists have used photography constantly since its inception. Photography is used all through the "hard sciences," where disciplined control of data is more of an issue that it is in anthropology. Botany, ecology, astronomy, physiology, psychology, and archeology all use photography in the collection, analysis, and explication of data for research.

Even after the development of methodology for visual anthropology, many ethnographers have continued to distrust photographic evidence. In recent years this resistance has increased. This has had a prejudicial effect on filming, for criticism is largely directed at film research which ideally forms the basis for ethnographic film. The central criticism, that surfaced eight years ago, is that the interaction of filmmaking so disturbs the natural flow of events that film records can be of little value to anthropology.

This disturbance has been labeled reflexivity. In critical dialogue reflexivity appears also to be associated with reflectivity, a projection of the practitioner-observer's values into the cultural record -- a spontaneous effect that is found all through anthropology. Reflexivity, the disturbing intrusion of the investigating observer, is a distraction most photodocumentarians are disciplined to avoid or correct. Even so, the personality of the filmmaker can still be detected in most documents; the schooled rapport and low-profile "invisibility" of the camera-person does not guard against observational se-

lectivity, and this continues to have a major distorting effect on ethnographic film.

Figuratively, reflexivity is a fisherman dislodging a stone into a quiet
pool teeming with fish that dart into the shadows; normal ecological process is interrupted completely. But if the fieldworker fisherman patiently
waits, in time the fish will return to their familiar haunts. Like fish, people
are independently programmed and will assume their normal behavior if the
intruder becomes a part of the scene. In my film research on schoolroom
culture in Eskimo education (1972) I also was worried about my filmic disturbance of the flow of the classrooms. I began by obscuring myself in a
corner, but I soon observed that in a very short time the routine behavior of
the classroom was resumed. Teachers may have tried to change their routines to please the stranger-investigator, but these efforts were short. Good
teachers continued to be good teachers, and inferior ones continued their
negative routines. Basically teachers know only one way to teach, and
pupils only one way to study and behave to please their observing disci-
plinarians.

My first contact with the issue of reflectivity in fieldwork came when I
joined the Department of Anthropology at Cornell University as a photographer. As my first orienting experience I was assigned to read the raw data
files of the project within which I was going to work, which dealt with the
mental health of French and English in the Maritimes of Canada. I was
amazed at what I found: only verbatim interview statements without a
qualifying sentence of description beyond the place, date, time of day, and
name of person interviewed. It was explained to me that the purpose of all
field observation in anthropology is to gather impartial records undistorted
by the bias or impressionism of the observer, so it was a basic discipline of
field observers to withhold personal opinions and impressions from the data,
to keep the evidence "clean" from what is now called projectivity. I considered then that "clean data" must be related to the white lab coats of laboratory technicians who strive for sterility.

I also observed other students' use of these interview files. How revealing was this optimal effort at gathering non-reflective information? Graduate
students were assigned to the files to develop their skills in using data.
Their task was to construct a typical Maritime man and woman, formulated
on the interview responses. Then the researchers met in seminar with field
personnel who had worked in the region, these experts sitting in judgment
as students gave their sketches of Maritime personality. Invariably the field
experts rejected the students' summations. It appeared that without supporting descriptive information the interview content was inadequate for such a
reconstruction.

Ironically, when Alexander Leighton, director of the study, wrote his
social psychiatric text, MY NAME IS LEGION (1959), he fulfilled exactly
the assignment asked of these students. Leighton traced psychosomatic illness through a contrived maritime man to illustrate the typical stress prob-

lems observed in this research. Fieldworkers were sure they knew this man--
though he never existed but was a montage of many case history personalities. Leighton had used literary nuance to present the circumstance of mental
illness. Of course Leighton, having lived and worked in the Maritimes most
of his life, had access to refinements that were unavailable to the students,
and so, regardless of other "data" he could construct a palatable individual.

It was this experience that first stimulated my concern for the development of responsible photographic recording for anthropology. Could the
camera correct the possible bias for the reflective eye of the human observer?

In 1978 a major challenge as to the value of film was made at the annual meetings of the American Anthropological Association. In a symposium titled "Portrayal of Self, Profession and Culture," papers charged that
the very presence of filmmakers disturbingly projected their values and biases, which destroyed the complete review before film could be used for research.

My reaction at the time was, why single out ethnographic film for the
charge of reflexivity when it affects all research and writing in anthropology? Of course the presence of the fieldworker can disturb the indigenous
circumstance, and of course photography can exaggerate this disturbing
presence. And manipulation in selection and editing can make film that is of
no use at all for anthropology. Yet I have been working for years on photographic methodology to help control the reflexivity or reflectivity so common in field observation, precisely because I consider the photographic imprint less manipulatable than field notes!

Reflectivity is humanly part of the rapport bridge over which fieldwork
is accomplished. The human transference so essential to interpersonal as
well as cross-cultural communication certainly affects the filmic-photo-
graphic relationship. But without this transference, photo-recording with
any humanistic depth cannot be made. The cry against reflectivity is only
justified in clinical research; hence it is bewildering that it has become an
anthropological issue.

Filmmaker Hubert Smith has worked creatively to make filmic fieldwork an honest and integrated part of his documentation. In the 1970s,
working in Bolivia for the American Universities Field Staff, Smith practically included his film crew in THE SPIRIT POSSESSION OF ALEJAN-
DRO MAMANI (1974), a record of an eighty-one year old Aymara suffering
from such stress over the crumbling of the solidarity of his family that he
announced his coming suicide. Smith's sound man reasons with the old
man, gives him sleeping pills, and humanly attempts to avert the suicide.
The sound track includes much of their dialogue, and their relationship is a
central part of the film. The camera records this interaction in such a
"natural" fashion that the film has never been criticized for distortive reflectivity.

Hubert Smith reports that Jay Ruby had been urging him to give up on "clean observation." So when Smith received a large grant from the Research and Public Media Programs of the National Endowment for the Humanities to make a television series, he decided to make his film and sound crews active subjects throughout the filming (personal communication). Jay Ruby encouraged Smith's innovative scheme. I believe Ruby's concept was that, by openly recording the human and judgmental influence of the filmmakers, a new genre of honest ethnographic film could be created. But did Ruby see it as a methodology to correct the reflexive distortions in ethnographic film that he was agonizing over at the time?

The resulting film series, which Smith called LIVING MAYA (1983), raises some interesting questions. What Smith recorded was the participant observation approach which is the basis of much fieldwork. Certainly Robert Redfield's thirty years of research in Mayan village ethnography was carried out with this sort of participatory relationship. Probably, though less formally, many successful photographic film studies have been similarly made. I am sure Smith has been an empathetic participant in all his film ventures, whether or not this has been a part of the visual record.

But as Ruby's symposium points out, ethnographic film is, however surreptitiously, as much an image of the filmmakers as the document of a culture. The question to be asked is, what did the documentation of the film crew add to the film? Largely it added Hubert Smith, honestly participating in the life of his collaborating Mayan family. Smith feels that the process "contextualized how and in what sorts of human relationships this data were gathered." What if the record of the film crew were largely edited out of LIVING MAYA? Would the Mayan ethnography have appeared more complete? Probably not. But audience response might be different. Smith notes that while LIVING MAYA has not received high media ratings, the people who did see it were "appreciative AND entirely accepting" of the film crew's presence (personal communication). In effect, Smith's visual and audial presence personally led the audience into the lives of the people. In popular eyes he may have been the star, the personality who introduced real people to the American audience. This may not be important to filmic ethnography, but it is very important to communication.

Will Smith's methodology open a new genre of ethnographic film? Possibly the direct character of the film could influence ethnographic film style. Because the film was edited around the interaction and Smith's continually recorded comments, there is no drifting from the order of events. The filmic narration is accomplished with unbroken commentary. But LIVING MAYA is far more than documentation, for each step is discussed with the Mayan family. Smith has relied on this constant discussion to give depth and ethnographic structure. If critics find it structurally weak, the fault lies in the film's visualization, not its reflexive content.

Wasn't Smith recording what usually happens spontaneously in the field when anthropologists become deeply involved in the lives of their subjects? Much scientific objectivity is left behind in the field journey; in my philosophy, anthropology is a "people to people" experience, requiring the sincerity of involvement demonstrated by Smith and his film crew. This reality may be seen as a flaw. But what does human reflexivity genuinely mean? Sincerity of human rapport, participant observation, ethical giving as well as taking, all reasonably take place in any productive field experience.

The critics of reflexivity can be found in all cultural investigations and in much ethnographic writing. Condemning ethnographic film only scape-goated the problem. I believe ethnographers, filmmakers, or any outsider-observers need the support of human bridgework to gain the cooperation of the people being studied. Significant insight can come only over this hu-man linkage. These contacts do promote transferences. But reflexivity is controllable, particularly to the degree that it is recognized. Scientific pro-cesses can objectively protect the data from the bias that usually occurs in sincere human interaction. Yet unconscious projectivity is a covert influ-ence that shapes the perspective of much anthropology and can, and often does, distort ethnographic film as well.

At the same AAA meetings after the symposium, "Portrayal of Self, Profession and Culture: Reflexive Perspectives in Anthropology," I asked myself, "What would be left standing if the charges of reflexivity were made against the complete body of anthropological literature?" Conversationally film was singled out, as an example of reflexivity misleading ethnographic record, where photography may be cleaner than the written anthropological reports which have even greater influence.

A more recent criticism of photography and film is an article by I.C. Jarvie in CURRENT ANTHROPOLOGY, "The Problem of the Ethno-graphic Real" (24:3:313-325). Jarvie attacks the content of photography and film as unreliable evidence for anthropology, claiming that filmic informa-tion is out of context, lacking the supportive information necessary for its use as data; that the fieldworker's notebook is superior, for the pencil can write down subject, date, time and place. Of course such data are essential for the use of any primary evidence. But is there any reason why film-log-ging could not provide this vital field notebook information? Is this not what film slates are for? Jarvie's criticism fails to recognize that the eye that organizes the photograph is the same reflector that manipulates the note-book's pencil.

At the same time, it would be naive to deny that the photographic im-age does reflect the attitudes of the beholder. What critics fail to recognize is that photography not only reflects the values of the camera-person, but that it can at the same time record undisturbed values of the film subject, and measurable circumstantial evidence as well. The disciplines we have devel-oped under the name of visual anthropology attempt to recognize this dou-ble reflection and to reject uncontrollable imagery so that only responsible visual evidence will be used in analysis. Such discrimination partially con-trols the reflective process by defining "photographic fact," which can be used either to substantiate or refute an anthropological hypothesis. Written evidence can be challenged only by returning to the field, but the photographic image, gathered as a responsible artifact, can be re-evaluated by further analysis at any time.

Still photographs may have only a limited impact, but moving images of film open up new areas of sensitivity to anthropological research. When the photographic image moves, it qualifies and refines our understanding of behavior, making possible refined insight on the quality of interpersonal relations. This is why I chose film over still photography when I was asked to provide data for research on Eskimo education for the United States Office of Education. Team analysis of classroom and environmental film found, among other things, a sharp contrast between Eskimo children's sluggishness in the Bureau of Indian Affairs classroom and their acuity outside in the snow (Collier 1972). Similarly, when we analyze film footage of modern stone age tribal people, we can recover human nuances that challenge classical views of primitive societies. We are likely to find tribal peoples who compare in signals of intelligence and sensitivity with the classical "wild" California Indian, Ishi (T. Kroeber 1960).

Three elements have distorted ethnography of non-Western peoples: (1) inconclusive and confused recordings gathered through pigeon-speaking informants (see Perera and Bruce 1981); (2) gross over-emphasis on material technology, since this is the sort of data that can be gathered by scientifically "clean" (though inhibited) methods of observation; and (3) far more seriously, the projective "superiority" of White Western colonial observers and ethnologists who created a "down hill" view of tribal and non-western people. This reflectivity creates distortions more serious than the reflexive intrusions of filmmakers. As Hubert Smith puts it:

> To assume indigenous groups are being "swept away" or "flocking to" the modern world is backhanded western chauvinism. They are, perhaps, "trying to sidestep it" or "looking for crumbs" after losing land and culture...(personal communication).

Intentionally or spontaneously, much early ethnography supported the concept of racial and genetic inferiority. Yet John Marshall's film records on the Kalahari visually contradict the stereotypic notions of "primitive" behavior. As an example, Marshall's short sync-sound film, MEN BATHING (1973), of five men assisting each other in a ceremonial bath in a desert stream, reveals that these Kalahari hunters can express considerably more human sensitivity for each other than is to be found in many American athletic locker rooms. These are the qualities of behavior and interaction that can be read through film analysis.

But the rejection of photography goes further, as David MacDougall clearly recognized:

> If anthropologists have consistently rejected film as an
> analytical medium, and if they have themselves often rel-
> egated it to subordinate record-making and didactic roles,
> the reason may not be merely conservative reluctance to
> employ a new technology but a shrewd judgment that the
> technology entails a shift in perspective which raises ma-
> jor problems for scientific conceptualization (Nichols
> 1981:243).

Both visual communication and visual evidence confront the literate-
biased value system of Western society. We are compulsively verbal in both
our communication and thought. Our memory image is codified--and now
computer organized! There is small room in our literate society for visualization; we feel that visual observation belongs to pre-literate tribal people.
Hence we distrust visual phenomena and look for the written directions to
guide our reasoning. This reality alone has largely discouraged the development of visual anthropology. In education classes at the University of
Alaska, Athabaskan and Eskimo students analyzed film and video recording
more accurately and rapidly than Euro-American students in the same classes
who generally were poor visual observers--probably because they come from
a primarily literate culture and have not been trained to conceptualize from
visual information (Malcolm Collier, personal communication).

How Impartial is the Ethnographic Record?

Critics of anthropological film are more fastidious about the accuracy
of the photographic record than they are about the authenticity of classical
studies in anthropology. What is ethnographically real? The prejudice, culture shock, and bias of many fieldworkers and writers in anthropology is
notorious, and many times these are reflected in print--sometimes spontaneously, but many times intentionally.

One classic case of variation in ethnographic description is to be found
in the writings of Robert Redfield and Oscar Lewis on the Mexican village
of Tepoztlan. Redfield's study (1930) was accepted as a classic ethnography
of a peasant community. Two decades later Lewis' LIFE IN A MEXICAN
VILLAGE: TEPOTZLAN RESTUDIED (1951) radically contradicted Redfield's characterization. When Redfield was challenged over this discrepancy,
he answered philosophically, "I always believed the 'good life' took place in
small organizations, and I went into anthropology expecting to find this to
be true. Now, Oscar Lewis is a New Yorker and dislikes small organizations. His TEPOTZLAN describes accurately all the negative experiences in
a small community. Read both books!" (Paraphrased from a conversation
with Friedl Lang). It appears that "The collection and analysis of cultural
data and its explication is funnelled through a paradigm of theoretical per-

spectivity." (This is Ronald Rundstrom phrasing; Hubert Smith expresses it, "We see that which we know.")

Where do we turn for cultural truth? To Zola, Dostoyevski, Conrad, Faulkner? Novelists can present the holistic human process which ethnographic filmmakers strive for. The novelist's process is creative invention. They are not searching for reality; they are inventing life's authenticity through literary means. But when filmmakers attempt similar invention, their dramatizations are no longer ethnographic. This raises the question, can audience-directed film drama, for example, Flaherty's MAN OF ARAN (1934), constitute an authentic cultural record? Are the contrivances and filmic reorganizations that critics challenge in ethnographic film the producers' efforts also to create reality?

Anthropologists, in their conclusive writings-- consciously or not--assemble their data into structured wholes. In evaluating reflectivity, the feedback loop between the data and the observer, this final step of organization must be appreciated. In anthropology we deal with projectivity in such works as Redfield's A VILLAGE THAT CHOSE PROGRESS (1950), Elizabeth Marshall Thomas's THE HARMLESS PEOPLE (1959), Elenore Bowen's RETURN TO LAUGHTER (1954), and Oscar Lewis' LA VIDA (1965). All these writings departed from the conventions of clinical procedure. Reconstruction in any field may be an act of recognition that demands all levels of intelligence. When doctoral fellows return from the field to write their dissertations, they paw through their data hour after hour seeking the spark that will ignite their material into an enlightened conclusion. I believe this spark comes from all their insights-- feelings and intelligence-- to reach understandings that lie beyond the outposts of their data. What is needed in this creative process is the development of self-correcting feedback--from the known into the exploratory unknown, repeatedly circling back. Responsible information is recorded, analyzed by reliable means, considered and reconsidered, and compared to incoming fresh observation, before it is finally projected into a conclusion.

To proceed, we must clearly separate data film from the conclusively edited records of ethnographic film. Just as there is need for basic descriptive ethnographic writing, there should be room for films that just present the cultural record. In teaching, such open-ended documents are very rewarding because they do not dramatize conceptual conclusions.

Whether in anthropological literature or film, conclusions must rest on foundations of sound data and research. But moving systematically through the factual evidence does not insure arriving at conclusive understandings. There is a point in all investigations where the trail of data collecting ends and a new process of reasoning must begin. We can call this the "inventive phase" in which the researcher-philosopher creates new concepts that can embrace and combine the data insights into organic relationships. This data-summation can be difficult in anthropology because of the disciplined nature of the information the anthropologist must work with. As stated, ethnographic observers are not allowed to filter field observations through their sensitivities as they are collecting their data, but their creative faculties must be used to the full later when they are tying together their research. Film records can carry this conclusive process further by extending the trail of tangible information, for the refinements of observation missing from raw written notes can be found reliably in film records. For this reason documentary data film offers further reliability to anthropological conclusions.

Is ethnographic film projectively distorted? Not necessarily, but often yes. Without structured discipline, film can reflect distorted attitudes of the filmmaker. Because of the pressure to produce audience film, ethnographic productions are rarely loyal documentaries but rather montages that are plastically edited to present the producer's point of view. It must be said again that this reflectivity runs all through the cultural record, but we are conditioned to be more accepting of the written word as authoritative. David MacDougall finds that the ethnographic filmmaker reaffirms the colonial origins of anthropology. It was once the European who decided what was worth knowing about "primitive" peoples and what they in turn should be taught. The shadow of that attitude falls across the observational film, giving it a distinctively Western parochialism. The traditions of science and narrative art combine this instance to dehumanize the study of man. It is a form in which the observer and observed exist in separate worlds, and it produces films that are monologues (Nichols 1981:266).

The Background of an Ethnographic Film

Robert Gardner's drama of the Dani, DEAD BIRDS (1963), is a film that by its subtle discrepancies points up the problem of authenticity in many ethnographic films. DEAD BIRDS is artistically fine filmmaking. It is honestly a personal statement of the producer about war in human development. Yet it appears that ethnography gives way to develop Gardner's philosophical concepts about the fatalism of perpetual conflict. A difference between DEAD BIRDS and other epic cultural films, such as THE NUER (1970) and APPEALS TO SANTIAGO (1966), is that Gardner is clear and explicit about his personal motives in making this extraordinary film.

In addition to the film on which they collaborated, Robert Gardner and Karl Heider published a visual ethnography of the Dani entitled GARDENS OF WAR (1968), which presents the background for DEAD BIRDS. Gardner wrote a revealing forward that traces his consciousness up to and through the film. He describes his fascination as a child with a World War I picture book (1968:xii-xiii), a fascination which may be at the roots of this film about aborigines who still carry on ritualistic warfare. There is also a study module prepared to accompany the film (Heider 1972), which includes a "filmmaker's essay" by Gardner. We are indebted to him for the candor with which he describes how he approached filming the Dani.

> I seized the opportunity of speaking to certain fundamen-
> tal issues in human life. The Dani were then less impor-
> tant to me than those issues. In fact, the Dani, except for
> a few individuals....were important to me only because
> they provided such clear evidence upon which a judgment
> about, or at least certain reflections on, matters of some
> human urgency could arise. My responsibility was as
> much to my own situation as a thinking person as to the
> Dani as also thinking and behaving people. I never
> thought this reflective or value oriented approach was in-
> consistent either with my training as a social scientist or
> my goals as the author of a film (Heider 1972:2-34; em-
> phasis ours).

Is this a distortive approach to filmic ethnography? The important issue
is, how does this effect the overview of Dani culture? In contrast to the
film, the book, GARDENS OF WAR, places warrior activity within the
context of Dani life, in its functioning position as only one of the labors
and skills of Dani men. Equal energy was dedicated to clearing agricultural
fields and canals. At one of the AAA meetings Heider showed a film record
he had made documenting the same Dani community building a spacious
pig sty a hundred feet long. Such collaboration was routine activity. The
book is an assembly from the ethnography gathered during the three year
period of filming, and it reveals the scope of insight available to the filmmaker. When the film, DEAD BIRDS was edited, this contextual content
gave way to the war activities and the epic funeral of a small boy said to
have been killed by raiders. Would the pig sty footage have been distracting
to the thesis of Gardner's film? Looking closely at the visual record of the
fighting, we may observe that the thousand years' conflict has been resolved
into a sophisticated ceremonial confrontation in which few people get hurt.
But while the war confrontation was well documented, its function as cere-
monially controlled ritual was not made explicit. The study module discusses the ritual aspect--the necessity for appeasement of ghosts--but the
shot log and the narration do not; this was not a key enlightenment of the
film. The battle is narrated as a battle directed to mutual destruction. There
is no suggestion that the conflict is hardly closer to outright "war," in our
understanding of the term, than is the Rose Bowl.

It is my reflective interpretation that DEAD BIRDS is a symbolic
statement of the fatalism of warfare, rather than an observation that conflict
might be moderated, and the sobering concept that some aboriginal peoples
may be more civilized in dealing with man's persistent drive for violence
than we are today. The film does not acknowledge this civilized develop-
ment--an omission that under-represents the refinement of these aborigines.
Why was this ignored? Was it blindness to ethnography, or simply the

artistic license and the acknowledged cultural self-concern of the film producer?

What is the place of artistry in anthropology? Is art in conflict with scientific inquiry? I hope not! For the art process appears essential in organizing insight and essential in forming dynamic conclusions. Is artistry a license to weight the record in order to express the personal projection of the author and filmmaker? In DEAD BIRDS Gardner made a choice to use film artistry to express his view of the human process. The same artistry could have been directed to an understanding of what the Dani had developed to meet the challenge of eternal warfare. The issues of authenticity may appear as minor manipulations, but I see the presentation of ritual warfare as combat to overwhelm the enemy as a major distortion.

THE AX FIGHT (1975), filmed among the Yanomamo of Venezuela by Timothy Asch in collaboration with Napoleon Chagnon, presents another example of anthropological reflectivity, though the conflict is very different from DEAD BIRDS. In this case the fidelity of the film image belies the view of the anthropologist. The film is a documentary recording of a spontaneous fight over adultery. The duel was carried out in fury that could have led to serious injury or death. Blows are exchanged--though with the flat of the axes at the least vital parts of the anatomy--and the duel ends without serious harm. As in the war games of the Dani, social controls reduce this confrontation to a ceremony of violence. The Yanomamo endure long bickering tribal conflicts that could lead to wars of extermination, but shared cultural values and procedures hold fatalities to the minimum. Napoleon Chagnon has titled his popular ethnography, YANOMAMO: THE FIERCE PEOPLE (1968), and though he is a meticulous ethnographer, his personal reflective judgment of their fierceness affects the film's interpretation, obscuring the more sensitive side of these forest hunters.

Asch has produced an extensive series of Yanomamo films, though most of these are less often viewed than the dramatic AX FIGHT. One film, A FATHER WASHES HIS CHILDREN (1973), follows a father bathing his young children in the river and later playing with them in the secluded jungle. Asch's footage contains records of Yanomamo behavior that reveal life ways of gentleness, humor, and human warmth largely missing from Chagnon's descriptions.

The demography of Yanomamo life today appears quite different from their life even seventy-five years ago. Traditionally the Yanomamo were not riverine people but lived back in the forest in small semi-migratory bands. Marvin Harris suggests that the Yanomamo violence that so impressed Chagnon may be a recent development following the Portuguese introduction of platano. This food source, while supporting a larger population, also called for settlements that had to stay close to the plantings for long periods. This in turn over-taxed hunting resources in the immediate area and pushed hunters into other tribal domains. Platano gardens also brought about a shift from a diet high in protein to one high in starch and carbohydrates. These social and dietary changes may have contributed to the inter-group hostility and aggression which Chagnon describes (Harris 1974:100-103).

The contemporary fierceness of the Yanomamo is also well-documented in the account of Helena Valero (1970), who lived for twenty years in captivity among the Yanomamo. From the first group she was forced to go with, which broke apart almost immediately in overt hostility, her report suggests to me that serious internal stress, probably exacerbated by population increase, had become close to unbearable.

Since the Chagnon and Asch's ethnography and films were completed, another writer has entered the field. Florinda Donner, a Venezuelan and a doctoral candidate at the University of California at Los Angeles, has published SHABONO: A VISIT TO A REMOTE AND MAGICAL WORLD IN THE HEART OF THE SOUTH AMERICAN JUNGLE (1982), purporting to be a true account of a year's habitation with the Yanomamo. Donner's writings cover much of the same occurrences described by Valero, as well as ethnographic material paralleling Chagnon's texts, but the behavior style described is in marked contrast to Chagnon's material and is synchronized rather with the more sensitive overtones of Timothy Asch's films. While it is seriously questioned whether Donner actually lived with the Yanomamo (De Holmes 1983:85:664-667, Picchi 1983:85:674-674), she certainly could have studied Asch's many films of the group. If Florinda Donner did indeed write from Asch's films, her contribution could be considered an interpretive study, a humanistic decoding of Yanomamo film records!

My own impressions of the Yanomamo also are drawn from Timothy Asch's films, and they relate to the writings of Donner and Valero. I find the Yanomamo violence as neurotic as it is deadly. But I also trust the sophisticated development of film research to reveal other sides of Yanomamo personality and behavior.

What are Ethnographic Films For?

The functions of ethnographic film have been dispersed among three genres: cultural documentation for ethnographic research, anthropological film for education, and cultural drama film for public consumption and profit. This diversity has further confused our focus. Can all these genres contain ethnographic integrity?

Regardless of criticisms prompted by reflexivity and reflectivity, ethnographic films can dynamically add to ethnographic understanding. Steps can be taken to preserve authenticity through the disciplines of visual anthropology. Film research methods define responsible and researchable imagery. Briefly, scenes should be held together intact, temporal order retained, and contextual relationships preserved. If any of these orders is seriously confused, the ethnographic integrity of the film is largely destroyed. Of course, any film can be used as data, including American soap operas, if the goals of research are properly established.

Filmmakers may object to these limitations as too restraining. Without them ethnographic film becomes largely an art process without scientific validity. In visual anthropology there are plastic ways to accomplish ordered relations that surely can be adapted to creative filmmaking. Ethnographic film ideally is a visual presentation of anthropology, but this function has been muddied by the counter currents of media production that compromise the primary goal. Professional filmmaking exerts a growing influence over the processes and structure of ethnographic film.

Teaching with film is the most pragmatic way to appreciate its value as communication. Timothy Asch, for example, has taught extensively with film, and his Yanomamo productions are clearly supportive of conceptual understanding. There are several kinds of educational films that should be considered. One is the informationally edited "closed" lecture type. These "how to think" productions provoke little comment, for they are edited to deliver a lectured message. Even though the image is faithfully projected, the message may be manipulated through inept or inadequate translation of what the people are saying. As an example, in a scene from the "Faces of Change" series, filmed in Kenya by David MacDougall, we see a partially clad woman sitting outside her indigenous brush shelter saying, "I want my son to go to college, get a Ph.D. and come back and lead his people." I asked Miller, the series coordinator, if she really said that. "Well, it went through five translations and this was the most accurate message we could get" (personal communication). In other films we also wonder if the editors are not putting their own words into people's mouths.

At another extreme are cultural epic films, such as DEAD BIRDS. These also have "closed" ends. In both cases producers have decided how audiences should respond. When the lights go on, students too often are numb with culture shock and drama and have nothing to exchange, for it has all been said for them. These structured message films are dominated by the producers' reflectivity, which blocks students' individual perceptions.

A third and more unusual type of film presents the cultural circumstance as an undisturbed reality. As one example, when MacDougall's records of Kenya cattle herders (1972, 1973) are screened, students are able to write down copious personal insights about the nature and ways of these people. Karl Heider's film of the Dani building a communal pig sty is another "open-ended" record with no reflective epic message, and therefore it offers students an open opportunity to make self-directed primary observations about an important focus of Dani culture.

A fourth, but rare, variety of ethnographic film is structured directly on pre-filmic research. One such film is THE PATH (1971), an ethnography of a Japanese tea ceremony produced by Don and Ron Rundstrom, a film edited and montaged directly on an authentic cultural core. A related example is

Timothy Asch's documentary recording, THE FEAST (1968), which is structured on a thorough analysis of uncut footage. Still imagery is taken directly from the film and used to introduce the sequential structure of this Yanomamo ceremonial occasion. Asch objectively edited this document to offer an educational experience in the classroom. Temporal context is meticulously preserved, which again allows students an open opportunity to experience the event with full intelligence.

A more structured but also educational film is TROBRIAND CRICKET: AN INGENIOUS RESPONSE TO COLONIALISM (1973). This production presents clear concepts about both acculturation and the persistence of culture by documenting a Trobriand village celebrating their independence with a magical cricket game that they have adapted from their British experience. The Australian producers supply the historical context by flashing back to British occupation, with future development projected in a sync-sound interview with a village elder. Yet Hubert Smith finds that audiences "respond primarily to the sheer performance aspects" of this film and "evince patronizing 'look at the houseboys playing with the master's golf sticks' attitudes" (personal communication).

The Development of Ethnographic Film

The authentic beginnings of anthropological photography and film were the recording of field observations made directly in the environmental circumstance. In effect, the initial use of photography was, and still can be, an extension of the field notebook. Getting undisturbed information was certainly the highest priority. The kinesics and spatial recordings of Gregory Bateson and Margaret Mead (1942) created one authentic style of anthropological photography, and the early film vignettes of the Kalahari hunters filmed by John Marshall, another equally dedicated effort to record ethnographic reality.

When Robert Gardner edited Marshall's films into the epic, THE HUNTERS (1958), we observe the shift from film as record to film as ethnographic drama. It is public knowledge that Marshall quarreled with Gardner over this dramatic editorializing, that motivated Gardner to overplay episodes that would shock Western sensibilities for dramatic effect. As an example, the key hunter, roving for game, finds a bush with nests of hatched birdlings, and proceeds to destroy the nests and the baby birds. The over-voice states that he will bring the hatched birds home to make soup for his children. Visually this is a long scene without clear ethnographic meaning, but it creates culture shock that can obscure Western eyes to other sensitivities and refinements of these aboriginal hunters. Considering Marshall's over-all documentation, the scene appears spliced in just for effect--because it shocked Gardner's sensibilities?

Do these criticisms suggest that artistry and ethnographic film are in conflict? Karl Heider (Heider 1976:5-7) states that filmically recording the "holism" of culture is a central accomplishment in ethnographic film. If filmmakers are to accomplish this whole perspective certainly artistry and ethnography *must* relate to each other. What we should be concerned about is *artistry out of context*. One example of artistic distortion is the exquisitely filmed APPEAL TO SANTIAGO (1966) which depicts a religious festival in Chiapas. Its sequences contain superb visual ethnography, but when finally produced, these scenes are montaged primarily for artistic effect with no respect for spatial or temporal context. The results of this manipulation is that it is impossible to follow the ethnographic progression of this festival. In contrast, Hilary Harris's film THE NUER, a co-production with Robert Gardener, contains none of this contextual confusion. THE NUER is a filmic translation of Evans- Pritchard's ethnography of the cattle herders of Ethiopia which both artistically and anthropologically presents the overtones and symbolism of a people whose whole life and ethos merges with their cattle. But in this film, artistry *is* in context and this cultural record could not have been made without the interpretive artistry that guided both the filming and the editing.

Beyond the confusions of editorial manipulation, it is the ascending technology of filmmaking that dims the research integrity of anthropological film records. This is mostly by default; it is still possible for a lone anthropologist-camera-person to make, independently, a silent (or later "voice-over") ethnographic record. But this rarely happens today. Film recording has become a team accomplishment in order to control the increasingly complex technology. This evolution does not have to rule out authentic insights or cultural structure. Technology can be the means to even richer anthropological ends, if the goal is real ethnography. But too often technological considerations take the camera away from the ethnographer and give it to the professional filmmaker. The ethnographer's role is reduced to that of consultant. Gone is the one-to-one rapport and communication bridge so essential to native collaboration. In place of personal relationships there is a team with necessarily limited anthropological discipline--or none at all--that flies in and out and, at least implicitly, tells the people filmed, when and how to act.

In the face of this production circumstance, Hubert Smith has a cogent comment:

> Filmmakers make films that viewers attend to. Anthropologists make films which are informed. When one learns the skills of the other, chances for good filmic ethnography improve. It is as unproductive to make an un-viewable film as it is to publish an un-readable book. It is as indefensible to make a misleading filmic utterance as it is to make a printed one (personal communication).

What, then, is the future of ethnographic film? Those concerned should first ask, What are anthropological films for? Certainly they are not travelogs, nor are they cultural dramas for entertainment or propaganda. Certainly they are educational in responsibly sharing the diverse ways of mankind. Educationally their foremost contribution is to share with students the primary experiences of anthropology. In content they can be illustrative records of ethnographic studies. They are oriented toward authentic research, which may be their most important characteristic. We can define ethnographic film from this description, for it separates cultural records clearly from dramatic or artistic narratives. Popular ethnographic films made with all the refinements of the industry lean toward audience entertainment about exotic peoples, but it must be reiterated that these cultural epics often have little value in the classroom. For ethnographic film to be of research value requires disciplined guidelines for filming, organizing, and finally editing the production. And for students to get a first hand filmic experience, to get real insights, they must be able to "research" films themselves.

It would be helpful to consider the achievement of ethnographic film in comparison with the writing of summary conclusions based on disciplined ethnographic study. As suggested before, valuable conclusions about culture frequently involve both subjective and artistic intelligence. It appears that responsible cultural summations require the full scope of intelligence-- including intuitive hunches! (Consider the writings of Levi-Straus.) Authenticity in cultural representations rests on agreed ends, as well as upon means, and these must be shared by the production team. When the artistry becomes an end in itself, then film on human behavior can become scientifically worthless.

Much confusion about ethnographic film results from an incomplete knowledge of the history of its development. Authenticity, of course, did not begin with Robert Flaherty, whose films were as much poetry as documentation. His images were powerful and his tradition is still with us. But it should be clear that documentary film is not necessarily ethnographic film, despite the documentarians' efforts to record loyally what, how, and where actions take place. Grierson, the English documentary filmmaker, broke with Flaherty when the latter re-arranged and tried to re-enact the culture process, as in his film MAN OF ARAN (1934). Flaherty was searching for cultural ethos and relationships he could not find in a strictly documentary approach. He was trying to go beyond the details of documentation to achieve the essence of the "life way" of Aran Islanders, so he partly contrived their drama. He might have produced a more authentic record with this artistic approach if he had appreciated the vitality to be gained by looking deeper into the reality of island life. MAN OF ARAN is a great epic but not an ethnographic film.

Flaherty developed a formula for making a cultural epic: "If you find the pain and danger in a culture, you can make a dramatic documentary film." But when Flaherty went to Samoa, this approach failed because he could not find pain in the idyllic islands. Then he observed the puberty rite of tattooing, and with the zeal of THE NUER filmmakers, Flaherty produced MOANA OF THE SOUTH SEAS (1926) around this rite. The fallacy was that this type of tattooing was not as painful as the film represented (John Adair, personal communication, ca. 1950).

Searching for the Ethos in Anthropological Films

Despite anthropological insight, most ethnographic film is an outside-in experience, which promotes the reflectivity for which it is criticized. In the 1950s I worked with Bernard Siegel on an ethnography of Picuris Pueblo. My contribution was to make an embracing set of photographs for Dr. Siegel to use as probes in interviewing. Picuris is a dwindling pueblo of the Tiwa language group, with perhaps twenty families. In their cycle of acculturation they were pleased to be studied by an anthropologist and a photographer. I had lived many years in this area of New Mexico, and Siegel was a scholar of Southwest anthropology. We both presumed that ceremonial dances were the heart of Pueblo religious life.

I photographed the Picuris environment with an "open" process, hoping to record material that would trigger new insights into tribal values. San Lorenzo Day, the Pueblo's summer fiesta, came during our research, and the Governor asked me to photograph the Deer Dance, for which the Pueblo was famed. The dance was theatrically exquisite. I also photographed the morning activities. After the Saint's Day Mass, the fiesta throng moved out of the Pueblo plaza and down to the river where the ceremonial foot races were held. I recorded all the runners in this relay, most of them elderly, and the race to my eyes seemed low-keyed compared to the beautiful Deer Dance.

However, when Siegel carried out his photo-interviewing, he found our pre-judgments to be completely wrong. The dance held a relatively low place in this day's ceremony, one collaborator stating, "We do this to please the White people." But when they studied photographs of the procession down to the river, the response was, "Now the solemn time begins!" We found that religious feeling centered on the running, a collective energy rite of greater importance than is recorded in Tiwa ethnography. Had we been making a film without this photo-interview research, we might have centered it around the photogenic Deer Dance and created another of the stereotypic blunders common to ethnographic film!

Interviewing with photographs, a central method of visual anthropology, is useful in searching for the themes of culture to be conveyed in ethnographic films. With the Polaroid camera, or with Porta-Pac video, proposed film scenes can be checked rapidly by interviewing. This collaborative feedback can supply an inside-out view of filmic circumstance that could correct the impressionistic presumptions of the filmmaker.

Franz Boas sought the inside view when he developed the process of working intensively with key informants, which gave anthropology its first inside-out view based on native intelligence. John Adair and Sol Worth experimented to discover the visual inside view by placing Bell and Howell three-turret 16mm cameras directly in the hands of seven Navajo men and women. Through the films they made, these Navajos were able, for the first time, to share visually their own perceptions of their processes and their world. The films, described in THROUGH NAVAJO EYES (Worth and Adair 1972), were genuinely inside-out ethnographic films--a revolutionary development of emic understanding.

In another attempt to get the inside view, Don and Ron Rundstrom used direct techniques of visual anthropology. They photographed students of Japanese Tea Ceremony performing the ritual, and then interviewed their master teacher with the still photographs. Then they used the insights from these interviews--plus continuing collaborative feedback--to create THE PATH (1971), a film record that is accepted as authentic by Japanese audiences.

Yet it is significant that these two successful experiments have not been repeated nor their methods incorporated into other ethnographic film productions. Is it that most film producers are not themselves anthropologists? Or because anthropologist filmmakers are too conservative to appreciate the possibilities inherent in these methods? There likely is a more human and culturally determined explanation: Surrendering the camera to the native is surrendering the Western ego. I suspect that only in theory do we want "the native" to have the authoritative judgment!

Visual Anthropology"s Contribution to Ethnographic Film

Anthropology remains visually illiterate, for both anthropological filmmakers and their critics appear equally uninformed on the disciplines and developments of visual anthropology, a field that has been devoted to bringing authenticity to the photographic record. Visual anthropology can help bring clarity to the meaning and function of ethnographic film.

The success of film rests on its function as communication, which allows its audience to read and share its content. Visual anthropology rests on the photographic recording of non-verbal communication. The basic elements of proxemics (Hall 1959, 1966), kinesics (Birdwhistell 1952), and choreometrics (Lomax 1969), together provide the visual research language of behavioral science. As one example of kinesic research, Paul Ekman of the Langley Porter Clinic of the University of California, San Francisco, has tested the facial expression of emotions, not only in the clinical setting but also among people of the highlands of New Guinea, and found that at least facial kinesics are an interculturally shared means of communication--though he points out that when a culture requires suppression or masking of emotion we can observe contradictory signaling (Ekman 1972).

Extended film research of cultural interaction has further developed the scope of understanding of non-verbal language. Knowledge of the language of kinesics can be of great assistance in the reading of intelligently edited ethnographic film. Edward T. Hall's behavioral research has demonstrated that, without awareness of the relationship of behavior to both time and space, we cannot comprehend the meaning of human action in cross-cultural research. These insights have revolutionized how research film is made and how filmic behavior is interpreted. I repeat, the fluency of film rests on communication, the viewers' ability to read and understand what is happening. If filmmakers interfere with interlocking kinesic signaling, scramble sequences, and chop up time, the fluency of ethnographic film is destroyed. The disciplines needed and developed in film research are communication guidelines to photographing and producing ethnographic film.

Where lies the integrity of ethnographic film? In part it rests on the viewers' ability to experience holistically and authentically the cultural circumstances presented. Even though ethnographic film, like all film, succeeds structurally by its organic artistry, yet this artistry is only a means, for the end is cultural authenticity. This suggests that the criterion for strength of an ethnographic film record lies in its research background and the retention, through production, of this research authenticity. When the educational worth of cultural film is considered as the criterion, it is the researchable content of film that is valuable. For students, reading and learning from film should be a research experience.

Visual anthropology clearly defines the content and structure of researchable data, and these criteria offer guidelines for producing readable and researchable ethnographic film. Anthropologists making film should be well-acquainted with these needs, for reasonably they are essentially the same as for all responsible data gathering: identification of the source of phenomena, and undisturbed spatial and temporal order of objects and occurrences. If filmmakers find these requirements too restraining, Robert Redfield, in THE LITTLE COMMUNITY (1955), offered a series of approaches that would allow them to retain researchable content systematically. Redfield stressed the value of building an organic model of cultural circumstance so that parts can be considered units of the whole view. Ethnographic interpretation requires an artistic synthesizing intelligence that can qualify and link together otherwise isolated cultural parts into organic wholes. But montaging cultural episodes only for artistic effect can destroy the organic structure of an ethnographic film. A resistance to a structural approach to cultural processes suggests a misunderstanding of artistic development itself--the ability to assemble organically complete form.

Visual anthropology can support the orientation and planning phase of making an ethnographic film. The anthropologist consultant or film director may have made extensive field studies in the area of the proposed film. But conventionally this research may have been predominantly verbal, and may have omitted many visual relationships significant to filmmaking. This will handicap the direction of a film, in which intelligence is primarily visual. Primary photographic surveying of environs visually unfamiliar to the investigator, and surveying of the visual shape and sequence of a proposed film can offer essential visual relationships for film planning. A month's intensive field photography, followed up by photographic interviewing, can give film planners extensive and accurate information on geography, ceremony, social structure, and the technology of survival. Native collaborators can identify and validate any unfamiliar visual information. Photographs from such a survey can be incorporated directly into the planning and storyboard of a proposed film. This can be done in the field prior to actually exposing film. A major value of such rapid visual orientation is that the filming can begin with an open process, that invites otherwise unknown visual circumstances to influence the theme and content. This approach can deflect prestructuring which might warp the authenticity of a film. The feedback facility of orientation photographs can also be a fluent communication bridge that allows native participation in filmmaking decisions, just as collaboration through interviewing with photographs created the authenticity of the Rundstoms' film ethnography of the Japanese tea ceremony.

Robert Flaherty attempted to use an open process with what he called "the roving camera," seeking themes directly in his rushes. He had faith that the realism of the film image could catch insights unavailable even to his own observations. But he did not involve native eyes in this filmic searching. Visual anthropology also exploits hidden dimensions of the photographic image which can be uncovered through disciplined research, particularly with the assistance of native photographic readers.

In the still image analysis of the cultural inventory, of homes or of village environment, observing detail within its context is essential to research understanding. This is of course equally true in archeology, where artifacts out of context have little data value. In film both spatial and temporal context are essential dimensions for analysis. Robert Redfield states that the holistic view in ethnography requires an understanding of cultural continuity. He suggests that behavior must be tracked through both space and time if an orderly understanding of culture is to be achieved. Redfield describes observational tracking as "like stringing beads on a necklace," that places all facts and activities in their functional order (1955).

Preserving cultural continuity can be essential in ethnographic film for two basic reasons. First, continuity through space and time retains the research value of film. And second, visual continuity is essential to non-verbal comprehension. In visual narrative each still photograph or scene is, figuratively, a word in a sentence, or a unit of paragraphic meaning. When images in film are moved, the visual message can radically change or seriously distort the order of understanding. Strictly artistic image-scrambling may create a work of art, but it can destroy the documentary and conceptual message. When ethnographic footage is cut and montaged for the wrong reasons, authentic communication is lost.

Anthropologists as filmmakers should, first of all, retain their roles as ethnographers and not surrender their film to media. Surely anthropologists must learn the technology of filmmaking, but at the same time they must retain their vital roles of cultural researchers and educators.

REFERENCES CITED

Asch, Timothy (1975).Using Film in Teaching: One Pedagogical Approach. IN Principles of Visual Anthropology, Paul Hocking, ed. The Hague: Mouton Publishers.

Bateson, Gregory and Margaret Mead (1942). Balinese Character: A Photographic Analysis. New York: New York Academy of Sciences.

Birdwhistell, Raymond L. (1970). Kinesics and Context. Philadelphia: University of Pennsylvania Press.

Bowen, Elenore Smith (pseud. for Laura Bohannon) (1954). Return to Laughter. New York: Harpers.

Chagnon, Napoleon A. (1968). Yanomamo: The Fierce People. New York: Holt, Rinehart and Winston.

Collier, John, Jr. (1967). Visual Anthropology: Photography as a Research Method. New York: Holt, Rinehart and Winston.

Collier, John, Jr. (1972). Alaskan Eskimo Education: A Film Analysis of Cultural Confrontation in the Schools. New York: Holt, Rinehart and Winston.

Donner, Florinda (1982). Shabono: A Visit to a Remote and Magical World in the Heart of the South American Jungle. New York: Delacorte Press.

Ekman, Paul (1972). Universal and Cultural Differences in Facial Expressions of Emotions, IN Nebraska Symposium on Motivation, J. Cole, ed. Lincoln: University of Nebraska Press.

Gardner, Robert and Karl Heider (1968). Gardens of War: Life and Death in the New Guinea Stone Age. New York: Random House.

Hall, Edward T. (1959). The Silent Language. Garden City: Doubleday and Co.

Hall, Edward T. (1966). The Hidden Dimension. Garden City: Doubleday and Co.

Harris, Marvin (1974). Cows, Pigs, Wars, and Witches: The Riddle of Culture. New York: Random House.

Heider, Karl (1972). The Dani of West Irian, an Ethnographic Companion to the Film, DEAD BIRDS, with narration and filmmaker's essay by Robert Gardner. Andover, Massachusetts: Warner Modular Publications.

Heider, Karl (1976). Ethnographic Film. Austin: University of Texas Press.

De Holmes, Rebecca B. (1983). SHABONO: Scandal or Superb Social Science? Review article, American Anthropologist, 85:664-667.

Jarvie, I. C. (1984). The Problem of the Ethnographic Real. Current Anthropology, 24:3:313-325.

Kroeber, Theodora (1961). Ishi in Two Worlds: A Biography of the Last Wild

Indian in North America. Berkeley: University of California Press.

Leighton, Alexander H. (1959). My Name is Legion: Foundations for a Theory of Man in Relation to Culture. The Stirling County Study of Psychiatric Disorder and Sociocultural Environment, Vol. I. New York: Basic Books.

Lewis, Oscar (1951). Life in a Mexican Village: Tepoztlan Restudied. Urbana: University of Illinois Press.

Lewis, Oscar (1965). La Vida: A Puerto Rican Family in the Culture of Poverty--San Juan and New York. New York: Random House.

Lomax, Alan (1978). Choreometrics.

Nichols, Bill (1981). Ideology and the Image. Bloomington: Indiana University Press.

Perera, Victor and Robert D. Bruce (1982). The Last Lords of Palenque: The Lacandon Mayas of the Mexican Rain Forest. Boston: Little Brown.

Picchi, Debra (1983). Review of SHABONO: A VISIT TO A REMOTE AND MAGICAL WORLD IN THE HEART OF THE SOUTH AMERICAN FOREST. FLORINDA DONNER. New York: Delacorte Press, 1982. American Anthropologist 85:674-675.

Redfield, Robert (1930). Tepoztlan, a Mexican Village: A Study of Folk Life. Chicago: University of Chicago Press.

Redfield, Robert (1950). A Village That Chose Progress: Chan Kom Revisited. Chicago: University of Chicago Press.

Redfield, Robert (1955). The Little Community: Viewpoints for the Study of a Human Whole. Chicago: University of Chicago Press.

Ruesch, Jurgen and Weldon Kees (1956). Nonverbal Communication: Notes on the Visual Perception of Human Relations. Berkeley: University of California Press.

Rundstrom, Donald, Ronald Rundstrom and Clint Bergum (1973). Japanese Tea: The Ritual, The Aesthetics, the Way: An Ethnographic Companion to the Film THE PATH. Andover, Massachusetts: Warner Modular Publications.

Thomas, Elizabeth Marshall (1959). The Harmless People. New York: Knopf.

Valero, Helena, as told to Ettiore Biacco (1970). Yanoama: The Narrative of a White Girl Kidnapped by Amazonian Indians. New York: E. P. Dutton & Co.

Worth, Sol and John Adair (1972). Through Navajo Eyes: An Exploration in Film Communication and Anthropology. Bloomington: Indiana University Press.

FILMS CITED

APPEALS TO SANTIAGO (1966). Duane Metzger and Carter Wilson. Color, 27 minutes. Distributor: McGraw-Hill Films.

THE AX FIGHT (1975). Timothy Asch and Napoleon Chagnon. Color, 16 minutes. Distributor: DER (Documentary Educational Resources).

DEAD BIRDS (1963). Robert Gardner and Karl Heider. Color, 85 minutes. Distributor: Contemporary Films.

A FATHER WASHES HIS CHILDREN (1973). Timothy Asch and Napoleon Chagnon. Color, 15 minutes. Distributor: DER (Documentary Educational Resources).

THE FEAST (1968). Timothy Asch and Napoleon Chagnon. Color, 29 minutes. Distributor: DER (Documentary Educational Resources).

THE HUNTERS (1958). John Marshall and Robert Gardner. Color, 73 minutes. Distributor: Educational Division, Films, Inc.

KENYA BORAN (1973). David MacDougall and James Blue. Color, two parts -- 33 minutes each. Distributor: Wheelock Educational Resources.

LIVING MAYA (1983). Hubert Smith.

MAN OF ARAN (1934). Robert Flaherty. Black and white, 77 minutes. Distributor: Contemporary/McGraw-Hill.

MEN BATHING (1973). John Marshall. Color, 14 minutes. Distributor: DER (Documentary Educational Resources).

MOANA OF THE SOUTH SEAS (1926). Robert Flaherty. Black and white, 85 minutes. Distributor: Museum of Modern Art.

THE NUER (1970). Hilary Harris. Color, 75 minutes. Distributor: McGraw-Hill Films.

THE PATH (1971). Donald Rundstrom, Ronald Rundstrom and Clint Bergum. Color, 34 minutes. Distributor: Sumai Film Company.

THE SPIRIT POSSESSION OF ALEJANDRO MAMANI (1974). Hubert Smith. Color, 27 minutes. Distributor: Wheelock Educational Resources. American Universities Field Staff.

TO LIVE WITH HERDS (1972). David MacDougall and Jane MacDougall. Black and white, 70 minutes. Distributor: Media Center, Rice University.

TROBRIAND CRICKET: AN INGENIOUS RESPONSE TO COLONIALISM (1973). Jerry W. Leach and Garry Kildea. Color, 54 minutes. Distributor: University of California Extension Media Center.

Third Eye:
Some Reflections On Collaboration
For Ethnographic Film

Linda H. Connor
Department of Sociology
University of Newcastle, Australia

ABSTRACT: In 1978, Linda Connor, an anthropology Ph.D. student carrying out field research in rural Bali, began an ethnographic film collaboration with Timothy Asch and Patsy Asch. The project, originally begun by chance, and conceived of as brief in duration, developed into a long term enterprise that is still continuing after nine years. Connor, as an anthropologist in the final phase of a long and intensive period of fieldwork, derived many advantages from sharing her field situation with an anthropologist who had not previously worked in Bali, and who, as an ethnographic filmmaker and someone not fluent in the local languages, was more sensitive than she to visual information about social relations. Problems arose over the burden of constant linguistic and cultural interpretation the anthropologist had to provide, over the anthropologist's lack of training in ethnographic filmmaking, and over the amount of time and energy the anthropologist had to set aside for the project, and also had to request of the Balinese participants. Just as important were the problems unanticipated by the anthropologist at the time of filming, foremost the necessity for even greater expenditures of time in the production phase, and the conflict of this activity with the demands of dissertation writing, and other forms of academic publication. Advantages for the anthropologist in the post-fieldwork phases of filmmaking include sharing a detailed knowledge of her fieldwork with two other people who have more than an observer's interest in it, and the stimulus to data analysis that the film and sound record has provided.

Many ethnographic films depend on collaboration between anthropologist and ethnographic filmmaker (and possibly others as well), but we find little written in the film and anthropology literature on the problems and advantages of this process. Has collaboration been so disagreeable as to discourage published reflection? Or do people take for granted that collabora-

97

tion is an uncomplicated process the success of which is guaranteed once the team arrives in the field?

In my own experience neither of these assumptions is warranted. Collaboration may succeed despite odds, or it may founder on the rocks of interpersonal and intercultural insensitivity and misunderstanding. The joint efforts of myself, Timothy Asch, and later Patsy Asch on the Bali film project should, I believe, be considered among the more successful collaborations, notwithstanding the obstacles involved. I shall outline the background of the project, what I see as the vicissitudes of collaboration in the field, and the important stages of production and beyond.

Background of the Project: A Narrative Account

In July, 1978, I was deeply involved in the final months of a two year research project as a doctoral student in the Department of Anthropology at the University of Sydney. I was living part of the time in a small Balinese village where I had spent most of the preceding 21 months and part of the time in a small town 7 kilometers from the village. I felt at home in my rural Balinese environment, had few contacts with other researchers or travellers, and was feeling apprehensive about leaving my comfortable pace of work and numerous Balinese friends to return to the rigours of an urban university environment and dissertation writing.

My research focused on the beliefs and practices of indigenous healers viewed in relation to island and nationwide processes of change. Because part of my work included detailed studies of individual healers and their patients, I had developed good rapport with several healers practicing within the district where I had chosen to live. (See Connor 1982 for further information about this research.) Since early in the fieldwork, my closest friend and greatest source of ethnographic information had been the spirit medium and masseuse, Jero Tapakan, who became the principal subject of the four films on Balinese healing.

My first meeting with Timothy Asch had taken place approximately 12 months previously, when he had spent a few days in Bali en route to Eastern Indonesia for another film collaboration project. We had talked about my research and his own work, and he had expressed interest in working with me if the opportunity were ever to arise. I had almost forgotten these words when Tim returned to Bali in 1978, again en route to film in Eastern Indonesia. Delays in the arrival of his colleague had Tim casting around for an opportunity to test some old film stock in Bali and to test his camera that had just been repaired. When Tim proposed that he and I shoot a small amount of footage on a topic that was relevant to my research, I enthusiastically agreed. Thus began a collaborative venture that was to fully preoccupy me for the ensuing six weeks and that as continued intermittently for nine years with still some work remaining to be done.

The initial selection of a topic to be filmed did not present us with any problems. Tim suggested that I choose a short event that was important to my research and that I would be interested in using for analysis and teaching. He did not want to use more than a few rolls of his film stock, which at that stage limited our ambitions. I immediately fastened upon the idea of filming one of Jero Tapakan's seances for the following reasons: I guessed that Jero would like the idea; a seance is a relatively circumscribed event or what Heider calls a "whole act" (1976:82-87); it can be brief (the range is about 15 minutes to 2 hours); and it seemed to me that seances were eminently filmworthy because far more information could be recorded on 16mm film than on slides and tape recordings with which I had hitherto been contented.

Jero, whom I had of course asked in advance, was only too enthusiastic about the project, and even more so after she had met Tim. Both Tim and Jero have an astonishing capacity to overcome communication barriers without a common language, and within a few days a mutually trusting and warm relationship was established, enhanced by my role as interpreter, of which more will be said later. I began by explaining to Tim as much as I could about the nature of seances in Bali: their structure, their purposes, the variety of locations and practitioners, and the quality of the linguistic interaction. Then we proceeded to observe some seances conducted by Jero Tapakan so that Tim could strengthen his acquaintance with her and analyze the event to be filmed more closely.

Tim was excited by the prospect of filming a seance, although taken aback by the restricted space in Jero's shrine house and the lack of adequate natural lighting. We spent some days organizing lighting and a work space for ourselves that would not be too intrusive for Jero or her clients. During this time, I was quickly tutored in the use of a Nagra 4.2 tape recorder and in basic 16mm filmmaking principles and techniques. At this point, my knowledge was dismally deficient, having never been exposed to the technical aspects of filmmaking. During the whole period of our collaboration in 1978, I never was completely sure, for example, what a "cutaway" was, despite my sympathetic murmurings whenever Tim complained that he was not getting enough suitable cutaways. Tim refused to be discouraged by my ignorance. He felt that anyone could become adequately technically competent in a short period of time and that my contributions as an anthropologist were what was crucial to the collaboration.

We had used five new rolls of film for the seance footage because Tim wanted to test the circuit board of the camera. He also decided to test some old stock that had been left in storage in Bali the preceding year. Thus a second film project evolved: a short film (only three rolls) of Jero treating her massage patients, a practice that she maintained on a different day from her practice as a spirit medium (see Connor, Asch, and Asch, 1986, for details). The aim of both projects was to produce some interesting audiovisual data for me to analyze when I returned to Australia and to use as a teaching resource for my own classes. Again, I explained to Tim as much as I could about massage sessions, and we spent a whole day watching Jero treat her patients planning how we would do the filming and discussing our ideas with Jero. A major advantage in filming events such as a seance or massage (which follow recognizable patterns) is that one can observe and analyze in advance the typical strictures. Our ability to predict what would occur resulted in greater economy and efficiency when we eventually shot the footage and more thorough coverage of the events. This was in marked contrast to the events we later decided to film.

Tim was enjoying his stay in the village, which was so markedly different from other field situations he had worked in. He was an interested observer of the everyday routines that constituted much of village life. Just after we shot the massage footage, Jero's son and daughter-in-law invited him to observe some ceremonial preparations in which they were participating. He returned to the house very excited about what he had witnessed: the early stages of a cremation ceremony collectively organized by a group of people in Jero's hamlet, including Jero's household. Cremation ceremonies, which were being held all over Bali during July, August, and September of 1978, were preparatory to a centennial ceremony of purification, Eka Dasa Rudra, that was to be performed the following year. All Balinese Hindus were required to cremate their dead (some of whom had been long-buried, pending the accumulation of adequate resources) before the time of Eka Dasa Rudra. Many people, especially those with few resources, organized the expensive cremation ceremony on a collective basis to reduce costs per household. This is how the ceremony had been organized in Jero's hamlet.

I had previously decided not to spend too much time observing the ceremony because of other research commitments that I had made for my remaining time in Bali. But Tim's enthusiasm forced me to consider my decision. Moreover, it was about this time that Tim received the news that his colleague would not be arriving in Bali for some weeks to come. He did not relish the prospect of several weeks of inactivity, especially when there was so much good work he could do with me. At the very least, he felt we should gather materials for a slide tape from our observations of the cremation ceremony and its preparations, which lasted several weeks. My interest in doing this was renewed by the thought that I would have a fully participating companion during what I knew (from previous experience of big ceremonies) could be long, tedious, and exhausting weeks of documentation. So Tim and I accompanied the group members every day during preparations which went on from sunrise to long past sunset. He took slides and tried to assist in the preparations whenever he could, while I recorded interviews and my own observations on the Nagra. But it was not long before Tim expressed the opinion that the material we were collecting was so interesting that it warranted filming. By this time, I could only agree and hope that permission to keep using film stock would come from Australia (which it did). In this way, we embarked on several weeks of intensive filming and documentation. We focused on several people that we considered were emerging as key personalities in the event. This endeavour proved to be more than a full-time job for two people.

Towards the end of Tim's six-week stay in the village, we decided to shoot some more footage of Jero Tapakan. The lab report from Australia on the massage footage reported that the film was solarized and virtually useless, so we elected to shoot another three rolls of massage footage. We had also decided to film Jero Tapakan talking with me about her past life, especially the events that led to her becoming a healer. On several previous occasions, I had recorded Jero telling me about her life. We felt her account, interesting in its own right, would enrich our other footage by revealing more aspects of Jero's personality and by placing her profession within the context of her life history, and the results were so interesting as to enhance the other healing footage we had, and perhaps assist in making the Jero films more understandable to a wider audience.

While we were filming the cremation (a total of 22 rolls in 1978), we began thinking about our work as something that may be of interest to a wider audience than just myself and a few of my colleagues or students. We began to strive to create a broader context for each film, both with regard to the healing footage and the cremation film. We belatedly began to think about ourselves as in possession of a corpus of "films."

Vicissitudes of Collaboration

Collaboration with an ethnographic filmmaker required his intense involvement in my fieldwork, in contrast to other visitors I had received. I derived many benefits from Tim's necessarily different perspective on the field situation. He asked questions about people and events that challenged me to find new answers or improve upon the information I already had. The presence of another anthropologist with more than an observer's interest in my fieldwork presented me with an ideal opportunity to explicate some of the theoretical ideas I had formulated. This process of review and explication enhanced my confidence in what I had achieved as a fieldworker. In retrospect, I can appreciate that this aspect of the collaboration also eased the transition that I was to make back into an academic environment. Tim's lack of local language fluency and his filmmaker's eye predisposed him to attend to non-verbal information in the social environment. His sensitivity to the visual nuances of interpersonal interactions and work activities provided me with new sorts of data to analyze and an adequate visual record to undertake this. I had worked hard in the early stage of my fieldwork to achieve fluency in Balinese and was less attentive than he to non-verbal information. While I am still of the opinion that good fieldwork depends first and foremost on adequate language skills, it can only be an advantage to learn from a filmmaker's perspective while one is doing fieldwork. The ethnographic film collaboration has changed the way I will do fieldwork in the future, even if no film project is involved.

However, this jointly conducted process of ethnographic enquiry had its problematic aspects too. The filmmaker's eagerness to learn about the new culture in which he was involved was wearing for me as the field anthropologist. Sometimes it seemed to me that Tim expected a constant running commentary in English about everything that was happening around him. Unfortunately there was no one to provide such a commentary but me. Often he would ask me to put ethnographic questions to the people we were with. I would resist doing this if I felt it would be at odds with the ambience or if the question was not appropriate for this person or if I was too tired to launch a pedagogical conversation and was enjoying listening to the flow of conversation about me. Although Tim never complained when his questions went unanswered, it was disappointing for him and difficult for him to understand the reasons when I did not have an opportunity to explain immediately. Despite the fact that Tim had read much of the published ethnography about Bali, what he really needed was quite specific information to provide him with a context for the events we were filming. Passing on lengthy pieces of information that were already well known to me, as well as interpreting back and forth between him and the Balinese, attempting to obtain new information about complex events, and operating the sound system often seemed to me to be more than one person could reasonably be expected to achieve. This problem is not a readily soluble one. The attainment of a high standard of ethnographic film depends upon all those involved having as much information as possible about the events and people being filmed. Unless collaborators start out a field research project at the same time and with the same language skills (a rare situation given time and funding constraints), there will always be an imbalance in the amount of ethnographic information each possesses. And yet specialization creates its own communication problems. I did not want to be merely a consultant to Tim's filmmaking enterprise, nor did he want to be just a consultant to my fieldwork. The same applied when the collaborating team expanded in the editing phase to include Patsy Asch.

Perhaps some of the load could have been taken off me as the anthropologist if our team had included a sound person, but situations where we could have taken advantage of such a person were extremely limited. During the shooting of the seance film, space did not permit a third person to be present and the intimacy of the situation mitigated against the introduction of two outsiders besides the anthropologist. In crowd situations (for example, large rituals) these considerations do not weigh so heavily. During both the seance filming and the shooting of the cremation footage, getting the best results with limited footage partially depended on understanding what was being said and being able to predict what was going to happen next. In 1980, when Tim and Patsy Asch and I returned to Bali, it still seemed more appropriate that I rather than Patsy record sound for the second-time filming of Jero's massage session (which became THE MEDIUM IS THE MASSEUSE) although Patsy was able to record the more straightforward interview material. We made this choice based on anthropological rather than film considerations. I was included in the images to show how I worked and the kind of rapport I had achieved with the participants in the event.

Another problem touched on above is the way in which collaboration influences the relationship that the anthropologist has with members of the group being filmed. My friends in the village were used to my undivided attention and took for granted my accommodation to the rhythm of daily life. I had tried to maintain a standard of living that was as close as possible to theirs, including a minimum of technical equipment. This changed when Tim arrived. The amount of equipment he brought to Jero's house (where we were staying) was mind-boggling, even to me. (There were more boxes stored in the nearby town.) Suddenly another strange and manifestly wealthy world had arrived in the village. And we had to spend a lot of time cleaning, maintaining and repairing. Not to mention the time I spent learning and practicing with the Nagra, and the frequent trips to town to recharge batteries (there was no electricity connected in the village) and to renew supplies. Whereas previously everything I had spoken could be understood by the people in the village, now I spent a lot of time having conversations in a foreign language, the subject of which they could not discern. Just as Tim always wanted to be filled in on any conversations I was having in Balinese, so did the villagers want me to tell them about what I was discussing with Tim, especially when we were laughing about something because they liked to share the joke. I was also besieged with questions about Tim's activities and equipment.

My feelings about the equipment were mixed. I had always been a reluctant photographer, readily laying aside the camera for what I considered a more direct participation in events. Occasionally photography became a diversion which helped me through the more boring stages of a long ceremony. I had made extensive use of simple tape recorders to collect data about seances and other ceremonies, as well as interviews. I was concerned that the filmmaking activities would impede observation and communication with the Balinese participants in the events. Certainly maintenance and repair took my time away from Balinese friends. But during the actual filming, the equipment did not seem to constitute a barrier between myself and events. The reasons for this were twofold. The healing sessions were routine occurrences that I had observed many times, and thus I did not feel I was going to miss anything new and important by concentrating on the recording process. With regard to the cremation, I would not have attended in such detail to this ceremony if it had not been for the possibility of making a film, so that the filmmaking actually enhanced my participation. Tim's and my efforts to record the event were well-received by the group members and added to the excitement generated during the ceremony.

Filmmaking required me to make new demands on Balinese participants, and because of my position as mediator, I usually was more reluctant
to do this than Tim. From my observations of other ethnographic
filmmaking situations, I am certain that Tim was more sensitive than most
cinematographers in this situation. Nevertheless, situations did arise where
he would want me to ask film subjects to accommodate their actions to the
dictates of good cinematography, for example, move some offerings that
were obscuring the camera's view; allow him to elevate himself a little
higher than was polite to get a good camera angle; repeat an action he had
missed on film; or move to a better-lighted position. Usually such requests
were granted with good will. In the case of the healing sessions, Jero was as
helpful as she could be, as were the clients once she had explained our purpose to them. Shooting the cremation footage was more problematic. The
complex coordination required and the inexperience of those conducting the
ceremony created many problems in themselves. It was more difficult for
me to make demands on people in this situation. Sometimes I refused, and
perhaps we missed a good shot, but at least mutual trust and friendship was
maintained throughout the entire six weeks. This sort of problem would be
further aggravated if the parties to the collaboration viewed themselves as
having specialized, non-overlapping functions, with radically different (and
possibly conflicting) commitments to the project.

Production and Beyond

Tim finally set out for Eastern Indonesia a few days after we had finished filming the cremation. I was left with two more months in the field,
part of which time I spent collecting extra information about the events we
had filmed. We had made no firm decisions about how we were going to
proceed with the next stage of the project. Patsy Asch had viewed much of
the workprint while Tim and I were in the field and we had received favor-
able evaluations from her. We were optimistic about the potential of the
footage to become a documentary resource for educational audiences but had
no clear plans about how we would set aside time or obtain sufficient funding to produce the films.

Early in 1979 I joined Tim and Patsy Asch at the Australian National
University to view the footage and discuss plans for editing. Tim had asked
Patsy to assist us as editor, although as the collaboration progressed, our
self-designations (editor, anthropologist, and filmmaker) became less
important. From the beginning of editing, we decided to take all decisions
collectively, even where individual competence varied. We wanted the final
product to be one for which we all felt equally responsible. Although time-
consuming, this way of working allowed an intensive transfer of knowledge
and skills among the three of us. I tried to provide as much additional
ethnographic information about the footage as I could, while at the same

time learning as much as possible about the technical aspects of editing and production. Tim had been through this process with other collaborators, and we were guided by his ideas on how best to proceed.

Our first step was to view all the Bali footage together, with Patsy taking notes and tape recording my comments and explanations. After one viewing, we decided to put aside the cremation material and to start on the films of Jero Tapakan, because these films were more relevant to my dissertation topic, shorter, and less complicated in structure. Tim and Patsy rightly supposed that I would be more interested in working on material that could also be used in my dissertation, my major preoccupation at that time. Eventually I incorporated an analysis of the filmed seance into my dissertation as the main part of one chapter. We decided to edit the seance footage first, as it was of most interest to me, and the event itself had a clearly defined structure that seemed to present no major editing problems.

The seance footage was difficult for Patsy and I as beginners to edit. We worked on it for about twelve weeks, over a six month period. We knew the footage was interesting, unusual, and worthy of wider distribution than just to our friends and other Bali specialists. The major problem was how to provide a context for this exotic event so that it would be comprehensible to audiences who had no background of Bali. The problem was to some extent created by Tim's and my vacillation over defining the scope of our project while in the field. This in turn was a consequence of the lack of planning. The problem also arose because of my inexperience in making film and my failure to think about ways we could have provided a more meaningful context for the event through film. But during the editing we came up with no solution to this problem. There did not seem to be any extra footage that we could have shot that would have improved the situation, except perhaps to have a little more of clients walking up the road and arriving at Jero's house. We improvised on this lack by including a series of freeze frames of seance participants. From the beginning of editing, we realized that material as complex as the seance could not stand alone no matter what sort of filmic context we could provide: a written accompaniment was required. I committed myself to writing what we then called a "study guide," a set of notes that would help others understand the film. We were also aware that the other films about Jero Tapakan would, if completed, provide a more meaningful context for the seance film and for each other. It was to this end also that we decided to use extensive narration in the seance film, a technique that we did not need to employ in the other films.

The process of providing an adequate context for the seance film was facilitated by the audience reaction technique that Tim had developed for other films he had made. Every version of the film was shown to groups of students and colleagues, who could be presumed to have some interest in the subject, but who were as diverse as possible. During each viewing (at which I read the narration and the proposed subtitles) we noted the audience's questions and comments. We would later discuss the audience reaction amongst ourselves and use it to make further changes. We gradually obtained a picture of what would be the most coherent version of the film (of course constrained by the original footage) and were able to avoid some of the worst pitfalls of ethnographic film: leaving out information that seems obvious to the filmmakers but is unknown to the audience and overloading the narration with information that is superfluous or too abstract.

A chronic problem for me during this period was finding enough time to work on the film. I had not appreciated the production time that would be involved when I had blithely agreed to collaborate with Tim the year before. Nor was I aware of the expense that was involved in ethnographic film production. The pressing need for funds if the other films were to be completed caused me to launch my grant-writing career, in which I was assisted by Tim's extensive experience. I was not being reimbursed for my work on the films, so I had to find time between the more pressing demands of teaching and dissertation writing. Both Tim and Patsy had much more time than I to spend on the films, and Tim was being paid a full salary as an ethnographic filmmaker. And yet there were long periods in the editing process when Patsy could not make any progress unless I was there to translate the sound track and advise on other matters. The lengthy and tedious process of subtitling could not go on without me. Our solution was to work in bursts of a few days to a week, when I would concentrate solely on the film work. We did this five or six times during 1979, supplemented by a frequent exchange of letters and phone calls.

If the finished film, A BALINESE TRANCE SEANCE, had not received such a positive response from most of the audiences to whom we showed it, I may have abandoned or postponed my filmmaking activities at that point. But the rewards were great, in terms of audience appreciation of Jero Tapakan as a healer, as well as in terms of the opportunity I had to discuss my work with people from diverse intellectual backgrounds. Moreover, the film record had spurred me on to a far more detailed analysis of the seance material I had collected in the field than would have been the case if I had been dependent on my tape recordings alone. So I was enthusiastic about the plan the three of us were formulating to return to Bali in 1980 for some more filming. Tim had promised the villagers that he would take the film back for them to see. We wanted them to take an active role in the filmmaking process by being given an opportunity to respond to the film images of themselves. We hoped that we would be able to record this feedback process, which could then be incorporated into our films. Tim particularly wanted to get some feedback material on the seance film. Criticisms of the film included accusations that the viewer did not learn enough about Jero's perspective on the event and was over-dependent on my narration for information about Jero as the subject. This indeed had been one of the problems of filming the seance, which is a highly structured event in which it is impossible to ask participants to comment on their own roles and experiences. The medium herself was possessed for much of the time, or else responding to very specific questions from the clients. Clients customarily would not talk about their purpose in coming before the seance and afterwards were anxious to leave lest they miss their bus. Moreover, western audiences suspected Jero of fraudulent practices, as the film provided little or no evidence that she believed what she said. Tim was convinced that we could get some valuable insights about Jero's perspective on the event from filming her conversation with me while she was sitting watching the seance film for the first time. So this became an important reason for returning to Jero with the finished seance film. We also wanted to film some more life story interviews with Jero. Our preliminary editing of the biography material had revealed that we did not have enough material to make a film. In addition to this, because of the poor quality of the massage footage from 1978 (which had been shot with old film stock) we wanted to film this healing session again, incorporating new ideas to improve the structure of the film.

We were successful in obtaining enough funds to return to Bali late in 1980, I for three months and Tim and Patsy for a few weeks, combined with another ethnographic film undertaking in Eastern Indonesia. We all stood to gain a great deal out of the trip. Patsy wanted to meet Jero Tapakan and the other villagers (she had been poring over footage of them for two years). I would be able to follow up some research questions from the previous trip that would assist me in completing my dissertation. We all looked forward to fulfilling our promise to show the footage to the Balinese participants, and we were eager to test Tim's ideas about the potential of feedback footage for ethnographic film. The finished seance film, plus rough cuts of all the other 1978 footage, had been transferred to video for the trip. We planned to operate our portable video equipment with batteries while in the village.

Whereas in 1978 I would have been doubtful about introducing an additional person into the field situation, I felt it was the appropriate thing to do in 1980. The people in the village had grown fond of Tim during his six weeks stay in 1978. I knew they would be delighted, and would consider it only natural, that he should return with his wife in 1980. As editor, Patsy already was familiar with people and events in the village, so she would not need the intensive orientation that Tim required when he first arrived. I was pleased to be relieved of much of the burden of equipment operation and maintenance. The presence of two collaborators meant that they could talk to each other when I was occupied. Thus I did not feel I was consigning another person to silence every time I participated in a Balinese conversation. Moreover, Patsy had learned some Indonesian and was able to have simple conversations. Rescuing her (and Tim) when they encountered linguistic difficulties became a source of amusement rather than frustration.

Our Balinese friends were overjoyed that we had fulfilled our promise to return and show the films. We first showed Jero Tapakan the healing footage, in a friend's house in the nearby town. Although I was sure she would be pleased with the content of the films, we wanted her to have the right of veto on having the healing footage shown to others, both in Bali and elsewhere. The first thing she viewed was the seance film, and that feedback session became the film JERO ON JERO: A BALINESE TRANCE SEANCE OBSERVED. As is recorded in this film, Jero was intrigued and delighted, immediately asking to see all the footage we had of her! She requested only that one small part of the life story footage not be shown, where she had mentioned in a bad light the names of two of her former creditors with whom she was now on good terms.

This first feedback session with Jero (at which Tim shot two rolls of film) was one of the high points of our trip. Although Tim and Patsy could not understand what was being said, they could see that Jero and I were absorbed in the experience. Jero's comments and responses to my questions were amusing and instructive, providing just the sort of context that I knew non-Balinese audiences would want. The results of other showings in the village were mixed. Large audiences crowded around the small video screen reacted with hilarity to the images of themselves and their neighbours on film, and this of course will be interesting to include in the cremation film in a limited way. Small group showings sometimes produced interesting spontaneous comments, but this situation was usually too distracting to allow any but the most superficial interviewing. The most successful viewings for my research were with one or two people who had a particular interest or knowledge of the event and could be prevailed upon to talk at length about topics raised in the film. Nevertheless we persevered with as many showings as possible in many different sorts of situations, both to test our method and to satisfy our ever-growing and enthusiastic audience. We shot nine rolls of cremation feedback footage.

This second field collaboration was in many respects much easier than the first. The time involved was shorter, and we undertook no arduous filming of long ceremonies. The workload was not so taxing when there were three people to share it. We were aware of our mistakes in the earlier footage and were able to avoid repetitions. We had a proper budget and adequate film stock to meet our needs. Before our departure, we had formulated a relatively specific set of goals that we wanted to achieve during this phase of what had by now become "The Bali Project." The Balinese participants had obtained a fuller appreciation of what we were doing, because of the video viewing sessions, so I felt better about making demands upon them. But problems did arise despite these advantages. Tim and Patsy had an exhausting schedule, dividing their time between two projects, and they were in poor health for the second part of their stay in Bali. More importantly, during the previous two years there had been a genuine exchange of skills and knowledge among the three of us, so that we all had strong opinions about the best way to proceed in any given situation, whether dictated by ethnographic or filmmaking considerations. Usually we were in accord, but when conflicts arose, (e.g., about the best way to film a scene or about whom or how to interview), they could be difficult to resolve. Tim and I had a serious disagreement about whether or not to film a second session of Jero watching the seance film on video. I thought that we had enough footage to make a film which would derive its interest from the spontaneity of Jero's comments. To my mind it was an imposition to ask Jero to go through the same experience again, and I did not feel we would get enough interesting new information to warrant using more film rolls. Tim, impressed by the success of the first showing, insisted that Jero would have even deeper insights the second time around. I felt she would merely be bored. Finally, I reluctantly asked her to sit through a seance feedback session again, but we never used the footage which was uninteresting. Patsy and I, having sat for hours at the editing machine puzzling over how to put together sequences with no adequate cutaways, were determined that Tim should compensate for his previous oversights and gave him no rest on this matter. Tim and Patsy went to great pains to make sure that I was getting all the relevant ethnographic information so that we should not be left with gaps in the material for our study guide. I was often annoyed by which I regarded as their unnecessary persistence in this matter, which seemed to me to indicate a lack of faith in my competence as a fieldworker. To be fair, however, they sometimes did prompt me to obtain information that I would otherwise have overlooked.

We returned to Australia with enough material to complete the whole project: the remaining three films on Jero Tapakan and at least one longer film based on the cremation footage. JERO ON JERO was quickly produced, at no great effort or expense. Despite the fact that we became more efficient at working together as a team as the project developed, limitations of time and funding slowed our progress, and the last two healing films were not completed until 1983. The cremation film, which is longer, costlier, and more complex, is still in production.

Completion of the written material to accompany the films has been a crucial element of the project and has also required intense collaboration. Our original plans for a small study guide to accompany each film gradually expanded into plans for a major publication that would be a comprehensive monograph based on the four healing films. As ethnographer, I undertook the major part of the writing, but Tim and Patsy each made substantial contributions, as filmmaker and editor respectively. In some ways, we reverted to our more specialized functions for the purpose of writing the monograph, but the process was one of mutual review throughout. The ethnographic film monograph was a time-consuming enterprise that in its several drafts occupied much time over a span of five years. It became apparent to us that the effort expended on a full-length book would be worthwhile compared to relegating smaller publications to the limbo of "study guide" with attendant problems of academic credibility and distribution. The process of producing films and monograph has been a mutually reinforcing one and has involved the three of us in an intensive and intellectually stimulating collaborative effort.

ACKNOWLEDGEMENTS

Fieldwork in Bali during 1978-1979 was supported by an Australian Commonwealth Postgraduate Scholarship, and the Carlyle Greenwell Bequest Fund of the Department of Anthropology, University of Sydney. 1980 fieldwork was supported by the Wenner-Gren Foundation for Anthropological Research. The author would like to thank Timothy Asch and Patsy Asch for comments on an earlier version of this chapter.

REFERENCES CITED

Connor, Linda H. (1982). In Darkness and Light: A Study of Peasant Intellectuals in Bali. Ph.D. Dissertation, Sydney University.
Connor, Linda H., Patsy Asch, and Timothy Asch (1986). Jero Tapakan: Balinese Healer. New York: Cambridge University Press.
Heider, Karl G. (1976). Ethnographic Film. Austin: University of Texas Press.

FILMS CITED

A BALINESE TRANCE SEANCE (1979). Linda Connor, Timothy Asch and Patsy Asch. Color, 30 minutes. Distributor: DER (Documentary Educational Resources).
JERO ON JERO: "A BALINESE TRANCE SEANCE" OBSERVED (1981). Linda Connor, Timothy Asch and Patsy Asch. Color, 16 minutes. Distributor: DER (Documentary Educational Resources).
THE MEDIUM IS THE MASSEUSE: A BALINESE MASSAGE (1983). Linda Connor, Timothy Asch and Patsy Asch. Color, 31 minutes. Distributor: DER (Documentary Educational Resources).
JERO TAPAKAN: STORIES FROM THE LIFE OF A BALINESE HEALER. (1983). Linda Connor, Timothy Asch and Patsy Asch. Color, 26 minutes. Distributor: DER (Documentary Educational Resources).
A BALINESE HAMLET CREMATION (n.d.). Linda Connor, Timothy Asch and Patsy Asch. Color. To be distributed by DER (Documentary Educational Resources).

REVIEWS OF THE ABOVE FILMS

Geertz, Hildred (1984). Review of A BALINESE TRANCE SEANCE; JERO ON JERO: "A BALINESE TRANCE SEANCE" OBSERVED; THE MEDIUM IS THE MASSEUSE: A BALINESE MASSAGE; JERO TAPAKAN: STORIES FROM THE LIFE OF A BALINESE HEALER. American Anthropologist 86(3): 809-811.

SOUTHEAST NUBA:
A Biographical Statement

James C. Faris
Department of Anthropology
University of Connecticut

ABSTRACT: This brief biographical statement recounts the genesis, filming, and production of the controversial film, SOUTHEAST NUBA (1982) from critical and personal perspectives of the anthropologist involved. A host of ethical and political questions addressed in the film are addressed to the film, and implications are drawn for anthropological filmmaking.

Background and Genesis

SOUTHEAST NUBA, of the BBC Worlds Apart series, was a painful film in the making--in events which motivated it, events in securing permission to film, in the filming itself, and in subsequent editing. Now that it is available in 16mm and has been initially screened in the United States (in March 1984, American Museum of Natural History),[1] it is appropriate to record these events, my part as anthropologist to the film, and my reactions, for, if nothing else, instructive reasons and advice to others.

After the publication of the book NUBA PERSONAL ART (Faris 1972), the German filmmaker, Leni Riefenstahl sought out the Southeast Nuba, recording her visit and her vision in a large picture book, THE PEOPLE OF KAU (Riefenstahl 1976).[2] Riefenstahl had earlier visited the Mesakin area of the southern Nuba mountains (some 170 kilometers west of the Southeast Nuba) resulting in an earlier volume (Riefenstahl 1974). She claims to have gotten the inspiration for the Southeast Nuba from a dream, and a quest (necessary to great art) thus led her to the region (Faris 1972, which has clear maps of the area, is conspicuous in her 1974 bibliography).

I first learned of her visit to the Southeast Nuba from a London Sunday Times color supplement in 1976 which breathlessly described the "lost tribe" and featured Riefenstahl's photographs. As my own work was quoted in the article in a manner that could have been interpreted as collaboration, I contacted the editor and was promised space to respond. This was never

111

forthcoming, however.

It was then that I was contacted by Chris Curling, a filmmaker I considered one of the more politically sophisticated and sensitive documentary workers (cf. LAST GRAVE AT DIMBAZA). We discussed a film project that would present another view of their cultural knowledge surrounding men and women, particularly treating their personal art, production and distribution. We planned no mention of what we regarded as Riefenstahl's caricature of local custom and practice, but felt our alternative view would stand on its own, sufficient in itself to counter--it was to be critical only by its example. No Nuba had any input into this decision, although Sudanese colleagues from Khartoum and from Kordofan urged it.

We seriously underestimated the dramatic events her visit precipitated as well as the consequences for future research and/or filmmaking in the area. We intended to begin work in 1977, while Chris Curling was producing for the DISAPPEARING WORLDS series from Granada Television. Despite appeals, the provincial commissioner at the time was firm that no further filming would take place, as he and many others had been embarrassed not only at Riefenstahl's publications on the Southeast Nuba, but also reports of local hostility engendered at the numbers of European tourists (both by Nuba and their Arab neighbors), principally German, that followed in her wake, anxious to capture her experience themselves.

The government's response to all this had been mixed, according to various local administrations. They attempted on the one hand to control tourism through permit and payment into a "development fund" for the area, and on the other hand by banning tourism altogether at times. Often it seemed that both policies were in force, but what was beyond doubt was the motivations of the vast majority of these Europeans. Their requests for decorated bodies, sport and dance created dissention between ignored elders (non-decorated) and the youth who had now become models for cash; and between Southeast Nuba and their Arab neighbors who were also dismissed by these tourists. Slight hostility erupted occasionally, and even those youth decorated often refused to cooperate (there was an attempt, for example, at one point to throw Riefenstahl's cameraman down a well).[3] And there were petitions from Islamic conservatives and others to authorities to stop tourists from "photographing naked people." In this atmosphere, our 1977 efforts under Granada sponsorship came to naught.

In 1979, however, Chris Curling, now producing with BBC, met with the Southern Kordofan provincial commissioner in London and finally secured his permission to film the project we had planned earlier. I had in the interim also met with the commissioner to discuss the project. Curling secured the finest crew he could muster--talented and experienced, these individuals (all free-lance, not BBC) were used to working in difficult conditions. Politically sensitive and sophisticated, they were the best people for the job, as it developed. Roger Deakins was the cameraman, with Barry Ackroyd his choice for assistant; Bruce White was responsible for sound.

Hussein Shariffe, a Sudanese filmmaker living in London was associate producer, as was Dr. Howard Reid, an anthropologist working for BBC. Deakins and White had worked with Curling before.

Curling, Shariffe, Reid and I arrived in Khartoum in early January 1980, to begin the complicated logistic arrangements, only to discover that recent political changes had yielded a new provincial commissioner (provincial commissioners are appointed by the President), who refused to honor the commitments of the previous administration as well as our extensive permissions and permits from the central ministries concerned. Meanwhile, an expensive crew sat in London as the four of us scurried around to attempt to change the commissioner's mind, go around him, or go over his head. No Southeast Nuba had any input at this point, nor did I know what it might have been.[4]

With, at least on my part, increasing distaste for the project, we persevered to the highest circles, finally securing what essentially amounted to an order to the provincial commissioner from the First Vice-President of the nation. The crew then arrived and we proceeded to southeastern Kordofan. Dr. Reid and I were yet forced to meet with the provincial religious authority, the vice commissioner, and the police commandant for the region (a copy of Riefenstahl's 1976 book was on the table when we walked into this meeting) to insure that our intention was not to "photograph naked people." We were to be, in any case, accompanied by an assistant commissioner and five security personnel at all times during the filming.

The Filming

But the delay--almost five weeks--was critically damaging. The productive activity on which we had hoped to focus--the harvesting, threshing and winnowing, had finished. In fact, save some herding and women's domestic production, essentially all productive activity had ceased as the hot dry season firmly set in. Moreover, we had just missed a crucial new fruits festival which was to be an important part of our earlier plans. Thus, the size of the entire group, and the unexpected hostility of local people (now mixed with fright at the heavy security presence) to yet another photographic expedition, all was quite sufficient for me to want to abandon the entire project at this point. The producer, however, persevered, confident that something worthwhile would (had to) come of it. He had, after all, been attempting to reach this area for now a number of years.

Moreover, I found myself in shock at the intrusive character of filming. Curling, as an experienced producer, is generally insistent on camera techniques that avoid the potential voyeurism of long-focus lenses. Moreover, as adequate sound requires similar contingency, there is little that can be done, and at least two people, with gear, are in the face of each event or interview in addition to the anthropologist, and, in the background, producer, assistants, government security. Though it was probably naive not to have anticipated this, it nevertheless came as a surprise and exacerbated an already strained situation.

We filmed every public event possible and several interviews. For some public events (decorating, dancing, the combat sports) we were required to pay to film by decorators, drummers, and referees, respectively. This was by now clearly standard procedure, and although we found it very uncomfortable, we would have otherwise simply not be allowed to photograph these events. Interviews were arranged with friends and were not paid. They were unrehearsed, though they were edited; questions were not usually written out, and though focused, they frequently simply followed conversation. With the dramatic differences in the local situation as a consequence of the recent tourism, and with plans to film productive activities dashed, we did pursue queries about tourists and Riefenstahl in particular in the interviews. But much time was spent simply waiting for an activity or event to take place, and then arranging to be able to photograph it, by payment if required. I was less than cooperative in this, and much of the payment negotiations fell to Hussein Shariffe, who could communicate with local bilingual people in Arabic.

At the end of each day's filming, the sound recordist would make a tape copy and deliver it to me, I would listen to it, and the producer and I would discuss directions interviews might take, what queries arose to pursue, and what we might possibly film the coming day. Conditions were trying. Already over budget and weeks behind, the discomfort of the continual security surveillance, the uncertainty of activities and events (dances and sports occur in no regular sequences during the dry season), were then compounded by discovery of thefts. The items taken were not important, but the producer realized that they might have been, and he went to the local government-sanctioned Nuba leader. This individual, anxious both not to have government officials and provincial security involved, as well as to impress such visitors with his own command and authority, convened a public moot to discuss the incident with all of the elders of the village of Kao. Suspicion centered on a few teenage boys that had always hung around and who often conspicuously displayed items of European origin on their person or for sale (we had been earlier offered for purchase several items of photographic gear--lens shields, battery packs and the like--presumably stolen from earlier European visitors). This added event (the moot) was filmed, and although little of it was to finally be included in the eventual product, it did impress upon me the extraordinary degree to which things had dramatically changed from my earlier field research--revealing, for example, the essential collapse of elder authority to effect events such as bride-service and decorating rules. No youth were ever apprehended and the items were never recovered--this, despite many hours of impotent debate by the elders over the situation.

No longer guided by a plan, work proceeded inductively. I had little idea of how a film might come from such chaos, but with the generosity of local people and the support of friends, we managed to continue. We filmed in all three Southeast Nuba villages--though interviews were principally with people in the village of Kao. The village of Nyaro, despite a new police post to monitor tourism and the site of the only small school of the area, had the largest group of young men decorating and willing to structure it for payment. And, of course, we filmed several events which never reached the final product, including a long funeral sequence, considerable husbandry practices around watering places, and various non-productive activities.

I was not very clear what considerations led the producer to decide when to leave, as my irresponsibility at this point for planning simply meant that I was glad when it was over. The crew left, and I returned to the provincial capital to translate and transcribe some 33 hours of sound. Later I returned to London to view all the raw footage, but this experience simply reinforced the chaos with which I viewed the project. I was at this point certainly too close to the project.

Editing and Final Production

But that is what producers are for. Chris Curling knew that at this point editing decisions would be unlikely, so further decisions were postponed until the semester break at Christmas 1981-82, when I went to Bristol to begin the editing process. By this time a full typed transcript was available, and Curling and I discussed how we might proceed. It was by now clear that one feature had to be Riefenstahl and the change precipitated as a consequence of her visit. We had, after all, been pushed into filming principally the dry season activities--the dance, decorating, and sport that were so paramount in her own caricature (Riefenstahl 1976)--so we decided to counter her view directly (and its implications) with the interviews about these matters, and our own reading of the significance of these flamboyant activities.

A factor which had to be mentioned but for which I was ambivalent was the role of the government in the changed circumstances. Curling felt many of our problems (delay, surveillance) as well as those of the Southeast Nuba were governmental in nature (which was true), but my own continuing interests in the Sudan, plus possibly a more generous view of Islam, meant that I was not very interested in seeing the film overly condemn Islam or the Sudanese government (the general outcome is still, I feel, overly critical of Islam as a factor in change--see below). In any case, our reading of the significance of local practices, the events of change, and the reaction to them by authorities quickly came to be the central core of the film. The very competent editor, Ian Pitch, and Chris Curling carved out some two hours of footage with which to work, in a process--magical to me--that is testimony to their talent and experience.

From this I fine-tuned translations and we began to write the voice-over narration. It should be mentioned here that my translations for the sub-titles continually underwent revision to make them both as literal and as comprehensible as possible. Today, in viewing the film, I still see some that could be clearer.

I could stay but five weeks, so we were continually rushed and overworked. Although I largely remained skeptical, the producer and editor were forever optimistic and enthusiastic. And although I left before final cuts had been made, sub-titles had been set, and a series of stills of Riefenstahl and by Riefenstahl had been inserted, the narration had passed through many drafts and was on its way to being final. I had no effective part in the film from January 1982. A few transatlantic telephone conversations were held to discuss changes in the narration, but removed from the footage, my input was only to veto impossible statements, hardly to truly edit further. I regret I could not have participated more and had more time to consider the narration script in concert with the footage. But flawed as the film is (and I consider it more flawed than do all others involved in its production), and though aware of its limitations, the producer, Chris Curling, considers it a successful film, particularly in its critique of Riefenstahl.

Reflection and Critique

A. Constraints

Apart from the numerous above-mentioned problems and constraints imposed during the project, as it was a BBC-TV production, some attempt was made to have the finished product appeal to a wider audience, insofar as it could, given its complex and esoteric subject matter. An executive producer viewed the near-final copy with a draft of the narration and suggested several changes to accomplish this. Vocabulary was changed in spots of the narration and some footage removed. He was also very much in favor of an emphasis on the critique of Islam (and the government) to balance the critique of Riefenstahl. The time of the final product did not seem to me to be a problem (that is, to be dictated by any external determinates). Although there is still much excellent and valuable footage (which I would hope might be made available to film archives), it was clear that it was inappropriate to the eventual product.

Commercial factors did not seem to matter in the production itself, but they did delay its appearance in a 16mm version with sub-titles for two years because, as I understand it, it was thought it would have limited commercial appeal. I was urged by the producer to write a small introduction to convince the distribution strategists at BBC, but as I could not see what simple theme might unite such pages, I consistently refused.[5] Without doubt the film is of limited appeal--its subject matter could hardly be other--and a decision was finally taken to produce the sub-titled 16mm version, presumably realizing this. After all, the WGBH Odyssey series, with ethnographic films of less complicated and quarrelsome character, was not renewed.

B. Motivations and Stimulus

The essential aim to counter Riefenstahl's presentation has been discussed. These were decisions taken wholly on our own, and as such are arrogant and presumptive (and not uncommon). Sudanese official reaction has been essentially positive, or neutral, depending on attitudes toward Islam, and the issues of presentation of "anthropological specimens" in new nations attempting to counter the European fascination with the Other--even, as is the case in the Nuba mountains, to reacting to the caricature Europeans have structured.[6] So it is in essence one more film dictated by interests of Europeans and their squabbles with one another. That it is an anthropologist's view, informed by intimate knowledge of local people and their language *versus* the view of a non-anthropologist seems of peripheral significance to me now, for I no longer think the issue is debate about a "correct" or a "truthful" view as opposed to an incorrect or untruthful view (one might assume Riefenstahl thinks her view is appropriate), but basically over political perspectives. This view is explored more thoroughly and in greater theoretical detail elsewhere (Faris 1985).

For this film in particular, however, I had been personally impressed by the film MASAI WOMEN (Chris Curling, producer; Melissa Lewellyn-Davies, anthropologist) in which Masai women were asked, in essence, to critique Masai culture. With less poignance, but equal success, we asked similar questions in interviews with Southeast Nuba. Their responses to these queries in part formed our reading of local culture (particularly surrounding divisions of labor between men and women). Otherwise, the general structure of the film (interviews in indigenous languages with precisely-translated subtitles, voice-over narration, mix of event and interview, anthropologist-not-visually-present, didactic style) are decisions and method essentially of the producer. I do not find any of them objectionable, on the contrary. And as it *per force* proceeded inductively, there was hardly any script that guided us.

C. Conclusion/Criticism

Many of the issues that might appear here are discussed above and in theoretical detail in Faris 1985. Suffice it to say I would not again participate in such a project. This is not simply because of the particular difficulties of this film, but in the entire exercise, I came to see that such a response must extend to other anthropological practices--it is certainly not a statement about the excellent crew, the producer, nor others involved in the project. Indeed, it is not uncommon that non-filmmaking anthropologists have such reactions to the intrusive nature of filming. My reasons are somewhat different and are detailed elsewhere. Let me focus here on specifics of the film in question.

There are aspects of the film itself about which I am not now very pleased. I think, for example, both the dance sequences near the beginning and somewhat near the end cater to the pastoral exotic image not wholly different from what Riefenstahl might have used. There are also a few side comments I wish were now subtitled--most that I could not hear sufficiently well at the time of the editing (as in the major decorating sequence) to make out, and at least one scene (young girls carrying water toward the camera) which I thought was to be subtitled, but it never appeared on the final print.[7] And there are some portions of the narration I do not like, although I had direct input and veto to the penultimate draft. A couple of items were slightly (but significantly) changed at the last minute, and others I can only now see the possible confusion and ambiguity in (for example, a line of narration that reads "what the Nuba really are" should more precisely read "what the Nuba think of themselves as.")

As noted, I was always uncomfortable with the way local authorities and Islam are treated. Certainly the positions are given adequate time, adequate freedom, and can thus be said to have condemned themselves. And as I have been reminded, local authorities are satisfied with their appearances, as are the guardians of Islam (see footnote 6). But the film is principally to be shown in Europe and America, and the interview and commentary on the government and Islam seem to me to reinforce the all-too-ready European stereotypes of Islam and prejudices about the Third World and new nations. Indeed, it was in anticipation of this that I refused to do the interview with the assistant commissioner (which is done in English), for I knew the producer wanted to elicit responses about flogging and imprisonment for offenses tourists promoted in local people. It seems to me that given European pre-dispositions, the most generous understanding of rural Islam is to be promoted, not, unfortunately the reverse. The entire narration also failed to address any cooperation (see footnote 7) that may exist between non-Muslims and/or authorities.

And, though I suppose it may seem disingenuous, I actually find the stills of Riefenstahl and Adolf Hitler, as well as the excessively bloody photographs from Riefenstahl's book (1976) too violent and very offensive. It indeed changes the quality of the film, and we become partisans of a position that uses the same blood and the same fascism ostensibly to argue the opposite. Certainly the critique of Riefenstahl I encourage (cf. Faris 1976; 1980; 1983; 1985), nor do I have an easy alternative to the stills used; it simply now strikes me as violent in the context and perhaps even too rhetorical and strident.

SOUTHEAST NUBA ought to be an instructive film (though certainly for filmmaking and anthropological audiences--I have no idea what non-specialists might think), for it raises many issues of concern. It perhaps instructs by negative example, but also positively, in that it espouses a specific political position, not another truth nor epistemological claim. It is my view that this is instructive to all anthropological practices.

NOTES

[1] SOUTHEAST NUBA was first broadcast on BBC-2 TV from tape (though it was, of course, filmed in 16mm) in Fall 1982, but uncertainty about its commercial viability delayed 16mm prints with expensive subtitling until 1984. It was reviewed when broadcast in Britain vaguely positively (Loizos 1982) and negatively (Ryle 1982). There may be other reviews with which I am unaware.

[2] Southeast Nuba is the ethnographic label given to the persons inhabiting three villages (Kao, Nyaro, Fungor) in the southeast--most of the Nuba Mountains of Kordofan. They speak a language mutually unintelligible to any of their neighbors, and today number something over 3000 people.

[3] Riefenstahl filmed in 16mm (or so did her cameraman, Horst Kettner) during her visit to the Southeast Nuba, but none of the footage has ever, to my knowledge, been shown. It is rumored that much of it was destroyed in processing (possibly sabotage?). Several other film teams, however, in the late 1970s did succeed, and I am aware of Italian, Spanish, Japanese, Dutch and German cine materials, which I assume have appeared commercially abroad, and some of which has appeared on American television.

[4] I had visited the area but once briefly (in 1977) since my fieldwork finished in 1969, but only to see friends and introduce a Swiss economic anthropologist who was to begin fieldwork (cf. Iten 1979). I heard at this time shocking tales of the behavior of Europeans, but did not query local reactions sufficiently nor ascertain what local people might have wanted done.

[5] I was paid my ordinary salary while on leave from the University of Connecticut. My contract obliged all of the described assistance in return for the salary and a 16mm print of the film. Despite the problems, I was well-treated by BBC, and have respect for all those with whom I worked.

[6] Sudan government officials (from the embassy in London) were invited to view the film before it was broadcast and during the final editing stages. And copies were made available (in tape, as I understand) to the relevant ministries in Khartoum. They could have perhaps had some input in the edited product (by way of objection), but presumably chose not to. Though I insisted upon their right to view the product before broadcast, I was not present at this time to discuss issues with them. Hussein Shariffe related they felt that it "ought to please the Saudis" presumably as a conversion was filmed.

[7] The subtitling at this scene should read "motherfucking Germans, I'm going to call the police!" as one young girl kneels to pick up a stick. This

subtitle is important not just for the hostility to European photography that it illustrates, for that is repeatedly noted throughout the film, but for an indication of collaboration and cooperation between local people (and these were decorated) and authorities. The film in general stresses or leaves the impression of the contrary.

REFERENCES CITED

Faris, James C. (1972). Nuba Personal Art. London: Duckworth.

Faris, James C. (1976). Fascism and Photography. Newsweek 88 (24):4 (13 December 1976).

Faris, James C. (1980). Polluted Vision. Sudanow 5(5):38 (May 1980).

Faris, James C. (1983). From Form to Content in the Structural Study of Aesthetic Systems. IN Structure and Cognition in Art, Dorothy Washburn, editor. Cambridge: Cambridge University Press, pp. 90-112.

Faris, James C. (1985). Image, Document, Power: Anthropology and Photography (forthcoming).

Faris, James C. (1988). Southeast Nuba Social Relations. Aachen: Rader Verlag.

Iten, Oswald (1979). Economic Pressures on Traditional Society: A Case Study of Southeastern Nuba Economy in the Modern Sudan. Bern: Peter Lang.

Loizos, Peter (1982). Review of SOUTHEAST NUBA. Royal Anthropological Institute Newsletter 52:10 (October 1982).

Riefenstahl, Leni (1974). The Last of the Nuba. New York: Harper.

Riefenstahl, Leni (1976). The People of Kau. New York: Harper.

Ryle, John (1982). Invasion of the Body Snatchers. New Society 549. (30 September 1982).

FILMS CITED

MASAI WOMEN (1974). Chris Curling, Producer; Melissa Lewellyn-Davies, Anthropologist. Color, 60 minutes. London: Granada Television.

SOUTHEAST NUBA (1982). Chris Curling, Producer; Jim Faris, Anthropologist. Color, 60 minutes. Bristol: BBC-TV.

MAJOR FILMS OF JAMES FARIS

SOUTHEAST NUBA (1982). A film by Chris Curling, Producer; Jim Faris, Anthropologist; Roger Deakins, Camera; Bruce White, Sound. 60 minutes, color, sound, English subtitles. Distributor: BBC Enterprises, London.

REVIEWS OF THE ABOVE FILMS

Loizos, Peter (1982). Review of SOUTHEAST NUBA. Royal Anthropological Society Newsletter 52: 10.

Ryle, John (1982). Invasion of the Body Snatchers (review of SOUTHEAST NUBA). New Society 549. (30 September 1982).

What To Tell And How To Show It: Issues In Anthropological Filmmaking

Solveig Freudenthal
Department of Social Anthropology
University of Stockholm

ABSTRACT: This article suggests four factors which must be taken into account when producing specifically anthropological films. First, the filmmaker must be aware of the effect of the particular type of technology on the kind of film which can be made. Secondly, he or she must command a broad and deep anthropological grasp of the culture being filmed. Thirdly, rather than obeying any preconceived cinematographic conventions, the filmmaker must consistently focus on the culture being filmed and allow that culture to dictate the flow and form of the film. Finally, he or she must at all costs protect the integrity of the persons or groups being filmed.

These points are discussed and their applicability analyzed in the specific context of a film produced by the author in a kindergarten for Turkish immigrant children in a suburb of Stockholm, Sweden.

In this article I want to present some of my views of filmmaking as an anthropological endeavor, and explore some aspects of my own experience as a filmmaking anthropologist. I will first deal with four specific factors which I think must be considered when aiming to produce edited anthropological films. I will then relate these issues to the film I made in conjunction with my fieldwork concerning Turkish children in a Swedish public kindergarten. Lastly, I will point out some of the possibilities and some of the limitations of this odd art, making films that are specifically, purposely and consciously anthropological.

My points of departure, and biases perhaps, are two: first, I believe that visual materials (still photographs, videotapes and film of all kinds) are important if not indispensable tools for the collection of anthropological field data. Visual data are special; they offer a unique and valuable opportunity for feedback from both informants and colleagues, and they enable us to disseminate our findings with a special and important kind of impact. My second bias is simply that I love to make films. Moreover, and I think this is significant anthropologically, I view the process of filmmaking as a collective one, that is, I cannot film at, but only with, people. I have therefore had few if any difficulties fitting filming into the framework of classical anthropological field methods, participant observation. Cameras need not stand in the way of asking questions, commenting, disagreeing and generally getting involved with informants. On the contrary, as I will indicate below, cameras can in fact facilitate that process: we can use them to collect more, and in some cases, more reliable information, including informants' comments, explanations and corrections of their own activities as they view them on the screen.

One other point must be raised in the context of my approach to anthropological filmmaking. I do not regard film cameras and the host of equipment involved in filmmaking as especially complicated or too difficult for most people to master. Whatever mystique films have (and they indeed have some element of half-mystical power) the mystique lies in the images, and not in the machines used to record them.

In my research on Turkish children and their very special experience in a Swedish kindergarten, I have used film and cameras in two different ways: first, as research footage for myself, analogous to (indeed an extension of) my field notes, and here I include still photographs, videotapes and 16mm film footage. Secondly, I have made films with an audience in mind, that is, films geared for public showings where my specific and conscious goal is to present the material as examples of particular anthropological concerns.

This distinction in the use of film has been made by many other anthropologists, most notable Heider (1976:x), MacDougall (1978:406) and Ketelaar (1983:178). In this article, it is the second of these functions which concerns me. My question is, in short, what, if any, are the distinguishing features of anthropological film, as opposed to ethnographic or documentary or other kinds of films?

I certainly feel reluctant to add to the endless discussions of definitions which seem to saturate anthropological literature. Let it suffice to say with Ketelaar (1983:182), that anthropological films are "scholarly endeavors that respectively document and interpret according to anthropological standards." I thus differ with those who would equate ethnographic films with anthropological films (Heider 1976:3). Anthropological films must be those which deal with, portray and present anthropological concerns, most specifically with the explanation and comparison of cultures and cultural events. While ethnographic films are clearly a related genre, I think they lack the explanatory ambition of anthropological films. Ethnographic film (as does ethnography in general) seeks primarily to reproduce, record and reveal on the screen what is happening, say, in the corn field or at the wedding or in the kitchen. Anthropological films go several steps farther: they attempt to clarify the systems of symbols and ideas which lie behind or en-

ergize the work in the corn field or the rituals at the wedding or the sex roles
in the kitchen. Such films must thus not only portray the activities being
performed, and give the viewer an idea of who is doing what; they must explain somehow the anthropological significance of these activities--most
particularly, though not exclusively, what things mean to the people involved.

Why bother doing this on film? The question must indeed be asked:
Why film? I do not believe that anthropological films will or should ever
replace written monographs, nor, indeed, that all aspects of culture are
equally amenable to visualization. Still, I do not think we can deny that
showing what we tell or showing while we tell has a very special and important impact. I do not merely refer to the fact that films carry messages to
the viewer differently from the way words carry messages to the reader, nor
even to the fact that anthropological films can carry anthropological concepts and conclusions to the viewer in a way that monographs cannot. What
I mean at a somewhat different level is that film enables us to experience, as
no other medium can, the "all-at-onceness" or what Geertz has called the
"thickness" (1973) of social life. Whether we view macro-events, those
which include a great deal of different kinds of action occurring all at once
(e.g. people eating and cooking, people dancing and watching dancers, people flirting, scorning lovers and scolding children) or micro-events (e.g. the
tears, bent back and frown of a single sad human being) the camera permits
us to confront the compoundedness of the activities. Moreover, it permits
us to experience the connections between the activities, the links between
the various sub-scenes. On film we can communicate the energy of all-at-
onceness and the power of connections which certainly from an anthropological point of view is the touchstone of all social life. No literary
description however apt, and no verbal formulation however exact can ever
connect the thousands of threads present in the most miniscule event as well
as the camera can. As writers, we are locked into two dimensions: we are
unable to say more than one thing at a time. The camera permits us to
break our dependency on lineality. It permits us to experience the multiple
dimensions of social reality, its all-at-onceness, as words simply cannot do.

Granted for the sake of argument that showing all-at-onceness is our
goal as filmmaking anthropologists, this does not tell us anything very
specific about anthropological film. Clearly, it is not my intention in this
article to exhaust that topic. What I do want to do is to present four factors
which I think must be considered when producing anthropological films: (1)
we must be aware of the constraints and effects of our technology, (2) we
must know our subject, (3) we have to film what the culture demands, and
(4) we must consider ethical issues.

The first issue is somewhat complicated. It concerns the whole topic of
technology and the possible effect of technical equipment, both on the kinds
of films we are able to produce and on the people who are being filmed.
Filmmaking anthropologists are often accused of interrupting the natural

flow of events due to our supposed increased visibility; once we appear on the scene with our cameras and cords and perhaps lamps and extra batteries, it is said that things and people are not as they usually are.

While it could be argued that the added weight and bulk of filmic equipment need not make us more visible (indeed, as established figures in the community and trusted members in the social setting we are *already* very visible) our equipment does make us clumsier. Cameras and tape recorders and microphones and lighting equipment and endless cords certainly can disturb the flow of natural events. Instead of trying not to be visible, clearly virtually impossible, we can learn to minimize the bulkiness and bothersomeness of our paraphernalia; we can try not to put strong lights in people's faces, avoid sticking microphones under people's noses, and refrain from having hordes of assistants running around checking sound levels and taking light readings while a family is, say, trying to get ready for a wedding.

I think we must also be aware of how our particular technical equipment can affect our final film product. If we choose to use, for example, simple spring cameras which must be rewound every fifteen seconds, and have in addition no access to synchronous sound equipment, we might have to use sound differently (treating it perhaps as a separate channel for information, and using it, as James Blue said, as a "transport mechanism" to link discontinuous material). If on the contrary we have access to the best synchronous sound equipment, easily maneuverable cameras and camera-wise informants, we will probably produce a different kind of film. Clearly, the final product will in some way be affected by the technology. My point is simply that what we can say is affected by what we say it with.

The second issue is perhaps the easiest to deal with. The sine qua non of all anthropological filmmaking must be that the filmmaking anthropologist is thoroughly familiar with the subject before he or she begins to film. Any shooting must be preceded by a good deal of fieldwork, fieldwork conducted as an anthropologist and from the point of view of anthropology. We must know, among other things, who is who among the participants, what they mean to each other, what they think they are doing, and perhaps even what is happening elsewhere. While I do not eliminate the possibility of surprises (indeed, while I do adore them) by the time we are ready to do the film, whatever happens should not be all that surprising!

My third point is stickier. How should we deal with verbal information? How should we present explanations? Many filmmaking anthropologists find anything other than synchronous sound and spontaneous dialogue unacceptable. Narration by an outsider (even the anthropologist) is said to remove some of the immediacy and direct sensory impact of the filmed event and create an unnatural barrier between the viewer and the action.

Whether this is true or not, I envision our task as anthropologists as something more than filming an event: we want to both see and understand an event; we want to combine the emotional experience of film with some amount of directed, conscious understanding. One feasible solution to this (our greatest) problem is to first show the event unexplained, and then to show it again with explanations. I will return to this issue below.

And interviews? Clearly, what people will say in front of a camera or what they will dare to say is affected by so many factors (their feelings for the anthropologist, for the audience, for their elderly aunt who is looking at them). Though some filmmaking anthropologists would do so, I do not think we need to take a stand on interviews as such; we must however be aware of the difficulties of interviews and of the kind of information we get (or do not get) in certain kinds of interview situations.

Another problem (which in fact might be a non-problem) is the acceptable ratio of visual to verbal information in our films. Some of us deliberately try to avoid situations which are "talky" and concentrate on those which are pictorial. I think somehow that this issue is not relevant. It seems to me that *our ground rule should be that anthropological films take us where our subjects want to go.* If we know for example, that our people talk and talk a lot, and that their culture values talk and lots of it, this must be permitted to come through in the film. Claude Karnoouh and Jean Arlaud, for instance, impressed us with the talkiness of French village life in their film entitled, oddly enough, "Jours Tranquilles en Lorraine." Conversely, in a film I made with Pekka Niemela about an elderly couple living on a farm in the middle of the Swedish woods, A WINTER'S DAY WITH EMMA AND VIGERT, there is little talk, not because we do not like talky films but because old couples living on isolated farms in the midst of the Swedish woods do not in fact talk very much. Whatever else is important to them, and this comes through in the film, talk is not. My point is a very basic one: anthropological films must be about their lives, they must move according to their rhythms and reveal what is in their heads. These considerations, and not any pre-established principles or guidelines about how films should be or look, must be paramount.

This dictum (that *our films must do what the culture demands*) also applies to the use of music. It is quite all right to use music in a film when people are listening to music or performing themselves, but I cannot accept using music to fill in all the empty spaces on the sound track because the filmmaker is afraid of the silence which might be there in real life. It is precisely because music influences our interpretations in a very direct way, and the same shot with different sound can give us vastly different impressions that we must avoid putting our music on their action and thus leading the audience our way instead of theirs.

Doing what the culture demands also means being quite careful about what we show. Anthropological romanticism is still very much alive; too many filmmaking anthropologists are busy capturing disappearing worlds, and filming only the most "exotic" aspects of cultural life (rituals, festivals and such). While I certainly do not deny the value of such communal rituals, I merely want to make a plea for filming everyday activities, particularly those which our informants consider important, if not quite spectacular. In the same vein, though I do so with tongue in cheek, I want to warn us (myself included) to withstand the temptation to make "nice" films. One hazard which accompanies our general ideology of cultural relativism is that we tend to make "nice" films about people who are not very "nice" at all. We will too often film the wedding ceremony with all its colorful gaiety, and shy away from showing the conflicts, confusion and contradictions which often precede and more often follow the ceremony and feasting. Clearly, showing what the culture demands necessitates a focus on both big and small events and on people and activities which are both "nice" as well as not "nice."

There is a limit however to how far we can carry this approach, which brings me to my fourth point. Not loading the film in favor of the "nice" and exotic does not mean that we should not respect the people we film nor that we should ignore their wishes. Ethical considerations must be of primary importance in anthropological filmmaking, and the uncompromising ground rule must be that we do not film things or people or events that people do not want to be filmed. The temptation to include such footage is often hard to resist; our urge to be artistic and make "good" films can sometimes be stronger than our desire to protect and show respect for our informants. I remember an instance of this kind: when I was making my film about the Turkish children in the Swedish kindergarten, I had to put some fascinating footage taken during a parents' meeting back into my archive and not include it in my film. For cultural reasons which I well understood, the Turkish parents who were present at the meeting did not want their participation in the meeting to become publicly known.

We must also consider the nature of the audience, and whether the film will be shown to a limited or an unlimited and diffuse audience. Even when the issues are unproblematic and the informants enthusiastically support the film, problems sometimes arise due to sheer public exposure. I am thinking specifically about my film about the elderly couple in the Swedish woods: for months after the film was shown on Swedish television, the old couple was visited by strangers who drove up to their lonely farm to gaze at them as though they were animals in the zoo. Living as isolated as they did, they feared that the strangers would harm them. Fortunately, nothing of the sort happened, but my film did result in some unnecessary amount of fear and worry for them.

Let us grant then, that as filmmaking anthropologists, we (1) are thoroughly familiar with our technology and how it influences what we can say, (2) know our subject and subjects well before we begin to film, (3) agree that our overriding concern and goal is to film what the culture demands, and (4) try as far as possible to protect and respect our informants' demands and preempt any negative effects of our films. With these four points in mind, I want to turn to my film about Turkish children in a Swedish kindergarten. I will begin my discussion with some general information about Sweden, particularly that regarding immigration and immigration policies in Sweden in recent years. I will then turn to my specific research problem and indicate why this kindergarten is interesting in light of these policies. Finally, I will turn to the film itself: why I made it and for whom, how I went about making a film in a kindergarten as an anthropologist, where I was able to follow my own four principles--and where I failed to do so.

Until several decades ago, Sweden was said to be a relatively homogeneous society, at least in terms of its ethnic composition. Although some non-Swedish ethnic groups did live in Sweden, and had been living here for generations and centuries (Finns, Lapps, Estonians, and Jews, to name only a few; see Arnstberg and Ehn 1976), their particular cultural heritages were publicly ignored; with several exceptions, they were invited to assimilate into the Swedish body politic and to participate in the construction and expansion of the welfare state. In the latter half of the 1960s, however, there was a distinct change in this benevolent though clearly assimilationist policy. It was at this point in Swedish history that large numbers of immigrants came to Sweden, immigrants from countries whose world views and life styles and languages differed very obviously from those of the Swedish majority. Instead of assuming, as had been done in the past, that these immigrants forget the specific "cultural baggage" which they had brought with them to Sweden, they were offered at public cost a large variety of programs (mainly though not exclusively related to native language instruction) which would lead to the maintenance and strengthening of this cultural heritage within the general structure of Swedish social and cultural institutions.

At the level of the pre-school, this meant that children from the same language group would be placed in the same kindergarten, and that they would be taught by bilingual personnel as well as by some Swedish-speaking personnel. One purpose of the program was to provide the children with an opportunity to continue to develop their competency in their native language (or as it was and is still called, their "home language"). It was thought that such a program would avoid or prevent the possible intellectual and/or emotional problems caused by a too-rapid transition to another language.

What interested me as a specifically anthropological problem was not only the language but the other skills, values and behavioral norms which I assumed were being transmitted to the children in this Turkish-speaking but Swedish-administered kindergarten. Little of the research then being done in these monolingual kindergartens focussed on anything other than language; the extent to which "home language" involved the transmission of cultural norms and values was generally ignored. My purpose therefore was to examine what kinds of values and behavioral rules and views of the universe were present in this ostensibly Turkish but from the looks of it very Swedish kindergarten, and what kinds of information were being transacted in the course of the encounter between the various members of the kindergarten. My view was thus purposely bifocal: I was interested in the messages being transmitted by both the Swedish and the Turkish participants.

It seemed to me that because this encounter was taking place in the rather limited space of the kindergarten, it was an especially attractive set-up for visual documentation. Thus, in addition to my pencil and paper accompanying me as I participated and observed, I also used a variety of cameras. I took endless stills of the walls of the kindergarten, and documented the variety of messages I found on them (e.g., maps, flags, drawings, posters from Swedish agencies, formal collections of "knowledge" alphabet posters, and posters of the days of the week and months of the year). I took stills of how the spaces were laid out and used and how their use changed from time to time, and of where the children's things were kept and how they were labelled.

More extensively, and more consciously perhaps, I also used video equipment. My interest here was to document the varieties of communicative codes which I posited were being used by the Turkish and Swedish and children and adult participants in the encounter. I have since used these tapes to study the non-verbal communication going on in the kindergarten (Birdwhistell 1970) and have sharpened my understanding of cultural differences in the use of movement and space (Hall 1959, 1966). As the fieldwork progressed, I shared the tapes with the children and the staff, and recorded their reactions to themselves and their activities and to me.

A year after I began my fieldwork, I was asked by the officer in charge of these bilingual kindergartens in the Swedish National Board of Health and Welfare (the governmental agency in charge of all pre-schools in Sweden) to produce a 16mm color film about "my" Turkish-Swedish kindergarten. The film was to be used to inform those in the field of pre-school education about the activities of this kindergarten as well as to provide a basis for discussing the general issue of pre-school education of immigrant children. I must add that I was given an adequate budget to work with, and few directives on the kind of film I was to produce, other than it was to be "informative."

With two significant exceptions, I did all my filming in the kindergarten. I did film in the homes of some of the children who attended the kindergarten, and, in connection with a lovely invitation from one family to accompany them on their annual summer trip to their village in Turkey, I filmed much of what went on in the village, particularly in the world of children. My trip to the village presented me with an invaluable opportunity to compare the lives of Turkish village children with those of their cousins in Sweden. Aside from these non-kindergarten sites, both of which did appear in the finished film, most of my filming hours were spent in the kindergarten.

Throughout the nine months it took me to shoot the film, I put myself as well as my camera into the action. MacDougall's excellent phrase, "participatory cinema" (1975:119), provided me with a needed conceptual model of what I was doing, as well as an important challenge for me both as an anthropologist and as a filmmaker. Clearly, my year of fieldwork in the kindergarten had anchored me to it as an accepted member of the staff. Because I was already accepted as a member of the kindergarten world, and had washed hands and picked up toys and served lunches for many months, my camera when it appeared on the scene was accepted as part of me, and was therefore equally welcome in the kindergarten. In a real sense, the social bond between anthropologist and informants was strong enough to bear the weight of the camera; it never made me move away from participating and into the role of a detached observer.

Moreover, because I filmed myself and used one of the Turkish staff members as soundwoman, no new people appeared in the kindergarten while we were making the film. The film thus retained the quality of being a locally produced, family-like product: everyone in the kindergarten contributed some input into the final film. My Turkish soundwoman, for instance, clearly more fluent in Turkish than I am, led me to the spots in the kindergarten where delightful bits of intense verbal action were going on (outside doll houses and inside darkened tents made of huge foam rubber pillows). The film soon became a part of the children's daily program: when they decided to sing their favorite songs, they sang them into the tape recorder, making sure of course that the camera's red light was on. Little Songul's birthday party preparations included directions to me as to where I should stand and whom I should film first. In the middle of the party, they waved gleefully into the camera, unhappy that I could not both film and eat the ice cream they offered me at the same time!

More often than not, however, the children were rather unconcerned with "our" film, quite as I had expected and hoped. To permit life in the kindergarten to go on as usual, I made my equipment as unobtrusive as possible. I solved the problem of lighting, for instance, and eliminated the bother (and danger) of cords and wires and bulky light fixtures by using rather sensitive film stock and by replacing the kindergarten's ordinary light bulbs with much stronger ones.

Though my budget was sufficient to permit me to bring my rather light sound camera to the kindergarten rather often, I found that I could cover the full range of activities (from daily "show and tell" sessions with the head teacher, to teachers' meetings, to special outings, to making lunch and taking naps) in a rather few shooting days. I say this not to boast about my filmmaking ability but to emphasize the value and the importance of knowing the field before starting to shoot.

Aside from using MacDougall's "participatory cinema" as my model, I found rather early on in the shooting stage that my previously banked images of what anthropological films were supposed to look like, and the cinematographic conventions which were supposed to guide their production meant less to me than my particular subjects, my particular arena and my particular purpose. These very local factors guided what I shot and how I edited the film. My "style" then, and I use the term as unpretentiously as possible, was more related to my "problem" than to my ideology as a filmmaker. Or perhaps, this is my ideology as a filmmaker or a filmmaking anthropologist. In this regard, Colin Young's words come to mind with special relevancy:

> There is no need to argue exclusively about one method. Conferences about method are arguments about power, representatives of one approach are racist about all others. This is obviously a waste of time. If different languages are being used, we just have to learn their rules to avoid confusion (1975:79).

I want to return to my four issues within the framework of making this film of the kindergarten, and to report the degree to which I could follow (and failed to follow) my own advice. Three of my four guidelines were rather unproblematic: I knew my subject well before I started to film; I managed to solve whatever technical problems I had to a somewhat acceptable degree; and I had succeeded in respecting the wishes of my informants, particular with regard to their demands for privacy. I had also allowed the culture of he kindergarten to move the film and to impose its special tenor and tempo on the images and the sequences. But what I found troublesome and difficult (indeed, what most of us writing about and making anthropological films find difficult) was how to explain the anthropological significance of what was happening in the kindergarten. However delightful the chatter of my children, and however spontaneous and honest their comments about themselves and their friends and their tea parties with their dolls, they did not and could not explain the anthropological significance of what was happening. Nor, must I add, could their teachers. That task remained for me, the anthropologist, to do.

I solved the problem of explanations with a voiced-over narrative, highly informative and, according to some viewers, anthropologically interesting. But I was not completely satisfied; my final product was not exactly as I had hoped it would be. The narrative had sometimes the unwanted effect of overdoing explanations. It introduced a pedantic tone to parts of the film which estranged the children and their activities from the viewer. Some of the scenes became something "cultural" rather than something "real," anthropological cases in point. Too often, in MacDougall's terms, the narrative heightened the film's illustrative qualities at the expense of its revelatory and observational qualities.

The narrative problem could have been solved (and was indeed later solved) by the publication of a study guide. It could also have been solved by translating directly over the explanations of the children and the Turkish teachers.

Still, the film, entitled BURDAYIM: I AM HERE has had the desired effect. It has contributed to the on-going debate about the education of immigrant preschool children in Sweden. It has, more importantly perhaps, added to the pool of information about the Turkish community in the city of Stockholm, and has thereby opened a previously closed ethnic domain and generated some needed empathy for the people there. On another level, it has provided a concrete example of some of the problems and possibilities of bilingual, bicultural kindergartens.

Granted that the narrative introduced concepts which were not really there: big brothers picking up little sisters at the end of the day became "sibling socialization;" little boys helping with the cooking became "changing sex roles" or "Westernized and urbanized family roles." Some of these explanations may have interfered with the viewer's delight at seeing a big brother escort his little sister rather nonchalantly out of the kindergarten; they may have also interfered with little Ergun's total involvement in mixing parsley with chopped meat as he prepared the Turkish *kofte*. Yet the comments also deepened the viewer's understanding of what was happening; they added a dimension of explanation which while it was not "really there" is in fact always there.

I think that this imposition of explanation on action is a necessary aspect of anthropological filmmaking. It is not enough for us to devise techniques which enable the viewer to participate directly and fully in the action. What we must also do is to find an acceptable way to back out of the scene and offer a comment about what it all means.

Perhaps this is what we filmmaking anthropologists owe to our audiences: not only visions of the varieties of cultural forms but some kind of deeper insight into what these forms mean to their practitioners and what they mean in terms of some admittedly heavy but important generalities about human societies.

The time has come to tackle the issue of explanation in more detail. It seems to me that we filmmaking anthropologists (and I think anthropologists in general) would greatly benefit from such an endeavor. How indeed can we tell about what we show? It might be that our lack of good answers to this question is one of the reasons that so few of our colleagues make films.

ACKNOWLEDGEMENTS

I would like to thank my friend and colleague Judith Narrowe for her constructive comments and stimulating criticism on this article.

REFERENCES CITED

Arnstberg, K-O and Ehn, B. (1976). Etniska minoriteter i Sverige forr och nu. LiberLaromedel, Lund, Sweden.
Birdwhistell, Ray L. (1970). Kinesics and Context. University of Penn-

sylvania Press.

Geertz, Clifford (1973). Thick Description: Toward an Interpretive Theory of Culture. IN The Interpretation of Cultures, Clifford Geertz (ed.). New York:Basic Books, pp. 3-30.

Hall, Edward T. (1959). The Silent Language. New York: Doubleday.

Hall, Edward T. (1966). The Hidden Dimension. New York: Doubleday.

Heider, Karl G. (1976). Ethnographic Film. University of Texas Press.

Ketelaar, Henk W.E.R. (1983). Methodology in Anthropological Filmmaking-A Filmmaking Anthropologist's Poltergeist? IN Methodology in Anthropological Filmmaking, Bogaart, N. and Ketelaar, eds. Gottingen: Edition Herodot, pp. 177-187.

MacDougall, David (1975). Beyond observational cinema. IN Principles of Visual Anthropology, Paul Hockings, ed. The Hague: Mouton, pp. 109-124.

MacDougall, David (1978). Ethnographic Film: Failure and Promise. Annual Review of Anthropology, Palo Alto, California. Vol. 7, pp. 405-426.

Young, Colin (1975). Observational Cinema. IN Principles of Visual Anthropology, P. Hockings, ed. The Hague: Mouton, pp. 65-79.

FILMS CITED

JOURS TRANQUILLES EN LORRAINE (1973). Jean Arlaud and Claude Karnoouh. Black and white, 55 minutes.

A WINTER'S DAY WITH EMMA AND VIGERT (1972). Solveig Freudenthal and Pekka Niemela. Black and white, 30 minutes.

BURDAYIM - I AM HERE (1981). Solveig Freudenthal, Color, 30 minutes.

MAJOR FILMS BY SOLVEIG FREUDENTHAL

A WINTER'S DAY WITH EMMA AND VIGERT (1972). A film by Solveig Freudenthal and Pekka Niemela. 30 minutes, black and white, sound (in Swedish). Belongs to Swedish Television, broadcast on Swedish Television, January 1973.

BURDAYIM - I AM HERE (1981). A film by Solveig Freudenthal. 30 minutes, color, sound (Swedish and Turkish). Distributor: Swedish National Board of Health and Welfare, Stockholm.

THE ARTIST AND HIS MOTIF (1981). A film about the Artist Olle Nyman. A film by Solveig Freudenthal. 30 minutes, color, sound. Distributor: Solveig Freudenthal, Langa gatan 10, 115 21 Stockholm, Sweden.

An Interview[1]

Maurice Godelier
Ministere de l'Industrie et de La Recherche
Centre National de La Recherche Scientifique
Paris, France

LS. How did you begin using film in your work as an anthropologist?

MG. In the beginning I planned to use pictures, slides and super-8 film as research tools, but did not intend to make films. At one stage in my fieldwork, I realized that very important events, such as the initiation ceremonies of the boys, were going to occur. I wanted to record these events on film. It was beyond my capacities as a filmmaker to do so. In addition, I felt that, as an anthropologist, I had to be involved in the ceremonies with a still camera and notebook. In some way the eye of a trained anthropologist captures more than a camera. I therefore wrote to a few people to see if they were interested: Marshall Sahlins, the Jablonkos, the CNRS, the Australian filmmaking unit. I got a positive response from the Australians, who knew about New Guinea and the importance of cultures in New Guinea. They offered to send Ian Dunlop. I was very pleased because I had seen his film DESERT PEOPLE. I also got a positive response from the Jablonkos. In this way was created a unit of production of knowledge, and production of culture: a combination of professional filmmakers and professional anthropologists.

LS. How did the working relationships between you and Ian Dunlop and you and the Jablonkos develop?

MG. Ian Dunlop came when something important, something impressive was happening, the initiation ceremonies of the boys. At that time I had been living for more than two years with the Baruya. After two years of working and interacting with the Baruya, I knew quite a lot about their culture. I knew the genealogical and political relationships among hundreds of people. Two years of knowledge stored. For instance, when the ceremonies started, I knew already much about them. I was expecting things which had been described many times before by men who had been through the initiations. When the ceremonies started, I could guide Ian Dunlop, who came with two chaps, the cameraman and the soundman. Ian

135

Dunlop was not the cameraman. He was the director, a sort of professional leader. But he did not really know what was going to happen. I had to explain the anthropological setting in every detail. For example: a man crosses the area; for Ian it was unimportant. For me it was extremely important. I knew why he was coming from there, going there, carrying a small leaf, meaningless to an untrained observer. I said, look! catch! take the camera, shoot! He is carrying a leaf, a sacred leaf. A couple of years later I went to Australia to work on the rushes with Ian. Then he told me that at last half of the pictures were meaningful. It was a success for me. The idea of combining a professional anthropologist, who is not a filmmaker, and a filmmaker, fond of anthropology but not an anthropologist, was a good idea. It was a good unit of production of knowledge and culture.

LS. Did you talk directly with Ian Dunlop if you saw something like the man with the little leaf that you knew was an important part of the ceremony? Or would you say that directly to the cameraman?

MG. To Ian. Ian was the boss. I never interfered with his job, except once. Once....this is an interesting anecdote. If you have seen the films, you remember the huge ceremonial house, the tchimia? The ceremony was taking place within. Hundreds of men were coming in and out, a crowd of people with inter-action, violence and so on. And I remember once something was taking place, a small ritual near the door. Imagine a team of three people: cameraman, soundman, plus Ian Dunlop. Plus the master or two masters of the ritual. Plus me. There was no space. I said look, I don't see anything. I have to take pictures, he said. No, it's not possible. I am the anthropologist. I have to see what you are going to shoot. I have to be there, because I can understand things you will not understand. So piss off! There was a clash. There was an objective contradiction between the necessity for him to take pictures, close pictures, and for me to be there to see the same things--and to take a few notes. A ritual is warm and tough, and violent and smooth and so on. Everything is important in some way. They don't repeat things. So you have to be there all the time and take a few notes. What I take is two words, the name of a chap, the name of a leaf, or he bends on the top of, and so on.

The Jablonkos came at a time when nothing spectacular was happening. Nevertheless, I wanted to take advantage of the presence of a team of professional filmmakers. I decided to construct something with them. I proposed to use part of their time to make a film about the job of an anthropologist. I wanted to show as accurately as possible the everyday life of an anthropologist, which is boring in many ways. Often, an anthropologist does things which are important by their accumulation. For example, it is important to have full genealogies of a set of families, and that is a sort of work which lasts for weeks. It is not very good for filmmaking. The kinship interview, I staged as a pedagogical film. The other film, which shows me working in the gardens, and re-enacts the clearing of a forest with stone implements shows outdoor aspects of an anthropologist's work.

In some ways it was frustrating working with filmmakers. When I saw the way the Jablonkos were making films, I felt frustrated. Even with Ian Dunlop. I understand why, and I don't accuse anyone. To me, the ideal would be to capture large scenes, hundreds of people interacting or 20 people interacting, and, at the same time, capture the details, an eye, the motion of a finger. Everything is meaningful. For instance, the Jablonkos were always making wide angle shots. Rarely trying to focus on one chap, sweating or interacting. That nice combination of large scale pictures that capture a society more widely, and at the same time, individual interaction. For me, that is the idea of cinema. Like for a book.

LS. Why was it that you didn't decide to take the camera, to capture those kind of things that only you could film?

MG. I don't know. Something to do with my own personality. Like when I was a child, I liked very much to draw and to paint. I stopped painting and drawing when I started philosophy. I was fascinated by philosophy. I thought I was good in philosophy and abstract analysis. I was not too good in drawing and painting, so I stopped. It was more-or-less the same. I thought I was much better with my notebook and my pen, asking questions, interacting with the people. What I was doing was selecting parts of reality to be shot. At the same time asking a lot of questions to people around me. Questions, answers, questions, answers. How can you do that with a camera? It is not possible. It is beyond the forces of somebody. During the ceremony it was better for me to decide what to do and to keep going with what I could do well, and not try to do everything at the same time. I had a still camera on my belly. From time to time I took pictures for myself and no more.

LS. What can filmmaking do in anthropology, that the written word cannot do?

MG. Many things. Even though I suggested what to shoot, since the filmmakers used wide angle shots, a lot of things which I did not select myself were on stage. A lot of anthropological data, social data, social realities were captured unintentionally by the cameraman. When you watch the same ceremony again and again, you discover new things each time. Another important fact, is that you can go back and show the films to the Baruya. The ceremony is eternal. We can show and show and show thousands of times the same pictures to the Baruya. They see many things that you do not see, and they comment. I insist on the fact that we, Ian Dunlop and I, brought copies of the films to the Baruya. We started a process of reappropriation, cultural, social, but partial reappropriation. That is very important. I had to convince Ian Dunlop, who is himself a democrat and very open-minded man, and he had to convince the Australian government filmmaking unit to give a copy of the nine hours, to the Baruya, to give them the possibility to use the films, at least in Papua New Guinea. I started the process. Discussing with the Baruya, discussing with Dunlop, Dunlop discussing with his boss. They found the money. They paid for a copy to be re-exported to Papua New Guinea. After, I staged a sort of ritual myself. I arranged for the CNRS to pay the fares of eleven people from the bush to go to the capital, Port Moresby, to negotiate with the government about the use and the storage of these films. With the assistance of the University of Papua, New Guinea (Waigani), the people were living at the university. Eleven Baruya, they came, they lived for one month in students' rooms, and they ate with the students in the cafeteria. It was very interesting. In some way the young, so-called evolved Papua New Guineans, 20 years old, university students; and probably some of these students were thinking of becoming ministers. And suddenly they see people coming from the bush, standing in line at the cafeteria. It was very interesting to see their reaction: the young people were very pleased to see people from the bush, in the university. It was something you do not do in New Guinea. You do not bring the people from the bush to the university. You separate university people from bush people. We did the opposite. We brought the people from the bush to live in the university. We visited almost all the ministers except the prime minister, Michael Somare, who is now back in power. Finally, the films have been stored in the Institute for Papua New Guinea Studies, sponsored by the Ministry of Culture. A contract was signed between the Institute and the Baruya. The Baruya fixed the rules for diffusion of the films in Papua New Guinea. I can tell you the rules. It's a bit shocking for many people. No black woman is allowed to see the films and specially the Baruya black women, because it's male initiation ceremonies. All the male people with responsibilities, like teachers or missionaries, or ministers, are allowed to see the films. Black and white. All women excluded in Papua New Guinea. But white women are allowed to see the films if they are in another country. It is very interesting. The Baruya have maintained the basic framework of their society. The initiation ceremonies are evidence. The way they dealt with the use of the films about the initiation ceremonies shows that they are willing to adapt to the new world outside and inside their tribe.

The minister, the missionaries and professors and teachers were allowed to see the films. In some way the Baruya were following the pace, the process of formation, of a new society. That was a good thing to do with films. I could not have done that with a book. The process of showing the films to the Baruya for the first time was interesting. We went back to Wonenara where we shot the films. We used the generator of the station, and we organized a screening of the film. That was very interesting. First the women were excluded. It was during the night, when it was dark. We found a large place, a storehouse of the missionaries. Men were watching that women did not show up. There were guards in the bush. It was male initiation ceremonies, only male. We were jammed into the house. We started to project. Panic started. All the leaders, the elders realized that among the 200 or 300 men, were men of all ages. There were people from the first stage, the second stage, the third stage, the fourth stage of initiation. The second stage of initiation could not see the third stage. A large panic started. It is not possible. Stop! Maurice, stop the bloody thing. They started to clear the room. You get out! Get out! Get out! You come back! Come back! It was a panic. It was fantastic. They had to deal with their own structure. It was too much. It became a chaos. At the end there were just 100 older men who had the right to watch. This first step was to bring the film back to the Baruyas themselves. Second step was find money and bring eleven leaders to Port Moresby. There, we worked on the films in detail. After, we organized a visit to the ministers and the leaders of the university and so on. The Baruya became more and more important, publically important. They were interviewed by the TV, the radio, the local newspapers. In some way, a cultural fact like male initiation ceremonies of a local tribe of 2,000 people in New Guinea, that cultural fact and the work of anthropologists became known more widely, nationally. They gained something in the nation at large. After things worked in their minds. They wanted to make a film one hour long to make money out of it. They asked Ian Dunlop to come back and to work now for them, to make a one hour film in order to make money. They wanted to eliminate from the film everything sacred. So, I said, that makes it difficult, it's on the initiation ceremonies. Yes, but we want to make money. You white people make money with your films. You pay for going to the movie. Even when you go to the missionary, the missionaries ask 2 shillings to sit down and look at the films. So we want to make a commercial film. You will be forced to exclude everything sacred? We don't care; there are other pictures. You've seen the films Dunlop has shot: a woman giving breast to a child, that is nice. But, I said, how could it be interesting for someone from another tribe to see a woman giving breast to a child? Everywhere women give breast to children. So, what is interesting at the end? If you eliminate everything which is the topic of the film, what are you going to sell to the people to make money? They are not fools. They are like you. They have babies, women, pigs and so on, and warriors. So that was the problem. The idea of making money bombed, it was finished. The possibility for Dunlop to work for the Baruya did not exist. So you see all the possibilities of evolution from making films, and large scale films.

LS. It reminds me of what you say in TO FIND THE BARUYA STORY. You advise the Baruya to take what is powerful from the white society and use it, make it their own. You did, in fact, give them a powerful tool.

MG. Yes, the most rewarding thing which occurred was in 1979 when we were there to film their first stage of initiation. Why? Ten years earlier, in 1969 when we shot the films on the second, third, fourth stages of initiation, a lot of young boys were going away to the missionary school. When they left the Baruya society, I talked to them. They were 14 years old, 12 years old. They told me: we piss on the customs of the ancestors. All these bloody things of piercing the nose! We follow the way of God and the missionary. They were dressed like me. Ten years later, only a minority of boys were going to school permanently. Fewer people were going to school than ten years before. Very interesting. More than half of the boys had their nose pierced. The others could not have the nose pierced because they were going to school--but they managed to keep in contact with Baruya society. The elders discussed politically and publically what to teach to the boys if they could not pierce their nose. They had to give them something of their culture. In the films that Dunlop and I shot in 1979, you can see some young men, 22, 23 years old who were the same who had left ten years before spitting on their customs. They had come back for the initiation ceremonies. One is a police officer, one a clerk and so on. They were dressed like Baruya. And they cooperated with me. We filmed them as they addressed a group in pidgin English and Baruya. There is a fantastic speech given by a young man explaining: Maurice is there with Ian. They make pictures of you. It is very important. You follow the road and the rules of the ancestors. When we go to work in towns, when we go to work in plantations, what can we do except to be strong? If you go to the town, you have no woman, you starve, it's difficult, you are alone. How can you do without? At the end he said, what we are doing here is (in pidgin and Baruya), what Maurice and the white people call "culture." It is wonderful. A young man of 23, who ten years before spit on his society. Falling in Baruya, and then suddenly I hear the word "culture!"

LS. What has become of the films outside of New Guinea?

MG. What does it mean "films?" The first time we worked, Ian Dunlop and I, the product was 9 hours of films on initiation ceremonies: second, third and fourth stages. Ian also has somewhere 2 or 3 hours of films never edited on trade between the Baruya and neighboring groups, exchange of bar of salt for bark capes. I have seen some rushes. It's not too bad, not too good, but something. You can store that, or give a copy of the rushes back to the people if they are interested in that. In some way, you store things for the future. It has its own value by itself. After, you have 9 hours of films. It's too long. For the public, it's too long. But for anthropologists it's ok, if they are patient. I remember in Cambridge they screened the 9 hours in one day. In U.S., I don't remember where, they did the same. They start in morning. 9 hours of ceremonies, people eating, drinking beer at the same time. That was anthropology for anthropologists. Now you don't screen nine hours of film for people living in the street. That is missing in the film I made with Ian Dunlop. I always wanted Ian Dunlop to make a one hour twenty minutes film, for millions and millions of people. We have such a richness. To talk to millions of people, literate, illiterate. I wanted to make that sort of film. A large public film. With the best pictures of nine hours, and with my own comment, because I think I can comment on films without putting people at a distance, I don't use too abstract words. That was missed. Dunlop never did that. Maybe Dunlop is working for "le musee imaginaire de l'humanite." We have now eighteen hours of films people have never seen. Fantastic films! Eighteen hours! And the Baruya and I have translated every piece of the eighteen hours. It took months. I don't know when you will ever see that. Never, maybe! We have nine hours on the second, third and fourth stage you know. Michel Tregger has made a four hour television version. But for the first stage of initiation, we have eighteen hours! We have all the details. Beautiful. In the mountains night and day. But in 1979, we still did not have the last piece of the social system. The initiation of the shamans. But in 1980 it happened (it happened every eight or nine years). Ian could not come. So I made a film with Jean-Luc Lorry and Pierre Lemonnier. The same structure again. I took the notes and Jean-Luc and Pierre made the films. He was carrying a small super 8 camera. We have something like one hour. Jean-Michel Arnold is going to give some money to see if it can be transformed into a film useful for anthropologists. It is very interesting. One hour initiation of the shamans. In the world, today to make a film on the initiation of shamans is very, very rare. Not the quality of Ian Dunlop's films. Just amateur. At least it is there. Imagine. We have nine hours on the second, third and fourth stage. We have eighteen hours on the first stage. I have pieces of female initiation. We have three or four hours on trade between two tribes, so-called primitive silent trade. And we have one hour of amateur films on initiation of shamans, female and male shamans. Plus a lot of miscellaneous three minutes films. So it's a sort of cathedral of films on one group. How it will be useful, for how many people, I don't know. There is not a film of one hour for the large public. And it is a pity.

LS. It is a terrible pity. I had the very strong feeling when I looked at the four hours, that I wanted to edit it to one hour or one hour and a half. I wonder what it would take to do that?

MG. It takes four or three months, at least.

LS. If you had it to do over again? Would you make sure that you have some rights on the film?

MG. I have an abstract right. No film can be screened without my permission. If it is screened to a learned public or university people, I have a sort of moral control which is in the contract. But, I have been asked for the first year, I have been asked two or three times for diffusion of the films in United States in universities. I have nothing to say against. Now, nobody asks me anything. You see, the situation of someone like me. Without me, no film. I don't belong to that commercial structure. I am completely separated from that. At the same time, you need that sort of structure to produce and diffuse things. For me, one of the main goals would be to have a 1:20 min. film for millions and millions of people in Europe or in Africa, everywhere. But you need also a sort of philosophy, a sort of political attitude. You want to transmit or diffuse or give access to millions of people to what you know. In the same way, not to do that is very elitist.

NOTE

[1] In order to include a contribution by Maurice Godelier, the editor of this book suggested that the material be included as an interview. The interview was conducted in France by Lynn Silverman, a colleague of Godelier.

Gone With The Gael:
Filming An Irish Village

Paul Hockings
Department of Anthropology
University of Illinois at Chicago

ABSTRACT: THE VILLAGE was a collaborative venture between Mark McCarty, a film professor, and Paul Hockings, an anthropologist, carried out when both were teaching at U.C.L.A. and trying to develop a new style of anthropological filmmaking. Their efforts, first in a Gaelic-speaking village and later in an editing room, led to a 70-minute documentary that was an early example (1968) of Observational Cinema. This project developed through several stages, each sketched out in the article, and each guided by the supposition that Gaelic-speaking peasants could explain themselves to the audience without the intermediary of a commentator. Methods of winning local co-operation, structuring an unscripted film, and elucidating the social structure are discussed, as well as the general rationale for making a documentary in this manner.

Selection of a Site

One day early in 1967 a phone-call to my office at U.C.L.A. began the sequence of events that over a year later came to be labelled simply THE VILLAGE. The man who had phoned was Mark McCarty, a professor of film; someone who had recruited himself into the film business after a degree in Classics at Berkeley, and a spate in the U.S. Army at Fort Worth during which he was so often confined to barracks for minor infractions that he got to see there all the oldest and worst films that Hollywood has ever released. Eventually this involuntary experience led him to conclude that *he* could make better films himself. Released from service in Germany he headed for Paris where he tried to study film academically, but ended up having to wash dishes to pay his way back to the States. After settling in at U.C.L.A. he came under the influence of Scottish producer and film critic Colin Young, and eventually found himself on the staff of the tripartite Department of Theater Arts there (film, drama, T.V.) during the heady 'sixties. He did minor and major tasks on numerous commercial and student films, in the more painful cases hiding behind such sobriquets as "F. Leverett Ar-

143

cane." But he was (and is) also a great teacher of film and a classic camera-man; and it was certainly fortunate that it was he who had called.

But why had he done so? A native of San Diego but of evident Irish ancestry (as was I in some small part), McCarty had decided to ask the University for a grant to study and film Irish pub life. The committee which decides on these things took him seriously enough to suggest he should track down an anthropologist or sociologist who might help him beef up the social science content of his proposal. Colin Young gave him my name as a likely candidate.

My qualifications in documentary film were rather more tenuous than those of most students in the film program at U.C.L.A. All my degrees were in Anthropology (Sydney, Toronto, Berkeley) and I had had little experience with the cine-camera. During the 'fifties I had broadcast a lot of my own radio scripts, and had even collaborated on one or two unmemorable T.V. scripts. From that experience and the reading of modern plays had come a few ideas about dramatic structure; but I had never studied film. Then in 1963, while doing fieldwork in South India for a doctoral dissertation, I had shot a small amount of footage for my own research purposes on a Badaga wedding and a Toda funeral. More was not possible because of the complete unavailability of 16mm film stock. My technique was nothing wonderful, but was at least practiced in the field with the help of an ancient Kodak that is now a museum-piece. After returning to Berkeley in 1964, I helped Sherwood L. Washburn, Clyde Smith, Suzanne Ripley and one or two others to develop a seminar on filming in the field for anthropologists.

These "qualifications," if they may be so termed, were all that I had to go on, but still we were able to radically reorganize Mark McCarty's original idea, and by spring of 1967 we had agreed on a general ethnographic account of life in one Irish village as the general subject for the documentary. Better yet, the Committee on Comparative and International Studies at U.C.L.A. agreed in their wisdom to fund it. I was to go ahead and scout out the countryside, to be joined later by McCarty and two graduate students. By now the project had developed rationalizations for locating itself in Ireland: the two graduate students were to be trained in field techniques, so that putting them in a very foreign, Gaelic-speaking village was seen to be highly desirable. But we also wanted to develop film and see the rushes while still shooting, and the proximity of London and its film labs made Western Ireland especially attractive. But as yet nobody knew where we would be working.

I flew to New York and then embarked in the grand manner on the old Queen Elizabeth. It was to be one of her last voyages, memorable for only one event: on the day we left New York, the Six Days' War broke out between Israel and Egypt, and on the day we reached Cork it was all over.

I rented a car and began snaking up the west coast of Ireland. By now I knew pretty much what I was looking for: a Gaelic-speaking, visually interesting village with all the basic social amenities, and with some published ethnographic or folkloric literature already available. Each of these requirements brought its own problems. Many of the villages were picturesque by any standards, something that should ensure that the film would at least be scenically interesting; but I quickly found that the established ethnographic authorities in the area, Arensberg and Kimball, were all too correct about the scattered nature of the settlement pattern. After driving all the way to Donegal and taking a look at perhaps 300 villages and small towns in the course of a three-week trip, I found that hardly any of the villages had a close clustering of houses that could *look* like a village in some establishing shot. Rather as our authorities had already made clear, farmers lived in scattered townlands so that from one farmyard you could scarcely see the next. This I knew to be one of the faults in Robert Flaherty's classic film, MAN OF ARAN (1934), which up to this time was the only serious documentary available on Western Ireland. It does contain a two-second shot of a nucleated village seen from half-a-mile away, but most audiences miss it and come away instead with a feeling of loneliness, isolation, and primeval-man-against-the-elements. Of course, we could have found hundreds of nucleated villages in the eastern part of the country, but it was entirely English-speaking. The only answer was to look for a hill with a village spread out beneath it (helicopter shots being beyond our budget, and besides, they frighten the cows).

The social amenities I was looking for were minimally a pub, a church and a cross-roads, since these were already known to be the prime places of public interaction in Gaelic villages. If we could also encounter a dairy, a shop, a post-office, a school or a cattle fair, so much the better. On the score of such institutions most villages filled the bill fairly well, but my other requirements were much more restrictive. First there was the Gaelic problem: nationalistic propaganda to the contrary, 95% of the Irish Republic is English-speaking; and here I was looking for little pockets called Gaeltachts which, when found, turned out to be uncomfortably like American Indian reservations in more ways than one. I quickly abandoned any idea that the Gaelic-speaking village I soon had to choose would in any way be representative or typical of rural Ireland. It was impossible, because the Gaeltachts were evidently backward in education and agriculture; but they did still have the traditional economy.

Finding places for which there was a solid body of literature was an even more restrictive venture. In 1967 almost nothing except two books by Arensberg and Kimball was known to the anthropological fraternity. The many important studies by Brody, Cressell, Fox, Messenger, Scheper-Hughes and others were not to appear for several more years. I therefore concentrated my search in County Clare, looking at both maritime and inland communities, in the hope that we could indeed bring Arensberg and Kimball to the silver screen. I did in fact find one of the villages that they had worked in back in the 'thirties, to be quite suitable for our purposes, although not much seemed to be going on there: it was more like (and very close to) Hugh Brody's village of Inishkillane (1973), which was inhabited by despondent elderly people in an advanced state of anomie. I did locate another likely village northwest of Galway town but still close enough to County Clare to justify our taking Arensberg and Kimball as our guides. Indeed it was Gaelic-speaking, whereas most of County Clare was not.

Of course the thought had crossed our minds, even before leaving Los Angeles, that we should film in the Aran Islands, perhaps recording the nature of cultural change since those months 34 years before when Robert Flaherty had filmed his masterpiece, MAN OF ARAN. Although perhaps a methodologically sound idea, it did not appeal to either of us, and indeed I did not bother to visit those islands. To have worked there would have left us fighting with the established position of Flaherty's film in the history of cinema, and our production would undoubtedly be dismissed as a "re-make" by all and sundry. We also feared that it would have proved extremely difficult to avoid a fishing scene, a storm scene, a potato-farming scene, and most of the other details that had already appeared in Flaherty's film. So no more about "Son of Aran."

Aside from the two acceptable villages already mentioned, there was one other that I felt did meet all my criteria almost perfectly: it was Dunquin (Dún Chaoín), by chance also the most westerly village in Europe. It was a place of 180 people, was spread out over two square miles along the coast of the Dingle Peninsula in County Kerry, was in a Gaeltacht, and 98% of the people really did speak Gaelic. Offshore were the twelve islands of the Blasket group, now uninhabited for fourteen years, and behind the village was the vantage point of Mount Eagle. Who could ever forget the breath-taking view of Dunquin and the Blaskets as one comes to the top of the pass over Mount Eagle?--it was one of the memorable shots in David Lean's spectacular M-G-M feature film, RYAN'S DAUGHTER, made just a year after THE VILLAGE, and largely at this place.

The attractiveness of the scenery and the possibility of recording the scattered settlement pattern from the mountainside were not all that commended Dunquin to me. The villagers were evidently characters who, while not quite stage-Irishmen, were unlikely to close up once they saw a camera. This consideration was clearly to be of great importance.

My final consideration--was there some literature to fall back on?--met a unique answer in Dunquin, unique for almost any peasant society. Let me first explain the local geography. Dunquin itself was on the tip of the mainland. Three miles out to sea was the Great Blasket, the only one of the island group to have a real village on it. This village, An Gob, probably dated back to Viking times, if not earlier, but in 1953 its population had become so small and elderly that they all were relocated on the mainland, mostly in Dunquin amongst their relatives. But back in the 17th Century the Great Blasket had been home to Piers Ferriter, one of the redoubtable poets of Gaelic. More germane to anthropological interests was the fact that early in the present century it was also the home of Tomás 'O Crohan,

Muiris ó Suileabháin (Maurice O'Sullivan) and Peig Sayers, three ordinary peasants who had done the most extraordinary thing by writing their autobiographies and getting them published, first in Gaelic and soon in English ('O Crohan 1929, O'Sullivan 1933, Sayers 1974). The existence of these books made the whole prospect of filming the community even more appealing, because classroom appreciation of the film could be fleshed out with detailed study of the accounts of these three treasured but regrettably deceased informants. Yet this was not all. The folklore of the area, long known to friends of the Irish Folklore Commission, was readily available in English through another book of Peig Sayer's, AN OLD WOMAN'S RE-FLECTIONS, and a delightful volume by Robin Flower, a classical scholar at London University. That book of his, THE WESTERN ISLAND, was as close to an ethnography as we could come; but having a great amount of material from my Indian research still awaiting analysis and publication, I wanted to avoid getting myself into a position where my colleagues would also demand of me a written ethnography on Dunquin, as well they might.

This brings me to an important theoretical point. At the time we are speaking of I knew all too well that the great majority of anthropologists took a dim view of ethnographic documentaries, even though some tended to use them in the classroom, particularly on the occasion of an unavoidable absence. I had too often seen people make a comment about someone's documentary that ran like this: "Nice film...now when are you going to write the book?" There was in the air the sense that film was an inferior medium for social scientists to use. In most universities, for example, a graduate student could not present a film as a thesis, and in many a professor could not officially claim one on his tally of "publications." This was as true in Britain, my homeland, as it was in North America. Teaching anthropologists in the 'sixties had themselves been educated twenty or thirty years before with high-school documentaries of pedestrian quality that depended on an ill-delivered, insincere-sounding commentary in which most of the information had been placed. Hence there was an unthinking tendency to expect that a modern teaching film would have nothing more to it than an Encyclopedia Britannica effort of the nineteen-thirties. It was an unjustifiable attitude that was to dog our steps once THE VILLAGE was completed; because we were not thinking of using a commentary at all. Both McCarty and I resented the professional commentaries we had so often been subjected to, performances which came across the auditorium like the Voice of God but, in the final analysis, stood between the audience and the picture and were only as accurate as was their writer. We preferred to make a film where the "characters" would speak for themselves, and where our job was only to record their ongoing behavior and speech, and then edit it all into a reasonable sequence. Any commentary would be extraneous and, we hoped, unnecessary. It was a style of film that was soon to be called Observational Cinema (MacDougall, 1975). With this end in view we were consciously courting the problem raised by working in Gaelic, a language neither of us knew, and finding a comfortable way of translating it for English-speaking audiences.

But let us go back to Dunquin. What we were not to know was that during the 'seventies there were to be two excellent monographs about the culture of villages in the immediate neighborhood of Dunquin (Scheper-Hughes 1979; Russell 1979). These, taken with the literature already mentioned and several other excellent articles (Symes 1972, 1973; Granlund 1976; Synge 1962, etc.), meant that the tip of the Dingle Peninsula was suddenly becoming one of the most intensely studied parts of Ireland--and I have made no mention here of the archaeological literature.

Getting Started in the Gaeltacht

My long drive through Ireland and sampling the hospitality of innumerable pubs had to come to an end the day Mark McCarty reached Shannon Airport. We quickly looked at the countryside in Clare and Galway, and again examined the villages I had selected. But once we went to County Kerry and ensconced ourselves in Kruger's pub, the only one in Dunquin, we immediately agreed that this was the place to work. Indeed, I could not think of a solid argument against the village, and reticent as the Irish peasant usually is with strangers, we were nonetheless made to feel warmly welcome. McCarty stayed at the pub, a sop to his original filming project, I stayed at the home of Mrs. Casey who, as a little girl, had been host to John M. Synge when her family lived on the Basket. We were joined by two graduate students from the Ethnographic Film Program, Mike Hall and Alex Prisadsky. Mike quickly and justly received a Gaelic nickname that meant Big Mike, and was very popular with the local lads, especially because he was a composer and performer of "folk" songs. Alex was a quieter, slower person, but one that people warmed to because he did not seem to threaten them. McCarty himself proved to be an amiable manic-depressive who punctuated events every two or three days by announcing, "It's a disaster, Hockings," a sentiment that was to ring in my ears right up to the day of our World Premiere. But he quickly put things right again, and regained his breezy equanimity by shooting some more film. The two graduate students stayed in a small rooming-house, our strategy being to spread ourselves around the village and keep all ears and eyes open.

The division of labour we agreed on was as follows. McCarty was the chief cameraman, and was seen constantly with an Éclair on a shoulder-brace. I was the main soundman, and Alex Prisadsky the second cameraman. Since I was the only anthropologist present, I spent a great deal of time in what we called social engineering (borrowing Comte's phrase), and so there were many occasions when Mike was busily recording sound. Although we had two cameras and two Nagra tape-recorders, we used only one of each most of the time we were shooting, for fear that we would disrupt with our saturating presence the delicate, often intimate small-group situations we were endeavouring to record. It cannot be emphasized too strongly that we were recording on-going behaviour as we found it, not shooting from a pre-pared script. There was effectively no director because there were no scenes to direct: we never told people what we expected them to do, did not inter-rupt events with clapboards and shouting, and usually were not able to shoot several "takes" of an event--unless of course it was repetitive. My main task as field anthropologist was to find out what sort of things were likely to be going on over the next day or two, and enquire whether we might film. If, as very rarely happened, people objected, then we did not force our way in where we were not wanted. One notorious family wanted a few shillings to be filmed at certain activities--a dangerous precedent, I feared--but other villagers who heard about this brushed it off as distasteful cupidity.

The question of whether to pay informants or "actors" in the field is only part of the general problem of relations between local people and the film crew. We felt that as we expected to be in Dunquin for perhaps three months we did not want to, indeed could not, pay everybody for every word and gesture. Aside from emptying our budget, it would have led to much unnatural behaviour. The question of payment was complex, for evidently nearly everyone we dealt with was very poor, and every family in the village (bar one) was either receiving the pension or the dole (unemployment pay-ments) from the government. We found that a gracious, unostentatious but productive way of remunerating our friends was to buy them drinks at the bar, something which most of them could ill afford. In addition we gave people rides to Dingle town, ten miles away, or did shopping errands for them; for besides Kruger, the innkeeper, we were the only people in Dun-quin to have a car at our disposal.

There was one group of people in the village who could not be consid-ered poor: these were the summer tourists, who were mostly from England and nearly all staying at Kruger's Inn. Mark McCarty befriended all of them, and it soon became apparent to us that these outsiders were an integral part of the economy and society at that time of the year. So instead of seeking a false ethnological purity by "shooting around them," we decided to include the tourists in our filmed account of the village community: this was to be something quite new in anthropological filming. It seemed out of question that we should pay these people to appear in scenes: they were urban and middle-class like ourselves, and were mildly amused by our activities.

Since McCarty has described elsewhere (1975) his general strategy in shooting THE VILLAGE, there is no point in repeating it here. But I too had to have a clear strategy in mind, for without a hired cast, script or story-board, I still had to ensure that we succeeded in two endeavours: (1) getting entree and full co-operation in any scene that interested us; (2) achieving ad-equate ethnographic coverage of all aspects of daily life under the very strict limitation imposed by our 20,000 feet of black-and-white film stock. The best way to get started was to tell everybody we could, exactly what we were up to. We emphasized that we were from the University of California and not Hollywood; hence our relative poverty. We visited the parish priest in a neighbouring village, wrongly believing that an audience with him would win us acceptance in Dunquin. We allowed people to watch us filming the most innocuous things, cows and hedgerows and hillsides, so that they could see that the camera was not really threatening even though it looked like an elephant gun. And, most importantly, McCarty and I began taking Gaelic lessons every morning. I can't say we made very great strides in what is perhaps the most difficult of all Indo-European tongues, but we could make small talk in the bar, McCarty had enough sense of a conversation not to turn the camera off in the middle of it, and I became adept at sitting outside buildings, when not wanted inside, and warning visitors "We are filming inside today"--which was the extent to which we prepared anybody for their moment on film. These simple procedures worked well, people were very co-operative, and altogether a third of the Dunquin population appeared in the film.

In the back of my mind was a checklist of the topics that might be covered in an anthropology textbook. I wanted to get some film coverage of each of these so that our final product could be a well-rounded ethnography. Of course, some of the events we expected to film never occurred: it being such a small community, there was neither marriage nor death during our stay. There was (fortunately) no great Atlantic storm like the one Flaherty's second crew had shot for MAN OF ARAN. But against these lacunae we can balance the annual regatta in Dingle Harbour, which the Dunquin team legitimately won; and the useful visit of Dr. Bo Almqvist, now professor of Irish folklore at University College, Dublin, which allowed us to glimpse how a folklorist goes about interviewing Peig Sayers' son, the local poet-philosopher. Another topic of great importance in Irish history, emigration, was adequately covered in the middle third of our film; Flaherty had not breathed a word of it in MAN OF ARAN, though its long-term occurrence explains much of the desolation seen in both that film and THE VILLAGE.

The Later Stages

In some respects the later stages of shooting were easier than the beginnings. This is understandable: as people got to know us better, they trusted our intentions and our discretion more, and they opened up (some of them, anyway) to these new-found friends. This was as true of the usually reticent English tourists as it was of the local villagers. It is also understandable that our film coverage of village life improved, in part because we knew now what to expect and what we might be able to film, in part because we could easily see where gaps in our coverage up to that point were, and so investigate the possibility of filling them in.

The more closely we looked at the community the better were we able to understand its structure and (as any anthropological field-worker learns), the more we were able to separate out the actual from the ideal. It was almost predictable that this latter activity would bring us into the realm of religious matters, and indeed it provided us with an experience worthy of inclusion in any textbook on research methods. I had noticed that the parish priest and his assistant, who lived in a village several miles away, never put in an appearance in Dunquin except once each Sunday morning when one of them celebrated Mass, and on many Saturday afternoons when they heard Confessions. A little questioning led me to suspect that they were not very popular people even among the faithful, and even though everyone in the village, film-crew included, attended every Mass. We had not been working in Dunquin very long when an informant let me know that one of the two Fathers had been there enquiring about what sort of people we were, and what we were really up to. Fortunately we were given glowing character-references, possibly embellished simply to spite the mistrustful priest. Only much later did I discover the source of his concern: it seems that several months before our arrival an itinerant journalist had passed through the area, made a few casual inquiries, and perhaps had his leg pulled a bit in the ineffable Irish way which was known as "codding." At any rate, a newspaper subsequently published the resultant article, which informed the world there was a thriving witch cult (which also means, to the knowing, a fertility cult) still being practiced back in the hills of the Dingle Peninsula. So far as I can tell (and without ever having seen the article) this was a piece of nonsense; yet the more we were reported to be filming the cows, the peat-bogs and the farmyards, the more the parish priest was convinced he knew what we were really up to. His suspicion rubbed off on the local innkeeper, who wrote the Chancellor of the University of California to ascertain if we were who we had claimed to be. Fortunately most people took our side against the allied opposition and things went well for us.

There came a time, however, when I knew we would have to confront the parish priest somewhere other than over the communion railing. Accordingly, McCarty and I dressed in our Sunday best, made a social call on the parish priest to explain our next step. We told him of what a warm reception we had received in Dunquin; we told him of our serious research intentions; we told him of the documentary film we would be leaving to Irish posterity; we told him how thorough the coverage of subjects had been to date; and then I sprang it on him: "You wouldn't want us to portray these villagers as being without religion, would you? Everything else of their lives is shown in the film." The ploy worked, and within minutes we had permission to wire the church for light and sound and film the next Mass. It was almost the only reference to religion in the film, since all the other events filmed were of a purely secular nature. Yet I had discovered that a belief in pre-Christian spirits (leprechauns and banshees) was still alive among some of the older residents: their folklore and behaviour made this clear.

While I was convinced this was basically the case, there seemed to be no way of getting any such material onto film without creating some kind of artificial scene. So instead I recorded on tape some folktales relating to this pre-Christian past and we edited some of the material into the soundtrack of the Mass, thereby implying that there were still *two* religious traditions in the community without, I hope, confusing the audience about what was being portrayed. The presence of prehistoric standing-stones and beehive huts in the area made it easy for us to present some quick visual references to times long past.

Indeed, such quick references were all that time would allow for in the finished film, simply because of the conventions of the medium. Although our tendency, and that of observational cinema in general, has been to rely on quite lengthy shots where some on-going piece of behaviour is allowed to play itself out, we did make effective use of many brief and tightly edited visual references, rather as contributors to this book append footnotes to their articles. Thus the film shows us--if we know where to look--the ruins of the homes of Tomas O Crohan and Muiris O Suileabhain which figure so prominently in their autobiographies; the abandoned Blasket school with desks now sinking into the earthen floor; the original emigration ledgers listing passengers who left at the beginning of the century; the local cross-handed method of rowing; a medieval house still being lived in by man and animals; and much else too arcane to mention here. These brief visual references become much more than mere research trivia however, in the middle of the film, where we deal with the motivations of the mostly English tourists. It was evident that these people were in a dreamworld while they stayed in Dunquin, so romantically unrealistic were their visions of local life. They actually said they liked it here because "You can successfully transport yourself back two hundred years" and "All the nasty, modern things aren't here." They explained away the evident poverty of the local people with Protestant incomprehension: "I suppose it's their Faith: they know that material things don't matter very much." Such comments were, I recognized, a distortion of the emic truth, but I could hardly intrude into the sound track to say so, and to leave out an important cue to tourist psychology would have been equally unacceptable. McCarty and I thus devised a way of intercutting this long discussion with brief glimpses of the hard work that lay behind daily survival, in an attempt to let the audience draw its own conclusions about how accurate the tourists' opinions were. Had we not done so, there was a clear risk that their pronunciamentos, just because they were delivered in crisp, middle-class English accents, might sound all too convincing to our audiences.

A Film is Born

Our work in Dunquin was punctuated by several trips across the

Republic to see our "rushes" in a small but excellent Dublin laboratory. We were thus in a position to discover if particular events needed further or "repeat" coverage. Our stay was also punctuated by occasional hunts for food, during which we ate at every Chinese restaurant in the West and every Indian one in Dublin (there were not many). Bread and boiled potatoes were otherwise an uninspiring diet, though usual in the villages.

The film editing was not done in Ireland. We all returned to Los Angeles, but had barely got back to U.C.L.A. when a nasty accident befell Mark McCarty. He had been at a small celebration for a student's M.A. and had just opened a bottle of champagne. The cork careened off the ceiling and hit him on the spectacles, smashing one glass and driving bits of it into his eyeball. When I found him heavily bandaged in hospital it looked as though he might never film again. Lamely he cracked, "I must be the only cameraman in the world with a built-in-split-image viewfinder!" But it wasn't funny. I was frankly amazed that the glass was all removed, the eyeball stitched up, and several weeks later the scar tissue came away and his vision was as good as ever.

Although back in Los Angeles, we had to wait for some months while Mike Hall methodically transferred all of the tape-recordings to 16 mm. sound stock, and "sunkup" (i.e. synchronized) this with the picture. Then over one lengthy weekend we all retired to Colin Young's house with a few filmmaking colleagues and some cases of sustenance, to project the entire fifteen hours of film on a screen. Shortly after, McCarty made a first essay on paper of the sequence in which we would edit the scenes. I looked it over, made a few changes in the sequence, and we had an outline of THE VILLAGE that we were able to stick with pretty closely. Then over the next few months the two of us sat in a smoke-filled little room with a moviola, racks of film, stacks of sound tapes, a garbage can, and the occasional sense that we were making film history. Once more McCarty's manic-depressive cycles swung into full gear, as we worked day after day, arguing, cutting, splicing and recutting, till a film slowly took shape. In fact we spent quite as much time in the editing process as we had done in the shooting.

In lieu of a story--for we had never shot to the requirements of a script and were not about to write a narration that would impose a story on the visuals--we had decided to order shots in the film to represent the events of a typical summer weekend, beginning with the milking early on Saturday morning, and continuing on through to the Sunday afternoon boat-race and its muted conclusion. According to this format most of the events "occurred" on the Saturday, only the last quarter of the film covering Sunday Mass and the regatta. We used a second organizational strategy too, because one of the most difficult things to convey in an anthropological documentary is a clear sense of social structure--unless perhaps a commentary presents the information in the form of an illustrated lecture. We decided to use the concept of social role to illustrate the social structure of Dunquin, and consequently the first ten minutes of the film showed a disparate sequence of people engaged in various activities: men rowing, a farmer milking his cows, an old lady baking bread, and so on. Subtitles gave the person's actual name and occupation, a nice way of acknowledging their participation in the film. But after seeing these opening sequences, the audience begin to recognize the same people in other roles: the boatmen are now in the bar, and the car-owner (there was only one) turns out to be the innkeeper, a character in his own right (he had been a bodyguard to Gloria Swanson, and later to Eamon De Valera). Later we see yet more of these people in other social and religious contexts, till the recognition of their various roles cumulates to a sense of the social structure in the mind of the viewer. It was, I believe, this editing strategy which allowed us to complete the film without resorting to a commentary to hold it together. And it was because the filmmaker and the anthropologist were always in the editing room together, arguing over the true meaning of every scene and the effect of every cut, that we were able to put into the film the totality of our knowledge of this and other Irish communities. In retrospect, the editing was a mutual education for us just as much as the fieldwork had been. I commend such a collaboration to all who would make anthropological films.

As we came near to concluding the editing, the influence of Colin Young, then Chairman of the Department of Theater Arts at U.C.L.A., became more marked. Scottish by birth, he had his own insights into Gaelic culture, and moreover he shared our vision of what observational cinema could be. Since he had handled the logistics of getting equipment and funds for us, and was now assuming a dominant role in giving the film its final form, it was appropriate that he should receive credit on the film as its producer. One of his biggest decisions was to insist on reducing our "final cut" from 90 minutes to 70. Both McCarty and I preferred the flow and coverage of the 90-minute version, but Colin Young's arguments about classroom use of the film prevailed.

We still didn't know what to call it. Friends and relatives dreamt up dozens of titles, one of which graces the heading of this article. It was only when Young was on the way to the laboratory with the edited negative in his car that he decided on the brief but easily remembered title, THE VILLAGE, a title that had been used thirty years before in a forgettable documentary produced, I believe, by the great Erich von Stroheim during his Hollywood days.

Our world premiere occurred at the annual meetings of the American Anthropological Association in Seattle, in December 1968. It was a large audience, perhaps 400, and a never-to-be-forgotten experience. Clearly many people were uncomfortable with a film that lacked a commentary. Anthropologists or not, they still wanted to be told what they were seeing, what to look for. We had felt, on the other hand, that a commentary would only come between the audience and the "actors," making it more difficult to see all that was really going on in the film. One middle-aged scholar on that occasion rushed up to the projectionist and attacked him, angrily shouting something about how this film was nothing but a vast accumulation of ordure. McCarty sat behind the screen chain-smoking, and readying himself for a question-and-answer session afterwards. One can imagine his mortification when the film came to an end and the darkened hall was filled with loud booing: it was the first time either of us could remember such an animated reception for a serious ethnographic film. But fortunately I was standing in that hall, and so could notice that the booing started quite suddenly during the final credits when a man was mentioned there who had nothing to do with the film's production but had been involved with its funding. It was the name of a well-known anthropologist. Any lingering doubts we may have had about the film were finally dissolved in 1972, when John Messenger published a sterling review of it in the AMERICAN ANTHROPOLOGIST.

Use of Film in Teaching

Most of us experience other cultures only through glimpses caught on vacations, in the pages of a book, or when seeing and hearing a film. Of anthropological films, however, many are little more than smoothly edited, authoritatively narrated travelogs: the viewer remains at a comfortable distance, essentially undisturbed by what he has seen and heard. Being disturbed at this state of affairs, our goal in making THE VILLAGE was to immerse the viewer in an alien culture and leave him perplexed, even shaken, and also eager for the answers to a hundred different questions.

We have, in fact, tried to eliminate the distance between the viewer and an alien subject. The viewer experiences much the same culture shock as would an anthropologist arriving in the field. He finds himself alone among strangers in a kitchen, a peat bog, a pub, a boat, even a church. No one guides him, tells what is going on, or even translates everything said. The viewer must try to put the pieces together himself as he returns again and again to the same places, the same people. Soon, like an anthropologist in the field, he finds himself almost unconsciously beginning to understand, to see patterns. He discovers that he appreciates and even likes these people--so much so that now he is jarred when suddenly confronted with a bevy of tourists and the threat they pose to the "purity" of the local way of life. Today the Gaelic speakers there are the focus of an annual invasion of amateur linguists and idyll-seekers from Dublin and even from overseas. More than anything else, it is these summer visitors whose needs are rapidly changing the local economy as they prompt subsistence farmers to cater to the tourists.

THE VILLAGE contains no acting and no directing. Everything that takes place would have occurred even if the cameras had not been there. The film covers a large number of discrete events which are held together by a certain cinematic logic and by the postulate that they represent the sort of things one would see going on in the community during a weekend visit. The approach is essentially etic.

The events (or scenes) have been very carefully chosen, however, so as to suggest as much of the ethnography as possible in one and a quarter hours. Each scene in some way represents a wider pattern of behavior or a more general attitude, the validity of which was established by other research. By filming altogether a third of the total population and by attempting to sketch the range of variation in any particular kind of local activity, the filmmakers have grappled as well as they can in 70 minutes with the problem of representativeness. Thus the film outlines the dimensions of the culture:

1. from poorest to most affluent household;
2. from households of one unmarried occupant to a large family;
3. from Iron-Age to 20th century architecture;
4. from foot to automobile transportation;
5. from ancient pre-Christian religious beliefs to modern Irish Catholicism;
6. from subsistence activities to cash earning;
7. from the landless to those with larger farms.

In addition to these topics the film focuses on three other pertinent subjects: the causes and consequences of emigration, the role of tourism in recent cultural change, and the nature of social interaction.

Anthropologist and filmmaker worked jointly on the editing of THE VILLAGE. Shots were selected for inclusion partly on aesthetic grounds and partly on grounds of their cultural content. As there was no script or story, it was expedient to string the shots together as a representation of what would go on in Dunquin during two days. This procedure led to a sort of dialectic, stressing comparisons and contrasts within the culture.

The intellectual activity that went into editing THE VILLAGE was in some respects like that of Marcel Proust writing REMEMBRANCE OF THINGS PAST. In ethnographic filming the quality of an event eludes the cameraman: his eye is fixed on a small dark image in the eye-piece, while his mind and body are concentrating on the technicalities of achieving a smooth and usable film sequence. If an anthropologist and sound-man are present, other immediate problems will be uppermost in their minds; for them too, the reality of the moment is elusive. It is hinted at for the first time when they look at the film rushes in the laboratory, and it grows with reflection, with research, and with repeated viewings in the editing room.

The rough parallel between the Irish film and Proust's work does not end here, however. Like Proust, the film editors had to discover a style of presentation which gave coherence to a potentially chaotic sequence of disparate events. This style had to achieve a formal beauty and a formal meaning that could stand for the aesthetic values and the social significance these events had initially held for their participants.

The simple device of presenting two days in the life of a community (actually distilled from three months of fairly frequent photographic and sound recording), thus becomes the framework for a more complicated structuring of events. The normal chronological order of the narrative is sometimes interrupted by the requirements of a contra-puntal logic intended to bring out similarities or contrasts between various personalities, various events and different social institutions or cultural forms within the community. A pattern is created, both in THE VILLAGE and in REMEM-BRANCE OF THINGS PAST, that depends not on a chronological sequence but on a sense of recurrence. It is this effect that allows both the film and the novel to suggest more than they present, and even to stand as total ethnographies when what is seen is only partial.

Much of the Irish film has synchronous sound, but this is often supplemented with local music and comments from recorded interviews. This treatment seemed to the editors more elegant than a drawling narration full of information more easily obtained from books. Such narrations are distracting: they keep the audience from observing and relating directly with the people on the screen.

THE VILLAGE nonetheless is didactic, intended primarily for university audiences. It is edited to give these audiences first a feeling of culture shock and disorientation, and then a cumulative understanding and sympathy for what is going on. This is precisely what would happen to any outsider going to an Irish village, and recalls what did happen to the film crew. When the film ends it has raised dozens of anthropological questions without giving complete answers to them. This "open-endedness" should, we hope, stimulate students to search for answers in the available literature on Irish society, or in a second look at the film. We certainly prefer this approach to an explanation lecture that tells the student precisely what to notice and leaves him with the feeling that there is nothing more to be said on the subject. A dogmatic narration is an unstimulating educational device: much better that the student experience for himself something of what the culture might feel like to an intelligent outsider.

When one visits a strange community he first sees various discrete events going on, one after the other. Only later do things fall into place and reveal the roles of people, the patterns of the culture. It is this sort of anthropological field experience that THE VILLAGE attempts in part to replicate. Such events, brought into the classroom, are a valuable addition to the usual training we can offer large classes in sociology or anthropology.

REFERENCES CITED

Arensberg, Conrad M. (1937). The Irish Countryman, an Anthropological Study. London: The Macmillan Company.

Arensberg, Conrad M., and Solon T. Kimball (1968). Family and Community in Ireland. Second edition. Cambridge, Mass.: Harvard University Press.

Brody, Hugh (1973). Inishkillane, Change and Decline in the West of Ireland. London: Allen, Lane, The Penguin Press.

Cresswell, Robert (1969). Une Communaute rurale de l'Irlande. Paris: Institut d' Ethnologie, Musee de l'Homme.

Flower, Robin (1944). The Western Island or the Great Blasket. Oxford: Clarendon Press.

Fox, Robin (1978). The Tory Islanders, A People of the Celtic Fringe. Cambridge: Cambridge University Press.

Granlund, John (1976). Coumenoole, Dunquin and Other Townlands. IN Folk and Farm, Essays in Honour of A.T. Lucas..., Caoimhin O Danachair (ed.). Dublin: Royal Society of Antiquaries of Ireland, pp. 72-89.

MacDougall, David (1975). Beyond Observational Cinema. IN Principles of Visual Anthropology, Paul Hockings (ed.); pp. 109:124. The Hague, Paris: Mouton Publishers.

McCarty, Mark (1975). McCarty's Law and How to Break it. IN Principles of Visual Anthropology, Paul Hockings (ed.). The Hague, Paris: Mouton Publishers, pp. 45-51.

Messenger, John C. (1969). Inis Beag, Isle of Ireland. New York: Holt, Rinehart and Winston.

Messenger, John C. (1972). Review of THE VILLAGE. American Anthropologist 74: 1577-81.

O Crohan, Tomas (1929). An t-Oileanach... (Trans. by Robin Flower, 1934, as The Islandman. Dublin: Talbot Press.)

O Suileabhain, Muiris (1933). Fiche Blian ag Fas. (Trans. by Moya Llewelyn Davies and George Thomson, 1933, as Twenty Years a-Growing. London: Chatto and Windus.)

Proust, Marcel (1934). Remembrance of Things Past. (Trans. by C.K. Scott Moncrieff.) New York: The Modern Library.

Russell, John Charles (1979). In the Shadows of Saints: Aspects of Family and Religion in a Rural Irish Gaeltacht. San Diego: University of California, Ph.D. dissertation in Anthropology.

Sayers, Peig (1962). An Old Woman's Reflections. Oxford: Oxford University Press.

Sayers, Peig (1974). Peig, The Autobiography of Peig Sayers of the Great Blasket Island. (Trans. by Bryan MacMahon.) Syracuse: Syracuse University Press.

Scheper-Hughes, Nancy (1979). Saints, Scholars and Schizophrenics. Berkeley, Los Angeles: University of California Press.

Symes, David G. (1972). Farm Household and Farm Performances: A Study of Twentieth Century Changes in Ballyferriter, Southwest Ireland. Ethnology 11: 25-38.

Symes, David G. (1973). Stability and Change among Farming Communities in Southwest Ireland. Acta Ethnographica Academiae Scientarum

Hungaricae 22: 89-105.
Synge, John Millington (1962). In West Kerry. In his The Aran Islands and Other Writings. New York: Vintage Books, pp. 211-267.

FILMS CITED

MAN OF ARAN (1932-34). Robert Flaherty, director. B and W documentary, 77 mins. Distributor, Films Inc., Wilmette, Ill.
RYAN'S DAUGHTER (1970). David Lean, director. Color feature film, 176 mins. Distributor, Films Inc., Wilmette, Ill.
THE VILLAGE (1968). Mark McCarty, filmmaker; Paul Hockings, anthropologist. B and W documentary, 70 mins. Distributor, University of California Extension Media Center, Berkeley, California.

The Controversy About Kypseli

Susanna M. Hoffman
Oakland, California

The projector shuts down and the lights go on. A woman of Greek
descent hits her husband over the head with her purse and says, "See what
I've been trying to tell you!"

Crying, a suburban Thousand Oaks, California housewife announces,
"You've just told me the story of my life."

A Greek man from Santorini says, "It's absolutely true. It's just the
way it is."

An anthropology professor says, "I can't tell you how important this
film is or how many classes it works for. I've shown it in introductory
classes, theory classes, peasant studies, Europe."

A philosophy professor and a woman studies professor, neither
anthropologists, show the film every year to every class.

Yet another anthropology professor sputters, "Why this isn't
ethnography. It's ...it's...analysis. It's only one way of looking at things.
Very controversial. You couldn't show it alone. You'd have to explain it."

An ethnographic filmmaker comments, "It's not a whole picture of how
the people live, and there are no subtitles!"

An a senator, thinking he could avoid writing a speech by borrowing a
copy from the National Endowment for the Humanities and showing it to a
Greek society, found himself in the center of an uproar.

Practically no anthropological film has stirred up the ado that
KYPSELI: MEN AND WOMEN APART - A DIVIDED REALITY has.
Many educators, lecture givers, students, and general public find it an
excellent film. It graphically shows theory. It demonstrates what an
anthropologist does, unfolding more than a people do, but what their
behavior means. Other teachers and viewers find the film disturbing. It
doesn't present a complete picture of the people's lives or tell how the
subjects themselves see the matter. It depicts only one aspect of their lives
and presents a preordained view.

The argument rages. The tale that KYPSLI tells is true, it isn't true. It
doesn't tell all. It tells what it's suppose to tell, and what it tells is
revealing.

The controversy surrounding KYPSELI in part has to do with what the
film is called. KYPSELI: WOMEN AND MEN APART - A DIVIDED
REALITY is an unusual film. It is classed with ethnographic film," those

161

films made by anthropologists and other students of human behavior that show how other people live. Ethnography means the description of a people's customs or habits. Most ethnographic films do exactly that. But KYPSELI isn't an ethnographic film. KYPSELI is an *ethnological* film. Ethnology means the "study" of how a people live. Ethnology involves analysis. And that is what the film KYPSELI does. It doesn't merely chronicle how the people of the village live, it examines their lives and draws a conclusion. It delves behind a people's habits and presents an explanation.

Anthropologists do both sorts of work, ethnography and ethnology. A lecture or article written by an anthropologist may well simply detail how a people dwell, what their culture contains, from their fish hooks to the religious practices. Other articles and lectures go farther. They attempt to extract patterns in human behavior, and to offer explanations. Few films in anthropology have been ethnological. Most are ethnographic. But KYPSELI was always intended to be an ethnological film. It was always meant to show not just the days, weeks, events and affairs of the island villagers in the images they present, but to reveal the possible explanation of their customs.

In the village of Kypseli it became apparent that people were of a Western cultural tradition, the same tradition as the rest of Europe and the United States, people long civilized, who read, write and have a tradition of literature, philosophy and Judeo-Christian religion, retain a very basic dividing principle to their lives. That principle is based directly on sensory perception, not on some abstract notion (for example an invisible birthing system which supposedly tells people which families were more noble than others, or a system of star signs, names, occupations, totems, or quantities of wealth). Though some of these other divisions also exist, a deeper one underlays all. It is based on a simple, although highly visible, fact of nature. There are two sexes of humans. On that simple natural fact the people of the culture (the same culture in essence as ours) built many notions that aren't natural. They are instead"cultural," ideas created by people. They created notions of dress and behavior for each sex, rules about which sex could do which chore, use which space, be out and about during which time segments, hold what power, have what character. Like the fact of two sexes, the villagers came to believed the ideas about sex were natural, and from that right and proper. Meanwhile the cultural ideas controlled and effected everyone's life.

Ethnology comes from ethnography, and that is what KYPSELI: MEN AND WOMEN APART - A DIVIDED REALITY comes from, too. The analysis of what underlay peoples lives took in-depth research to realize. It took an extended stay and intricate knowledge of the villager. Only after I studied the village a long spell, did all the pieces come together, and did I realize what was going on behind the day to day interactions. Only then did I see that in Kypseli one could actually see the core cultural pattern. The underlying principle by which people separated reality, formed their notions and conducted lives, lay visible to the naked eye.

My stay in the village of Kypseli spanned close to four years. The main stretch lasted over 2 years. I arrived one December day with two donkey loads of belongings, and that was all I lived with the entire time. I added only a straw mattress, some bricks and boards for shelves, and a few new books and tapes. I had visited the village twice before my arrival: once when I was deciding which of Santorini's 12 villages to live in, to look the community over, and once to rent an abode. At first I had wanted to live with a family, but the villagers would have none of that, not with a stranger. In the end I rented a four room house, the temporarily deserted dowry home of the storeowner's sister. I paid $6. 66 a month for it. He offered me his own wife's house first, as they lived next to the store. But it was off to the side of the hamlet. The sister's house was right in the center of town where I could oversee almost everything. Of course, that meant that the villagers could oversee me at all times as well. Ah, well, nothing without it's price.

I chose to live in and study Kypseli for a number of reasons. The village was "typical," holding 350 tilling people, a store, a school, one phone. It was isolated. It was not touched by tourists and had no paved road. It was considered backward and traditional by the town and beach communities, a place where the women "still wore scarves." It was divided in an upper and lower portion, each having it's own collection of families, each bearing a certain sense of superiority and animosity toward the other Lastly, it was within walking distance, only some 5 kilometers, of town (a budding metropolis of 1, 200 people, but that at least had the supplies I would need) while the only other isolated, divided village was a long and dusty 5 mile trek away.

The villagers were both fascinated and dismayed at my arrival. They had no idea what I was about or what to do with me. It turned out later they thought I might be a prostitute setting up for business. (When they finally told me, I pointed out that with the amount of spare cash they had, I'd have starved to death in a week.) My Greek was practically non-existent, at least in terms of the island vocabulary of fields, goats, and chickens and the local dialect. I had hired an assistant in Athens to help me the first few weeks, but she lasted only the boat trip to the island, found a excuse to return to the mainland, and never came back. No islander could help me since none knew English. So there I was.

It was the proverbial blessing in disguise that I was so alone and waif-like when I entered the village, though I will never say (not even now) that it was easy. Because of my solitude and muteness, I learned the village from inside out, bottom up, like a child growing to an adult. To the villagers, I was like a piece of unformed clay that had to be honed and shaped, shown and trained, until I became a proper human and Kypselian. I tripped over, I think, probably every subject possible during my stay, and learned about everything. I was there a long while and I was ever present. The only thing they apparently tried to hold back form me was village politics. Perhaps they thought it was too complex for a woman, or more likely they feared it was too revealing. At any rate, that subject too came tumbling down by the end, with the not-so-startling revelation that village political factions were based on family (not political party) and people voted for their relatives.

Fortunately, I pulled off a great, unwitting coup my very first day in the village. Scared out of my mind, unable to speak, and having nothing to do, I dragged a chair into my courtyard and began to knit. Now, I can knit patterns with holes, turn loop-do-loops, and make whirly gigs with yarn in a way that not a single village woman could do. In no time at all I had a huge audience, and the foundations of my first friendships. I also quite unconsciously triggered the notion that I might indeed be an O. K. woman. I got patted and chatted, invaded and examined. They began to accept my presence. If nothing else, I would provide entertainment.

What happened over the next two years was like learning an ever more complex song, one posed in counterpoint between their purposes and mine. I was a single woman, so at first they hustled me into that group to which I seemed most suited, the gaggle of unmarried maidens. Too old to be children, not yet married, having little to do until they were dowried and married, these women ranged in age from about 15 to 30. They were my first clue into the web of male and female lives in the village. If any group there knew nothing, or at least was at a point where they could not speak or show what they knew, or had little power, it is this group. I dallied with the "girls" some months through various Sundays, numerous saints days, and gatherings by the square until I realized what had happened to me, how tidily I'd been tethered by the place the villagers so snugly ensconced me.

It was then I made my first purposeful social breach. (I'd made others not on purpose and some the villagers tricked me into, mostly by teaching dirty words I innocently then used in conversation.) I departed the maidens, and sat myself down with the married women. At first a few of the married women tried to shoo me off with the maidens again, since I didn't fit their category. But I steadfastly persisted. I joined the young mothers around the village square, hovered with the grand dames in church, and followed mothers of all ages about their chores (the laundry, the goats, the fields, the shopping). I refused to be entertained in any more formal living rooms. I plunked myself down on broken kitchen chairs while the ladies were cooking. I let it be known I knew the secrets of married life. Soon I was more than tolerated, I was incorporated. I remember the day I realized I'd made my second breakthrough (the first was when I cracked my first pun in Greek), and it was all because I'd joined ranks with the married women. I was about four months into my stay and my now I was understanding quite a bit of the conversation. Sophia let go with a rather nasty crack about another woman and her fancy acting family. Remembering I was present, she quickly covered her mouth and said, "Oh, I shouldn't have said that with you around." Then she continued with an, "Oh, well, you might as well hear. We can't keep watching what we say. You're always here." They had been censoring village intrigues, gossip, and less than rosy sentiments from my ears, and it had become too hard to keep it up.

From then on I heard about everything. Dowries, fights, sex, curses, money, power, jealousy, shopping, clothing (the ages one could wear red, when one switched to blue), mourning, who was too conservative, who was too free, who was doing what to whom, what the traditions were, how people should behave. I worked my way 'round and 'round the married women's group, from the new brides to the matriarchs, young daughters-in-law that only received food, old mothers-in-law that only gave it, the fertile and the barren, the modern and the scarf wearing, the farmers' wives and the mates of poor mule drivers.

I broached the widows next. They talked of men and marriage and life. They kept tabs on fortunes and knew the ins and outs of dowry exchanges. They made *kolliva* for the dead, performed cures. They monitored their sons and daughters while tending their grandchildren. They were as rich a source and as vital a gang as anyone could even encounter. It was in a widow's house surrounded by a troop of her kind that another revelation occurred that I shall never forget. I had been growing increasingly restless and, I'll admit, cranky. Suddenly sitting there I realized why. There I was on a chair by myself and across from me were about 20 Greek women on a couch built for 2. I hadn't been touched for months! They were so close and I was so distant. I was so clearly from a different cultural tradition about physical proximity and it was time for it to end. I gave a great cry and jumped into the huddle. They were a little startled, but also quite amused. Forever after I never sat in an isolated chair again. I always headed right for the middle of the sofa.

By now my whimsical breaching of propriety had become *de rigueur*. I was so well behaved most of the time. Then every now and then the notion to do something contrary would strike me. It was then, a year or so into my stay, I decided to break the final and major social barrier. I started hanging out with the men. I marched into the fields and wine vats. I followed them to market and wiled away the Sunday in the tavern. I sat in courtyards with them in late afternoons, when courtyards were men's own. I don't know if I ever became "one of the guys," but a great comfort grew. They liked to "tell" me things more than the women did, what the customs were, and why. How the village functioned, what the beliefs were. We discussed everything from bank accounts to politics and why girls shouldn't go to high school. (It was co-educational and no decent father would let his daughter stray there, though eventually the store owner, an arch conservative, let his daughters go because the youngest was my god-daughter). We talked of hunting rabbits, musical talent, splitting fields among children, continuing relations among brothers, as well as war stories and ghost stories.

As I traversed every social segment, it's true I developed favorite friends and families. I suppose any anthropologist does. But I could drift in and out of any house, seek companionship from anyone, and join any group in the village. And I did.

I can never thank the villagers enough. They allowed me access to their hearts, minds, homes, and knowledge. They also oversaw my survival. They gave me so much food, starting at dawn and the 6 A. M. goat milking, I couldn't finish it and decried the waste. Finally, I simply started dropping into one house or another at mealtime. They always knew where I was, and once sure that I was provided for, they would stem their flow of food stuff.

The first weeks I couldn't even get my bucket into my cistern. Once lowering a bucket to the water, it seems you must rest the bucket on the water's surface for an instant. Then you give the rope a quick smart jerk. Otherwise, the edge of the pail never cuts into the water and the bucket never sinks. Marketousa one day saw me come up with my fifth paltry cupful of the precious liquidwhile trying to wash my hair. She took me in hand, talked to me like a child, and showed me the trick.

They had endless patience. They put up with my idiocy and even my occasional irritability, which they put down to too many books and too much thinking, without rebuke. Most of all they had grace. Within a short time after my arrival, they developed a system of altering their definition of me so that I was always fitting and all right in their eyes. When I was behaving properly they called me, "our Susanna." When I was out of line, when I was sitting with men, indulging ribald jokes with matrons, or when strangers from other villages criticized me, they called me "our foreigner."

In the end they showed me more than they themselves saw. They could live as men and women, but they couldn't see the separation. They could hold power, but they couldn't see the pattern to their interplay over it. Only an outside observer could do that. Perhaps only a social scientist trained to see beneath the surface could have seen and extracted the reiterating sequence a male and female segments that cut across the church to the square to the courtyard, that intersected daylight to night, purity to danger. And that is what led to the film.

When I returned from Greece I knew I had chanced upon a rare place and an uncommon experience. I had living in a site where the underlying organization of peoples' reality showed quite out front, quite discernibly. True, KYPSELI is also a"telling" film. It relies heavily on narrative. Any film that attempts to demonstrate theory or analysis must. "Showing" abstract subject matter is difficult. The pictures don't necessarily demonstrate what is being said. Sometimes they do, other times (as I believe happens in KYPSELI) the pictures reflect the exposition while it's being stated. The images corroborate the treatise. There is much more evidence on the separation of male and female realities in Kypseli than I could show in a film. There are kinship terms and complex references concerning who married into a family and how. There is language use and subtle interaction. There are quarrels and the pattern to them, who fights what way and how, and there are intimate moments, so thoroughly hidden because they contradict the public separation of the sexes, that the confirm the pattern by their absence.

Returning to Kypseli to make the film I knew what I wanted to present. The script was by and large written before shooting the film, a fact that has often been the focus of both speculation and criticism of the film. Indeed, KYPSELI received funding exactly *because* it was pre-scripted and exactly *because* it intended to present theory graphically. I also had already planned many of the pictures we would take. After all, it was because of the spatial arrangement in the village square, church and houses that the film could show it's thesis. I didn't know whose name day we'd show, which healers, or that Maria wringing her sheet would be the final shot. I did know the sorts of events that occurred in Kypseli. I had lived there a long while.

The film's crew consisted of what I hoped would be an unobtrusive three. When I returned to the States after my long stay in Greece, well before even I wrote up my study of the village, I already knew I wanted to film the revelations about their and our culture I found there. I contacted an anthropologist colleague, Richard Cowan, who had written several anthropology films and knew how to write them. I looked up a filmmaker, Paul Aratow, to query how to launch a film and what I'd need. It was the same two people who joined me in the project, and with whom I decided to share full credit. We had hoped to have more help, but I was so convinced of the importance of making KYPSELI and determined to make the film, I insisted we attempt it, money or no money. We left in late Spring with 11 metal cases numbered with bright florescent numbers so we could always count them before we heard if we had been funded. On Columbus Day, almost finished with the film, we finally got a wire announcing our grant from the National Endowment for the Humanities. We bought the only bottle of what passed for champagne we could find on the island and celebrated. Three weeks later we packed up our cameras and left.

I believed when I first decided to make KYPSELI that theory could be shown and taught in film, that anthropology films could do more. They could demonstrate analysis, show insights, demonstrate underlying codes. They could present what the social scientist deciphers, as well as merely how the people behave. Of course, what sort of explanation or treatise the anthropologist presents also triggers controversy. Are the explanations right or wrong, the theories correct or incorrect? That is the other part of KYPSELI'S controversy. Is the explanation presented correct of incorrect?

I happen to believe the analysis of Kypselian life present in the film is correct. The separation of men and women is as plain, clear, and moving as the camera shows it. I further believe every ethnographic film actually presents an analysis. DEAD BIRDS contains only one explanation of what rules tribal interaction in New Guinea, and it's a very filmic explanation.

TROBRIAND CRICKET gives us only one aspect of male life on the island. It depicts a very competitive aspect and we learn nothing of women. All film has a point of view. So called cinema verite has. The ethnographic films that attempt to depict pure description by merely following say, the action around a camp fire, do. Even travelogues have. I remember walking out of a ghastly film called Mondo Cane II once. It was supposedly a cross cultural extravaganza film, though admittedly commercial, if not exploitative. In it the cameraman followed a woman who had allegedly speeded the death of her horribly deformed thalidomide child, while the narrative asked, "One wonders, does she feel guilty?" That's was surely a skewed point of view.

It's difficult to judge the correctness of an analysis execpt by whether it is efficient, that is, it explains much of the material, that it is elegant, that is, it makes the explanation the simplest terms, and whether it enlightens. The pattern in Kypseli is simple. It appears and reappears on numerous levels. And for many it's viewers, it appears the KYPSELI: WOMEN AND MEN APART - A DIVIDED REALITY is enlightening. That is why, I feel, a woman in Thousand Oaks cries. A Greek woman has corroboration for what she has been trying to tell her clearly, tolerant mate. A philosophy and a woman studies professor show KYPSELI every year. The film finds use in many sorts of anthropology classes. And if it's controversial for both it's presenters and its audience, all the better. That is what any good article or lecture should do, and that is what our films should do, too.

Ado or no ado, something about Kypseli must work. "It's been E. M. C.'s best selling film for 15 years," says its distributor.

Readings On Kypseli

Allen, Peter S., et al. (1978). Five Views of Kypseli (a film review). Reviews in Anthropology 5(1): 129-142.

Hoffman, Susanna M. (1976). The Ethnography of the Islands: Thera. Proceedings of the New York Academy of Sciences, Number 268, pp. 264-275.

Hoffman, Susanna M. (1976). Discussions of the Film Kypseli: Women and Men Apart, a Divided Reality. Proceedings of the New York Academy of Sciences, Number 268, pp. 382-385.

Hoffman, Susanna, and Richard Cowan (1978). Kypseli: A Marital Geography of a Greek Village. Lifelong Learning, volume 45, Number 58. Berkeley: University of California.

Hoffman, Susanna, and Richard Cowan (1978). Comments on the Reviews of KYPSELI: WOMEN AND MEN APART - A DIVIDED REALITY. Reviews in Anthropology 5(1): 129-142.

New Guinea In Italy: An Analysis Of The Making Of An Italian Television Series From Research Footage Of The Maring People Of Papua New Guinea

Allison Jablonko
San Francisco, California

ABSTRACT: In 1980 Allison and Marek Jablonko joined an Italian writer and editor to produce a television series on the Maring people of Papua New Guinea. The footage had originally been shot in 1963, 1964, and 1968 as material for behavioral research. The challenge in 1980 was to use the footage to produce films for the general public.

This paper is an overview of the differences in approach and the complementary skills which became clear during this collaboration between research anthropologist and film professionals. Various problems inherent in making films of one culture for viewers of another culture are examined, among them the reversal of the relationship between script and background, culturally programmed scripts and cross-cultural invisibility, the need to balance repetitiveness and behavioral rhythms with the cutting rhythms expected by the viewers, and problems of authenticity and verisimilitude in the construction of image, sound effects, and commentary. Audience reaction is touched on, and bottlenecks to production are noted. It is suggested, in conclusion, that more such joint projects need to be undertaken and then used analytically in the teaching of anthropology. In this way, new generations of anthropologists will be able to expand their skills from a predominantly verbal approach to the multi-media approach of film, and communication among anthropologists and the general public will be greatly enhanced.

In 1963 and 1964 my husband, Marek Jablonko, and I took 63,000 feet of film among the Maring of the Simbai Valley as part of the Columbia University Expedition to study the human ecology of the New Guinea rain

169

forest. The footage covered general observations of gardening, ceremony, village, and family life with special attention to child behavior. This footage was silent and the original was subsequently archived at the National Institutes of Mental Health (Sorenson and Gajdusek 1966). In 1968 we returned to the Simbai Valley with synchronous sound equipment to shoot footage specifically oriented for research in non-verbal communication. We took 48,000 feet, this time concentrating on 11-minute uninterrupted sequences. My husband did most of the camera work, while I handled the sound and made as full a written documentation as possible.

In March, 1980, after we had been residing in Italy for ten years, an Italian TV director, Ezio Alovisi, who had heard of our footage, obtained a contract from RAI-TV (Italian National Television) to make an eight episode series from our footage to be broadcast by their Scholastic & Educational Department. On September 19, after initial planning discussions with Alovisi, who was the writer and over-all director of the project, we were joined by a young editor, Filippo Bussi. It took three full months to complete the series, which was entitled MARING: DOCUMENTS OF A NEW GUINEA PEOPLE. The series consisted of the following episodes: (1) Introduction; (2) Life with the Forest; (3) Individuality and Social Relationships; (4) Ritual Cycles; (5) Crops and Food Preparation; (6) Children; (7) Space and Time; and (8) External Influences. The episodes were broadcast at one-week intervals from November 12 to December 31, 1980. While the first in the series was being broadcast, later episodes were still being completed. The challenge for each of us, coming as we did from such diverse backgrounds as theater and research anthropology, was to answer in a practical way the question: "Can a TV film for a general public be made from what was originally shot as anthropological research footage?"

Our project, shot as it was in the early and late 1960s for research purposes, and edited in 1980 for a general audience, bridged a 20 year period of considerable development in the field of ethnographic filmmaking. When we first went to the field in 1963, the only films of general ethnographic interest, as I remember, were Flaherty's NANOOK and Marshall's THE HUNTERS. More usual were exotic documentaries, such as SKY ABOVE AND MUD BELOW, which I was trying to counteract. I was convinced that it would be possible to take footage useable for anthropological research and then to edit films from it for the general public. This assumption, that I could kill two birds with one stone, as it were, seemed eminently sensible given the expense of filming. My training had been with Margaret Mead, spiced with touches of Birdwhistell, and my aim was to use film as a recording device for situations which were too complex to be captured with paper and pencil alone. After we returned from the first field trip in 1964, the Program in Ethnographic Film (PIEF) was formed, marking the first organizational awareness among American anthropologists that film is an important presentational device. But the hope that this would lead to greater awareness among anthropologists at large of film as a serious tool for learning and teaching was not fulfilled at that time. What could have become a concerted three-pronged effort to develop the use of film as a research device, as a medium to present anthropological thinking, and as material from which to build theories of visual anthropology, concentrated predominantly on the last of these possibilities. Film was used as a research tool only in specific anthropological sub-disciplines and there was little methodological cross-fertilization. With very few exceptions film was not used for serious presentation either among anthropologists or between anthropologists and the public. Generally, departmental or class film screenings were interpreted as recreational in nature and consequently were perceived as less substantive than lectures.

In the 1960s theoretical considerations of visual anthropology were still in their early stages of development. However, during the 1970s more ethnographic films were being shot than before. Due to the availability of lighter-weight equipment, there was less disruption of local behavior by large, intrusive film teams. The use of synchronous sound with subtitles was introduced by those ethnographic filmmakers who wished to let the subjects speak for themselves about the images of their own lives (for instance David and Judith MacDougall). These new films were very different from anything my husband and I had imagined when we had first started shooting footage in New Guinea.

The theoretical basis of ethnographic filming has been greatly improved since then. It has far outstripped practice in providing films for the general public. In this paper, therefore, I will not attempt to add to current theory, but rather to report on our own experience with television, hoping thereby to encourage more people to embark on projects of this nature.

Development of the Project

Our multi-faceted project was an unusual "field situation" in itself. We, two Americans from the sub-culture of research anthropology, worked together with Italians coming from a commercial filmmaking sub-culture. Our mutual goal was to create, from the footage shot in New Guinea in the 1960s, some understanding of the Maring culture for general Italian viewers in 1980.

My background in research filming had left me with a mistrust of editors and professional film style. While filming in the field, our working style had been based on minimal interference with on-going action and we had introduced no subsequent editorial changes to the film record. We felt that the selectivity introduced by the cameraman's choice of angle and timing was quite sufficient interference. Our original footage was safely archived for the use of any interested researchers and for posterity. However, anthropologists had not yet developed a lively use of research footage as a device for mutual investigation of shared problems (a resource of which medical researchers were already taking full advantage). Only one researcher besides myself had made any significant use of this "treasury of information" on Maring life (Byers 1972). Therefore, I was eager to experiment with the creation of a bridge between the archived material and a wider public, knowing that the original material was safe and sound and uncut for future reference. I had no doubt that to reach the general public, cooperation with professionals was a rational, if uncomfortable, move. I hoped that among professionals there would be those eager to work in new, exploratory ways with this unique footage, and that some people in the general audience would welcome the opportunity to look at "real time documentation" of daily life in another culture. I expected the writer and editor to deal flexibly with the TV medium, using their tools to bring out the "best" in the footage, not just in a cinematographic sense, but also in terms of the anthropological message that I would be sharing with them.

Immersed as I was in the production process, I took running notes covering the most varied aspects of the experience, from lists of edge-numbers and transcriptions of taped sound, to remarks on my colleagues' work patterns, and references to relevant theory. For me it was a trial by fire of Hall's point that to truly learn about one's own culture, one must confront a different one. I sharpened my perceptions about visual anthropology by a short and intense confrontation with the sub-culture of commercial filmmaking (Hall 1977).

During initial discussions I found that the writer understood the project as a means of satisfying the "natural curiosity of people about each other" by giving them the opportunity to look at people living another way of life. I was suspicious that the "natural curiosity" was rather an emotional pull to the exotic, an opportunity to project on "others" many unconscious or stereotyped elements of our Western culture. It seemed to me that in response to this curiosity, anthropologists could share the tools of their discipline so that interested viewers could go beyond curiosity to a fuller and more satisfying understanding. A presentation of anthropological perspective together with the images and sounds of the culture in the film could help viewers to develop their innate ability to perceive different culture patterns and respond to these differences consciously rather than unconsciously (Hall 1977).

I was working with two contexts: anthropology and Maring culture, both of which were unknown to the potential viewers. I expected the second to be more difficult to share than the first, because the first is a product of Western civilization and is neatly codified in our languages. I discovered, to my chagrin, that communicating "the culture of anthropologists" to non-anthropologists takes a great deal of time and effort. Anthropologists have all gone through long periods of academic preparation and fieldwork. It is too easy to forget that phrases and concepts that we anthropologists now take for granted may be quite unfamiliar to the general public.

In making an anthropological film of one culture for a general public of another culture, anthropology enters the project as a third culture, a culture as different from the viewer's culture as that one is from the filmed culture. Nothing can be taken for granted. Concepts must be wrestled with until they can be presented in as plain language as possible. No shortcuts are possible. Some concepts, those which are the result of long study, will just have to be avoided, or slowly built up with examples in the course of the program. On the other hand, without being mentioned, anthropology can be used as a foundation for the whole film. This is the direction most anthropological/ethnographic films currently take.

For the TV series, I had to introduce not only the particulars of Maring culture, but also the basic notions of culture. The images and sounds on film had to transform concepts which I had long since taken for granted into living examples. The materials we had at our disposal to fill each 27 minutes of TV program time were the already existing moving images and wild and synchronous sound, plus voice-over commentary and video-taped interviews to be created.

As part of each episode I envisioned video-taped conversations between the writer and ourselves in which we would speak about our role as anthropologists, discuss the contribution of anthropology to the understanding of the world today, and share the notion that there is no "one objective reality," but that people perceive in terms of the categories they learned in the culture they were born into. I wanted to explain that the documentation on the screen had not been automatic but was a result of the interplay of our anthropological and cultural assumptions and of our own personal interaction with the Maring. I felt that such discussions on screen could make the whole subject less remote and academic.

I asked the writer whether we would ever put direct questions to the audience, to encourage them to think and compare what they would be seeing and hearing in the film with their own familiar life. Would we let viewers do some thinking for themselves before putting out all our own explanations? Would we do this to various extents in the different episodes? Some sample questions I suggested were: (1) How does this space compare in size, content and organization to the space in which you meet your friends? (2) How does the way the Maring use their space differ from the way you use your space (e.g., who sits where, how close, who stands)? (3) Do Maring touch more or less than you do? (4) Do Maring talk louder or softer than your friends? (5) Do Maring speak one at a time or simultaneously? I was curious to find out what possibilities the writer saw for conveying these ideas, since, in his role as coordinator of the whole project, he would be responsible for creating a final format that would be acceptable to RAI.

We developed a general outline which indicated that each episode would consist of a two minute introduction to the entire series, a five minute interview with us concerning the particular episode, three minutes of documentation with slides, objects, diagrams, and tapes, followed by ten to twelve minutes of uninterrupted film illustrating the main point, and a final

five minutes of video-taped conversation between us. The writer did not
want to present "an illustrated lecture," but rather to awaken interest by a
series of surprises: "How will the next point be made?" "What will be
shown next?" He spoke of presenting anthropological "tools": starting with
the anthropologists themselves as observers, then showing how they aug-
ment their abilities with tape recorders, still cameras, film, notes, objects,
maps, questions, comparisons with their home culture, and cooperation
with other specialists. The writer's idea was to show that anthropologists
both learn and communicate what they learn by using this large array of
possibilities.

I found that the writer viewed the whole project as very "avant garde," a
project that would open new possibilities which would only be widely understood some time in the future. "The fact is," he said, "ten years ago RAI
would have given money for this sort of serious, informational program for
only one 40 minute episode." Therefore, sponsoring eight 27 minute
episodes was a great step forward.

Although the project had been initiated by the writer, after our first
conferences he appeared only intermittently at the work scene (one of the
cutting rooms of Cinecitta, in Rome). For the next three months I worked
almost daily with the editor. My learning about "TV culture" from practice
began.

Emerging Observations

1. Basic Assumptions: My earliest filming assumption had been that our
   footage would convey information about the Maring. The second assumption, which I embraced after the convincing theoretical analyses of
   the 1970s was that, obvious content to the contrary, the footage tells as
   much about the people who shot it as about the filmed subjects. It was
   only in the dramatically different world of TV filming, that I became
   aware that a third basic assumption is necessary: "Footage must be
   looked at in terms of the viewers," and in this case "viewers" meant
   "general public." What would they see when shown the film? My
   guides in this "new world," the editor and the writer, assured me that
   they would "see nothing," but quickly switch to another channel, unless we reshaped the footage into a dramatic kaleidoscope of ever-
   changing images following each other with something intriguingly
   called "correct rhythm." Given my respect for the footage as a document
   of Maring rhythm, I was none too keen to see this transformation, yet
   it was an inevitable part of what I was to learn. I was curious to explore what exactly the audience would think it was seeing, once the
   "correct rhythm" had managed to affix its eye to the screen. I had been
   eager to give others a chance to use their powers of observation to interact with an unknown situation, to let their minds begin to generate

questions, and, finally, to satisfy them with an explanation of the unfamiliar in terms of the Maring cultural background rather than their own cultural presuppositions.

What quickly became obvious in working with the editor and writer was that people in our culture (including most anthropology students) have minimal time or ability to just watch anything in an open-ended way. Any scene is immediately either "domesticated" by being naively explained as analogous to something in our own culture, or it is dramatized and appears as a projection of unconscious or suppressed elements of our own culture. People only "see" what they already have in mind. To change what people have in mind, so that they can begin to see things previously unfamiliar to them, is a great challenge.

A film editor has skills which can be used as powerful tools in helping people develop new ways of seeing. I was delighted by our editor's lightning visual perception, his grasp of visual information, and his ability to make a flowing and animated film from sometimes skimpy, fragmented, and dry material. I was less delighted by his comment, "It is too bad that you didn't take a professional cameraman with you." I ruminated darkly about the time strictures and shooting habits of professional cameramen which would have precluded the basic data collection our filming had achieved, even though it would have produced more malleable raw footage for the editor. Nonetheless, we developed a satisfying working procedure. I would introduce him to each filmed event, explaining both the particulars of behavior or technology which were not visually self-explanatory, and the context of the event in Maring culture. Then I watched as he translated my explanations into action with his splicer, rearranging and shortening the footage to create a concise version which was visually easier to "see" than the original. Viewing his rough cut, I could head off most misunderstandings he might have had, and the edited version could be corrected to correspond as closely as I knew how to Maring culture norms and the actual filmed event as I had witnessed it.

2. Reversal of the Relationship Between Script and Background: I began to think about the relationships between "general background" and "particular script" in films. Film and TV scenarios are usually situated within a cultural context which is familiar to the viewing public. The scenario is focused through a particular script whose details are unfamiliar. It is these details, therefore, which are explained and elaborated as the film proceeds, while most of the visible "surface" of the film (setting and on-going action as distinct from story-line action) forms an unremarked and unquestioned background. This relationship is reversed when a film is shown outside the culture in which it was made. Viewers do not share the cultural context, and the background is

not thus anchored in familiar assumptions, but begins to float in a sea
of questions. For the outsider, attention to the script becomes difficult
if not impossible, since attention is pulled instead to the unexplained
and puzzling images of the "foreign visual surface." If the film ignores
questions caused by the unfamiliar background and instead, moves ahead
with the intended script, foreign viewers will predictably lose interest,
or begin to interpret what they see in terms of their own expectations.
My colleague, Thomas Blakely, recently shared a dramatic example
with me. While he was working in the USA with his research assistant, Faila Mwa'a, a Bahemba woman from Zaire, 50 years of age and
mother of 8 children, they watched the film "H.G. Wells and His Time
Machine" together. When she saw the efforts made by the hero to rescue the heroine from Jack The Ripper, she asked, "Is that his sister?" If
the man and woman had been brother and sister,the hero's concern
would have been comprehensible to her, but as they were only
prospective husband and wife (or even had they been married) she could
not perceive any believable motivation for this central dramatic idea of
the script. Among the Bahemba such behavior occurs only between
people who belong to the same patri- or matri-lineage. In our culture,
with its historic roots in the tradition of courtly love, we take for
granted that such behavior can be motivated by romantic love. By contrast, since Bahemba stories frequently include unrealistic, super-natural
occurrences, the element of time travel in the H.G. Wells film did not
puzzle Faila Mwa'a at all (Thomas Blakely, personal communication,
1983).

Ethnographic films, at least the ones which set out to be bridges
between different cultures or subcultures, must consciously deal with
the fact that the "visual surface" is unfamiliar to the intended audience
and has to be explained to some degree before any story lines are developed or any abstract concepts are explored. If not, the unfamiliar visual
material completely distracts attention from the intended text. An example of this difficulty can be seen during North American screenings
of TO FIND THE BARUYA STORY, a film documenting the work of
a French anthropologist in the Eastern Highlands of Papua New
Guinea. The viewers' curiosity about the Baruya people, starting with
the unusual costume of the men, prevents them from concentrating
whole-heartedly on the activities of the anthropologist, who is, after
all, not as eye-catching to a Western viewer as are his informants. Yet
there is no way to film the work of an anthropologist *without* showing
a foreign background unless one makes diagrammatic animated cartoons, or films anthropologists whose field locations are in the Western
world.

This reversal of priorities for dealing with cultural context and
specific script is related to the fact that visual images, with the possible
exception of diagrams, are always specific. Particular people are in a

particular place at a particular time. In writing, a general statement can be made which excludes particulars, and a level of abstraction can be reached which is not possible in the film medium, at least given most present viewers' modes of "reading" film.

3. The "More Behind the Image": In viewing Maring footage with the editor, I soon learned that it was not enough to explain from the point of view of Maring culture (as I understood it) what was "behind" any given image. My explanation had, in addition, to take into account the editor's assumptions about "native cultures," for these assumptions were inevitably triggered when viewing the film. Furthermore, I realized that I had been considering a viewing audience as a *tabula rasa*, openly and eagerly awaiting new information. Most viewers however, have what we might call "instant capsules of comprehension," ways of "reading" film so as to reduce the confusion and uncertainty felt in viewing an unfamiliar scene. Stereotypes about native cultures are used as "capsules of comprehension," for example, "Technological simplicity equals poverty."

Thus, there is "more behind the image" in two respects. On the one hand, there are the detailed explanations of the images from the point of view of the filmed culture. On the other hand, there are the cultural preconceptions of the viewers, which can lead to perceptions having nothing to do with the reality of the filmed culture. One of the audience preconceptions that I felt would skew any informed viewing of the Maring footage was the opinion prevalent in Italy that people with a material culture like the Maring are "poor and backward savages." To the general Italian viewer, the life of agricultural people in New Guinea looks similar in certain respects to the life of Italian peasants, dependent upon heavy manual labor and relegated to the lowest rung of the social hierarchy. Reasoning within this framework, viewers assume that the Maring are also on the lowest rung of a social hierarchy and are in consequent need of help and/or progress. A variant of this preconception was: "Buildings made of wood show a lower level of cultural development than stone buildings, since stone has been used to produce the finest examples of architecture." This was the statement of a person born and bred in a Mediterranean environment and I rather doubted that it would have occurred to anyone from northern climes where wood is the superior material and has been used to build magnificent religious structures. To replace the ubiquitous comparisons with "superior Western ways," I wanted to provide a fresh context showing that simplicity, functionality, and harmony with the environment are qualities to be considered in their own right.

Another stereotype I wanted to unsettle was the way people think of the ground. For many Westerners, sitting on the ground or working at ground level are considered uncouth. Such images evoke feelings of being dirty. The Maring are immediately fitted into this stereotype: it is "obvious" that "such simple native people" would sit on the ground. For example, it took the editor many viewings to notice, in a scene of mixing pandanus fruit, that the mixing took place not on the bare earth, but on a leaf. We had shot this scene after long acquaintance with the Maring, never thinking of the misperception we were fostering by not framing the image with sufficient emphasis on the leaf. Our viewers' preconceptions were blinding them to its actual visible presence. During the editing we had to make up for such shooting oversights. Sometimes our rough and ready camera angles had not mitigated impressions of the ground being "lowly." For example, we were in doubt whether to keep a sequence of a mother napping on the ground with her baby playing over her because of the possible associations with "starving beggars lying in the streets in India." The Maring are, in fact, extremely conscious about "dirt," and, though the ground is their "chair and table," they never put their food directly on it and they take extreme care to wipe any unwanted soil off their skins.

A further example of "seeing through the eyes of one's own culture" was the editor's perception of Arum. Arum was a five-year old girl who appeared in a long sequence of a family eating an evening meal. After viewing the entire sequence, the editor decided to incorporate it into one of the episodes. He was enthusiastic about the scene "because Arum is so lively..." Later, after several hours of editing the scene, I was amazed to discover that the editor had been thinking all along that Arum was a boy. I had neglected to explain what was so self-evident to me: girls wear fringed loincloths and boys wear woven ones or none at all if they are as young as Arum. When I said that "he" was a girl, the editor was in turn amazed, insisting that she was much too lively to be a girl, because "girls are calm." I took this opportunity to explain to him the learning of gender-specific behavior: Italian girls are calm because they have *learned* that calmness is appropriate and not because they *are* girls. Would we be able to get that vital point across to the audience?

4. Rhythm: After a week of intensive viewing and cutting, the editor verbalized the major problem he was having in cutting our footage: the Maring would begin an interesting movement or activity, but before it became fully clear or was completed, they would pause, sometimes for minutes on end, before resuming that action or starting another one. It was this characteristic of Maring behavior that had made shooting very difficult for us. That the editor perceived this characteristic unaided, simply from viewing the uncut footage, was an example of the value of research footage as a tool for studying non-verbal characteristics of behavior.

But the question was "How many viewers would be able to see this sort of thing in the footage?" Few people consciously know how to "look," and I myself had originally became aware of this particular characteristic through live interaction. Film editors, as a group, are probably more able than anthropologists to see such rhythmic characteristics in footage, since, in order to make any kind of appropriate-looking cuts, they must depend on their ability to perceive the physical basis of action visually. Our editor, although able to *see* this characteristic of Maring action in the footage, was loathe to include it in the edited film. We had to work with the reality that a viewing public which has half an hour a week to watch a film from another culture will not be able to understand that culture as fully as an editor who can look at the footage for eight hours a day for several weeks. The editor, in turn, will not be able to understand as much as the anthropologist who lived immersed in the other culture for a year or more.

The editor's working assumption was that montage must be lively: the only reason to let a sequence run on longer than indicated by "correct rhythm" would not be to let Maring rhythm unfold, but to give time for a commentary. But at this early stage we had no text yet for two reasons: (a) We could not compose a definitive commentary until we were certain what scenes were visually usable; (b) the writer had to compose the Italian text and would do it after the editing was complete. Knowing the richness of accompanying information, I knew that no matter how long a scene was, I could compose an effective text, so I kept pressing for slower paced editing. Nevertheless, in some episodes such small portions of original scenes were used that the film began to strike me as a series of snapshots. The stretches of uninterrupted activity had been consistently made shorter, thereby violating whatever had been captured in the original footage of Maring rhythms of life and movement. These rhythms consist not only of the dramatic, swiftly moving highlights, but depend also on how these highlights are embedded in a larger movement context of sustained action, desultory attention, relaxation, interruption, etc. Human behavior takes place in an "observable time grid" and can be examined in terms of this grid, just as it can be examined from the point of view of the symbolic content of the visible behavior. It was the capacity of film to capture "observable time" that I wished to use to allow people of another culture to learn about the Maring. I wondered whether viewers would accept the discomfort of watching film with a different rhythm than they were used to, aware that their discomfort was due to cultural differences, rather than poor editing. This would be a pervasive, if undramatic, way of creating culture shock with film.

I hoped to bring this cultural perspective to the editor's skills so we could explore the middle ground between the research assumption that footage is a tool with which to pay attention to "what is going on" and the assumption that film must be "exciting" in order to catch the

viewer's attention. Both in the shooting and the viewing of research
footage one learns to find "drama" in what might seem to be very minor sorts of events, perhaps because more overt drama is rather scarce in
daily life. The drama in daily events may sometimes lie behind the visible surface, and to see it, one must know the significance for which
the visible scene is just a marker. But how could the editor, only barely
familiar with Maring life, know the significance or the drama in any
shot? I began to suspect that many of the sequences he omitted were
discarded not because of technical or rhythmic imperfections, but simply because they meant nothing to him.

5. Cultural Scripts and Cross-cultural Invisibility: As a filmmaker in the
   field, I had encountered more often than I would have wished what I
   called "locational invisibility." The action would be going on behind
   something, or there would be hardly any light, or the action would
   move out of range. Now, at the other end of the filming process, I was
   confronting what could be called "cross-cultural invisibility." I had to
   come to grips with the fact that if something is "not visible," for
   whatever reason, then a film sequence quickly becomes boring. There
   are very few people, of whatever profession, that are natural "sleuths of
   looking." Cross-cultural invisibility can be just as effective as locational invisibility in leading viewers to conclude that "there is nothing
   worth watching." At that point they cease to look.
       At the beginning of the selection process the editor often said, "It's
   too long, nothing is happening." This impression is based on a
   particular cultural experience of the world. Within each culture, as well
   as individually for each person, only certain scripts are perceived. If a
   sequence triggers such a script in a viewer's awareness (thought and
   emotion), then the viewer's attention is caught and the sequence becomes both visible and interesting. People's minds are filled with such
   scripts, programmed by participating in culturally patterned interactions
   among culturally defined actors in culturally recognizable settings. Especially in our literate and media-rich culture, awareness is further programmed by countless repeats of standard scripts in books, films, television, etc. Our ability to take in something through our eyes is so
   strongly affected by these scripts that we may have difficulty actually
   seeing the space-time framework of an event. We tend to look at this
   framework last, if at all, and at the "meaningful content" (as defined by
   an often unconscious script) first.
       In shooting research footage, we had specifically paid attention to
   the space-time framework, so that viewers could see from the film document the way Maring behavior is coordinated within this framework.
   Could we catch the interest of a general audience at this level? The culturally programmed scripts expected in daily action or in media presentations catch our interest and involve us emotionally, connecting us to

an event so that it jumps out of invisibility and we are able to "see" it. What I "see" when looking at a film is very often a story or variations thereof which is already in my head.

For me, as a cameraman/anthropologist having shot footage at my own field location, a related problem arises: since I know the lay of the land and am acquainted with all the subjects, I "see" the footage not solely in terms of the images on the screen, but also in terms of the wider context that is already part of my knowledge. I see a simultaneous blend of images coming in from the film and the images already "in my mind's eye" from my experience on location. If I proceed to edit the footage myself, there is a great danger that I will take the larger context for granted. The resulting film will trigger a story in my head but will not communicate this story to the viewers who were not present at the filming location. The visual images in the film can't possibly be triggers to a story they don't have in their heads to begin with. It is difficult for researchers who have been present during shooting to perceive the footage as if they had no information about the 360° space within which the filmed scene was embedded. This may be a danger of editing footage one has shot oneself.

There will also be parts of the visible scene, which, because of other scripts in my head, I will ignore. An amusing example of this is a scene of a family returning to their yard carrying many items. The writer asked, "What's *that?*" I replied, "A bamboo tube containing feathers." He answered, "No, no, not *that!* That *bag.* What's the young man doing with an airline bag? Where did he get it?" Here was an example of my systematic avoidance of seeing introduced European items in the scene. I had taken the bag for granted and suppressed it, at the same time "knowing" (though I never specifically inquired) that he got it when he was working on the coast. The QANTAS bag is, in fact, what any "normal" Western viewer notices first in that scene, and it must be explained in order to free the viewer to notice the more traditional Maring details.

6. Repetitiveness: It had been our feeling when shooting in the field that nothing ever repeated itself and any opportunity we somehow bungled was lost forever. Looking at the footage with a view to editing, we found this perception had been only partly true. The editor perceived unbelievable numbers of repetitions, and pressed them into his service. Each repetition presented an opportunity to cut and shorten the action, presumably without "breaking the rhythm." This raised several questions in my mind. Are there two orders of "repetitiveness" in events, one which the editor was looking at and one which I was looking at, so that we were not actually talking about the same thing? Or were we looking at the same thing with totally different perceptions? Only a detailed analysis of the original footage could answer such questions. Us-

ing repetitions, the editor could omit mid-sections and return to an action at a "repeat point" further along. In this way he discarded masses of good quality footage as "too repetitive," insisting that viewers got bored fast if they had to see "the same thing" twice. As I encouraged him to leave in long sequences of interaction, he would reply, "It's too repetitive." One day he expanded, "It may seem to the audience that we keep showing the same thing and the same people over and over again. They may even think we are showing them the same footage. To counteract this danger, we must mention that there are only 80 people and they all take part in village life. Their lives consist of gardening, hunting, cooking, and dancing. There isn't very much variety."

This notion was puzzling to me, and I really didn't understand what he was getting at. I wondered whether it was based on some sort of general assumption that Western culture is richly varied, in contrast to "simple native cultures," or whether there was an implicit expectation that documentary films should glide over the most varied surfaces of a foreign culture. The more *I* thought about it, the more it seemed to me that films and TV series of our own culture make us look at the same things again and again: the same scripts, the same actors, the same sets...Clearly this was another kind of "ethno-centricity of looking," operating in the editor's mind, and it would have to be taken into account as one of the formative elements of the film. The editor was not able to distinguish small variations in the behavior of people from another culture (an "all Chinese look the same" syndrome), although he was highly attuned to slight variations of Western behavior in essentially repetitive scripts. This was not just a case of "stubbornness" in adhering to TV norms, but was yet another example of cross-cultural blindness.

What I couldn't understand was how viewers were ever going to be able to learn about the unfamiliar culture of the Maring if they were never given the chance to see anything more than once. From my own experience in the field, I knew that by seeing a scene once, one can do no more than understand it in terms of the "already familiar" of one's own life and culture. Making films for viewing within one's own culture, one counts on a kind of instant understanding. One cannot count on such instant understanding in making cross-cultural films. I began to envision a film which would be full of "repetitions," a way of creating time for viewers to begin to understand the scene from the point of view of the filmed culture. This kind of film would play with repetition as poetry does, and would create an opportunity for what I would call "haptic" learning, learning by bodily identification.

7. Some Advantages of Editing: The editor's job was made particularly difficult by the way our footage had been shot. Our research shooting and viewing guidelines were entirely different from the guidelines of most

cameramen. We were attempting to record visible behavior, rather than to construct a preconceived story, so we had been "shooting to record" rather than "shooting to cut." Because our footage was part of a fuller, written documentation and because we were already so used to the Maring scene, we took much of the visible environment for granted and focused on activities rather than on actors. Our resulting footage has more images of hands and feet than faces, and catches only in passing such ubiquitous elements of the scene as pigs and their feeding, the making of string bags, and the carrying of toddlers.

We had shot two kinds of footage using the two cameras at our disposal: an Arriflex-BL and a reflex Bolex. Arriflex footage had been shot from a tripod and consisted of relatively long, stationary takes. This footage tended to be cold and distant, recording wide scenes, but rarely affording detailed shots which could be used as cut-aways. Bolex footage, on the other hand, had usually been shot hand-held. It consisted of relatively short close-ups, and it tended to be intimate and lively, but usually failed to record the wider scene. The editor preferred this more eye-appealing Bolex footage, although some of the best sequences were broken by flash frames caused by a faulty battery contact and, consequently, had to be "patched" with cutaways. Although we had planned to intercut the Arriflex and Bolex footage, the editor found it difficult to create a unified impression from two such different styles of filming.

Seeing the editor at work with these challenges, I learned some of the advantages of editing. First, editing can improve the ease of viewing, and increase the access to visible information by lessening the confusion created by the cut-up nature of footage which was not filmed continuously. During the actual shooting of an on-going event, a cameraman does his best to follow smoothly, but there are always unexpected vagaries in the action. The footage, as shot, may need a great deal of clarifying, so a viewer will not misinterpret it or simply remain confused.

One of the reasons montage developed was the necessity of constructing an intelligible continuity from all the short shots that were the inevitable result of technical limitations in the early years of filmmaking. In recent years (with the availability of longer-lasting batteries and larger rolls of film) a new style of shooting, characterized by long-uninterrupted takes, has become possible. In 1968 we were at the early stages of shooting long takes with the Arriflex. New styles of editing are developing on the basis of these long takes, however, it seems that it is hard for viewers foreign to the scene to concentrate for a long enough time to really take advantage of this technical improvement. Uninterrupted footage, though interesting for a researcher, may appear as endless meaningless detail to a general viewer.

Another advantage of editing is that activities in very dense or fast-moving events can be "stretched" to allow viewers to see them better.

Some action is so fast on the original footage that there is not even time for commentary. The editor can split parts of such action with cutaways, making the scene long enough for needed explanation in the sound track. Conversely, a "visual summary" can be "condensed" from several diverse, longer events.

8. Verisimilitude: Throughout the editing process, I was the only one present who could "represent" the Maring, and I began by fiercely sticking to "authenticity." Bit by bit, however, I understood that compromises were necessary, not just to humor the media world, but in order to create an overall impression in the mind of the viewer which would be as authentic as possible.

I find it helpful to call this "constructed authenticity" by the term verisimilitude. This was the point Margaret Mead made at the Margaret Mead Film Festival in 1979 when she spoke of the difference between "facts" and "truth." The best example of this in the Maring series is showing an airstrip in the Eastern Highlands to represent the airstrip at Simbai. We had simply neglected to film the Simbai airstrip, and it made more sense to have some New Guinea Highlands airstrip for people to see, rather than none at all. Should the film ever be shown in New Guinea, this construct would soon be noticed.

As cutting modified the original footage, I weighed many of the on-going decisions which I had to make against what I thought our Maring friends might say. On one side of this cross-cultural bridge would be Maring responses, especially instant reactions like "That's not the way we would have done it!" On the other side would be the responses of European viewers indicating either understanding or misunderstanding.

9. Sound: I felt that my ability to control authenticity and verisimilitude was weaker with sound than with image. There were several reasons why we could not always use synch sound in the editing. First of all, the lively footage shot in 1963 and 1964 had all been silent, but the completed film could not be presented silent to a TV audience. Secondly, in many cases where we had shot synch sound, the combination of Maring patterns of conversation with my recording technique had actually resulted in portions of sound track that seemed to bear little relationship to the visual images: the camera had been focused on one set of people in a large yard, while the mike was picking up lively conversation from another set beyond the camera's range.

Since my research intention was to document the "total sound pattern" of an interacting group, we had methodological reasons for not coming in close with camera and mike for lip-synch sequences of individual people. But the "total sound pattern" includes things which virtually never appear on the screen: crying children, peeping chicks, men chopping wood, outbursts of anger or laughter.... The sound track and the visual track of some events seem to represent two different worlds. The sound track is the more inclusive of the two. On the tapes many clearly perceptible planes of sound can be heard: the closest, the middle, the distant, and the very distant. These different planes occasionally overlap because of the Maring style of sudden vocal outbursts. However, we created a paradox for ourselves by thoughtlessly combining such a multi-depth synchronous soundtrack with footage which focused on a middle- or long-distance view of the situation. The occasional visual close-ups were a result of zooming in to a distant detail, creating "close up shots" which were not, however, close to the microphone. The synchronous sound footage we created is in accord with the multi-dimensionality of the actual event, but the sound and image do not combine neatly in editing a film of the event.

In editing, therefore, sound track had to be created both for the originally silent scenes and for the many scenes in which the synch sound bore too vague a relationship to the image. Because most of my recording had concentrated on conversational situations, I had almost no authentic sound for garden scenes and scenes outside of village yards. The writer went to a sound library and found an effects track of birds. Though I'm neither a bird-watcher nor a bird-listener, these birds had a distinctly non-Maring sound to my ears. I christened the track "English countryside in the morning," and was considerably astonished to hear these melodious tones over the Maring scenes, the more so since the writer had laid in the track during the final mix without consulting me. There was no way I could get those birds off again, short of missing the broadcast deadline. For future episodes I made it clear that I did not want to use this birdsong track any more, even though the editor tried to assure me that they were tropical birds. I replied that they weren't the sort of birds that sing around Gunts, and particularly not at that time of day. However, I realized my own shortcoming in paying so little attention to the sound environment of the Maring and thought with pleasure of Steven Feld's contribution in this domain (Feld 1982). We would not have had to resort to such wildly diverse sound tracks had I been more technically aware and sound-conscious during the field recordings. Creating a good wild sound library for various spaces, times of day, and activities is a crucial part of field filming.

I learned a great deal about how effectively wild sound can be used. The use of wild sound is a forte of the Italian film industry. They customarily do not shoot on location with synch sound, but always create the sound track later. They claim this gives the sound a perfection which can never be attained in the field, and they rate such technical perfection higher than authenticity.

To achieve verisimilitude in the sound track, I found that the editor had to examine as much synchronous sound footage as possible before beginning his constructions. Having gotten the feeling of a given Maring sound environment, he could proceed visually, and then, at the end, lay in a reasonable sound track. But this procedure did not always work. There are some Maring activities in which the coordination of sound and movement is so totally different from anything in our own culture, that there is no way of constructing verisimilitude. The only solution is to stick with the authentic synchronous sound. A good example is the courting dance. The editor started by cutting the scene visually with no reference to sound. He then laid in the on-going sound of singing. This made the dance look totally nonsensical. Trying to doctor it up according to "what looked right" led nowhere; we simply had no feel for how this dance actually fits with its music. We finally had to put the cut-up film back together in chronological order and lay in the synch sound. Then we could see that the dancers move almost twice as fast as the song rhythm, giving us the impression of two loosely-related strands of activity. At the beginning of the dance there are 2 or 3 or 4 sways per long syllable. Later, when the dancers start rolling their heads together, the movement phrases become longer and tend to synchronize with the song phrases. Even so, the couple at the far left often does two turns to the next couple's one. It became abundantly clear that constructing a sound match for this activity is something no non-Maring editor could possibly achieve, so that using the actual synchronous sound was the only possible solution for us.

The more one works with uncut synch-sound footage, the more skeptical one becomes of edited films as material for behavioral research. No researcher should begin before receiving a complete description of the processes leading to the film in consideration. No matter how "authentic" a piece of behavior on film appears, it can easily be several steps removed from a straight-forward record of the actual behavior.

So far, I have been discussing the sound on the effects track. This is the sound that gives the scene a three-dimensional quality and introduces the viewers to the sound atmosphere of the scenes filmed, hopefully adding the sound qualities of the culture to the visual rhythms of movement and interaction. There are rarely any comprehensible words in the effects track, but it provides a rhythm which affects the perception of all the moving images.

10. Commentary: There is a second sound track which is of equal importance, the commentary. Its overt functions are different from the effects tracks, but the factor of rhythm affecting viewers' perceptions of the moving images is the same. The commentary, however, is far from being a background. In fact, certain kinds of commentary tend to cancel out visual comprehension: the viewers hear the words while the images pass virtually unnoticed. In Italy, documentary films are customarily

edited after a commentary has been written. They may even be shot using a rough draft of the commentary as a shooting script. This is impossible when shooting research footage, which follows the flow of ongoing behavior. In this case, the commentary must be tailored to the available footage. One seeks a balance between the length of commentary and the length of images. The images are always longer. How much longer depends upon the familiarity of the audience with the subject matter. The commentary for a film of a foreign culture must always take into account the viewer's need for explanation and context. Yet, there must also be enough time for viewers to take in the scene visually with no verbal component. Silences, in turn, must not be so long that viewers will become bored or confused.

The editor, fearing that there wouldn't be enough commentary, consistently cut scenes shorter than I wished. I knew there was enough material to make as long a commentary as necessary. I also wanted scenes to be left as long as possible so the viewers could pick up Maring rhythms. However, most of the cutting was done with the visual images alone, and the action seemed to move much more slowly in silence than with the sound track. The editor, therefore, lacking the extensive dialogue in my mind which would eventually be developed into commentary, tended to cut scenes short. Since our work proceeded from a general idea through visual version to written commentary, and the commentary was never composed until the scenes were already cut, I had to lay a restraining hand on the editor's cutting rhythm. Only animated diagrams were designed and shot with the exact commentary and timing known in advance.

An editor deals primarily with footage at a visual, non-verbal level, working with the images physically: shortening, lengthening, re-ordering. A writer works at a verbal level, supplying the commentary which operates in a variety of ways on the image: explaining, calling attention to, linking concrete with abstract. In this Maring project, it was the editor's job to create the montage, the writer's job to create the overall form and accompanying Italian commentary, and the anthropologist's job to communicate the cultural information necessary. The editor and the anthropologist worked together daily. The writer spent less time with the project, viewing the footage at the beginning and making some basic selections, then viewing completed sequences when they were ready for the commentary. Nevertheless, he came up with a number of inspirations from this blend of research footage content and mass media TV form. He thought of beginning the episode on ritual by playing with the "sensational movie image" of Maring dance, and then pulling the image back to its anthropological context. He conceived of the final visual summary at the end of the series. He also imagined the electronic transformation of Maring music into a unifying musical track for the whole series, and commissioned a well-known composer to thus "acculturate" Maring sounds by passing them through a synthesizer. When he first presented this possibility I was highly dubious, feeling that all sense of authenticity was going out the window. But as I began to see so much authenticity being changed, hopefully to "verisimilitude" rather than to plain distortion, the idea of "Maring electronic music" began to intrigue me. I finally gave my consent, thinking that the Maring themselves would be pleased to see their music accorded the same "respect" as Western music rather than being treated as a museum piece. I thought they would appreciate this opportunity for their own music to "go modern."

I was delighted at the way the writer's mind played with the material available and came up with units which European viewers could easily follow at the fast pace of TV. My thinking tended to be pedantic and academic, staying close to the concrete events as I saw them happen, and his ability to synthesize the whole into concise, general statements was absolutely necessary to the project. My husband and I wrote eight to ten pages of background and explanations for each edited episode and my husband translated it verbatim into straight-forward, grammatical Italian for the writer, but we soon saw that he found these more of a burden than a help. He preferred to work directly viewing the picture while I gave a rough and ready Italian explanation of the main ideas I wanted to express in any given scene. Often I would tell him everything of interest that I could see in each shot and then he would synthesize the details into a general statement which could link to a Western audience. This system sometimes resulted in very poetic commentaries, which followed the images but introduced little of the structure that had been in our minds as we constructed the episode. The discrepancy sprang from the disjunction between the flowery Italian literary style, which has been thoroughly programmed into virtually every Italian who has been through high school and university, and our straight-forward, factual presentation of an idea with the minimal number of words. We had to content ourselves with the knowledge that language is not just a matter of content but very much a matter of a culturally-appropriate form. Much as the flowery literary style of Italian irked me, I couldn't help but wonder whether Maring oratory might not be better mirrored by this Italian style than by a dry American statement.

Professional Differences in Work Style and Approach

1. Shared Codes: In my work with research footage, I had found that shared numerical codes are an indispensable tool enabling several people to coordinate activities and information with a high degree of exactitude. In this project there were codes which could link the work of editor to

anthropologist, editor to laboratory, anthropologist to animator, animator to writer, etc. As the project unfolded, I began to notice a systematic non-use of such codes. The editor did not use the chronological numbers of the original film rolls, the basic means of identification I had used as a researcher. Nor did he use edge-numbers, the basic technical identification needed by the laboratory for later printing. The lab technician complained of this lack, but nevertheless completed the job. His ability to deal with the situation as it had developed was, for me, an example of the Italian genius for improvisation. The editor relied on his memory to locate images, rather than relying on references to roll- or edge-numbers. This ability no doubt makes possible fast and inspired synthesizing of vast numbers of images, but shared forms of identification and location of images are equally important when work involves more than one person.

The animator, on the other hand, worked with precise lists of split-second timing so that the diagrams he created would coordinate exactly with the text. I also used these lists to coordinate the English commentary with the diagrams. The writer, however, ignored this exact timing in composing the Italian commentary for the diagrams. This resulted in a presentation which, to my mind, was often haphazard. His reasoning escaped my understanding. The most curious thing to me was that the non-use of shared codes did not seem to bother anyone involved in the project but myself.

2. "Haptic" versus "Disembodied" Film: As a movement-trained anthropologist I had frequently looked at footage as a series of visual cues for bodily movement, cues for a kinesthetic experience which was much more comprehensive than the visual impression alone. Since, in my research, film had not been simply a set of visual cues for instantaneous mental operations, I had never before realized what an exclusively visual medium film can be. The constant striving of the editor and writer for variation, for non-repetition, for a lively cutting rhythm, and for an ever-changing sound background created an experience for viewers which made "bodily" or "haptic" communication with the subjects extremely difficult for them. The fact that haptic identification is nevertheless a strong element in viewing became clear to me when I finally had a chance to be present at screenings. The scenes which called forth the most intense and immediate reactions from viewers were indeed those involved with bodily sensations, for example, a boys' mud-game and the hand-mixing of pandanus fruit. These activities contrasted with what Western viewers have been programmed to feel is acceptable. Other body movement patterns involving activities unmarked by a conflict with Western expectations were generally overlooked in the swift onrush of changing images, even though they were just as characteristic of Maring behavior.

3. Feedback: Work organization involved minimal provision for feedback. Many solutions for problems were improvised instantaneously, and were put into effect without trial. Given our production schedule, there was no time to look at solutions "in draft form" and decide whether or not to use them. We had at our disposal only four days to edit and to write the commentary for each of the last two episodes. This gave us no possibility to polish or to adjust image to commentary. The process, totally eliminating the constant checking and rechecking which is characteristic of research projects, became entirely linear. Had I not stayed physically present throughout as many stages of production as possible to correct misinterpretations, the on-going process would have incorporated even more flaws into each finished episode.

No time was provided for looking at any episode from a conceptual point of view before broadcast deadline. If an episode flowed by reasonably smoothly as an aesthetic surface, it was accepted. I had hoped for a relationship between words and images which was not limited to verbal description of what was already plainly visible, but which combined on-going explanation with specific ideas which could enhance what one saw at particular moments. Since my commentary had tight time strictures, I wanted to check each episode as a completed whole to be sure that nothing had been omitted or misplaced. The writer/director, however, did not provide for such a final check as part of the production process. He was apparently satisfied to perform this checking process in his mind, trusting his imagination to unify the joint effect of images and commentaries, plus the video-taped interviews which were to be made still later. Or perhaps he simply trusted that the linear production process would satisfactorily fill 24-27 minutes of viewing time, even if some of the results were not totally predictable. In contrast to the "holistic" style I had expected, I would call this working style "linear." I couldn't guess whether the stylistic difference between me and the writer was professional or cultural, however, taking such differences into account will greatly improve our understanding of similar collaborative projects.

The Audience

Having explored some of the aspects of the production of a TV film and the interface between anthropological and media considerations, I now wish to consider briefly the audience. The viewing public cannot be considered as a massive indeterminate group. There are many degrees of interest among different segments of the public. Some people may never want to look at film about life in another culture unless it is wrapped in an easily recognizable package. Others may welcome the opportunity to look at something which "really happened" somewhere on our planet, and will not need slick TV packaging with its perfect, grainless image and lively cutting. They are more interested in content than form. There is no one recipe.

At the present time it is the standards of the film professionals which seem to have the overriding effect on actual productions. I do not know how RAI-TV makes final programming decisions, however, some of their decisions are based on audience research. One of their surveys works with 9,000 typical families, who are rewarded with consumer goods for filling out a daily report on how they liked the programs they saw. Since documentaries and educational films are usually shown at hours when most working adults are not at home, their reports of preference can cover only a narrow portion of the actual range of programming. A polling system of this nature could lead to a reduction in the range of programming. I would like to know whether any networks utilize polling methods which would extend to the viewing public the courtesy of finding out preferences over the whole range of programming, let alone interest in potential kinds of programs that haven't yet been tried.

My knowledge about audience reaction for the Maring series comes from three sources: what I heard from film professionals; being present during screenings arranged by us; and reports of acquaintances who had seen some or all of the episodes. This latter feedback was as random as the feedback from polls is predictable. Naturally it was skewed by the fact that only people who knew us told us their reactions, and most were too general to be of much use (e.g., "It is very interesting"). The barber in the small town where we live was a most avid viewer because he had spent some years in the South Pacific. A retired journalist from Norway who tuned in from the Italian part of Switzerland had one of the most illuminating comments. She commended us for the excellent use of music in the series. Her view was that the synthesized Maring music created a familiar bridge for viewers between their own culture and the "visual foreignness" of Maring culture.

Filmmakers' efforts to create films which a large viewing public will like may be offset by such factors as scheduling by the network. If a film is broadcast only once, and at an off-hour, the audience will be small, and somewhat unrepresentative of the millions of potential viewers. Our series was part of the RAI Educational Program which was always broadcast every Wednesday at 1:30 p.m. At this time, high school students, presumably an important segment of the audience, are actually in the streets on their way home for lunch. It did not seem to be the most well-chosen time for an educational program. The series was rebroadcast during the summer of 1982. As we were then out of the country, we do not know whether it was scheduled at a time more convenient for interested viewers.

I had expected to receive some feedback from RAI, an evaluation from their point of view of how the series turned out and how it was received. Looking back, I now realize that this expectation was unrealistic. Nevertheless, I believe that feedback is an essential part of the development of our field. In the future, if I am not convinced that there would be an appreciable audience for a film, I may not be willing to invest my thinking, energy or available funding on a similar project for three months. In the present situation of media abundance, I was left with the feeling that our project had been swallowed in a vast, anonymous sea.

Wanting to compensate for the lack of feedback from RAI, we decided to use video-cassette copies of the series for showings in our local town (pop. 3,000). The first evening, during which we showed the first two episodes, was attended by seventeen people, four of whom had seen some of the episodes previously and now wanted to see the whole series. The audience consisted of several university students, a number of young working people, a married couple, and three elderly peasants. Reactions were in the form of questions and comments while the film was being shown, and questions and discussion afterwards. There were the predictable questions about our personal experiences: how long we stayed, what we ate, whether we felt safe, etc. Then there were questions about Maring environment, family structure, politics, social organization, religion, and recent progress. These were all subjects which had not been covered in the first two episodes as they were treated in later episodes.

The most interesting observation that emerged for me during the evening was the contrast between the peasants and the university students. The university students immediately plunged into intellectual questions of a highly abstract nature. The film provided them with conceptual material for wrestling with the difference between natural history observation and the Marxist research models which they were offered at the university. The peasants, on the other hand, reacted to such tangible images as nettle treatment, pig castration, cooperative house-building, and the distribution of spoonsful of salt and matchboxes. They murmured that their own life was much the same only fifty years ago, when there was no money, and people made their own slippers and spun their own wool. They had lived simply and worked hard. "Now our children say we were stupid to have stayed under the land owners. They say we should have been independent like they are now, going out to work for themselves. But there were no jobs then and the landlords weren't rich either." Basing their perceptions on their own life experiences, the peasants accepted the Marings' life of almost complete self-sufficiency, seeing nothing stupid about it. The students, on a different track altogether, experienced our observational approach as an alternative view to the one offered by some of their professors, one more appealing to their non-Marxist bent. It became clear that members of the audience identified with the film in terms of their personal life and concerns. Such a range of reactions would be unlikely in a more homogeneous audience, such as an anthropology class, where viewers are expected to share a particular focus.

The TV public, far from being an anonymous sea of homogeneous viewers seeking only fleeting entertainment, is made up of many diverse groups. Now that cable TV has started and video-cassettes can be purchased, new parameters reflecting the actual audience diversity will come into being. People will not have to depend upon the scheduling of networks, but will themselves select the viewing time and the subject matter. Ethnographic films will hopefully more easily reach the people who most want to see them and slick packaging may no longer be necessary. The use of less expensive techniques may then lead to a more even balance between the time, energy, and resources necessary for the production of a film and the actual use of the film by a reasonable number of viewers. What a "reasonable number" would be is, of course, a matter of individual judgement. But when film projects must be supported after being made, by actual sales, rather than beforehand by grants, a serious consideration of what such a balance might be is definitely encouraged. In the case of this Maring project, 33,000,000 Italian lire (equivalent then to U.S. $40,000) were spent over and above the initial travel and production expenses in New Guinea. This cost was partly the result of making internegatives so the original footage could remain intact. Various laboratory fees, animation, video-taping of interviews, and a nominal payment to the editor were all covered. No money, however, was left to pay the writer or anthropologist for their time.

At present I see three problems hindering the development of anthropological filmmaking. The first is the high cost of production. The second is the difficulty which interested viewers have in actually locating and seeing existing films. The third is the small number of anthropologists who actually take seriously this challenging field of producing cross-cultural films.

Conclusions

My reservations about the "film industry" were not unfounded. The differences between research footage and film for a general audience were greater and more recalcitrant than I had imagined. I learned that the only way to deal with these differences was not by staying as far as possible from confrontation with film professionals, but by actually going through an apprenticeship and seeing clearly what the differences are and why they exist. Seeing, understanding, and maneuvering these differences is not easy at the fast clip of usual professional production. A great deal of more patient collaboration will be needed to achieve the kind of interface between cultures that I feel TV is capable of.

I became acutely aware of the fact that, as an academic, I had assumed that I could learn about anything by reading about it. Long ago I thought that being told "how to film" would be all that I would need in order to produce a satisfactory film. But film, whether used for research or for viewing by a general public, is a complex medium. If we come from an academic background, we are not trained in its use to the extent that we are trained in the medium of words. Instead, we are taught to move "quickly and efficiently" from the realm of observation to the realm of words. These words are simply markers of the mental constructs with which we work. We are hardly taught to work with images or to broaden our ability to observe. My initial assumption about being able to "kill two birds with one stone," by shooting one set of footage for both research and public viewing, proved faulty. A number of stones may be necessary to kill one bird. Our T.V. series leaned heavily on the didactic as a means to escape exoticism. But I think it is time to explore strategies for escaping exoticism using less pedantic means. For the most effective cross-cultural communication, imaginative new formats will have to be conceived to create films for the general public. Footage will have to be shot with these new formats clearly in mind, and research footage incorporated only in particular well-defined cases.

In films shaped by the understandings of anthropology, not only will the visual and verbal content deal with culture but the film construction itself will support and enhance the views presented. At one level, this congruence is always present in spite of ourselves. A canny viewer of the Maring series may see and hear all the elements of cross-cultural interaction that I have been reporting. By looking at film as a multi-media event and examining in detail the various strands, the message of the film becomes clear in a way which is impossible if attention is given to content alone. Few anthropologists are used to working with films within such an inclusive framework. Fewer still are able to handle the various components consciously and deliberately, at the level of practice, in order to create films in which the congruence between form and content are consistently visible.

This multi-stranded realm is too complex to be learned by analysis and discussion alone. We cannot draw up a "scientific procedure" which can serve as a framework for creating any given new film. Though anthropology is an intellectual pursuit, many other strands are basic to its inspired practice, both in written anthropology and especially in film anthropology. The actual film production process requires multitudinous and sensitive reactions to a complex whole, the final synthesis coming from both anthropologists and filmmakers as whole human beings. The role of the creative human being, already familiar in anthropology, and essential for the fieldwork experience, is crucial in making anthropological films. As challenging as it may be for the anthropologist to create a verbal synthesis of the field experience, it is all the more challenging to create a multi-media synthesis.

Only as we move beyond our competence with words and mental constructs, will fully competent, anthropologically valid films for general audiences become a vital means for anthropologists to communicate their best thinking. To reach this goal we shall need to incorporate into the time and scope of our training and research, new ways to explore the larger realm where our mental constructs interweave with those of other audiences, and where our words interweave with sounds and images.

REFERENCES CITED

Bateson, G. and Mead, M. (1977). On the Use of the Camera in Anthropology. Studies in the Anthropology of Visual Communication 4(22):78-79.

Birdwhistell, Ray L. (1970). Kinesics and Context. Philadelphia: University of Pennsylvania Press.

Byers, Paul (1966). Cameras Don't Take Pictures. Columbia University Forum 9(1):27.

Byers, Paul (1972). From Biological Rhythm to Cultural Pattern: A Study of Minimal Units. Columbia University, Ph.D. Dissertation.

Feld, Steven (1982). Sound and Sentiment: Birds, Weeping, Poetics, and Song in Kaluli Expression. Philadelphia: University of Pennsylvania Press.

Hall, Edward T. (1977). Beyond Culture. Garden City, N.Y.: Anchor Press/Doubleday.

Jablonko, A. (1967). Ethnographic Film as a Basic Data for Research. VII-me Congres International des sciences anthropologiques et ethnologiques. Moscou (3 aout - 10 aout 1964). Moscow: Izdatelstvo "Nauka": pp. 168-173.

Jablonko, A. (1968). Dance and Daily Activities Among the Maring People of New Guinea: A Cinematographic Analysis of Movement Style. Doctoral Dissertation, Columbia University.

Ruby, Jay (1978). Seeing the Native through the Eyes of the Anthropologist: Reflexivity, Anthropology, and Film. A paper submitted to the Commission on Visual Anthropology, International Union for Anthropological and Ethnological Sciences, New Delhi.

Scheflen, A.E. (1973). Communicational Structure: Analysis of a Psychotherapy Transaction. Bloomington: Indiana University Press.

Sorenson, E.R. (1967). A Research Film Program in the Study of Changing Man. Current Anthropology 8:443-469.

Sorenson, E.R., D.C. Gajdusek (1966). The Study of Child Behavior and Development in Primitive Cultures: A Research Archive for Ethnopediatric Film Investigations of Styles in the Patterning of the Nervous System. Supplement to PEDIATRICS 37(1, Part 2):149-243.

Sorenson, E.R., A. Jablonko (1975). Research Filming of Naturally Occurring Phenomena, IN Principles of Visual Anthropology, Paul Hockings (ed.), The Hague: Mouton, pp. 151-163.

THE MAJOR FILMS OF ALLISON JABLONKO

KEREPE'S HOUSE: A HOUSEBUILDING IN NEW GUINEA (1967). A film by Marek Jablonko, Allison Jablonko, and Peter Smollett. 16mm. 50 minutes, color, English commentary. Distributor: The Pennsylvania State University, Audio Visual Services, Special Services Building, University Park, PA 16802.

MARING IN MOTION: A Choreometric Analysis of Movement Patterns among a New Guinea People (1968). A film by Allison Jablonko.

16mm, 17 minutes, color, English commentary. Distributor: The Pennsylvania State University, Audio Visual Services, Special Services Building, University Park, PA 16802

UNDALA: Rhythms of Life in a Hindu Village (1968). A film by Marek Jablonko and Peter Smollett. 16mm, 28 minutes, color, original musical score by Harold Schramm. Distributor: The Pennsylvania State University, Audio Visual Services, Special Services Building, University Park, PA 16802.

HER NAME CAME ON ARROWS: A KINSHIP INTERVIEW WITH THE BARUYA OF NEW GUINEA (1982). A film by Marek Jablonko, Allison Jablonko, and Stephen Olsson. 16mm. 26 minutes, color and B/W, sound, English sub-titles. Distributor: Documentary Educational Resources, 5 Bridge St., Watertown, MA 02172.

TO FIND THE BARUYA STORY: AN ANTHROPOLOGIST AT WORK WITH A NEW GUINEA TRIBE (1982). A film by Marek Jablonko, Allison Jablonko, and Stephen Olsson. 16mm, 64 minutes, color, sound, English narration and sub-titles. Distributor: Documentary Educational Resources, 5 Bridge St., Watertown, MA 02172.

REVIEWS OF THE ABOVE FILMS

Asch, Timothy (1983). Review of TO FIND THE BARUYA STORY. American Anthropologist 85(3):751-752.

Asch, Timothy (1983). Review of HER NAME CAME ON ARROWS. American Anthropologist 85(3):752-753.

Sorenson, E. Richard (1968). Review of KEREPE'S HOUSE: A HOUSEBUILD-ING IN NEW GUINEA. American Anthropologist 70(1):183-184.

On the Making of
EZE NWATA - THE SMALL KING[1]

Sabine Jell-Bahlsen
Ogbuide, Ltd.
New York, NY

ABSTRACT: EZE NWATA - THE SMALL KING is a condensed version of the film trilogy, DIVINE EARTH - DIVINE WATER; these
films were produced during the author's fieldwork among the riverine
Oru Igbo of South Eastern Nigeria, in 1978/9. The present paper examines the author's experience relating to film production: in the
field, during post-production, and with the audience. The paper addresses specific questions which arise from filming in a non-Western
culture, and from trying to translate the field experience in that culture to a broad Western audience. The film, EZE NWATA-THE
SMALL KING presents a particular approach to the question of perspective while representing images from another culture, on film,
which is addressed in the paper, and related to the growing field of
visual anthropology.

Film and Fieldwork

When I originally planned my fieldwork in Nigeria, I was not very
much concerned with film. On the contrary, I was quite suspicious about
the combination of film and fieldwork for several reasons: I was not familiar
with many ethnographic films at the time, and I was also uncertain about
what kind of an effect filming might have on the field situation. Above all,
I was somewhat prejudiced against films that deal with foreign cultures, as
many of them tend to be exploitative (whether for scientific reasons, or for
mere voyeurism) and treat the documented people as mere objects rather than
as persons. However, it seems unfair to apply this generalization to all
ethnographic films: there are efforts to use film as a means of two-way
communication, documenting the lives of real people, both at home and
abroad, and giving these people an opportunity to express their views and
perspectives to a wide audience, on film.

When I set out for Nigeria, I would have preferred to stick to my pen and notebook, and at the most, take a still camera and cassette recorder and avoid sophisticated technical equipment. Yet, on the basis of my previous travel experience, I anticipated that living in an African village for a year would have such an impact on my own personal development that this might entail a disruption in my personal relationship with my partner, if we were not to share the experience. My husband, Georg, agreed, and joined me for most of the time during fieldwork.

Georg, who is an architect, was at the time concerned much more than I with visual conceptualizations of the social environment. He had previously taken film courses in New York, and decided to take a motion picture camera to Nigeria, more or less with my consent. However, since I had not planned to make a film during fieldwork, there were no provisions for film in our budget. Consequently, we had very limited resources for filmmaking and thus had to keep the film project technically as simple and as inexpensive as possible, a situation which many anthropologists who decide to take a film camera to the field encounter.

We bought a used, spring-wound 16mm Bolex camera, fifty 100 foot rolls of 16mm color negative film, one lens, and a tape recorder. In addition, we took our two still cameras, a Polaroid camera, and a Sony cassette recorder. The latter was intended for data collection during interviews, rather than for film sound. But as it turned out to be the most reliable piece of equipment under tropical conditions, we ended up using much of the back-up sound material recorded with this machine for our film.

We thought at this point we had spent all funds set aside for the film project before even starting to film. However (as more experienced filmmakers know) the real expenses came much later, during the post-production phase.

We began our filming only after having lived in the village for six months. By then, we felt that enough mutual confidence had developed between ourselves and the villagers, which enabled us to add a new dimension to our presence in the village without causing major disturbances in our relationship to the local people, as well as among the villagers themselves. Only at this point did I feel confident enough in my own familiarity with the people and the location, to be able to anticipate local reactions and assess the effect of taking pictures.

Urban Nigerians are often very sensitive to photography, taking offense when an outsider takes a picture of something that belongs to their "traditional past." Yet, the villagers took quite the opposite position: they were self-confident, proud of their own culture, and also trusted us enough not to fear any misrepresentation. The problems we encountered in filming were thus more of a technical, rather than a psychological nature--in spite of the colonial past.[2]

We were very well received after we had been introduced as researchers from the University of Nigeria.[3] In addition, many suspicions were allayed after it became evident that our interest in traditional religious beliefs was a

genuine one. It was evident that we were not intending to missionize anyone. Also, we demonstrated our good intentions when participating in certain events (e.g., ritually sharing kola nut), taking part in which was believed to entail harm to persons with bad intentions.

Although the village was rather remote and had neither electricity nor
running tap water, the villagers were familiar with photography. There was
a local photographer in a neighboring town, and some compounds proudly
exhibited framed photographs of their elders and prominent members, posing in their most prestigious outfits. The photographer's place was crammed
with baby photos he made to order. We were often asked to take pictures of
people posing, and whenever we traveled and stayed in a hotel with electricity and running water, I would spend the night enlarging black and white
prints in my field lab to be taken back to the people in the village as gifts.

We had originally brought the Polaroid camera in order to be able to
hand out instant prints when taking pictures. We had assumed that these
color prints might be appreciated as looking more realistic than black and
white prints. However, the villagers did not like these little pictures very
much. The Polaroid pictures were too small to be framed to adorn the compound. Also, the elders in particular kept turning the little pictures around,
seemingly unable to distinguish up and down; they would look at the Po-
laroids upside down, politely pretending to enjoy the gift.

On the other hand, the water priestess, Eze Mmiri, would call on me,
asking me to take an instant picture of one of her patients in his deranged
state of a seizure. She wanted to be able to show the patient the picture
later, after he regained his senses. The priestess had a whole album full of
pictures of former patients, and also of individuals, who had happily given
her photographs of themselves after being successfully healed. One man
called me to take an instant picture of his dead child before she was buried.
It was a very hard task for me: the dead girl, who was of the same age as my
own daughter, had been dressed up in her best dress and was placed in a big
seat in the compound's parlor room. She looked almost alive.

Only one or two of the younger men had been to a movie theatre in the
city. Thus, most people did not differentiate between a movie camera and a
still camera. One very conscientious woman froze in the middle of dressing
her baby so as "not to spoil the picture" when we were filming her.

Most people liked to pose for pictures, but they did not like to be photographed while at work. It was thus considered highly appropriate for us to
film/take pictures during rituals and special events, when everyone was
dressed at their best.

Participants paid very little attention to Georg when he was filming
during these rituals, as everybody present was too preoccupied with too
many other things. But, when allowed to attend, we had to participate fully
in the event, sharing everything with everybody present.

Thus, when the drink was shared, someone would suddenly walk right
into the camera with a glass of palm wine in his hand, which had been

blessed for Georg, offering it to him and insisting that Georg drop everything and drink the wine immediately.

In the case of EZE NWATA, the film was made under very different circumstances. We had traveled to the shrine of the Ibo river god, Urash; a place which is located in a secret grove by the river bank, and could only be reached by a half day canoe trip. We went there on a special day which is sacred to the river god, and we expected many water worshippers to visit the shrine to celebrate the holiday.

We went with my interpreter, Francis. Francis had previously performed a sacrifice to the goddess of the lake in appreciation of the birth of his first son. Francis brought his junior kinsman along, Eze Nwata, an apprentice in water worship. It was considered appropriate for a competent person to accompany us, making offerings to Urash on this celebrated day.

The secret grove of Urash is a very special place, where no plant may be hurt. A huge tree in the center of the grove gives it the feeling of a natural cathedral. Visitors must take off their shoes when disembarking from their canoe to enter the grove. Whoever enters the grove with shoes must leave them behind when he leaves. The secret grove is a dark, cool and quiet place; the voices of birds and insects are intense, and at times overwhelming. Local people come here whenever they wish to make an offering and pray to the river god, Urash. The place is littered with offering trays, and with gifts for the deity. Red and white pieces of cloth are tied to the bushes throughout the grove, as these are the water deity's favorite colors.

A person could offer to the river god anywhere in the grove, calling the deity's attention by sticking four little branches into the ground. However, the most prominent place is a shrine in a square uphill, which could be reached by climbing up on the shoulder of the river bank, the big tree's roots forming natural steps.

When we were visiting the shrine of Urash on that holiday, it was unusually quiet there. Nobody came for a long time, and nothing happened for hours. When we arrived, Eze Nwata made some offerings to the water deity on the beach. Then, Eze Nwata and I climbed up the hill inside the grove to the shrine above, while Georg and Francis stayed at the waterside. We sat at the shrine for hours, meditating, praying to the deity, and staring into the greens. While we were sitting there, Eze Nwata started to tell me his story.

I had only a small cassette recorder with me, which I always carried around, recording stories and conversations. Eze Nwata was telling his story in English. He knew that I had a tape recorder and that I was taping our conversation. But he was in a delicate state of mind; the presence of his deity and talking about his illness, his dreams, and his vocation were emotionally stirring him up. I placed the recorder between us on the ground, but I could not have used external microphones, or attached a lavalier microphone to his shirt. The resulting sound recording was not very good, and we later replaced it with a studio recording of an American English speaker, reading the transcript of Eze Nwata's narration in the film.

The interview with Eze Nwata was not planned, nor had we planned to make a film about him. Also, I could not have anticipated what Eze Nwata was going to tell me at the shrine of Urash. Georg took some pictures of Eze Nwata, of the grove, and of the river. He was filming when a woman arrived with her little son, for whom Eze Nwata performed some rites at the waterside. However, we decided to make a film about Eze Nwata only much later, after I had transcribed the entire tape and brought it in relation to everything else.

The Editing Process

We returned from Nigeria and lived in New York City, where I was writing my dissertation,[4] and Georg started working on the film footage. It was only then that I started to appreciate film in conjunction with field-work.

Returning to New York, we were not happy. We felt socially deprived and lonely after the intensity of village life. We missed all the people we had come to know and like. Seeing them on the screen helped a little. Although the screen could not bridge the physical separation, it could help us feel closer. We looked at the footage day and night, and night and day; fast, slow, at regular speed, forward, and backward. We did not want to see anything or anybody outside the editing room. The only movies we went to see outside were ethnographic films, which we felt had little to do with our footage.

I finished my dissertation as fast as possible in order to be able to devote more time to the editing process. The dissertation, by then, appeared as a mere skeleton to me compared to the "real" people on the screen. Yet, at this point, we also started realizing how much the technical properties of film determined the images on the screen, and the extent to which these images differed from the reality we had experienced during fieldwork. The pictures seemed to be only a fragment of that larger live experience.

We wished we had had technically more sophisticated equipment when shooting the films. Such a technical improvement would have been an electrically operated camera which would have allowed longer takes without interruption and also, the recording of synch sound interviews on film. The longer we worked on the footage, the more we realized how much film is an interpretation of reality, and to what extent this interpretation is influenced by the tools and techniques employed during production, post-production, and moreover, the filmmaker's intention, perception, and stylistic choices.

Due to our limited financial resources, and due to the remoteness of the location, we had been using a hand wound Bolex camera. This camera does not require batteries to transport film; it is very reliable, and its film transportation mechanism hardly fails to work in any climate. We had no electricity available on location, nor could we have bought, stored, or recharged large batteries. Batteries are sensitive to tropical heat and humidity, which may cause an unexpected weakening of the battery's power. If the battery of an electrically operated camera is not fully charged, then the speed at which the film is transported inside the camera could be slowed down, which results in the filmed motion appearing too fast, or even jerky, on the exposed film. A hand wound camera, on the other hand, is not susceptible to electrical disturbance, and thus, is less prone to a distortion of the depicted movement.

However, a camera that does not use electricity for its motor cannot be used to generate a synch tone necessary to record synchronous sound. Instead, sound and picture are recorded separately. This "wild" sound is then added to the picture in the editing process, just as synchronously recorded sound is. Wild sound can be recorded simultaneously with the picture being taken but (since camera and tape recorder move at slightly differing speed) there is no lip synch in the picture unless the magnetic registration of the recorded sound is aligned with the recorded picture with the aid of an electrically generated synch signal.

In addition, a spring wound camera runs for only 30 seconds at a time. Then it stops running, and has to be manually rewound before the cameraman can continue filming. In the meantime, the object has changed its position relative to the camera. Thus, if the cameraman were simply to continue filming after rewinding the camera, from the same position and with the same angle, then the audience would later perceive a very disruptive "jump." This jump would even be perceived when the cameraman was filming a quiet object, and it is highly distortive in filming a movement, which would appear jerky with all the jumps in it on the screen. In order to avoid these jumps, the cameraman may choose a different position or a different camera angle (e.g., a close-up following a long shot, etc.) which would later facilitate the editing process towards the rendering of a continuous flow of motion without perceptible interruptions. Yet, each time the cameraman changes his position or location, he has to take new light readings and readjust the focus (a very difficult task to perform every 30 seconds, under the most demanding conditions, and without assistance). An experienced cameraman might, therefore, film continuously, disregarding "jumps," and then take "cut-aways" separately, which could later be intercut between the individual shots, in order to avoid "jumps" in the editing process. On the whole, the restriction in the length of an individual shot in a spring wound camera has an impact on the editing style, which tends to favor short cuts, a more rhythmical editing, or a montage of shots.

On top of all this, a spring wound camera does not take film rolls that are larger than 100 feet (about 3 minutes of projected film in total). Thus, the cameraman must open the camera and change film very often, a very distracting process which admits the possibility of many sources of technical error. Each time, the exposed film has to be removed and stored safely and quickly, so as not to expose it to light, heat, or humidity. The same care must be applied to the new film taken from the can. In addition, dirt or dust might enter the open camera, which should ideally be cleaned each time before loading. The camera's gate is an especially vulnerable point because the tiniest piece of dust or a hair on the gate would later appear in the picture and constitute irreparable damage to the original footage. Also, there is always a chance of misthreading, or of the camera not picking up the film properly when loading.

Moreover, the camera's body must be closed carefully after loading, to make sure that it is properly sealed. If the camera is not properly closed (a common problem with the Bolex) then light might enter on the side and strike the film, resulting in irreparable red flares on the sides of the picture. Since this problem is so common, some cinematographers who are experienced in filming with the Bolex camera recommend taping its lid down each time the camera body is opened for loading film.

We were not aware of all the technical problems at the time of filming, and as a result, many of our shots had red flares on the side. Since there was no possibility for developing and viewing the footage on location, all the material was shipped out of Nigeria as fresh as possible and developed back home. We saw the footage only months later when we returned.

Another unpleasant surprise was that some of the footage turned out to be extremely grainy, due to damage of the film stock. Negative film is very sensitive to heat and moisture, and ought to be stored in a dry, cool, and dark place. None of these conditions were available to us on location because we had no electricity, and subsequently, neither a refrigerator nor a fan. We took great care in storing the film in a tightly sealed metal box that was insulated with styrofoam, and in addition, filled with dehumidifying bags. However, we were storing the film stock for a least six months in this way before we started filming. The temperature was at an average of 98 degrees and the humidity was 100% all of the time. The first rolls we removed from the box seem to have come out all right, but the last ones had been spoiled. Apparently, the dehumidifier was no longer sufficient once the box had been opened. There may have been no problem if the box had been kept sealed. Reversal film stock is said to be less susceptible to damage, yet it has a different latitude and may thus be too contrasty for such extremes as we encountered in terms of lighting.

We realized the consequences of these technical problems only after returning to New York. There, we were confronted with new challenges in the editing process. We hired an outside editor, only to realize that he saw entirely different things in the footage than what we saw. In addition, our objectives seemed worlds apart: the editor was more concerned with form, while we were more concerned with content. At this point, the long, painful process of translating the content began.

The editor saw the footage with totally different eyes than we did--a normal and desirable process in filmmaking, as we later learned. Neither did the editor recognize the persons we knew so well, nor did the depicted events make any sense to him--while all these people, places, and events were full of meaning to us, as well as to the people directly involved. We had recorded everything very faithfully, careful not to misrepresent anything; yet, the pictures did not seem to make any sense to the outsider, and needed translation; the editing process would give the images a meaning that would be intelligible not only to us and to the people directly involved in the action on the screen, but also to total outsiders, who had never been on the location, and who did not know anything about the people in it.

In addition, the editor had different preferences than we did. He wanted to take out all the shots that were technically weak (e.g., grainy shots, or those that had red flares on the sides). Some of these shots were not so important, so that we decided we could live without them. Others were vital parts of the depicted events and they had to stay, from our point of view--as opposed to the editor's. We were at this point, not so much concerned with the audience, but rather, with the people in the films. Our obligation was in the first place to them, so that we were careful not to omit any essential parts. Consequently, we decided to leave all the shots in the film that we felt were necessary for a proper portrayal of the film's content even though some of these shots were technically unacceptable, and distorted the film's form.

Although we were not editing the films for any particular audience, we did realize that the films were not only made for the people in the films but also for outside observers. Thus, we had to take into account that an outside audience might not be able to understand the film's contents without explanation. An explanation of some sort seemed unavoidable in order to evade possible sources of misunderstanding or misinterpretation. The more often we showed the footage to our friends and colleagues in New York, the more aware we became of the necessity of some explanation.

At the same time, we did not agree with the more conventional ethnographic films we saw. Many of those earlier films would simply show a portion of native life, and add to these pictures an explanatory narration, solely from the observer's point of view. We felt that this kind of narration would do some sort of violence to the people on the screen, who were thereby prevented from expressing themselves.

Furthermore, a film's explanatory narration would always fall short of a book, which it could not replace because it operates on a different level. We decided not to render the films' explanation in a way that would pretend to substitute for a book. Instead, our comments are kept as minimal as possible in the films themselves, while a study guide with more exhaustive information for the seriously interested student is planned.

Looking at the transcripts of our sound recordings, we found that the people involved were very adequately describing the depicted events in their own words. Moreover, the ritual texts were very beautiful and full of metaphors. By comparison, our phrasing of the contents would sound dull and dry.

During the sacrifice of a ram to the water goddess, Uhammiri, shown in our first film, the priest, Obiadinbugha, blesses Francis, his child, his gifts to the deity, and all participants in the event:

OBIADINBUGHA: ...Good health, good wealth, and child raising to him! (F.) Anybody who wants to use charm to kill him--let him die! He, who wants his existence should exist!

GROUP: ...ise![5]

. . .

OBIADINBUGHA: ...This is what I have to tell you, Uhammiri, and your husband, Urash (the water deities).

GROUP: ...ise!

OBIADINBUGHA: ...what we ask is what you should manifest to us: we ask for child raising, wealth, and life.

GROUP: ...ise!

. . .

OBIADINBUGHA: ...Life to all of us here!

GROUP: ...ise!

OBIADINBUGHA: ...We shall all reach our homes with life, as we leave here...

GROUP: ...ise!

OBIADINBUGHA: ...to meet our wives and children!

GROUP: ...ise!

OBIADINBUGHA: ...and myself who is officiating, so shall I meet my wife and children!

GROUP: ...ise!

OBIADINBUGHA: ...and my life shall be extended and not have an end!

GROUP: ...ise!

OBIADINBUGHA: ...The lives of the younger ones shall be completed too!

GROUP: ...ise!

. . .

OBIADINBUGHA: ...The one who kills the lizard for nothing--let the war of lizards encircle him!

GROUP: ...ise!

. . .

OBIADINBUGHA: ...we have all assembled here to kill a ram now!
GROUP: ...ise! ise! ise! Obiadinbugha! Obiadinbugha!

. . .

OBIADINBUGHA (blessing the meat of the sacrificial animal): It is to
be enjoyed by each and everyone of you!
GROUP: ...ise!
OBIADINBUGHA: As with us: what is meant for one man, is to be
enjoyed by each and everyone of you.
GROUP: ...ise!
OBIADINBUGHA: That is how you (god) have created each and every-
one: to enjoy eating!
GROUP: ise!

We decided to use these texts, rather than our own commentary, for two
main reasons: first of all, the texts do provide an explanation of the ongoing
events; secondly, any narration replacing these texts would be an abstraction, and thus, a form of interpretation. Since the texts can be explained at
various different levels, such an interpretation could more adequately be
given in writing. A deeper interpretation requires more space than a film
could (and should) provide, for verbal information.
We decided to start the first film with an interview. Though not lip-
synch, we had filmed an interview with Francis with sufficient "cut-aways,"
which enabled us in the editing process to cut away from the speaker as
soon as sound and picture would run out of synch.
In the interview, Francis explains in English the circumstances leading
to his offering a ram to the goddess of the lake, Uhammiri. We then filmed
Francis buying the ram in the market, him and his wife getting ready for the
sacrifice, the procession of kinsmen to the shrine, and the ritual itself.
At the shrine, all the attention focusses on the priest. He is an elderly
man who, in his blessings and prayers, communicates his and his followers'
concerns to the goddess. Although the background and the proceedings are
well known to all human beings present, the deity still needs to be informed, and is thus, detailed by the priest in his first blessing at the beginning of the ritual. He calls the goddess' attention, and explains to her why
he and his followers have come to her shrine, what they want from her, and
what they are going to give her in return.
The priest explains all these things carefully to the goddess, as if to an
outsider. His words provide a much more appropriate explanation of the depicted event than our own comments, and we used the priest's own words as
an explanation for an outside audience.
However, the priest addressed his deity in Ibo, rather than in English.
We were thus facing another problem: how to render the English transla-

tion?

At first glance, several options seemed available: dubbing the text (a practice commonly adopted in Europe) did not seem very attractive to us, as we did not want to imply that the priest spoke in English. Another possibility would have been a voice over: the sound track would start with the priest's voice speaking in Ibo, which would then be lowered, to be replaced by an English narrator's voice. Although this might be the easiest solution in a straight speech, it posed a problem in our case. The priest was not the only speaker, and his lines would alternate with responses from the entire group. Together, they would create a rhythm out of the back and forth between the priest and the other participants, which would have been difficult to re-enact with an English narrator; yet, this rhythm is an important stylistic element of the event, which could not be omitted without distortion.

Subtitles might have been the most elegant way of solving the dilemma. However, subtitles which are done in an optical house are very expensive and were beyond our budget.

Another possibility were written texts, which also seemed adequate to the technical standard of our equipment. The Bolex camera was originally used during the days of silent film. Such texts could be seen in some silent films, where they are intercut between sections of moving images, providing additional explanations for the scenes.

Flaherty, in his 1922 documentary classic, NANOOK OF THE NORTH, has used such explanatory texts, which he intercut with the depicted scenes. Since our budget and equipment compared more to the stage of film technology of those days than to modern synch sound equipment and subtitles, we decided to use this older stylistic means of rendering verbal information. However, although taking Flaherty as a starting point for using texts, we deviated from his way of using the texts in various respects.

First of all, Flaherty's texts are his own interpretations of the Eskimos and their culture. By contrast, our texts are translations of live speeches recorded simultaneously with the picture. Very few comments of our own are rendered in the same manner wherever this seemed necessary to introduce persons, places and events.

Secondly, NANOOK OF THE NORTH is a black and white film. Therefore, white texts over black backgrounds (which actually have faint images) are not perceived as too disruptive. By contrast, we were using color film stock, and black and white texts would have provided a very harsh and disruptive contrast. Therefore, we decided to use color stills from our large slide collection taken in the field as background for the texts.

We chose stills which would relate to the contents of the spoken word, or to the live action itself. The texts were then superimposed over these pictures in large letters filling the screen.

As we could not afford to have these superimpositions done in an optical house, we had to experiment to create the desired effect on as low a budget as possible. We used a horizontal titling stand[6] and mounted the Bolex on one side, facing the back-lit slide on the opposite end. We would then film the slide for a distinct number of seconds, counting the exact number of frames. Then, we would disengage the motor and backwind the film in the camera manually, up to the beginning of the shot. We would then film the white text on a black background over the same footage with which we shot the slide, thus superimposing the burnt-in titles right in the camera. These productions were then intercut with the live sequences.

We liked the resulting effects best of all available options of rendering the translations. First, the stills would enable the observer to rest his eyes on one picture, which would help familiarize him with the unfamiliar environment. Secondly, the background images would help understand the texts, relate them to their own context, and provide glimpses at the immediate location's wider environment. Thus, when the priest prays for himself and his followers to return home safely, we would show a picture of a village compound as a background for that text, so that an outsider would know what kind of a home is implied.

Film Truth and Reality

In comparing our own films with Flaherty's NANOOK, which was made with similar technical means, there are other distinguishing points which relate to differences in the approach and in the field situation itself.

Flaherty's NANOOK has been both admired by some, and scorned by others. On the one hand, the film is a true masterpiece of early documentary cinematography, regarding the composition of individual shots, the variety of camera angles and positions, and the masterful editing. It also testifies Flaherty's deep sympathy for the people he filmed. On the other hand, the film has been criticized by some anthropologists for being staged. These critics also charge that Flaherty's image of Eskimo life is too subjective, and too idealized.

Our own films share Flaherty's sympathetic approach to the subjects under consideration. However, there are great differences in cinematographic means of achieving this end. These differences in the cinematography relate in part to our then less developed cinematographic skills, and in part, to the field situation itself.

Our filming became an integral part of my fieldwork, in which I used the method of participant observation. Consequently, we considered ourselves as primarily participants in the events, while our taking pictures of these events was of secondary importance, to ourselves as much as to the other participants. Thus, we had to sit in a distinct place during most of the events, which had been ascribed to us in accordance to our age and our ranking as visitors. We were not free to move around and choose camera positions from a filmmaker's point of view, for the sake of the picture and its future reception by the audience. The only exceptions were during the relaxing phases of eating and drinking and chatting, which were as much a part of the rituals as everything else. Therefore, portions of the filmed rituals may appear to the observer like on a stage, because he sees the scene from the same position all the time (like in a theatre as opposed to a movie). Skillful cinematography for a movie (such as Flaherty's) captures the audience by constantly changing angles and positions, which make the depicted events appear more "real." The opposite effect may result from the cameraman being restricted from moving around. Thus, although nothing in our films is in fact staged, portions of the rituals in particular may appear so to the audience, because of our own place as participants.

Conversely, Flaherty's NANOOK, which seems very immediate and "real," was in part "staged." Since the "staging issue" is a very relevant one for documentary film and ethnographic film, I will explore it a little further, setting it in relation to my own fieldwork.

Documentary film has traditionally been defined as a genre that depicts "real people" and "real events," as opposed to actors and staged events.

Well-known documentary filmmakers have, nevertheless, at times staged portions of a real live event, or of a critical situation which they felt they needed to show in order to give a complete picture of the event/culture/character, etc. they wanted to show. Examples are the letter sorting on the train in Grierson's NIGHT MAIL, Nanook building an igloo in Flaherty's NANOOK, the president's dinner in Yates' WHEN THE MOUNTAINS TREMBLE, as well as various sound track creations, e.g., in THE SPANISH EARTH by Ivens. All these instances happened in real life, but could not easily be filmed for technical reasons, and were therefore staged, as the filmmakers freely admit. Unless otherwise told, the audience might accept such a staged event more readily than a possibly distorted real life sequence. The staging would also help the filmmaker to present his interpretation of real life.

Conversely, as most anthropologists know (although they do not always admit it) the mere presence of a fieldworker, or the act of recording (whether on paper, tape, video, or film) changes a situation and adds a new dimension to real life. In addition, film is in itself subject to so many technical and stylistic choices, that the mere act of filmmaking may be considered as a form of staging.

African Pygmies, not knowing that Flaherty had staged parts of NANOOK, asked whether the Eskimos knew that they were being filmed. Being told that Nanook knew all about it, the Pygmies commented: "Oh well, then it is all make-believe."[7]

Against the background of my own fieldwork, "staging" is not as easy as one may assume, and also, it may not have the desired illuminating effect, as the following incident illustrates.

None of the events in our films were staged, as we tried to document the real events as they took place. However, when we were filming the sacrifice to the earth goddess, Ani (the second part of the DIVINE EARTH trilogy) we missed an important part of the ritual. We had set up the camera near the shrine and the blessing had already begun, when suddenly all the men present got up and dashed forward, tightly surrounding the shrine, the priest, and the sacrificial goat, turning their backs to the camera. Not knowing what was going on, we stopped filming, as we assumed that the participants did not want us to see/film the ritual killing. Later, we discovered that this incident had been an important regular part of the ritual, in which all participants must touch the animal to be presented to the deity as they are blessed. We filmed the remainder, including the actual killing of the goat, realizing too late what we had missed.

The next day, the same men were setting out to offer another goat to a different deity, this time a water god. We asked them to stage the previous day's situation for us, which we had missed. They agreed to fake that part of the blessing for us, so that the picture would "look right." However, this time, the men did everything purposely wrong, so as to confuse the deities.

First, they said that they could not pretend an offering at the actual shrine of the earth goddess. If they did this, then they would have to follow through and make another real offering to Ani, whereas this goat was for another deity, a river god, whose shrine was located somewhere else. The ritual for that river god was to take another form. Moreover, his shrine was located in a far away sacred spot, where no cameras were allowed.

They chose a spot near the village, where there was no shrine, and which resembled only remotely the location of the earth-goddess' shrine. There, the priest and his men sat down for a few minutes, touching the goat as on the previous day. However, they would do everything in the exact opposite way of the other day: e.g., hold the goat on the priest's right hand side, rather than on his left, etc. Everything was done in exactly the opposite way than in the real ritual. No deity could have possibly mistaken this for a real offering.

The Audience #1

After two years of editing, we finally completed the three films and started showing the result to different audiences, with very contradictory results.

In the first place, it turned out that American English speakers unfamiliar with Africa could not understand the interview in our first film because of the speaker's Nigerian accent. The same accent would not pose a problem for non-English mother tongue speaking audiences in Europe.

The reaction to our rendering of the translations with texts superimposed over stills was mixed. Some audiences found the texts themselves very interesting and felt that the slides did facilitate comprehension. Others said that there were too many stills and texts, that there was too much reading involved, and that the stills were too disruptive to the flow of action. Some found the timing of the texts too fast for reading, others found it too slow.

In addition, there seemed to be a major discontent in some audiences with the aesthetics of the films with regard to their structure, especially in the two films on rituals. The structure of these films is dramatic rather than deductive or inductive. Above all, the films follow the internal organization of the depicted events, trying to capture their real timing.

The actual sacrifice to the water goddess, Uhammiri, lasted an entire day. It had very distinctive parts: such various blessings, relaxed pauses, and mounting tension, leading slowly up to the ritual killing, a climax after which there was a relaxing period of drinking and sharing food, with interspersed blessings, slowly wrapping up and finally concluding the event in a distinct way. This structure of the ritual itself had its own dramatic curve, corresponding to local aesthetics.

In reproducing an image of this live event, we felt obliged mostly to the people who had performed it, who had created its aesthetics, and who took it very seriously. Therefore, we tried to represent the ritual and its structure as accurately as possible, so as not to distort it. Although we could not have filmed the entire day, we tried to give an impression in the film of how the real time was spent on that day, proportionwise. Thus, we would show a bit of each of the parts that made up the whole event in their original sequence. We would attribute to each of these portions as much time as they had in proportion to each other in the live event, on film, thus trying to capture the proportions of the ritual's dynamic curve, in miniature.

Some Western audiences seemed to have different expectations. They would have liked to see the climax sooner, with little preparation, and not much beyond. We felt that doing this would totally distort the aesthetics of the occasion however contrary these might be to what we are accustomed to at home, and what an ethnocentric viewer might wish to apply to another culture.

On the whole, we found that there was not much difference between the reactions of the general audience, on the one hand, and anthropology students, on the other hand. Filmmakers were the most critical audiences. Yet, the films appealed to those who had a genuine interest in the subject and in the depicted people (whether anthropology students or not). Others (including students) could simply not relate to the foreign images, and still others felt offended by some of the things they saw on the screen (e.g., the intestines of a slaughtered animal). Many observers stated that the films had aroused their interest in the Ibo, and that they would like to read more about these people; a response which we appreciated.

Yet, the above mentioned technical problems jeopardized the films, especially where we had decided against the editor's advice to leave bad shots in the picture for the sake of the content. Audiences who were sympathetic with the content never complained, or stated that they found the technical shortcomings distracting. Filmmakers would point out all the mistakes, and exhibitors were so preoccupied with the films' form that the original DI-VINE EARTH trilogy was never accepted for a festival, nor did it ever sell.

EZE NWATA - THE SMALL KING

After these mixed experiences with screenings of the DIVINE EARTH-DIVINE WATER trilogy, we had nevertheless not given up hope to get the films distributed and recoup some of our money spent on the films. Since European TV stations have often proven helpful to independent documentary filmmakers, we offered the films there.

The response was encouraging. After looking at the films, the program director said the films were certainly interesting, though not suitable for a general audience in their present form. He recommended re-editing the three films into a shorter and more concise version, for which he offered his assistance. Since we had already made an internegative that would allow us to preserve the original version and draw further copies from it, we agreed and started working on what became EZE NWATA - THE SMALL KING.

In the DIVINE EARTH-DIVINE WATER trilogy, we showed people from a different cultural system than our own, who act within their culture, while incorporating changes brought about from without. A priest, for instance, is shown offering a sacrifice to the ancient Earth goddess, customarily asking the deity for good prospects in farming, but also, for her assistance in training his and his followers' children in colleges, building a two story building, and for a safe journey to the visiting whites. In addition, many of the objects shown in the rituals are imported from Europe and the USA and given a new function within the local African setting (e.g., red wool hats as symbols of prestige). Audiences picked up on these indications of change in different ways: while some were disappointed about not being presented with the pure images of native life (which they had expected to see), others appreciated our emphasis on culture contact.

We chose Eze Nwata's story (which formed the third part of the original trilogy) as a baseline for the new version, because it is the most personal and easily accessible part. EZE NWATA addresses the problems of post-colonial interaction directly, as his account expresses the internal conflict caused by the resulting social and cultural transformation. Furthermore, Eze Nwata's story relates directly to modern life, a confrontation which caused a problem for him, as for many third world communities. The issue is interesting for a Western audience, as it increases the awareness of our interaction with the third world. We edited the film for an easy comprehension by a general public audience without, however, distorting the story.

Eze Nwata's account represents a particular perspective of a participant in one African cultural system, and moreover, of a particular cult pertinent in that culture area. This perspective is contrasted with our own viewpoint

(that of the participant observer, who comes from another cultural background) and furthermore, with the viewpoint of the prospective audience
(targeted or not) who will see the film from a non-participant
Euro/American perspective. The film is an effort in pointing at these distinctions, and it takes account of these different perspectives on three levels:

(1) Eze Nwata's own words, which represent his subjective views;

(2) the images which we (the participating outsiders) chose from his
social environment to illustrate his account. These images are not always
images from his subjective life experience; but they are part of the general
cultural setting that forms his background, out of which we chose pictures
that would facilitate comprehension of his environment by a non-member
(e.g., the lady we show when he talks about his pregnant mother is not his
real mother, since he was apparently already born; the little boy we show
when he talks about his childhood is not himself, since he is apparently
much older; the fisherman we show when he talks about his father going
fishing is not his actual father since his father died).

(3) Our explanatory comments, which we felt were necessary for the
non-participant audience to understand the narration, are rendered as written
texts, thereby clearly distinguished from Eze Nwata's own (narrated) account.

EZE NWATA differs from our own previous films, the DIVINE
EARTH-DIVINE WATER trilogy, and also from other contemporary
ethnographic films. First of all, technically, the film could hardly be compared with recent films that were made with more sophisticated tools (e.g.,
synch sound equipment and electric cameras). Secondly, in the film EZE
NWATA, we gave special consideration to the question of perspectives
(e.g., insider's versus outsider's viewpoint).

Eze Nwata's own first person account provides the guideline for the
film's flow of information rather than being based on our own explanatory
narration, or our concept of Ibo culture. Since Eze Nwata's story is the
dominant source of transmitting the film's contents, greatest possible clarity
of the narration and of the story is crucial for a comprehension of the film
by an outside audience.

As mentioned earlier, I recorded Eze Nwata's account during our visit to
the shrine of Urash. The interview was not planned, nor was the sound
recording meant to be sound for film. The recording was not very good; furthermore, we had learned from screenings of our previous films how difficult the Nigerian accent is for an American audience. Consequently, we decided to have the transcript of the original recording of Eze Nwata's account
rendered by a narrator, to ensure greatest possible clarity.

In addition, the original tape recording of my conversation with Eze
Nwata was almost an hour long. We did not have enough images to cover
the entire time. Also, some parts of the story were rather confusing, and not
helpful in illuminating Eze Nwata's life experience. Thus, I edited the story
down to approximately 15 minutes, leaving various confusing side aspects

aside, and rearranging individual paragraphs in a chronological sequence so as to facilitate comprehension of the narration by an audience not familiar with Eze Nwata's background.

There is no explanatory narration beyond Eze Nwata's own words in the film. A few of our comments (which we felt were necessary to introduce persons, places, or events) are rendered as short texts, superimposed over stills, in the above described way. The film uses this stylistic device to distinguish clearly between the insider's point of view and the outsider's viewpoint. The insider's words are (Eze Nwata's) rendered in the narration, while our outsider's explanation is rendered in writing.

This explicit distinction of viewpoints is found in a few other films, notably the MacDougalls' WEDDING CAMELS, where explanatory texts are contrasted with subtitled translations of original speeches; and also in Marshall's N!AI.

We avoided an explanatory narration in our film EZE NWATA because we feel that such a narration would overemphasize the outsider's point of view. Instead, we dedicated as much space as possible to Eze Nwata's own account which we illustrated with pictures from his life.

The film, EZE NWATA - THE SMALL KING, is an attempt to make one Ibo man's story accessible to an outside audience unfamiliar with that man's world. Thus, we have used pictures from his world, rather than words of our own, to illuminate his points. The pictures are live images from all three of the original films which were taken in Eze Nwata's village, and which form part of his social environment. These images are contrasted with stills from the city where he worked. The city images may not be as shocking to us as some of the pictures of third world metropolitan slums we are used to seeing on TV; but from Eze Nwata's rural viewpoint, these pictures are quite alienating.

The live sequences from the village are used differently than in the original films: all these events may in fact take place simultaneously and they are part of the individual's consciousness. The scenes from the individual events are intercut with Eze Nwata's account. As the film's emphasis is on Eze Nwata, rather than on any of the other occasions, these episodes are not rendered intact, but rather as glimpses, or short sequences of portions of Eze Nwata's social environment. The film also features rather surrealistic superimpositions which are illustrations of Eze Nwata's dreams, and also, scenes from the water worship in which he got involved during the process of being healed. All this is set against the background of Eze Nwata at the shrine of Urash, the original location where he told me his story.

The film's overall tone is not oriented along the lines of an objective presentation of reality from the outside. Instead, it is oriented toward Eze Nwata's own, somewhat surrealistic account, which forms the guideline for the presentation of all other (visual and verbal) information.

The Audience #2

EZE NWATA - THE SMALL KING was much better received, and it is much more widely shown, than our original three films. EZE NWATA was initially shown during an exhibition featuring a wide range of West African sculptures relating to culture contact, Voodoo, and Mami Wata, in the City Museum of Munich, Germany. Three films were permanently screened on video during this show: LES MAITRES FOUS by Rouche (1953), a film on VOODOO, HEALING, AND POSSESSION IN TOGO originally produced in Super 8 by Wendl and Weise (1981), and our own film, EZE NWATA - THE SMALL KING (1982). There was a great interest in the audience in seeing live sequences that related directly to the objects on exhibition.

The three films presented quite a spectrum of different approaches: Rouche's early film provides an imperious commentary for which it was previously criticized by African students. As a consequence of this criticism, Rouche developed his renowned style of "Cinema Verite" (Eaton 1979). The Super 8 film takes a strictly observant position, supplemented by a narration. EZE NWATA provides a well received contrast to both films in its presentation of another viewpoint and in confronting the audience with different perspectives.

EZE NWATA was also shown at scientific conventions for academic audiences in the U.S. and Canada, as well as during museum festivals on ethnographic films, for a general public audience. In each case there were interesting discussions after the screening, most of which centered on the phenomenon of Mami Wata, its history, diverse origins, and impact. Interesting questions were raised by the audience as to the situation of native people in rapidly changing Third World countries. Many observers expressed a desire to learn more about the subject after seeing the film. Some would have preferred to see a more comprehensive illustration of the water priestess' work as a healer, and details of the healing procedures, which will be the subject of a future film. Students who saw the film responded to its special approach to the question of ethnographic perspectives. In general, there seemed to be no major understanding problems, judging from audience feedback and the screenings provoked the interest of TV stations, schools, museums, archives, and hospitals.

Prospects

EZE NWATA - THE SMALL KING is a subjective film in a double sense: first, it illustrates one Ibo man's perspective; secondly, this illustration is conceived and rendered by us subjectively, making distinct stylistic choices in its presentation.

The man whose life history forms the baseline of the film, Eze Nwata, was a patient and worshipper of the water cult, Mami Wata. Before the treatment, Eze Nwata was perceived by his townsmen as a madman. He himself became aware of his illness, and this awareness is part of the healing process, which began when he was submitted to the healer, Eze Mmiri; as he became her patient, he became her follower, joined her cult, and became a fellow worshipper of the water deities. A patient of the healer/priestess, Eze Mmiri, Eze Nwata also became an apprentice of the water cult. His initiation into the worship, as well as his knowledge of the art of healing are still incomplete. Once healed, Eze Nwata will no longer be considered a patient, but rather a healer/priest, himself. The film on Eze Nwata does not intend to, nor could it, give an objective general description of the phenomenon of Mami Wata. Such an attempt would have to be left to a book in which the film seems to stimulate an interest. A comprehensive description of Mami Wata was neither intended, nor feasible for us when we produced EZE NWATA - THE SMALL KING. EZE NWATA is a piece in a puzzle; a puzzle which requires more work.

I am, therefore, currently planning a new film on Mami Wata, which will present the subject from a different angle. It will focus on one water priestess, her worship, and her achievements as a healer. The film will focus on the "native doctor," rather than on one of her patients, and it will document the complexities of Mami Wata and its relation to social change. Native perspective and local viewpoints will be as prominent as in the previous films, and distinguished from my own interpretation. The proposed film will, however, use more sophisticated techniques, which are necessary for a more comprehensive portrayal of Mami Wata.

The healing of psychic disorders by Mami Wata worshippers involves such diverse aspects as group therapy, music, dance, drama, ritual, social reintegration, and herbal medicine. It will, therefore, be necessary to use an electrically operated camera that allows longer takes and uninterrupted sequences of music and dance, as well as synchronous sound interviews. This will require collaboration with a professional crew for sound, picture and (later) editing so as to relieve the anthropologist/director from technical duties. Such a project will only be feasible with a much higher budget, which in turn raises a whole range of issues related to fund-raising.

Conclusion

Film production, post-production, and distribution efforts are experiences which have helped me to broaden the perspective on my own field work, and to learn invaluable lessons from both film and field work.

Film is a means of expressing a subjective live experience, which carries the potential of transmitting this experience to a wide audience. Film adds a dimension to writing in illustrating non-verbal aspects of human life, which we sense visually or acoustically. Film can do so by using its own language, to which some refer as "film-language." The latter is subject to the technical properties of film, as well as to the individual filmmaker who chooses various techniques and stylistic means to communicate contents. Yet, how successful a film is in communicating the filmmaker's intentions to the audience depends not only on the film's technical quality, but also on the audience's background: their training in film, their expectations, preconceived opinions, world view, viewing habits, etc. Thus, an image from contemporary America may elicit an immediate association in an American audience (e.g., hamburger-lunch) but not in an African or European audience. Cross-cultural images do not communicate as clearly as analogies drawn from visual information within the same society. This creates a special problem for filmmakers dealing with subjects from another culture, or subculture, than the audience's. The anthropologist/filmmaker, who tries to communicate an alien life experience faces the additional problem that Western film audiences tend to accept film more readily as "reality" than writing. Audiences are conditioned to distinguish between documentary and fiction films, and they tend to disregard the differentiation between a film's interpretation and reality within a documentary. Yet a merely mechanical reproduction of reality on film is technically not feasible. The same event appears different when filmed by different filmmakers. An objectively complete replica of reality on film is not possible, as each film is subject to the filmmaker's choices. Film truth carries the author's interpretation as much as writing.[8]

The anthropologist/filmmaker who is aware of these distinctions faces various tasks: a faithful representation of the images from another culture, a translation of their meaning to the audience, and an awareness of his/her own part as an interpreter. The latter raises the issue of perspectives, which seems crucial to visual anthropology dealing with images in a cross-cultural setting.

On top of all this, the way of life of entire populations is rapidly destroyed the world over, as indigenous cultures disappear when absorbed by the modern worldwide economic system. Anthropologists who are engaged in research on peoples of Third World countries are constantly confronted with problems that relate directly to the transition caused in these societies by their entanglement with the modern world. The anthropologist/filmmaker working in this setting chooses to either produce a faithful representation of a world in transition, or to invoke images of untouched native cultures.

Although it may seem easy to omit those facts in writing that tend to disturb a model image of an intact traditional society,[9] it is not so easy to extract indications of change from a photograph (see Collier 1967). In this respect, "pictures do not lie." Yet, a film is an assembly of many individual pictures. In the editing process, many pictures are taken out, a necessary procedure for giving a coherent statement on film. The filmmaker creates an interpretation of his raw footage during editing, and it is largely during this phase of post-production that the degree of a film's authenticity is determined. In the editing room, the filmmaker decides whether he wants to create an ideal image of an unaffected exotic culture by taking out all "impure" shots, or whether he wants to take account of the contact situation and resulting changes in the documented society by keeping all those pictures in the film that attest to the process of social change.

During the research, scripting, and planning phase, as well as during the production phase on location, the filmmaker decides already on what to film: "pure" images of a disappearing traditional way of life only,[10] or the lives of real people. As indicated earlier, Flaherty has shown (and staged) more of an idealized image of Eskimo culture, rather than dealing with the Eskimos' contemporary lives, in NANOOK. Recent Japanese films have carried the staging of a traditional past of various peoples to an extreme, e.g., asking natives of New Guinea to stage tribal warfare for a film which supposedly illustrates these people's traditional past. These efforts seem to point in the direction of fiction film, rather than documentary. Ethnographic fiction films aim at satisfying the audience's expectations about catching a glimpse of man's rapidly disappearing past, nourishing the illusion that this would still be possible. Ethnographic filmmakers have often been caught by the temptation to present/sell seemingly intact images from another world, the continued and unchanged existence of which may be their hope, but which turns out to be a product of their fantasy (e.g., fiction).

Anthropologists studying contemporary peoples all over the world and committed to reporting their true findings (beyond the models they might expect to prove) find a powerful aid in pictures. Film is particularly suitable for documenting social issues of burning urgency, both at home and abroad. Due to the immediacy of moving images, documentary films of anthropological concern may have an opinion-forming impact on wide general audiences that often exceeds writing.[11] Film is thus uniquely capable of eliminating prejudices. Yet, conversely, the suppression and censorship of filmed material attests to the sensibility of those responsible against unwanted publicity.[12]

Film is an expensive medium because it requires the collaboration of various technicians and professional services. Consequently, film is highly dependent on funding. Anthropologists who intend to use film as a means of effectively communicating the social issues with which they are confronted during research, face two major obstacles: first, it is extremely difficult to obtain funding from the more prosperous nations for a presentation of issues that relate to the interaction of rich and poor in the third world. Second, it is even more difficult to reach saturated audiences at home, who do not want to be confronted with problems elsewhere. As there are enough problems at home, audiences prefer to escape into a dream world and do not wish to face any additional problems. Film, which is traditionally associated with the "dream factory," Hollywood, falls an easy victim to such preferences. Films that do not meet the dream expectations tend to be eliminated already in the planning stage. Visual anthropology presents a great promise in the form of film; yet a promise hard to keep, due to the costly medium's extreme dependency on financing.

NOTES

[1] EZE NWATA - THE SMALL KING is an abridged version of the film trilogy, DIVINE EARTH-DIVINE WATER, which originates from my fieldwork in an Ibo village of Southeastern Nigeria in 1978/9. The films in the trilogy were photographed by my husband, Georg Jell, and were later jointly edited by us in New York City.

The first film of the trilogy is subtitled: A SACRIFICE TO THE GODDESS OF THE LAKE, UHAMMIRI. It deals with the ritual offering of a ram to the water goddess. The sacrifice is performed by the traditional elderly priest of Uhammiri, on behalf of a young man, Francis, and his relatives, in appreciation of the birth of Francis' son, Ebiri. Baby-boy Ebiri is a reincarnation of Francis' late father, Ebiri, a widely known diviner and priest of the river god, Urash.

The second film in the trilogy is sub-titled: ANNUAL SACRIFICE TO THE EARTH GODDESS, ANI. It shows two separate rituals performed by the villagers: one performed by the men, the other by the women, respectively.

The third film is subtitled: MAMI WATA. It is based on the life history of a young Ibo man, Eze Nwata, who became psychically ill after living and working in the Nigerian capital of Lagos. He was subsequently healed by the water priestess, Eze Mmiri, successor of the late priest Ebiri, who was mentioned in the first film. The priestess leads a group of Mami Wata worshippers serving both water deities, the goddess of the lake, Uhammiri, and the river god, Urash. Eze Nwata's story forms the baseline for the composite film version entitled, EZE NWATA - THE SMALL KING, a personal narrative and ethnographic documentary.

[2] The only white persons who had been in the village before us were two colonial officers, so we were told. One of them was remembered for his brutality and nicknamed as "the man who cannot bear children's crying." He is said to have had any child that cried in his presence shot immediately.

[3] Many thanks to Professor Dr. Ikenna Nzimiro, then of the University of Nsukka.

[4] Sabine Jell-Bahlsen: "Social Integration in the Absence of the State: A Case Study of the Igbo Speaking Peoples of South Eastern Nigeria," Ph.D. dissertation. The New School, New York, 1980; University Microfilms, Ann Arbor, Michigan, 1980.

[5] "Ise" is a term used by the group of persons assembled during a ritual offering. The term "ise" might be translated as "yes," or "Amen," or "so it shall be." It is a group response to a priest's blessing. "Priest" (in this context) means any person who is officiating (e.g., blessing the kola nut, or any other offering made to a deity).

[6] An easier way of shooting the slides would be to mount them directly on the camera with a special piece of equipment, which was not available to us at the time.

[7] From an interview with Tavernier in THE VILLAGE VOICE, Jan. 11, 1983.

[8] As Goethe wrote, "The highest wisdom would be to understand that every fact is already theory," a statement which holds for film as much as for writing. (Quoted in Stanley Diamond 1979: 114).

[9] Very few monographs take account of the overall political and economic situation of the people under consideration. Evans-Pritchard, for instance, did not mention the presence of colonial government enforcement agents near the site of his fieldwork, a source of friction with the subjects of his research.

[10] There is the ever present story of natives being asked to take off their wristwatch when being photographed by foreign researchers.

[11] For instance, the wide impact of the TV airing of HARVEST OF SHAME by CBS in 1960 is opposed to the effect of various newspaper publications on the same issue, which had preceded the TV screening without resulting in any significant public outrage about the condition of migrant farm laborers in the USA (see Barnouw 1974: 227).

[12] For instance, the original film footage from Hiroshima and Nagasaki was kept secret from the public for twenty-five years--the crucial period during which the atomic weapons industry took shape (Barnouw 1974: 200).

REFERENCES CITED

Barnouw, Erik (1974). Documentary. A History of the Non-Fiction Film. New York: Oxford University Press.

Collier, John (1967). Visual Anthropology: Photography as a Research Method. New York: Holt, Rinehart and Winston.

Diamond Stanley (1974). In Search of the Primitive. New Brunswick: Transaction Books.

Eaton, Mick (1979). Anthropology, Reality, Cinema: The Films of Jean Rouch. London: British Film Institute.

Evans-Pritchard, E. (1980). Social Integration in the Absence of the State: A Case Study of the Igbo Speaking Peoples of South Eastern Nigeria. Ann Arbor: University Microfilms.

FILMS CITED

DIVINE EARTH-DIVINE WATER, parts 1, 2, 3 (1981). Jell-Bahlsen, Sabine and Georg Jell.

EZE NWATA - THE SMALL KING (1982). Jell-Bahlsen, Sabine and Georg Jell.

HARVEST OF SHAME (1960). David Lowe.

LES MAITRES FOUS (Masters of Madness) (1953). Rouche, Jean.

HIROSHIMA-NAGASAKI, AUGUST 1945 (1970). Barnouw, Erik and Iwasaki Akira.

NANOOK OF THE NORTH (1922). Flaherty, Robert.

N!AI. THE STORY OF A !KUNG WOMAN (1979). Marshall, John.

NIGHT MAIL (1936). Grierson, John, Harry Watt, and Basil Wright.

THE SPANISH EARTH (1937). Ivens, Joris.

TURKANA CONVERSATIONS TRILOGY (THE WEDDING CAMELS; LORANG'S WAY; A WIFE AMONG WIVES) (1977). MacDougall, David and Judith.

VOODOO: HEILUNG AND BESSESSENHEIT IN TOGO (Voodoo: Healing and Possession in Togo) (1981). Wendl, Tobias and Daniela Weise.

WHEN THE MOUNTAINS TREMBLE (1984). Yates, Pamela and Thomas Siegel.

THE MAJOR FILMS OF SABINE JELL-BAHLSEN

DIVINE EARTH - DIVINE WATER (1981). A film by Georg Jell and Sabine Jell-Bahlsen. 82 minutes (divided into three films: PART I: A SACRIFICE TO THE GODDESS OF THE WATER, UHAMMIRI, 35 minutes; PART II: ANNUAL SACRIFICE TO THE EARTH GODDESS, ANI, 27 minutes; PART III: MAMI WATA, 20 minutes), color, sound, English titles. Distributor/Producer: Ogbuide, Ltd., 487 Broadway, New York, NY 10013 (212-226-7854).

EZE NWATA - THE SMALL KING (1982). A film by Georg Jell and Sabine Jell-Bahlsen. 29 minutes, color, sound, English narration and titles. Also available in German. Distributor/Producer: Ogbuide, Ltd., 487 Broadway, New York, NY 10013 (212-226-7854).

REVIEWS OF THE ABOVE FILMS

Ottenberg, Simon (1984). Review of EZE NWATA - THE SMALL KING. American Anthropologist 86(3): 801-802.

Filmmaking
As Teleological Process

George J. Klima
Department of Anthropology
SUNY at Albany

ABSTRACT:Filmmaking is teleological in the sense that the film-maker's short-term and long-term goals have a causal efficacy in bringing about the present and necessary conditions and events for their realization. Directionality in filming is maintained by a pro-cess of self-correcting feedback through the use of a "shooting-agenda" which updates and upgrades the need for a coherent film ca-pable of being comprehended by a future audience. A parallel process of progressive awareness and ethnographic understanding of the so-ciety and culture being studied and filmed determined the content and structure of filmic events necessary for the realization of short-term goals. Missed opportunities in filming were corrected by a "shooting-agenda," thereby resulting in logically-complete se-quences. Short-term goals of filming, such as obtaining footage which would serve as visual "fieldnotes" for later use in writing an ethnography, were arranged in an order of priority (when possible) leading toward the realization of long-term goals -- the needs and expectations of future audiences, professional and general public. In this way, the parallel processes of ethnographic writing and filming became mutually-reinforcing, corrective, and complimentary.

The following is a mental reconstruction of the events, choices, and decisions that went into the filming and editing of my film, BARABAIG. Since a considerable period of time has elapsed between the initial filming in the field (Tanzania, East Africa) and the final product, there will be some lacunae and blurred recollection of the processual events which structured my choices and, ultimately, the shape and content of the film. However, what follows is, I believe, an accurate account of problems I experienced during the filming, editing, and projection stages of BARABAIG and some of the choices and decisions which contributed to the final result.

When I arrived in Barabaig territory, I had certain conceptions and ex-

pectations of what I was going to encounter in the field situation in terms
of significant objects, events, concepts, themes, and problems common to
cattle-herding societies generally. I had studied a number of ethnographic
accounts of pastoralists, especially Evans-Pritchard's THE NUER, and Gulliver's, THE FAMILY HERDS, but I had not seen any film on cattle-herding societies. Therefore, as far as I am aware, decisions on what to film, and
why, were based more on my reading knowledge of ethnographies on cattle-
herders and on my immediate experience in the field situation rather than on
considerations and emulation of scenes and sequences of previously-viewed
ethnographic film. From a seemingly unstructured mass of events occurring
before my eyes, I would attempt to discern pattern and meta-pattern deriva-
tive of individual and collective behavior among the Barabaig, patterns
which could then be synthesized descriptively and filmically into a "gestalt"
or integrated whole capable of comprehension by an American audience. In
many respects, cattle as a dominant metaphor were the metapattern which
gave meaning and significance to most aspects of Barabaig life. It also
served as an organizing frame within which to shoot and edit my film.
Through filming and editing, I attempted to establish an isomorphic relationship between the significant world of the Barabaig and the immediacy of
the film viewer's perception of that world. Of course, any such attempts are
bound to fall short of expectations, something I would learn later when
American audiences only superficially perceived the existential focus or epi-
center on cattle around which most of the customs and institutions of the
Barabaig rotated and gravitated. But at least some "exposure" to information
about a differing life-style, based on the all-importance of cattle, might
generate some comparative and reflective thought about what constitutes
meaningful and significant activity and goals in American culture and society. At the same time, I hoped that viewing my film might raise the level
of awareness on the relativity of human values and beliefs in societies with
differing but equally valid life-styles.

Filming and Ethnographic Fieldwork

During the course of my ethnographic fieldwork, which included filming a few months after my arrival, a number of communication problems
arose out of my initial inability to speak the local language. I had learned
Swahili, the lingua franca of East Africa, before arrival in the field but had
little knowledge of the Barabaig language which, up to that time, had not
been studied or recorded, except for brief vocabulary lists compiled by European travellers and sojourners.

Having succeeded, after a few weeks, in locating a Barabaig informant
capable of translating Barabaig into Swahili, which I would then translate
into English, the problem of how to make known my intentions remained.
The Barabaig had no experience with a stranger living in their midst and no

knowledge of graphic art, especially photography, although some plastic art was practiced by children modelling clay figures of bulls with large horns and fatty humps. However, other forms of representative art were non-existent, which made it difficult for me to use analogical or comparative references in discussing my plans to make an ethnographic film. Consequently, ethical considerations about open disclosure of my intentions to film their behavior became problematic. I had to postpone decisions regarding ethical questions surrounding my filmmaking until such time as my fluency in the Barabaig language reached a point where I could clearly communicate my plans and motives. Barabaig knowledge and experience regarding European technology was so rudimentary as to make it almost impossible to communicate the necessary information so that we could discuss the short-term and long-term consequences of my filmmaking in order to secure their approval. To them, my camera and recording equipment were as strange as my behavior in residing and doing fieldwork among them. I had not brought along any pictures or film to show them what the product of my labor would be like. Also, since I had brought no projection equipment, I never saw any of the exposed footage in the field. The exposed footage was sent directly to Kodak in Rochester, New York for processing and then forwarded to a photographer-friend who would periodically write letters informing me about the quality (e.g., color, exposure, movement, etc.) of the exposed film. Therefore, neither the Barabaig nor I saw any of the film while I was in the field.

One of my key informants in his youth had attended a boarding-school outside Barabaig territory and had seen photographs before. He assured me that my filmmaking would be acceptable and non-problematic. I later received additional approval from other Barabaig elders, which only raised a question in me regarding how many individual opinions and approvals I would need to have in order for these to constitute a consensus or societal approval. Having received what I believed to be sufficient evidence and assurance that my filmmaking would not be problematic and objectionable, I proceeded to film public events, such as major rituals, rather than activities of individual Barabaig, the latter being filmed only with their permission and with as much information about what I was doing as I was capable of communicating either directly or through Barabaig interpreters.

To refer to my filmmaking, and to explain it to themselves and others, the Barabaig used their word for "measuring"--a word which I suspect they had previously used in conjunction with the past activity of an European surveying crew which, years ago, had cut a dirt road through their territory. Perhaps, the similarity of the surveyor's transit and tripod and my camera and tripod were equated. Evidently, any negative feelings or consequences associated with the road-building were not transferred to my filmmaking, which was rather quickly and readily accepted and later almost totally ignored. However, I continued to remain self-conscious of my presence among them and tried, whenever possible, to avoid being intrusive or obtrusive.

Use of a telephoto lens made it possible to be "near" yet distant to the action thereby diminishing the influence of my presence but never quite eliminating it.

From the beginning, I was aware that I would be filming behavioral events which would become an historical record or pictorial document of Barabaig social and cultural life. I frequently felt a sense of urgency about recording as much as possible of Barabaig culture, knowing full well that cattle-herding was destined to become one of the rapidly-disappearing cultural life-styles, its extinction being only a matter of time.

Briefing Sessions and Filming

To be better prepared for the events to be filmed, I held briefing sessions with key informants who accompanied me to various locations where ritual events were scheduled to take place. These briefing sessions proved to be invaluable not only in gaining knowledge and sharpening my expectations and perception of upcoming events but also in later revealing unexpected variations and deviations from my informants' accounts. Their post-facto explanations of differences between what I was supposed to see and what actually happened sometimes revealed that these changes were not due to accident or chance but rather were due to the existence of norms and rules which required that certain patterns of behavior be either eliminated or placed in a different sequence because of protocol or precedent set by previous circumstances in similar events. Thus, the briefing sessions and filmmaking contributed to my ethnographic data-gathering by revealing questions about protocol and pattern variability which might not have been obtained through interviews and questionnaires.

Filming among the Barabaig was a never-ending series of unexpected happenings. These occasions yielded information which might otherwise have been "passed-over," or at least not obtained until a certain level of sophistication on my part had been reached. Sudden revelations were numerous and I will cite just one instance which is indicative of how the act of filming generated new information about Barabaig society and culture. It was also one of the few times when my filmmaking presence proved to be intrusive, a fact I would later regret.

During a briefing session on an upcoming funeral of a very important clan elder, I tried to elicit from my informants the most comprehensive description of what I was going to see and film the next day. Continuous interrogation led me to conclude that we had exhausted the subject of who was going to do what, how, where, and when. That evening, I devised a shooting plan which would take into account the various camera-to-subject positions to be followed in sequential order. While I allowed for certain flexibility in the positioning of the camera relative to the subject, I decided that, aesthetically and dramatically, certain camera angles would be more effective than others. On this occasion, however, concentrating on camera angle proved to be almost disastrous! An important part of the ceremony called for a black bull to be led through a gate and into the homestead of the deceased clan elder. Inside, a tall monument, about 15 feet high, made of wooden poles plastered with a mixture of mud and cow-dung, had been erected over the grave. The bull would be sacrificed by strangulation next to the monument in honor of the deceased. Knowing that the bull would be herded through the gate, I decided to locate the camera and tripod inside the homestead but somewhat to the side of the gate so as not to interfere with the sacrifice. When the time came for the bull to be herded toward the homestead, I quickly filmed an exterior shot to establish locale and then went inside to my planned position for a front-angle shot. As the docile bull started to go through the gate, he took one look at me (and my white skin?), snorted, and started to run away. Up to this point, a Barabaig elder who had been drinking a considerable amount of honey-beer, had viewed my filming efforts with some interest and amusement but when he saw the bull's reaction, he came towards me shouting, "He's ruining the ritual." He was about to hit me over the head with his herding-stick when he was quickly grabbed by several bystanders and restrained. It was only later that I learned about the reasons for his violent reaction to my filming. From the moment that a sacrificial bull approaches the homestead until it is captured inside, its actions will be carefully observed and analyzed. Barabaig believe that a docile bull is a reflection of the good, moral character of the deceased clan elder. If a bull "acts up" by refusing to go through the gate, or attempts to run away, this will be interpreted to mean that the bull is unwilling to submit to the sacrifice, that is, to give up its life, because of the bad personal character of the deceased. This knowledge I learned only post facto and, although I was forgiven by the Barabaig, I regretted having caused an incident which detracted from the serious nature and importance of the ritual sacrifice. I vowed that in the future I would be even more exhaustive in my questioning of informants during the briefing sessions, sessions that I found to be so productive and now so essential to my understanding of the social and spiritual contexts into which my ethnographic curiosity and filmmaking were taking me.

Instead of a shooting script (which would have been next to useless because I could not direct any action, nor did I care to) I adopted a filming strategy I call a "shooting-agenda." The agenda contained an itemized list of behavior, events, and event contexts which would receive future priority treatment, depending on gaps and "misses" experienced in previous filming situations during both ritual and non-ritual occasions. As a general rule, whenever I missed a particular opportunity to film certain behavior that had occurred suddenly and unexpectedly (despite the briefing sessions), I would immediately jot down notes about the event and make it a point to investigate it further with my informants. A brief description of the event would be placed on the shooting-agenda to be filmed in the near future. In this way, the process of filming took on the character of a cybernetic or self-correcting loop, with missed opportunities serving as feedback and input into the filmmaking decision process. Through a system of numbering and identification, I took scrupulous care to make sure that later, when the "corrective" footage was inserted during the editing stage, it would be in proper sequential order, that is, the order in which it would have normally occurred even without the filming. Additional footage used to fill the gaps was never obtained by asking the Barabaig to repeat their actions because I had missed filming it the first time. Therefore, with a few exceptions, such as a tilt-up shot at the beginning of the film, showing a young Barabaig man holding a buffalo-hide shield and walking away from the camera, no action was directed by me. Actions filmed were, for the most part, sponta-neous, candid, and one-time phenomena and not the result of any deliber-ately planned "staging."

Although I kept a daily journal or log to record my particular thoughts and feelings about daily events, and the progress of my ethnographic field-work, I was remiss in not keeping a similar log regarding my filmmaking activities. I now believe that a separate, written record of filming experi-ences, with reflections and assessments on problems, decisions, and results, would be an invaluable aid in any future mental re-construction of the cir-cumstances under which my film, or anyone's film, took the trajectory and structure it did.

Film as Data

Film as a technical aid in data-gathering during ethnographic fieldwork was an integral part of my study strategy. I realized long before I started fieldwork that there would be events occurring so fast and intensively that they would not be amenable to ordinary observation and notetaking. Not only would details of actions be lost but peripheral actions supporting the main actions would be lost as well. Descriptions of complex ritual behav-ior, for example, could not have been possible without the aid of photogra-phy. Also, certain problems of quantification and identification were made easier for me through the use of cinematography. For example, determining the size of various Barabaig cattle herds, and their identifying brands and markings, could not have been accomplished by visual observation alone without incurring suspicion. Barabaig believe that anyone staring at a cattle herd for more than a few seconds may be casting a spell on them by staring with an "evil eye." To avoid being accused of bewitching their cattle, I used a movie camera to film a slow pan shot of an entire herd and recorded on film not only the number of animals in a particular herd but many of their physical features and cattle-brands as well. I could analyze this visual data later during the final organization and writing of my ethnography, THE BARABAIG: EAST AFRICAN CATTLE-HERDERS. None of this footage, however, was incorporated into my film BARABAIG, since its main function was research data.

I decided early in my fieldwork that I would not shoot a film around a central character or attempt to impose a story-form on the footage. Nor would I create fictional situations, use actors, or directly influence any action or event. I considered my filmmaking to be a "mission" of historical preservation, the preservation of existing traditional culture rather than a filmic restoration of past behavior (as was the case in Edward Curtis' film, IN THE LAND OF THE WAR CANOES, Robert Flaherty's, MAN OF ARAN, or more recently, the Staal-Gardner film, ALTAR OF FIRE, which is a pictorial record of a Vedic ritual re-enactment in Kerala, India). My order of priority in filming Barabaig culture was (1) to obtain footage of rapidly-moving events which would be a kind of visual "fieldnotes" stored both economically and efficiently on film for later reference in writing my ethnography, (2) to treat filming as the recording of historical footage for future reference available to the Barabaig and to others interested in the ways of a cattle-herding society and (3) to obtain footage which would communicate certain anthropological concepts, such as "cattle-complex" and "rites of passage" to a general audience. Although I did not strictly perceive particular filming opportunities as necessarily productive of footage destined for one type of audience rather than another, I assumed that a certain amount of choices and decisions would have to be made at the editing phase of film production. The ordering of filming priorities was the result of both intuitive prompting (based on a growing comprehension of Barabaig culture) and on conscious, deliberate planning--planning that was structured according to a dialectic between my ethnographic fieldwork requirements and my perception of the needs of an American audience. Generally, I tried to concentrate on what the Barabaig themselves had sorted out as having meaning and significance and not my perception and conception of the situation. For example, the presence of cattle served to symbolize and concretize the importance and significance of various ritual events associated with stages in the life cycle of individuals. Birth, puberty, marriage, and death required the ritual use of cattle as an integral part of the rites of passage in Barabaig society and culture. I, therefore, devoted more time to filming these events rather than to mundane activities, such as milking a cow, which were filmed but without any definite plan for their future inclusion in the film. Similarly, I did not film scenes of inactivity or "quiet moments" because the need to conserve film was of continual concern. I even had dreams about observing spectacular events only to have the filming opportunities slip away because I had previously exposed the last roll of film!

Communication of anthropological concepts was one of my long-range goals, whereas, the filming of ethnographic visual data was of more pressing concern. I chose to concentrate on the filming of major Barabaig rituals as they related to the cattle-complex, the cattle complex being a meta-pattern connecting various periods and patterns of behavior as these progressed through time and space. The cattle-complex of the Barabaig (the emotional identification with and extensive ritual and non-ritual use of cattle) would, presumably, become more apparent to a general film audience. Cattle as a cultural and existential focus would emerge as a structural element or common thread running throughout the film, thus providing a kind of successive and cumulative imagery necessary for viewer retention and comprehension. Using filmic images to make another culture more intelligible to a general audience almost requires a filmmaker to adopt a uni-directionality or point of orientation--either starting from the individual and proceeding toward society or focussing on institutional networks as these encompass individuals. I chose to concentrate more on the order and network of relationships among Barabaig institutions rather than on individual cultural behavior--its mini-history or biography. In this respect, I regard filmmaking as not unlike the ethnographic problem of generating a level of understanding of another culture by either concentrating one's analysis on individuals, their actions, beliefs, and feelings OR showing how institutions in society X relate to each other (e.g., their implications, co-existence, contradictions, integration, and re-enforcement). This problem has been admirably analyzed by F. Allan Hanson in his book, MEANING IN CULTURE, but its resolution has yet to be accomplished. Suffice to say, the problem seems to follow the Heisenberg principle where the study and measurement of one aspect of a phenomenon precludes the possibility of studying or measuring other aspects of the same phenomenon.

Technical Considerations

During filming and editing, choices were infused with technical, aesthetic, and conceptual considerations, the latter taking precedent over the former. This is not to say that technical decisions were not made. For example, knowing that certain kinds of shots either slow up, maintain, or speed up that mystical quality of film called "movement," I planned to include a number of close-up and medium shots rather than adopt a "whole bodies--whole acts" approach. The latter perspective or approach I had assumed would produce a sense of remoteness and restlessness in a general audience. In addition to decisions about types of shots to film, a conscious calculation concerning the length of shot necessary for viewer interest and comprehension often became part of the decisions and justifications governing the resultant footage. This was especially true when filming and editing certain non-ritual behavior that did not require any lengthy presentation. By shortening the lengths of shots and scenes, the chronological time of an event was "condensed" in terms of viewing-time without losing the essential imagery necessary for comprehension. This is especially apparent in one scene in my film, BARABAIG, showing two women pouring cow's blood into a pot of milk cooking over a fire. By using short, direct cuts, rather than lengthy dissolve shots, I tried to deliver a visual message that would say "this...and this...and this" rather than use long lengths of shots that might produce tedious "filmic discourse" in places where quick comprehension was possible. This decision, and others, was directly influenced by my having read Alvin Toffler's book, FUTURE SHOCK in which he discusses the accelerated pace at which information (i.e. incoming sense-data) is being transmitted and received in ever-increasing increments (Toffler 1970:162-168).

Knowing that humans seem to have a universal interest in the faces of other human beings, I decided to include enough close-up shots to provide the kinds of information that generate an empathic understanding that sometimes comes from "studying" a human face with its varied expression. Wide-angle shots and normal one-to-one perspectives were used when it was necessary to provide visual information about the physical and social contexts in which the main events occurred. I felt that viewers should have wider reference points from which, and to which, their associational thinking and capacity for imagery might be encouraged.

One problem in film production is to create a filmic structure, linear or mosaic, which can be apperceived by a general audience without the need to explicitly refer to it. My choice of structure was influenced by several considerations; namely, my progressive understanding of Barabaig culture during fieldwork and on my comprehension of the expectations of future audiences (general and anthropological) and their previous viewing experiences with non-fiction film. Thus a basic dilemma existed between attempting to satisfy the needs and requirements of anthropologists and those of the general public. Whereas an audience of anthropologists, or those with a social science background, might be content to view long, uninterrupted shots of mundane activity, such as herding cattle, or the milking of cows, a general audience might grow impatient and become bored with the slow pace of presentation. Young audiences, especially college students, accustomed to the fast delivery of modern filmic and video imagery, have come to expect audio-visual presentations to be a rapid flow of image and information. Therefore, problems of pace (timing) and rhythm (flow) were considered cinematically rather than purely ethnographically and I chose to keep shot lengths relatively short so that the action on the screen would impel the viewer toward a more rapid comprehension of the imagery.

Composite Film as Generalization

Being alone in the field, it was inevitable that I would miss opportunities to film certain segments of a behavioral sequence and, therefore, I had to rely on later exposed footage of a similar event to serve as a "substitute" for the missed footage. Since I did not have a sound movie camera or any means of synchronizing camera and tape recorder, I had to alternate between the two, resulting in material which would later prove difficult to synchronize during editing. This was especially problematical in filming a ritual when it was necessary to reload the camera while the ritual action continued inexorably. However, as I mentioned in my discussion of a "shooting-agenda," I made it a practice to quickly write down a short description of the portions I missed and would later film these scenes or sequences during similar rituals. Thus, I was able to film the "same" ritual at different periods of time, and in different places, to form a composite pictorial record of the ritual event.

Much criticism has been levelled against those filmmakers who have taken "bits and pieces" of scenes filmed in different locations and different times and who then synthesize these portions into a composite picture of an event. Because of extenuating circumstances they might not have been able to film a ritual in its entirety and opt instead to film the missing portions during future occasions of the same type ritual. What will be presented to a film audience is a composite film sequence in the form of a pictorial generalization, much in the manner of a written ethnography when multiple observations or various informants' accounts are generalized to characterize or typify the customary behavior patterns of a society. Such generalizations as "The Trobrianders avoid......" are common in ethnographic literature and are accepted as legitimate. Karl Heider, in his book, ETHNOGRAPHIC FILM tells of audiences feeling "betrayed" when they learned afterwards that the giraffe hunt in THE HUNTERS, or the battle scenes in DEAD BIRDS were constructed out of footage from similar events at different times and then combined to form a single whole (1976:12). Heider also points out that "a comparable construction is done in ethnography" (1976:12). The question of whether this editing approach in film is any more a distortion of "reality" than presenting a character study of an individual and then having the viewer or reader generalize or logically extend this behavior as "typical" of others in the same society must remain for others to answer. Granted, there is generally no continuous, isomorphic correspondence between the images on film and actual physical reality. Nevertheless, I am inclined to side with those who believe that filmic generalization, as in composite filming and editing, is no less legitimate than the kinds of verbal generalizations found in ethnographies. There must be room in visual anthropology for composite film--film which contains a combination of footage that typifies an event. Why is typification considered a legitimate form for presenting literary material but is seen as distortion in ethnographic film? Why must standards existing in one medium be applied to judge other media? If the presentation of cultural imagery is understood by the filmmaker to be a humanistic rather than a scientific approach to the communication of information about a society, why then judge it as "faulty science?" The problem of what is, or is not, "legitimate" in so-called ethnographic film has yet to be resolved and continues to be vexing and intractable.

Editing Decisions and Levels of Information

A filmmaker must decide on the levels of information (visual and verbal) that are to be maintained throughout the film. Visual images and verbal support material, either sub-titles or narration, carry different levels of information and assume different levels of sophistication in the film audience. Film imagery should generate an understanding of the situation in which the purposes and meanings of what is occurring on the screen "makes sense." Being aware that a film audience can experience "information overload," I tried to avoid producing an edited film and sound track which might result in audience confusion rather than enlightenment. I allowed the visual images to "speak for themselves," as much as possible, by not making verbal reference to objects and actions patently obvious to any viewer. Excessive use of sub-titles or narration tend to slow down the tempo of a film and render it pedantic, thus detracting from its own reality. Of course, not all visual images, whether objects or events, will be self-evident and it is in these instances that verbal materials become necessary.

During the editing of my film I was faced with the choice of using either sub-titles or narration in explaining what was happening on the screen. I believe that sub-titles divert attention away from the visuals because they require a shift in the visual mode of processing information whereas this type of oscillation is avoided when narration carries the explanation. My personal preference to use narration was not, however, based on any scientific study of sense modalities (their complementary or antagonistic qualities) but rather on a common-sense notion that any visual shifting would be both distractive and detractive. This is not to say that narration may not occasionally produce the same results. Narration may also detract from the visual eventings on the screen by calling attention to itself because of an overly-poetic or rhapsodic quality, as in the film, THE HUNTERS, when viewers are told that a wounded giraffe "turned slowly and ran eastward....into the night." Or, when the narrator informs us of the inner thoughts of the hunter. While a literate script is generally desirable, forced lyricism and conjectural narrative are a disservice to the viewer who should recognize the difference between factual statements and inferential statements. Viewers should not be left to wonder whether, in fact, the narration was an accurate report on what had transpired.

A narration performs a number of functions simultaneously. From a cinematic standpoint, it provides a means of creating filmic continuity by "flowing" over various shots, linking them into a smooth, coherent whole. On the other hand, narration has a cognitive function when it explains unfamiliar images and sounds and when it discusses things that are not evident in the picture but necessary for a better understanding of it. It keeps the audience thinking along certain lines, and it influences the viewer of massive details and "eventings" to focus attention on a specific area of the screen and to ignore other visual phenomena occurring within the film frame. In sum, a narration should be explanatory, anticipatory of viewer questioning, and complementary in that it completes the experience by providing something that may be lacking in the visual imagery.

It seems rather obvious to state that the choice of words used to refer to or complement the visual images may either raise or lower the level of understanding and meaning for the viewers. For example, anthropological jargon, as a kind of "short-hand" way of talking about something, may make it more intelligible and meaningful to other anthropologists but may obfuscate and confuse viewers without the necessary knowledge of terminology peculiar to the anthropological profession. Use of jargon in narration does not appear in my film, although at one time I considered the possibility of preparing two different sound tracks (one for a general audience and a second for an audience familiar with anthropology). I believe that, to some extent, visual contexts may be comprehended differently depending on the referential nature of the narration, but any testing of this assumption must await further study. Suffice to say, selection of certain words for use in narration may raise or lower the level of abstraction and, therefore, alter our level of understanding. The problem then becomes one of maintaining a continuity of level whenever there is a tendency to oscillate or fluctuate between different levels of abstraction. If the maintenance of abstraction levels is not possible, then we should at least try to become consciously aware of how we shift cognitive and emotional levels during the abstracting process, both as filmmaker and filmviewer.

Ethnocentrism and the General Audience

Certain standards, values, and attitudes are always part of an experiential mix within a viewing audience. American audiences seem to be prone to negative reactions (revulsions) when viewing scenes of butchered animals or body mutilation of humans. The slaughter of pigs in the film DEAD BIRDS, or the killing and butchering of a giraffe, in the film THE HUNTERS, are only two instances where an American audience experiences discomfort and, sometimes, nausea. Similarly, I recall many such reactions of audiences to the sub-incision ceremony of the Australian aborigines in a film by Norman Tindale, the tapping of blood from the vein in the arm of an aborigine in the film EMU RITUAL AT RUGURI, or scenes in the film, NUER, showing large gashes being cut into the foreheads of Nuer boys during an initiation ritual. Having seen various films on bloodletting of one kind or another, I faced the problem of how much to film whenever I encountered similar situations of bloodshed during my fieldwork among the Barabaig. I decided that I must film the events but reserve judgment about inclusion or exclusion of potentially controversial footage until the editing stage. There were three scenes in my film which I felt might cause adverse audience reactions. Rather than delete them entirely, I included them in an attenuated form so that the audience would not be unnecessarily barraged and assaulted by a steady stream of sights and sounds in scenes of bleeding bulls, bulls being hit with sticks, and in scenes of young boys being circumcised. Although I filmed these scenes in their entirety, I edited out most of the bloodiest portions. I simply could not justify presenting a complete sequence in the name of science, or to satisfy any presumed requirement of an ethnographic film. To deliberately shock the sensibilities of an audience, or to shake their composure, was not part of my intentions. Questions about what kinds of film content might shock or greatly annoy American audiences were only partially resolved by self-censorship during the editing stage of film production.

Filmmaking is teleological in the sense that the filmmaker's short-term and long-term goals and intentions serve as feedback, determining the structure and process of the emergent film. Short-term goals, based on (1) need for complete sequences and (2) need for visual data to support ethnographic fieldwork, took precedent over the long-term goals of providing a filmic account of the Barabaig for an American audience (general or anthropological). In the field, the choices and decisions about what to film were shaped by my increasing awareness of Barabaig cultural life around me, whereas, the final structure of the film was mediated by assimilated field experience and determined in the film lab.

One recent trend in anthropology has been toward greater self-examination of its epistemological assumptions and consequences--the self-examination referred to as "reflexivity" (Ruby 1982). While the endeavor to make implicit assumptions explicit is highly commendable (and long overdue), the process by which ethnologist as filmmaker project their personal conception of pattern and order on external, cultural phenomena remains elusive. It is to be hoped that the present volume will contribute toward a deeper understanding of the dialectic process that is generated when the filmmaker and film inter-penetrate to affect each other.

REFERENCES CITED

Evans-Pritchard, E.E. (1940). The Nuer. Oxford: Clarendon.

Gulliver, Philip (1955). The Family Herds. London: Routledge & Kegan Paul.

Hanson, F. Allan (1975). Meaning in Culture. London: Routledge & Kegan Paul.

Heider, Karl (1976). Ethnographic Film. Austin: University of Texas Press.

Klima, George (1970). The Barabaig: East African Cattle-Herders. New York: Holt, Rinehart and Winston.

Ruby, Jay (ed.) (1982). A Crack in the Mirror. Philadelphia: University of Pennsylvania Press.

Toffler, Alvin (1970). Future Shock. New York: Bantam.

FILMS CITED

ALTAR OF FIRE (1977). Robert Gardner and Frits Staal. Distributor: UCEMC (University of California Extension Media Center).
BARABAIG (1979). George J. Klima. Color, 39 minutes, Distributor: PCR Pennsylvania State University.
DEAD BIRDS (1963). Robert Gardner. Color, 83 minutes, Distributor: Phoenix Films.
EMU RITUAL AT RUGURI (1966-67). Roger Sandall. Color, 33 minutes, Distributor: UCEMC (University of California Extension Media Center).
THE HUNTERS (1956). John Marshall. Color, 73 minutes, Distributor: Mc-Graw-Hill Films.
IN THE LAND OF THE WAR CANOES (1914-47). Edward S. Curtis. B & W, 47 minutes, Distributor: UWP, (University of Washington Press).
MAN OF ARAN (1934). Robert Flaherty. B & W, 77 minutes, Distributor: McGraw-Hill, also UCEMC.
THE NUER (1970). Hilary Harris, George Breidenbach, and Robert Gardner. Color, 75 minutes, Distributor: Phoenix Films, also UCEMC.

Structure and Message in
TROBRIAND CRICKET

Jerry W. Leach
Falls Church, Virginia

TROBRIAND CRICKET was made during a period in anthropology when attention was, and still is, focused on the message-bearing aspects of social behaviour. This dominant concern is expressed in the film and this paper is about how messages were built into the whole film through the interrelations of its basic parts, images and words.

The backbone of the film is the relationship between the images of which there are 316 (296 moving and 20 still). These were selected from about 2500 images available when editing began. In anthropological films, it is because one can do little to expand the available set of images after the field period, while the verbal level of the film can be continuously re-shaped to the end of editing, that the relations between pictures tend to form the basic framework of most works. And to obviate the obvious, the medium is film, not written pages.

The framework of images in TROBRIAND CRICKET, however, does not rest on a natural chronology of events. This means that the basic sub-divisions of the film are not related to each other because event X of the subject matter happens before event Y. There is, however, natural sequencing of images within the sections of the film, especially the game block. The major linkages among the sections, though, are conceptual and came about, consciously and unconsciously, in the filmmaking process. What is presented here are the synchronic results of decisions taken diachronically and in a piecemeal fashion. Those decisions unfold diachronically in the film but are intended to lead to a synchronic reconstruction of the meaning of the film in the mind of the viewer after seeing the whole. This paper presents what that intended reconstruction is while fully accepting that each viewer, because of his special interests, will understand the film in some variant way.

Major Messages

There are three basic ways of looking at how the images and verbal statements of TROBRIAND CRICKET are sub-divided and how these sub-

divisions are related to each other. There are, in other words, three simultaneous structures to the whole and the major messages of the film occur
through the imposed sequencing of the parts and the interrelations of their
verbal and visual contents.

Message level 1. Here the film is built on an opposition between Block
A, the opening one minute 32 second section ending with the title, and
Block B, the remaining 52 minutes.

Block A is based on two presumptions: (1) that viewers know they are
going to see something about cricket, and (2) that they have some preconceptions about how unfamiliar and unlike themselves the behaviours of remote peoples are. Block A panders to that stereotype saying "Here is
cricket--but with near-nudity, painted bodies, perpetual noise, dancing, bent-
arm bowlers and slugging batsmen! Is this not proof of how other-than-
yourself these distant people really are?" The intended effect of "chaotic and
ridiculous behaviours" in Block A is enhanced by choppy shots, a slight
shrillness in the sound track, and wobbly camera work plus the lack of any
verbal statement explaining the images. If achieved, the effect should have
viewers at the end of Block A saying "I can never see myself doing what I
have just seen" or more simply "How absurd!"

A nuance of editing in Block A deserves mention here. The opening
image is a ball on the ground, followed by a painted and feathered bowler
who, with arm bent, throws a full toss. The closing image of Block A is a
batsman poised in a roughly familiar fashion in front of a wicket, followed
by his wildly gyrating swing at the ball. The major message of Block A is
here played again in a minor mode, punctuating the beginning and end of
the section. The superficially familiar becomes jarringly something very
unfamiliar, reinforcing the distantiation between the viewer and the players.

Block B, the final 52 minutes, is a continuous attempt to break down
the distantiation of Block A and the stereotype which lies behind it. The
near-nudity is seen in a context of tropical heat and is further explained as
war dress now adapted for a similar type of ritualized competition but also
having stimulus value with female spectators. Body painting becomes a
conventionalized consciousness-changing device allowing players heightened
courage in the game and extra-normal freedom in entering the eroticized
relationship between players and crowd. Chants and dances are a part of that
eroticized relationship as well as the new purpose for playing, i.e. displaying rather than winning, while at the same time being a syncretic re-emergence of customs (harvest dances, tug-o-wars, and chants) formerly opposed
and under threat of extinction. Bent-arm bowlers are found to be behaving in
the natural manner of Trobriand spear throwers. Slugging batsmen fit the
rhythm of the game and become understandable in light of having runners
do the scoring, having batsmen face so many fielders, and having the hitting
of sixes as the main road to individual distinction.

Every element of Block A should stand verbally and visually explained
by the end of the film. It is a part of the process of breaking down

distantiation that each Block A image be seen in close-up and from different perspectives in Block B, allowing the viewer to build up a perceptual grid of how to perform each action. In addition, Block B turns the personalityless object-people of A into subjects who have names, speak idiomatically, have a purpose for being in the film, and feel joy and pain where viewers presumably would too. The intended effect of Block B, the opposite of A, is for viewers to come away saying "I can do what they are doing and wish I had the chance" as well as feeling "I would like to know those people." Otherness becomes cognitively and emotionally familiar, a representation of something already there in the mind of the viewer.

Message level 2. The second of the three simultaneous levels of basic structure in TROBRIAND CRICKET comes through another binary division. The two divisions are Block M, the first 20 minutes up to the date, and Block N, the remaining 33 minutes. The relationship between the two parts is, however, not that of opposition but of complementarity.

The principal reason for this division is that Block N could be, with a re-written commentary, a self-contained short film in itself. A condition of the sponsorship of the project by the Government of Papua New Guinea was that the results be presentable to the people of the many societies of that country. The built-in short form of the film was a safeguard in case the long form did not have sufficient appeal.

This aspect of the structure is not message-bearing of course. At another level, however, the M-N division does have message intent. Block M's main task is to explain Trobriand cricket in advance of seeing it in full chronological form in Block N. Block M is relatively timeless, i.e. outside of real time, because it carries the greater part of the burden of explaining the abstract form of the game. The beginning of Block N ends this sense of timelessness with a precise date which also signals the shift from non-chronological to chronological structure in the images. Block N continues, however, to explain the abstract form of the game while mixing that level, in a relatively balanced way, with explanation of the actual events of the 1974 game.

There are 17 fundamental points about the game and film in the whole 53 minutes and 12 of these occur in Block M. They are:

1. Only men play;
2. Two sides equal but no fixed number per team
3. War dress;
4. Bowlers throw in spear-hurdling style;
5. Runners, not batsmen, score 1-6 runs per hit
6. Outs by being caught, bowled out, run out;
7. Dances to enter and leave field symbolize the theme of a side;
8. Dances and chants celebrate every dismissal;
9. War magic adapted to cricket;

10. Games happen because of political strivings of leaders;
11. Exchanges in valuable foodstuffs follow game and reciprocate everyone for services to the event; and
12. Game evolved from British original.

In Block N come the five remaining points fundamental to the game and film:

13. Games take one day;
14. Umpires, like former war magicians, act for and control their own sides;
15. Games occur in "seasons", i.e. many visiting teams against one host, during harvest period;
16. Formal-informal victory convention; and
17. The film is a sponsored event.

Except for points 15 and 16, each of these fundamentals is repeated at least twice in the film in order to make them retainable after viewing. The 12 points of Block M are all re-stated in different ways in Block N and in some cases, namely dancing, magic and exchanging, their meaning is expanded considerably. Almost all the fundamental information has been presented by the beginning of the game in Block N. Point 17 'The film is a sponsored event' appears at the beginning of N, so as to clarify the status of what is being watched, and at the end of the exchanges, reiterating the message and climaxing it with a statement of the Trobriand purpose for the film, i.e. "to show their fellow countrymen their game" hoping, it might be added, that others would adopt it.

While almost all the fundamental information is being presented two or more times, one crucial piece, the formal-informal victory convention, is held back until near the end of the game in Block N. This serves as a kind of denouement satisfying the audience's expected curiosity about winning and losing. To make this point stand out the image background is very bland. The game winds down immediately after this conceptual climax.

One further point about the complementarity between Blocks M and N. Because Block M's basic function is to explain the abstract form of Trobriand cricket, it contains 53% of the verbal information (commentary and sub-titles) of the film even though it is only 38% or 20 minutes of the whole. Section N by design has more unverbalized space to allow viewers to get more 'feel' of the game.

Message level 3. TROBRIAND CRICKET's third level of simultaneous basic structure occurs through a division into five parts. These parts variously relate to each other through opposition, complementarity, and redundancy. Block V is the opening one minute 32 second section ending with the main sub-title AN INGENIOUS RESPONSE TO COLONIALISM. Block W is the British-international cricket section. Block X is the history-abstract game section ending with the explanatory dance and chant material just before the date. Block Y, starting with the date, includes the preparation-game-exchange sequence. Block Z is the children's game including the credits.

It is impossible to cover here all the interrelations among the five blocks. The following three, however, are of considerable importance:

Block V	Block W	Block X	Block Y
	Block Z		
unfamiliar	British	history-	preparation-
	children's		
"cricket"	cricket	abstract	game-exchange game

|____1____| |_____2_____|

|_____3_____|

Concerning relation 1, the British cricket section is primarily there to give viewers in the non-cricketing parts of the world a brief image and account of the game. The section is, however, also intended to contrast with Block V, the opening version of unfamiliar "cricket." Block W is silent, but for commentary, as opposed to V's irrepressible noise. Block W contrasts as well by having white images, fully clothed players, less dynamic body movements, great distance between players and spectators, and relative emptiness on the playing field. From the startling unfamiliarity of Block V, the eye and mind return to the more familiar order of things briefly and the problem set is "How could the opening section's cricket" bear any relationship to 'our' cricket? The similarities seem so superficial."

An imperfection of Block W should be noted here. The section ends with the line "The game is known for its slow pace." In its context, this line seems to suggest that slowness is fundamental to the game, an assertion that many people would dispute. There is meaning, however, in this "mistake," or as it should be labelled, this editing compromise. First, coupled with the accented, i.e. outsider's, commentary voice, this line and section should suggest that British cricket is susceptible to the same kind of analysis that Trobriand cricket is receiving. Secondly, the line has to say in words what is not "said" in the images, i.e. that cricket Trobriand-style does contrast in pace with British cricket. The shots available while making Block W did not allow the images alone to convey the "slow pace" message. Thirdly and most importantly, Trobrianders say that many changes they introduced into the game they were taught came about because the original game was too slow for them. Unfortunately, none of the discussion material on the yamhouse or the field included this key point so the second-best choice of having the commentator make the point had to stand.

Relation 1, the contrast between Blocks V and W, should generate the question "How could their cricket bear any relationship to our cricket?" Relation 2, linking Blocks W-X-Y, is a kind of answer to this pictorial question. Another diagram will help reveal how the "answer" is structured.

Block W	Block X	Block Y
British	history-	preparation-
cricket	abstract form	game-exchange

| our game | becomes | their game |

The "ourness" of "our game" places all viewers together as outsiders to Trobriand society due to the greater familiarity they will feel, even if they are non-cricketers, with the activities of Block W as opposed to Block V. Taken together with the opening minutes of Block X, especially the colonial pictures, "our game" is taken to be a representation of what was actually imposed in a much larger process of cultural imposition. The colonial pictures also locate the process in historical time, setting up a time framework, i.e. 1903 today, so as to understand how long it took for the Trobriand transformations to take place.

Most of Block X is about the transformations. The main points of primary transformation are, in order of their appearance in the film:

1. Added chants and dances;
2. Changed mission dress of first cricket to former dress of war because few people owned mission clothes and because cricket was fought something like war;
3. Changed from blocking with the bat to swinging to increase pace, display, and fun of the game;
4. Changed from larger to smaller ball because of injuries;
5. Fielders changed from standing silent and stationary to psyching out opposing batsmen to increase pace and spectacle and to give fielders something to do;
6. Changed to Trobriand-style competition putting play under control of leaders because European-style competition caused too many quarrels and fights. Giving control to Trobriand leaders politicizes game by attaching it to their status-building processes thereby leading to the need to reciprocate people for their services to the event, hence exchanges begin;
7. Expanded sides to allow all men of a community to play;
8. Pre-game pair-off became necessary to equalize sides (this rule retained from parent game) but done in ritual war formations as if facing each other across a battlefield;
9. Replaced wooden bails with hand bails because wooden ones were an unnecessary nuisance ;

10. Closed the three stumps of a wicket to make it a smaller target because bowlers were too accurate with the small ball;

11. Overarm bowling became spear-throwing bowling because this was more natural and masculine;

12. Changed from batsmen running to runners running to allow batsmen to swing vigourously, to speed up the game, and to allow old men to bat;

13. Replaced batsmen's running with bats by runners carrying decorated sticks for reaching over the crease;

14. War magic adapted to cricket to give greater control over unpredictable events and enhance performances;

15. Adapted traditional dance movements into new cricket dances to escape opprobrium of missionaries and to increase the pace and the display of the game;

16. Gave each team a name and theme, expressed through its chants and dances.

Numerous of these points appear again in Block Y, the preparation-game-exchange section. The new points of primary transformation found in Y are:

17. Rain magic now used in cricket;

18. Scoring done in a coconut frond in traditional manner;

19. Bowling alternates from either end to increase pace;

20. Changed umpire's role to approximate that of former specialists in war magic;

21. Added one new type of six, a ball hit above the coconut trees, because high and long shots are the most masculine and the best spectacle;

22. Changed games so they are not basically one-off affairs but occur in sets with numerous visiting sides facing a single host but on different days, the size of the set being related to the economic resources of the hosts and ultimately to their political ambitions;

23. Developed the formal-informal victory convention so as not to insult the host and yet allow some competition in playing.

This demonstrates what is intended by saying that Block X stands for "becoming" in the structural paradigm "our game becomes their game." The hoped-for result is that "their game" in Block Y becomes as sensible as "our game" in Block W though the two remain different. The crucial change in attitude should be that "their game" is not longer repelling but has become attractive. The total message "our game becomes their game and though they are different both are attractive" surfaces delightfully near the end of the game when the young student asks the old extroverted cricketer if it isn't "our kind of cricket" now.

A point about the Trobriand discussions in the film deserves note here. None of the discussion material was gathered by direct questioning but only in response to the directions "Please talk about cricket." The sub-titles are fairly literally translated and represent about 80% of what is being said. The remaining 20%, the least interesting remarks, do not appear because the speech speed in the sound track is faster than the reading speed of the audience.

Finally, concerning relation 2 and the transformations of Block X, a caveat deserves sounding here. The yamhouse discussion of Block X presents a folk history and folk model of Trobriand cricket. The anthropological commentary following the discussions illustrates what has been said and then adds to it. At one point a divergence of interpretation between the folk history and the observer's historical model is gently indicated. The Trobrianders in the film suggest that all the transformations were made on Trobriand initiative while historical investigation gives prominence to the Polynesian missionaries, especially those from Samoa, as catalysts in certain changes.

Relation 3 (see p. 4) connects Block V, the one minute 32 second opening section, with Block Z, the one minute 19 second closing part which centres on the children's game. The relations between the blocks are those of complementarity and redundancy.

A form of open-ended thematic complementarity in time is intended as one basis for the Block V - Block Z relationship. Block V shows scenes of an adult game in progress, the "now" of the game considered in relation to time. Block Z shows a practice game by young boys accompanied by the statements "Trobriand cricket has evolved from the parent game over the last 70 years" and "The game is still evolving." The section then suggests the "predicted future" of the game, the underlying message being that the game of the film represents only one point in a series of continuous transformations through time and that this process will presumably not stop now. The boys are the future players who will make something yet again of the game.

There is in the film an example of the "continuous change-never freeze" nature of the game. The 1974 timed event was the first ever to have a mascot. The mascot was terrifically popular with all concerned due to his role-switching antics. He marched as an unserious "pilot" with his "plane" but later became the gawking "tourist." Unseen in the film he also mocked the cameraman by staring back at him through the wooden binoculars-cum-eye-glasses-cum-camera. Apparently, the mascot, an ordinary villager who borrowed the bright clothes from a medical orderly, dreamed up his function on his own. It was so popular that one suspects his innovation might catch on elsewhere.

The thematic redundancy in the Block V - Block Z relationship occurs through the linkage between the main sub-title AN INGENIOUS RESPONSE TO COLONIALISM and the penultimate line in Z about the game's being a "creative adaptation of tradition to contemporary circumstances." Almost everything in the film should have a relationship to this grand theme and provide information for the viewer's questions "How is it ingenious? In what way is it a response to colonialism? How have Trobriand traditions been adapted to meet new circumstances?"

How is it ingenious? As mentioned, nearly everything in the film is part of the answer but the main points start with the Hula cricket section. Cricket was introduced all over Papua but largely remained the international version but for the Trobriands. The viewer should understand he is seeing a singular phenomenon which could have happened elsewhere but did not. Part of the meaning of "ingenious" lies in this contrast with other like societies. Another part of its meaning comes through correspondences with the development of British cricket seen in the history section. British cricket evolved through phases--as did its Trobriand counterpart. Forms of bowling changed to increase the pace and excitement of the game--as with Trobriand cricket. Bats were once curved (for hitting into the ground)--while Trobriand bats became curved the other way (for hitting into the air). Scoring was by notching sticks--analogous to using coconut fronds. The film suggests some parallels in the creativity at play of the British and Trobrianders.

More significant, however, in relation to the "ingenious" question are the creativity echoes found throughout the film between the statements of the grand theme "an ingenious response to colonialism" and "a creative adaptation of tradition to contemporary circumstances." They are:

1. "...the game has undergone a remarkable cultural transformation."
2. "...dances and chants have been especially created for the game."
3. "People have added so much...decorations and all..."
4. "...and then they made it our kind of competition."
5. "So the mission game was already behind us."
6. "And sometimes the words have double meanings."
7. "People are always inventing new chants for cricket."
8. "People are really clever about these things."
9. "on the surface, the players make fun of themselves--but underneath they taunt their opponents--you'll see how blind we are!"
10. (Seen in relation to the thrusting actions of the "tapioca" dancing spears) "Tapioca is a common phallic symbol and scraping it for cooking is an idiom for sexuality."
11. "...PK relates the sure-handedness of the fielders to the stickiness of chewing gum" and is "...a male term for a prostitute" here possibly meaning "I (we) can take on anybody."
12. (Seen in relation to the Aeroplane march-dance, especially the take-off) "A village on whose land a wartime airstrip was built call its team 'The Aeroplane'."
13. (Seen in relation to the dance-swooping bird images) "As an out-dance the team symbolically becomes predatory sea birds."
14. "The mascot imitates a white tourist gawking at the people."

15. "Which makes it our kind of cricket. Absolutely! It's ours now. So white man's cricket...They've rubbished white man's cricket!"
16. The formal-informal victory convention (presumably relatively novel in relation to the world's games).
17. "The leaders of the political movement who sponsored this film wanted it made to show their fellow countrymen their game" (presumably relatively novel in light of the purposes of other similar films).

These are the main parts of the answer to the question "How is it ingenious?" It should be noted, however, that the why question, i.e. "Why have Trobrianders been able to do all this while other groups have not?", is not answered in the film because that remains the major unanswered question in the minds of the filmmakers.

In what way is it a response to colonialism? Here the answer is based on a juxtaposition between inside and outside. Everything that comes from outside the islands is considered part of colonialism. Without repeating the basic transformations lying behind today's cricket, which are responses to what was introduced, the following will note what the outside, i.e. colonial, conditions are as presented in the film:

1. The form of cricket seen in the British cricket section was approximately what was introduced by missionaries.
2. "...British colonialism arrived in New Guinea" (seen in relation to flags and white masters).
3. "Alien institutions were imposed on the people" (seen in relation to gunboats, naval officers, and exploring officials).
4. "Missionaries brought their own moral values..." (seen in relation to fully-clothed bodies, a Western-style husband-wife relationship, big houses, and domestic servants).
5. "...some of these institutions have taken hold in their familiar form--parliamentary democracy in the House of Assembly..."
6. The cars and modern forms of dress that come with colonialism as seen in the images.
7. The "...international equipment and techniques" plus the "overarm bowling" which come with introduced cricket.
8. The first players "...just wore their mission clothes" (later seen in a still photograph).
9. At first "...the bats were the white man's kind."
10. "When Mr. Gilmour taught people cricket they would block the ball with the bat."
11. At first, "...the mission converts used the white man's ball" because '...white men had shown them that way."
12. "...Fijian missionaries...added ideas about how the game could be played."

13. "The first players were early converts to the Methodist Church."
14. At first "The game was played on the grounds of the mission head-quarters."
15. "Government control...was through resident officials--and the Papuan police force."
16. "Traditional warfare was stopped" (by implication, just about the time cricket was introduced).
17. "...mission games were introduced for entertainment, as a substitute for warfare, and to encourage a new morality" (by implication, the new form of competition would be nicer and less violent).
18. The games were first played with 11 players plus a reserve, "the 12-player business."
19. European-style competition meant face-to-face competition out from under the control of traditional leaders which somehow was not supposed to mean anything politically after the competition ended and the victor was clear.
20. "...mission teams weren't allowed magic."
21. The next intense phase of colonial imposition was World War II when land was taken, new machines first came, and new kinds of organization and activities among people were experienced.
22. Outsiders opposed "immoral dancing" (and by implication, "immoral chanting").
23. The introduction of chewing gum brings a new quality to tactile experience.
24. By implication, modern imposed conditions coming from outside generate a political movement internally.
25. Outsiders come to make a film about cricket.

To repeat, it is what happens in relation to these conditions from the outside that is the "ingenious response to colonialism." Obviously, no particular feature or act of Trobriand creativity is being singled out. It is the quantity of such features as a total package which deserves the accolade "ingenious response" in general terms.

How, then, have Trobriand traditions been adapted to meet new circumstances? How is it a "creative adaptation of tradition to contemporary circumstances?" The answer exists in what has gone before but these are the basic points:

1. Dancing has been given a new context.
2. Dances are created out of some traditional dance movements and are representational the way some pre-cricket dances were.
3. Chants have been given a new context, having been formerly associated with tug-o-wars.
4. Chants have been linked up with the themes of the dances and the teams.

5. Bats are painted like war clubs were.

6. War dress has been maintained by carrying it over as the uniform of cricket.

7. War magic has been carried over to cricket performing functions similar to those in warfare such as changing the course of the ball, formerly spear, in flight.

8. The custom of village corporateness in political affairs, mainly warfare, has led to the notion that men of a community should all be able to play cricket, therefore ending the 12-man rule.

9. Spear-hurdling, i.e. masculine, style of throwing has been maintained in bowling.

10. Trobriand-style competition has been integrated into the game, meaning traditional leaders have come to control the entire event and have to reciprocate people for their services to the event, hence a new context for the ceremonial exchanging of food. "Competition became ritualized--and also political" and is called "kayasa."

11. Cricket has given leaders a new domain, similar to kula exchanging, gardening and formerly warfare, within which to compete for reputation.

12. The role of war magician has been maintained through merging it with that of umpire, changing both former positions considerably.

13. The tradition of festivities at the harvest period has been maintained by attaching "new" dances and chants to the game the missionaries introduced and have been proud of, making opposition hard to sustain.

14. Rain magic has been given a new context for performance and belief.

15. Counting by coconut frond has been maintained.

16. The reward exchanges of betelnut (seen during the post-game yam exchanges) have been given a new context.

17. Traditional leaders have come to head a political movement.

Finally, there is an intended message in the grand theme, "an ingenious response to colonialism" and "a creative adaptation of tradition to contemporary circumstances," which is above and beyond cricket or Trobriand Islanders. It is related to the question "How does any of this have any relevance to me, the viewer?" The grand theme, if looked at beyond its space-and-time-bound anthropological context, says "Eve imposed changes can be handled creatively" or put another way "Imposed conditions need not be always alienating because they can be given new meaning." At this level of generality, the grand theme becomes, hopefully, a proposition about facing social change, especially when that change is imposed, seems out of control, or creates con-ceptual or emotional difficulties in orienting to unasked-for circumstances. Thusly generalized, the grand theme would seem to be particularly relevant to facing the problem of neo-colonialism in Third World countries, i.e. whether or not things emanating from the outside world are to be rejected or accepted and, if so, how. In addition, it should be food for thought in the trying circumstances of any individual's life.

Minor Messages

Minor messages are not necessarily related to the structure(s) of the whole of TROBRIAND CRICKET, but are messages, intended for special audiences, which may come from a single line or image, a particular section taken in isolation from the rest, or from the total configuration of the whole. The following are some of the most important ones.

First, for ethnographic filmmakers, is the idea that the people who are the subject matter can participate actively, not passively, in the filmmaking process. The notion lies behind the lines "...the political movement which organized the activities for this film" and "...(they) wanted it made to show their fellow countrymen their game" but most importantly it lies in the credit "With thanks for support, ideas, and organization to--The Kabisawali Movement."

Second, for ethnographic filmmakers and anthropologists, TRO-BRIAND CRICKET suggests a solution to the frequent complaint among Third World peoples that outside academics treat, or at least present, the people being investigated as objects. Film is an excellent medium in which people can be subjects who speak for themselves and have personalities. As a medium, film is probably more immediately appreciable than written pages in Third World settings. This is not to suggest that the conventional written core of academic anthropology, in style or content, should be replaced or altered. It does suggest, however, that film is a supplement to that core which fulfills certain valuable purposes better than the core itself. After all, the era is passed when anthropologists could assume that their research results would not be seen or understood by the peoples investigated.

Third, for filmmakers, the commentator of ethnographic films should be the person who understands the subject matter best for reasons of nuance in tone and expression. The original plan of the film was to have an English-speaking Trobriand commentator but when the sound-editing ended up in London this became impossible. The director, the actual commentator, became the second choice.

Fourth, for anthropologists, the magic material in TROBRIAND CRICKET draws attention, by implication, to one weakness in Malinowski's theory of magic. Malinowski wrote of magic as conservative in all its facets implying near immutability in its rites, spells, conditions of performance, purpose, and whatever. The film displays among Malinowski's own people how war magic has been taken over into cricket while retaining its verbal form and showing conservative parallelism in function.

Fifth, for students of anthropology, the film shows how intertwined are the observer's interpretation of events with those of the participants. At least in the fieldwork-based tradition of anthropology, in which this film rests, the observer's analysis often begins with participants' interpretations, i.e. explanations of what something means or is all about, and even though the observer may go on to find unarticulated significance and new interrelations in his facts, his participants' interpretations remain a kind of check on his theorizing.

Sixth, for those who may need to know, TROBRIAND CRICKET carries the message that dark-skinned people are intelligent and creative. This message should come through their hopefully intelligible explanations of their activities, the quantity of changes they have made to cricket to make it theirs, the word-play and image-play of their chants and dances, their seizing on the film for a purpose of their own, and the credit which thanks them for their ideas.

And seventh, for Papua New Guineans, there is the dual message that some white people do admire village-level customs and that in Trobriand cricket there is a model of how to take parliaments, schools, money, canned food, cars, bureaucracy, English and make them one's own culturally.

Conclusion

This paper makes explicit, in a moderately formalized way, what some of the intended messages of TROBRIAND CRICKET are. The actual messages to any given viewer or audience are, of course, another matter and open to further investigation. It is pleasing, however, to record in closing that the Trobriand sponsors of the film viewed it in January, 1976 and gave it their approval as an accurate representation of their game and of themselves.

ACKNOWLEDGEMENTS

While this paper has a single author, the film itself has two, and grave injustice would be done to Gary Kildea were the reader not aware that many of the above ideas are his or were produced in an intense dialectic between anthropologist and filmmaker during 1974-1975 when the film was in its production stages. This acknowledgment is also a tribute to the amicable dedication of an excellent partner.

TROBRIAND CRICKET also recognized the informant contributions of John Mwakwabuya and Kalitoni Pulitala plus the assistant directors' contributions of Gerald Beona and Bernard Mwayubu, all of the Trobriands.

Dr. Harry Powell deserves thanks for his permission to allow TROBRIAND CRICKET to include excerpts from his film THE TROBRIAND ISLANDERS and Mr. A. Nisbett of BBC-TV is gratefully acknowledged for help in acquiring authentic 1943 war footage from the Trobriands and for help in polishing the commentary.

The author wishes to thank Professor Sir Edmund Leach for teaching him what little he, the writer/filmmaker, knows of the relational theory of meaning, which lies in part behind the message structure of the film.

This paper is a modified version of the Notes to accompany the film TROBRIAND CRICKET distributed by University of California, Extension Media Center, Berkeley, CA 94720. It was originally written for the symposium "Problems of Anthropological Filming" in Section H of the British Association for the Advancement of Science, University of Lancaster, Sept. 6, 1976.

Autobiographical Filming As An Ethnographic Tool

June Nash
Department of Anthropology
City College of the
City University of New York

ABSTRACT: The experience of filming in a mining camp depicting those events described in the autobiography of a miner enhances the awareness of what gives value to life in the dangerous and arduous work in the mines. The life history provides the unifying theme for showing the rituals that brings meaning and motivation in work and family life. The remarkable persistence in culture traits and practices meant that these current scenes could be the backdrop for remembered scenes of a quarter century before.

With an extremely low budget, the author worked with the filmmaker to produce a documentary on Bolivian tin miners that reveals both the joys and the tragedies that the people face. The persistence of rituals reciprocating the hill spirit Huari for the riches of the mines dramatizes the inalienable ties that these Quechua and Aymara speaking cholos retain with nature even while they enter revolutionary movements.

When I was doing fieldwork in the tin mining community of Oruro, Bolivia I became interested in life histories as a means of analyzing how miners put together their experience with consciousness of their condition, ideological persuasion and action. One of the miners whose life history I was recording, Juan Rojas, was forced to retire because he had contracted one hundred percent silicosis, the lung disease that affects all workers. He gave himself a retirement party on his forty-fourth birthday, using a good part of his severance pay for the celebration. When the neighbors, working companions and relatives he had invited to the feast were gathered around the table for the feast, he began to tell them the story of his work life. As I listened to him relate the story of his 35 years of work in the mines, I sensed fully the triumph and tragedy of his life and felt that a documentary based on it would convey the experience to a wider audience.

The following year I applied for funds from the Social Science Research Council and received $5,000. I found a filmmaker, Roy Loe, willing to do

253

the filming on such a low budget. We went to Oruro, the tin mining center at 14,000 feet altitude in the Bolivian highlands, in July 1971. Because of the limitation in funds, we decided to combine documentation of what was happening in the community with limited dramatization of the events to illustrate his life history. I had completed editing Juan's autobiography, HE AGOTADO MI VIDA EN LA MINA (Rojas and Nash 1976), and I selected those events that seemed to encapsulate the life of a mining community.

The scene I had witnessed at the birthday party the year before became the entry into the life history. Juan again invited neighbors and friends to celebrate with him the end of his career as a first class driller. The force and vitality of the people, which had so impressed me in my year of life with them, comes through in the vigorous dance scene with which the film opens. People are not "camera conscious" in this culture that lacks television and even still cameras. The presence of a camera and sound equipment did not disturb the rhythm of their lives.

In order to introduce viewers to life in a mining camp, I selected an incident from Juan's childhood when he was lost just after the family moved to the Patiño mines of Siglo XX. Juan persuaded a neighbor's child to play his role in childhood. The child was very self-possessed in entering an unfamiliar scene in Siglo XX and improvising on his own with little instruction. He joined a group of kids playing marbles without being instructed to do so. As he wanders through the encampment, we can see the row on row of housing, built from the twenties up to the forties, that captures an earlier way of life that still goes on.

Among the events which I had selected from the autobiography for dramatization was an accident Juan had seen when, at the age of eight, he started work as a "parrot," one who warns workers in the tunnels of a landslide from the slagpile. In the remembered event, Juan had seen an explosion which caused the death of a man burned from head to foot. He was asked to accompany the man to the highway to catch a ride to the hospital some forty miles away. The man died on route, and Juan returned to work. The next day he fell asleep from exhaustion and woke up to see men flying in the air as rocks fell from the slagpile where he worked. He thought they were dying and that it was his fault because he had failed to blow the whistle. He asked to go home after he learned that the men were not injured, but on the way, he felt a paralysis come over his legs. He was treated in the mine's clinic, but his mother carried out a soul-calling ceremony with a yatiri, or curer, without him being present.

We got a good deal of cooperation in dramatizing this sequence. The "agonizing" man was the father of the actor who played Juan as a child. The men who rescued him were working in an abandoned shaft that we chose for the site of the accident, and they were glad to fake an accident when they had experienced so many real ones. A psychoanalyst and ethnographer, Mario Erdheim of Switzerland remarked after reading Juan's autobiography that he had never known people who faced death as directly and without fantasy as those in the mining culture as shown in Juan's autobiography. The people confront the most horrible accidents without forgetting a detail or repressing the incident. What Juan, as a child, could not handle without supernatural assistance was the guilt he felt in being participant at the accident and not having prevented it.

Juan attributed his cure to his mother's soul-calling ceremony with the yatiri. I had visited a yatiri the year before who served the mining community. I was impressed by his house, stuffed with items he had picked up at carnivals and in the junk pile of the camp: battered toy airplanes, a kewpie doll, a man's skull, along with dried herbs, llama foetuses and the other stock in trade. Our Bolivian assistant in production, Eduaro Ibañez, regretted that he was too acculturated--he wore a mechanic's jumpsuit and knit cap. But he was the kind of practicing curer whom the miners choose, and it would have been an ethnographic error to search out a non-acculturated yatiri who worked with peasants. Our curer was totally matter-of-fact in his approach to the supernatural, going about his business like a drill repair mechanic in the mine. He chose to speak in Quechua with Juan's "mother" and in Spanish to the skull, possibly because the skull, which he said represented the source of his power, must thereby be a representative of the Spanish-speaking power holders in the society.

In order to film the inside scenes, we had to get a generator. Production was held up three days as we looked for one to borrow. The Catholic mission had one, but it was being repaired. The mine administrators would not lend us any of their overtaxed models that were constantly in use pumping water out of the mines. Finally we decided to buy one, using one-sixth of the grant for the purchase. The first night we tried to use it in the yatiri's house, it would not start. The yatiri, who was a diviner as well as curer, had advised us that it would not before we even began priming it. The next evening he was more optimistic and it did start.

We were lucky in having events happen in our brief two-week stay that illustrated the life of the mining community. The fiesta which is the background for the betrothal scene took place in the chapel of Chiripujo (cold place) that miners frequent on the south side of the town. It is a small chapel at the site of the enchanted stone reptile. A myth miners tell about the early years of mining with the Inca relates that Huari, the hill spirit, was angered by the exploitation of the mineral riches he controlled and sent out four monsters to destroy the people. They were saved by the Inca Virgin who turned the monsters to stone and turned an army of ants to sand, all of which can be seen in the perimeter of the town. These enchanted figures appear in the opening scenes of the film. I asked one of my compadres, a young couple just starting their family, to enact the betrothal of Juan and Petrona which took place at a similar fiesta twenty-five years before. The automobiles shown in the fiesta date from the forties, like most of the operating vehicles in town, so we do not have obvious anachronisms. However, in the year 1946 when it was supposed to have occurred, there would have been even more archaic autos.

The ritual of the k'araku, or sacrifice of an animal to the "Uncle" (the familiar name for Huari) was filmed by Eduardo Ibañez in a small mine we visited on July 31, the eve of the Month of Huari. Roy had already left and Eduardo filmed the sequence of the sacrifice of the llama with an old camera with which he was not familiar. It is overexposed, but probably the only ethnographic filming of open-heart surgery on a llama in existence. The palpitating heart, which is the gift of miners to Huari in return for the riches he yields from the hills, was too important to drop despite technical weaknesses. In this sequence, we try to capture the time in Juan's life right after the revolution when he persuaded the engineer in charge to carry out the sacrifice in order to find some new veins and then, as an explorer driller, came upon a key vein which is still yielding mineral.

We decided to do the interior shots in Siglo XX because they are more prepared to receive visitors. Fortunately it was during the presidency of Juan Jose Torres and just before the military coup of Banzer that took place the following month. With the greater liberalization and the support miners had from the president, we had entry into the mines. The administrators were expecting some visitors from the Soviet Union, and when we entered, most of the men thought we were Russians so we had a warm welcome. With a great deal of effort, we got the generator down to the lower levels, and in the process attracted a large group of security technicians, foremen and workers. When we got to the work site where the advance drilling was going on, we had so many headlamps focused on the operation that Roy decided we didn't need the generator. "We just brought it to show the technical superiority of the United States to the Soviet Union," he quipped. The headlamp lighting did succeed in preserving the sense of obscurity that a miner lives with, and this would have been destroyed with full light.

Our real problem came when we returned and had no money to edit the film. The Social Science Research Council granted me another $5,000, but film costs and reproduction rose dramatically in 1975 and we were just able to put the film together without sound synchronization. Finally I took out a personal loan of $3,000 and we got a Spanish version put together. Our problem in editing was that we did not have taped narration that perfectly matched the visual parts. This was corrected in the English version by drawing material from the autobiography and having the English-speaking impersonator of Juan fill it out, but the Spanish version will have to rely on the audience's ability to bridge the gaps with his or her own imagination. I found some documentary photos from earlier times in the New York Public Library and added these along with newspaper clippings to suggest the political events Juan had experienced when the military occupied the mines and stood with rifles cocked as workers entered to work.

The complexity of the political and economic events was impossible to render with words or direct visual representation. I finally decided to use a song I had recorded during the celebration of the sacrifice to the Uncle. The sob in the soloist's voice as he sang of the military repression changes to laughter as his work comrades join him, clapping to the cueca dance tune. We ran it with the footage of headlamps playing on the devil figure that Roy filmed in our trip to Siglo XX mines. The miners' militancy, derived from the collective spirit generated in such rituals, comes out in the clapping and laughter as they sing of the Generals Barrientos and Ovando who posted the army in the mines and carried out the massacres of the workers and their families in 1967. By timing the clapping just at the point when the car-carrying workers come out from the dark tunnel into the blinding light of day, the film captures some of the impact of the political events and how miners respond to it without depicting it as graphically as was done in Sanjines film, THE COURAGE OF THE PEOPLE.

We decided to end the film with the birthday celebration rather than the despair Juan feels knowing that he is going to die and will probably not get his pension from the company to keep his family going. It is a celebration of Juan's victory and that of the mining community--the victory over dehumanization in the work process and over the attempts by a military-industrial repression to crush the spirits of the workers. Juan's life parallels that of the rise and fall of the national revolution. He was made a first class driller when the mines were nationalized in 1952. He contracted silicosis in 1965 when General Barrientos sent the troops into the mines. He celebrated his retirement just before the military coup of Colonel Hugo Banzer who instituted seven years of the most cruel repression Bolivia has experienced in its long history of military coups and exploitation. It is, as Juan says in his toast at the birthday party, a story not only for the family, but also for all mining communities and the nation, and maybe even for the world.

THE MAJOR FILMS OF JUNE NASH

I SPENT MY LIFE IN THE MINES: THE AUTOBIOGRAPHY OF A BOLIVIAN TIN MINER (1976). A film by June Nash and Roy Loe. 42 minutes, color, sound, some English subtitles and voice over as well as a Spanish version. Distributor: Cinema Guild, 1697 Broadway, New York, NY 10019.

REVIEWS OF THE ABOVE FILM

Kearney, Michael (1985). Review of I SPENT MY LIFE IN THE MINES. American Anthropologist 87(2): 484-485.

Filming The Fidencistas:
The Making of
WE BELIEVE IN NIÑO FIDENCIO

Jon L. Olson
Department of Anthropology
California State University, Los Angeles

ABSTRACT: WE BELIEVE IN NIÑO FIDENCIO resulted from filming a Mexican Spiritist group two years after initial fieldwork. Informants' knowledge of the filmic process influenced both the content of the film and the goal, which they perceived as the promotion of cult activities. Anthropologist-informant reciprocity resulted in the counterpart of a *promesa,* an obligation to present the participants' point of view in the film. Even though there were severe limitations imposed by budget and equipment, NIÑO FIDENCIO has been a useful teaching film, and continues to provide insights into the questions about the nature of film and reality, the depth and complexity of culture as expressed in magico-religious practices, and the importance of reciprocity in the network of anthropologists, informants/participants, and students/audiences.

In October 1971, Natalie and I returned to the site of my first field research in Northern Mexico in order to shoot some 16mm color footage of life in the area, particularly the activities of the Niño Fidencio spiritist groups with whom we had worked in 1968-1969. The Fidencistas are a charismatic spirit possession cult similar to other groups throughout Latin America. They believe that they can be possessed by God and other spirit beings, who give them the power to perform miracle healings for their followers. They base their beliefs on the teachings of one man, Fidencio Constantino, who has become a folk saint in the area since his death in 1938, and whose tomb has become a shrine to which the faithful make periodic pilgrimages.

We wanted to get footage of the October pilgrimage celebrations that I could cut into short films to use in lectures, and that could possibly be edited into a film for general distribution. To this end we had purchased two old spring drive Bolex H-16s with some turret lenses and some outdated stock from a discount film supply house. We were anxious to get back to "our" village; we knew many people in the area and we looked forward to renewing friendships. One of our closest informants was a leader of one of the cult groups, and we felt excited about doing our first film project with the people we had become so familiar with and had left two years earlier.

I was a beginning assistant professor at California State University at Los Angeles, and we had little money to mount a major film project on our own. I had the fall quarter off, and since we were returning to do some follow-up fieldwork, we thought that it would be a good idea to do some filming. We had investigated various educational film groups in the Los Angeles area for possible backing to no avail. We had no track record as yet, and apparently a first film on such an esoteric subject as a Mexican mystical cult seemed too risky. We felt that we didn't want to attempt the lengthy grant process because we didn't know when we would have another opportunity to return to Mexico. Besides, we had thought primarily in terms of the initial filming only, and we had enough money for that. If the footage was good we could arrange for more funding later.

During our initial field research we had both done extensive still photography in both 35mm and 2 1/4 inch formats. In California we had taken an ethnographic film production class organized by Arthur Niehoff, who was then chair of Anthropology at California State University at Los Angeles, and which was taught by an experienced educational filmmaker. We felt that with our anthropological and photographic experience and our $450 worth of film and equipment we could get some useful footage.

We decided that our basic approach should be a straightforward recording of as much behavior as time and film would allow. We would use two complementary cameras when we could. Natalie would also shoot stills and record interviews and wild sound. We would use the tripod as much as possible to minimize distractive movement. We would try to get complete processes and acts within the limitations of the approximately 20 second spring run time and 100 foot (about three minute) reel, and we would try to avoid the then-current filmic fads such as extended extreme closeups of hands and faces, rotating cameras, shooting up from the floor and the like.

We arrived in town (Mina, Nuevo Leon, population about 1,000) in the middle of a Charriada, a local fiesta which features horsemanship competitions, trick riding, a beauty contest, and the usual eating-drinking-dancing. A special event was the Norteño (Northern Mexican) riders' competition during which a live goat is dangled just beyond the reach of horsemen who try to grasp it as they gallop underneath at full speed. The behind-the-scenes activities also had filmic possibilities. Children played at their own versions of the adult activities, women socialized, and men politicked.

We spent a hectic first day in Mina shooting as much footage of the Charriada as we could. The footage is good, but we have yet to produce a short film on the subject. The next few days we reestablished contacts with friends and informants and planned the film/research logistics. We shot footage of goat herders, again with thoughts of cutting a short film on rural economic activities in Northern Mexican villages. We visited our friend, the local Fidencista curer, Cayetana, and arranged to film one of her Sunday healing sessions. As always, Cayetana was cooperative.

Cayetana's ritual sessions are typical of the Fidencista cult. She has built and decorated an altar in a room in her house that is devoted to cult activities. A supporting group of women adherents prepare songs and prayers which supposedly call upon God to allow His spirit to possess Cayetana's body. She is then able, with the help of the Power of God, to perform diagnoses and healings for the assembled congregation. An account of some of the other functions of this local cult group can be found in Olson (1977).

Cayetana's house is very small, and the room containing her shrine becomes extremely crowded during her Sunday sessions. We set up flood lights to illuminate the altar-curing area, but we were unable to move about to any great degree during her ceremonies. Most of the filming was done within 5 to 10 feet of Cayetana, which resulted in some good close-ups, but which limited the variety of the shots.

Cayetana repeated the ritual we had seen many times before. As the congregation prayed and sang special songs to Niño Fidencio, Cayetana appeared to be taken over by the spirit of the Power of God, and she began to show the mannerisms and voice that supposedly indicated the depth of her possession-trance. She then began to treat the members of the congregation, still in possession-trance, but repeatedly whispering aside to us, "Is this what you want me to do?" or "Are you getting this all right?" We assured her that we were doing well and that she should just do what she would if we were not there shooting film. This turned out to be a continuing problem during the other filming sessions as well. The people of this area have full access to television in the towns and villages, and to commercial film in the cities, and are thus quite sophisticated in the mechanics of film production. We found this to be particularly true of the "possessed" practitioners, who have a strong sense of showmanship and who almost invariably played to the camera. This also confirmed our suspicions about the depth of their possession trances. Some of the footage from that Sunday session appears in WE BELIEVE IN NIÑO FIDENCIO (1973), the film that eventually resulted from the trip.

After the Sunday session, we talked to Cayetana about going with us to the Fidencista shrine in Espinazo (Nuevo Leon) the next week for the annual ceremony commemorating Niño Fidencio's death. We felt that she might act as the central character in our footage and thus give continuity to any edited version of the film. However she had decided not to go that year because of local commitments and because the week-long festivities were too hard on her. She was then in her late 60s, and was not as active anymore in cult activities outside the town.

We also talked to a previous acquaintance who was suffering from throat cancer and who was undergoing radiation therapy at a social security hospital. Although a non-believer, he was going to attend the ceremonies on the chance of a miraculous cure. He was willing to have us film his pilgrimage, but we felt that he was doing it out of a sense of courtesy and friendship to us, and that he really wasn't very enthusiastic about the idea. We decided not to intrude into this very personal matter, and we declined to include him in the filming.

Ultimately we decided to go unaccompanied to the ceremonies. We decided to collect recorded interviews (as we had done previously), and take footage of the various activities without concentrating on any particular central character. We made out a rough shooting script in which we would try to film as much as we could to give an overall view of Fidencista activities. On paper, we allocated about 4500 feet of our film to activities that we knew we wanted to capture, leaving about 1500 feet (25%) for eventualities, a margin for errors and accidents, and for unanticipated opportunities. As it turned out, these initial estimates were pretty well on the mark.

We drove our camper-truck over almost-impassible muddy desert trails to a small ranch near Espinazo. We stayed with a family with whom we had had many dealings previously. After greetings and some filming of the family goatherding activities (some of this footage appears in NIÑO FI-DENCIO), we began to visit Espinazo in order to film the preparations for the ceremonies. The older children of the family with whom we were staying invariably accompanied us to town and introduced us to many of the people involved in the cult activities. We made sure that people clearly understood our purpose for being there, our connections with the local family and the people in Mina, and our general interest in cult activities. Many people remembered us from our previous work in the area, and offered to participate in the filming.

Guided by our rough shooting script and footage allocations, we began. Occasionally we were able to use two cameras so that we could get complementary angles, and so that we could overlap the times required to rewind and to change rolls of film. However, most of the time I filmed with a single camera, while Natalie shot stills, did tape recording, and dealt with the people who were either curious or wanted to offer their help and advice.

The most difficult and aggravating part of the filming (beyond the very oppressive heat and humidity) was the short run time for each camera wind. The spring-driven Bolexes only provided about 20 second bursts per wind, interrupted by 20 to 30 seconds of winding between shots. Each roll contained about three minutes of available footage, and with another two minutes or so required to change film, it was very difficult to capture an unbroken "whole act" (Heider 1976:82-86). Since the Bolex H-16s were completely manual, proper exposure and focus was also a problem. We partially solved this by Natalie reading off distance and exposure from her through-the-lens SLR, but it was a clumsy procedure at best. Amazingly, less than five percent of the approximately 6000 total feet exposed was unusable because of focus or exposure problems; predictably, this was mostly footage taken indoors or at night in low light settings. Another exasperating technical problem was the "flash" incurred along the edge of the film while loading the camera, especially in bright sunlight. Even though we tried to change rolls with a change bag over the camera when shooting outdoors, the light still crept in, and flash appears on some of the best footage.

During the week of filming at Espinazo we tried to record as much of the activities and as many of the groups as possible. We decided to work for a broad coverage of the festivities in order to gather enough information to do a later series of comparative studies of stylistic differences, kinesics, contrasts in dress and visual symbolism, etc. We realized that this approach might lead to continuity problems in editing a film for general audiences, but we opted for comparative overview rather than a more narrow coverage of a single group or individual. Ideally it would have been best to do both, but we realized that because of the limitations of time, resources, and the size of our "production crew," we had to decide between depth and breadth coverage.

Like Cayetana, the participants in the festivities were cooperative. Many were interested in what we were doing and commented on the benefits of producing a truthful, sympathetic film of Fidencista practices. When we asked if they thought that anyone would be offended by our filming, various people commented that most of the people knew who we were and why we were there. Besides, it was really up to Niño Fidencio; if he didn't want the film to be made he would fix it so it wouldn't come out.

We were particularly well-received when we stated that most of the people that would see any resultant film would be students. There was an attitude that the beliefs and practices of the Fidencistas should be more widespread, and that we had a communications function to serve. It was during these discussions that we found ourselves entering into a kind of *promesa* relationship with the followers to make a film about the cult as closely as possible to their own point of view. This reciprocal relationship with informants strongly influenced later production decisions, and continues to be part of our basic ground rules in filmmaking. One episode will illustrate the point. One evening we were invited to participate in a possession-healing session of one of the groups. As is the customary belief, the spirit of Niño Fidencio supposedly entered the leader and enabled him to perform a series of miraculous cures for his followers. As is also customary, Niño Fidencio delivered a speech-sermon through the mediumship of the cult leader. That evening the message went approximately as follows ("approximately" because we were not tape recording):

> "My children, you may ask yourselves why I (Niño Fidencio) have permitted these two North Americans here to film my celebration...I will tell you why...I pulled them down here from their homes in the United States with my magic cords...(He makes a gesture as if he is controlling the strings of an imaginary marionette)...so that they can make a film about the truth of Niño Fidencio...and after all

the people of the world see the real truth they will believe
in me and in my Father in Heaven...and there will be no
more racial discrimination in the cities...and there will be
no more violence in the cities...and there will be no more
war in Viet Nam...and there will be peace."

This was followed by specific directions to the congregation to be helpful
and cooperative with us because we were there by the Niño's own desire "to
tell the story of Niño Fidencio."

In another episode, we had set the camera up near the railroad depot in
order to film the arriving crowds. A group of Matachine dancers in full ceremonial dress descended from the train and began to dance to the accompaniment of their drummer. We had just focused the camera on them when
their leader gestured to us not to film. I walked over to him, introduced myself, explained that I certainly would respect his wishes not to be filmed,
and apologized if we had offended him or his group in any way. He quickly
explained that it wasn't that at all. They had just introduced some new dance
steps into their routine, and they wanted to iron out the mistakes before
they performed in public in front of the shrine area. They certainly wanted
to be filmed, but only during a good performance at the proper location. We
agreed, and the group appears in NIÑO FIDENCIO.

If anything, the people could be said to be too cooperative. Performance
is such a large part of religious ritual generally, and the Fidencistas tended
to overdue in some cases. We overheard one medium, who supposedly was
in deep ecstatic trance, as he whispered to his assistants, "Are they ready?
Are they ready now?" We were fumbling about as we tried to extract a
jammed roll of film from the camera. We signaled "ready," and the medium
went even deeper into his trance.

The Fidencista celebrations are to a large part folk drama, and we think
that although there may have been some playing to the camera, basically
the film records the same behaviors we have observed during our various
visits without film equipment. The reciprocal relationship we felt with
them compelled us to film them as they would have outsiders see them...at
the peak of their performances. There is some behind-the-scenes contextual-
ization in the resultant film, particularly in the narrative voice overs, but
WE BELIEVE IN NIÑO FIDENCIO intentionally presents the Fidencistas
as we think they would want to see themselves. In short, we hope that the
distortions of reality are primarily those of the participants rather than those
of the anthropologist-filmmakers; our *promesa* became to tell their story in
their terms, recognizing the fact of their knowledge of, and in some cases,
manipulation of the filmic process.

After spending a week of shooting in Espinazo, we returned to Monterrey to rest up, to visit friends, and to shoot additional footage of urban life.
We particularly wanted to get footage of the Social Security hospitals and
other health care alternatives to use in comparison to the Niño Fidencio
practices. Upon arriving in the city, both Natalie and I became ill with in-

testinal distress which progressed into colds and flu, probably a result of overwork, little sleep, and exposure to pathogens in Espinazo. After an additional week of recovery, we filmed the scenes we needed and left for Los Angeles, again stopping off in Mina to bid farewell to our friends and to get some final establishing shots.

We depleted the last of our funds in getting the film developed in a professional lab in Hollywood. The technical quality of the rushes was good enough so we decided to go ahead and try to cut the footage into a film for general distribution. As we had taken the fall quarter to do the filming/research, I had to concentrate on my teaching and on completing my dissertation during the next two quarters. The editing would have to wait until summer, so we concentrated upon assembling the script from translated interviews and recording various readers to use for the sound track.

It was at this time that the fundamental decisions were made; perhaps "reconsidered" is a better term. The projected audience was to be college students, particularly anthropology, sociology, psychology, and nursing students. The film should be 30-40 minutes long to allow time for discussion during one-hour classes. Most importantly, we wanted to keep our promise to the Fidencistas. This meant little or no "anthropologizing" in terms of theoretical interpretations, functional analyses, comparative statements, and the like. It also meant the inclusion of the semi-mythic account of Niño Fidencio's life and career with no anthropological footnoting.

We considered our basic approach to be a mixture of etic and emic perspectives as discussed by Harris (1968) and others. The "etic" aspect of the film would be the visual footage and wild sound where appropriate, which would give the viewer an idea of the events and participants during the Fidencista celebrations. The "emic" component would be comments translated from taped interviews and read by individuals whom we judged were close to the tone, attitude and voice quality of the original informants. By using only informants' accounts, we thought that the viewers would gain an insider's view of the practices, and that this would be most consistent with our overall goals.

As we might have anticipated, the etic-emic goal to make a film close to the informants' point of view (with no informants around to help us out) brought us quickly into some pragmatic and profoundly philosophical problems and decisions. Shall we include the cuts with "flash" on the edges? (Yes, when they are crucial to the film; no, when they are at all expendable, even when they may be some of our "favorite" shots.) What should be the basic structural order of the film; the real-time chronology of events? The sequence of the filming? The unfolding of the story in a way that would make sense to both audience and Fidencistas? We chose the latter option, even though it probably required the greatest distortion of reality; the other two approaches would have lead to overly-segmented discontinuity. Should we include information about Cayetana's (and others') playing to the camera? Here we felt that the "truth" about their showmanship would distort and betray our emic commitment; the issue could be dealt with outside the context of the film.

As editing progressed we began to have doubts about the relationship of the film to the actual events. Did a particular segment really show the way it happened, when it was assembled from cuts taken at different times, places, and with more than one group? We knew that juxtaposition was necessary in virtually all film editing, and that such time and sequence distortion was a usual point of discussion about such pioneering ethnographic films as NANOOK OF THE NORTH (Flaherty 1922) and THE HUNTERS (Marshall 1956). Yet we were concerned that the ethnographic reality was somehow getting lost in the editing process. Judgements were made on the basis of how "close" the segment was, or how "well" it communicated an event with proper mood and "meaning." Were we getting anything close to a complete picture of the Fidencista practices and, more importantly, their own understanding of what was going on? Our answer had to be: No. We came face to face with the fact that cultural systems are multilayered processes, and that the symbols and meanings of Niño Fidencio contain depths of significance and nuance that we probably will never fully appreciate, let alone communicate in a film.

Editing proceeded throughout the summer, again limited by lack of funds. Most of the rough cutting was done without the aid of a moviola or any other motorized editing table. We borrowed some manual rewinds and a 16mm viewer and proceeded by carefully keeping track of footage/timing; only occasionally would we take the film to a local small production studio to get an idea of the continuity and flow of the scenes on a moviola.

Money was a continual headache. The titles had to wait until we could save the two hundred dollars to pay for them. On various occasions, footage or an answer print would wait in the lab, sometimes for weeks, until we had accumulated enough cash to bail it out. We became friends with an editor-producer of educational films who, besides doing small jobs at a cut rate for us, offered free advice and use of his lab as long as our work didn't interfere with his activities. As he commented, he couldn't make a porno film for as little as we were spending on NIÑO FIDENCIO.

By fall, 1972 (one year since the filming) I had finished my dissertation and we had a timed answer print of WE BELIEVE IN NIÑO FIDENCIO. We went to the meetings of the American Anthropological Association to present a paper and to get feedback on our efforts on the film so far. The film was generally well-received and we were grateful for the constructive criticism offered. It was here that Professor Barbara June Macklin introduced herself. We knew that she also had been working in Northeastern Mexico, and with Fidencista groups in particular, so we had made a special point of inviting her to the preview. She was angry and offended that we had gone ahead and produced the film without consulting her, and that she thought that we had used her name as an inroad into contacts in Espinazo. In fact we had heard of her work in the area, but had not met her previously. While in

Espinazo we had been asked if we knew her; we had answered that we didn't know her personally, but we knew that she was also an anthropologist interested in Niño Fidencio. It was indeed an oversight that we had not contacted her previously, but that was one of the purposes of bringing the film to the convention.

We left the convention upset and disappointed about the new development with Professor Macklin. After a series of letters in which we apologized and tried to clarify our intentions, we came up with a tentative agreement to collaborate on a later work on the history and practices of the Fidencistas, with a chapter which would stand as a guide for the film. We met once more at another AAA convention, where we talked again about a possible collaboration. We never completed the work, primarily because I became involved in other studies. Although we both have presented and published subsequent works on Niño Fidencio (Macklin 1974, Macklin and Crumrine 1973, 1974; Olson 1977), the draft stands uncompleted.

In early 1973 we spent our last money for a set of release prints. Up to that point, NIÑO FIDENCIO had cost us about $3,000. We decided to distribute the film ourselves because distributors in the Los Angeles area were hesitant to deal with a film that they perceived as having too limited and specialized an audience. Natalie's father had run his own mail order business for years, so he offered to try his hand at film distribution. We had never intended to make large amounts of money from the film (also part of our *promesa*), but the film has done moderately well in the last ten years. WE BELIEVE IN NIÑO FIDENCIO broke even in the third year of distribution, and the rentals and occasional sales continue to provide activity and a small supplemental income for Natalie's father during his retirement.

The greatest benefits from NIÑO FIDENCIO have been in the area of teaching presentations. In addition to my own classroom use, the film continues to be incorporated primarily into medical anthropology programs throughout the country and in universities in Mexico and Canada. We have guest lectured at various universities where the film conveys aspects of Mexican folk culture and spiritist practices that are difficult to communicate by lecture alone. The film inevitably elicits active discussions, and viewers often express ambivalence about the "unexplained" or "inconsistent" aspects: how can they be Catholic and Fidencista at the same time? Are the leaders really in trance? Do the cures work? What do non-believers think of Niño Fidencio? How is this similar to or different from faith healing in other cultures? The emic nature of the film gives viewers little interpretation or analysis of what they are observing so that they must think about what it means in their own framework of understanding. To some people this seems to be disturbing; I think that these people would rather have the film interpret for them what it is all about and why the people do what they do. For others, NIÑO FIDENCIO stimulates their curiosity, and I believe gives them a more relativistic experience than if the film had done the interpretive analysis for them. Fortunately, those who have been stimulated in a positive way have outnumbered those who have been disturbed.

We have shown the film in Mexico to spiritist and non-spiritist groups, and again the reaction has been reassuring. Most viewers have responded that the film does indeed accurately capture not only the practices but something of the mood of the Fidencistas. Some interesting criticisms came from a group in Oaxaca (Southeastern Mexico) who are spiritists, but who are not followers of Niño Fidencio. They appreciated the technical aspects of the film, and they thought that it was a generally fair depiction of spiritism. Their complaints were: (1) That it wasn't proper for Niño Fidencio to imitate Jesus. (They don't.) (2) They wondered why the Fidencistas were possessed only by Niño Fidencio and not by the spirit beings (*seres*) that they were familiar with. And (3), that some of the Fidencistas were not showing proper trance behavior and therefore were probably fakes.

Now that ten years have passed since the first release prints, we have an ambivalent attitude toward WE BELIEVE IN NIÑO FIDENCIO, as I am sure most other filmmakers do toward their "first film." It would have been a much better film if we had had more film experience, more money, better equipment, a trained crew, etc., etc. But I think that our experience reflects the condition of many anthropologists, especially those who are close to their first fieldwork, whose first concern is ethnographic research, but who are intrigued by the possibility of making a film. It is these people who are the sources of the proverbial cans-of-film-lying-forgotten-on-the-shelf.

But it is also these people who have made important contributions to the library of ethnographic film when they have been able to carry their film projects through to completion. I see WE BELIVE IN NIÑO FIDENCIO somewhat in the genre of THE TURTLE PEOPLE (Weiss and Ward 1973), a film that may have some technical/production problems because of the financial limitations and inexperience of the anthropologist-filmmakers, but which is an important film nonetheless. We cannot expect all ethnographic films to reflect the skills (and funding) of the Yanomamo series (Asch and Chagnon 1970) or of Gardner's films (1963, 1970, 1974).

This is not an excuse for low quality films, nor am I arguing against a pursuit of excellence in ethnographic filmmaking. It is simply a realistic recognition that those anthropologists in the best positions to make a film contribution may not be the best funded nor the most skilled. Nor may they want to make filmmaking a major thrust in their careers. They may be motivated by the challenge of trying to make a film and by a desire to visually communicate a cultural way of life to their colleagues and students. Their work is valuable, and this paper is partly a plea and an encouragement for them to complete the task and then to do it again.

Since NIÑO FIDENCIO we have participated in a number of film projects, some in 16mm (LITTLE WARRIOR, BROKEN BOTTLES), but mostly videotape exercises in the Los Angeles area. The lessons learned from NIÑO FIDENCIO and from subsequent experiences are consistent with those expressed in the literature, particularly by Karl Heider (1976), and warrant repeating. Leading the list is the necessity of thorough fieldwork before filming, followed by as much film/video experience as possible. There is an obvious benefit in the greatest possible technical competence both in anthropology and filmmaking, but there is an equal need for seasoned flexibility in the inevitable on-the-spot decision making. As in all documentary filmmaking, the best laid plans (and shooting scripts) are bound to need changing, occasionally in mid-shooting. The anthropologist-filmmaker has to have an understanding of the events and cultural setting to know where a change in filming plans will lead in relation to the goals of the film. For example, when we were in Mina during the week before the ceremonies in Espinazo, we were invited to film in the local health clinic, and particularly the activities of the local midwife who assisted the visiting physician. This would have been important and interesting footage, but we knew the extensiveness of her activities. To film her adequately would use up too much film and would limit ourselves because we were friends. She would insist on our filming all her activities that she knew were of interest to us. We declined. It was the proper decision; after Espinazo we had just enough film to film the remaining scenes in Monterrey and a few establishing shots besides.

It almost goes without saying that the best equipment and the most film/tape possible should be obtained. Through-the-lens focusing, synchronized sound, and automatic exposure are part of most film and video systems today, so the question is usually not about the inclusion of these technical features, but about their quality. Starting costs are usually only the tip of the iceberg, and a realistic estimate of total production costs is imperative. Therein lies a crucial decision; if filming is to be a supplemental part of fieldwork to some area where there is little chance that the investigator will be returning in the near future, my position is that footage should be obtained if at all possible, and the costs of completing a film can be negotiated upon return. If the field situation is more accessible, I advise my students to get the basic field study completed first, while making notes on filming opportunities for the future. In this manner the investigator has time to reconsider and plan back home as the ethnographic account emerges. Not only can the filming budget be planned more accurately, but the anthropological-theoretical perspective can be clarified, hopefully resulting in a more coherent film than would result had the investigator done the filming during the first time around.

What has also become clear to us is the importance of the social networks that are related to ethnographic film production. The relationships among the filmmaker and the informants and subjects of the film are primary, followed by the networks of co-filmmakers, colleagues, students and other viewers. Few people in the modern world are naive about film, and their goals and understandings must be considered. To this end, a great deal of insight can be obtained from Worth and Adair's work with Navaho filmmakers (Worth and Adair 1966, 1972).

Other documentary film orientations, particularly so-called "docu-dramas," may be based on rationales of intentional slanting in order to make judgements or to manipulate viewers into a specific value/political position. In contrast, I think that with anthropological film there is a basic obligation to be ethnographically truthful. But the anthropologist's truth may be different from the protagonists'...and there is a good chance that the subject people will, and indeed should, see the film. I feel most comfortable with the emic-etic combination approach discussed earlier; the film should reflect in a fundamental way the subjects' perspective and understanding of their way of life. The anthropologizing can (and probably will) come later. No gimmicky shots, no extreme angles, no extreme effects that are bound to become cliche. In other words, there should be nothing in the content or style of the film that would offend the subjects or that they would not understand. I fully realize that this doesn't result in a value-neutral or "objective" film. It is our position that since all films express intentional and unintentional value orientations, ethnographic truthfulness requires that the film reflect the orientation of the subjects as closely as possible. Not only is this most fair to the subjects, but also provides the additional emic dimension for the viewer, who is then free to make his own interpretation.

In summary, in a larger sense, making NIÑO FIDENCIO has had a significant impact on the progress of my career in anthropology. First is the benefit of learning a craft and the challenge of making tapes and films of diverse cultural happenings. It has been great fun. Second is the profound appreciation of the fragile quality of "reality" and "truth" as we try to assemble visual projects pieced together from selected shots and angles edited into the necessary time compression, and then when we experience the inevitable frustration and guilt that the film isn't quite the way the events and people really were when we filmed them. Does reality really have a beginning, a middle, and an end?

The third (and perhaps most unexpected) benefit gained from the filming experience is the realization of the complexity and interrelatedness of cultural systems. Can we see and film events in a way that we can later make into a film that makes sense to both observers and subjects? What are the various levels of meaning in a symbol like Niño Fidencio? How do we come to understand and then communicate such complexity? What are the insights we might gain into semiotic processes by comparing cultural meanings (theirs and ours) as represented in film compared to the meanings communicated in written material? The struggle of cultural understanding and translation inherent in ethnographic filmmaking has provided me the insight of the depth of differences in cultural systems, and an appreciation that we anthropologists may approximate but never really "translate" the total levels of meaning of one cultural system into the meanings of another.

Finally, we have come to appreciate the nature of a *promesa,* not in the sense of a promise to a supernatural force, but the obligation and reciprocal respect for people and what they value. Visual anthropology is minimally a three way communication system: subjects/informants, anthropolo-gist/filmmakers, and audience. The anthropologist/filmmaker is the middle link in the chain and so is under the obligation of truth and respect to both the other parties. For us, this communication system is based on the im-plicit *promesa* that we will communicate from the subjects to the audience with the minimum distortion and with the maximum effort to tell the sub-jects' story the way they would if they could speak to the audience them-selves.

REFERENCES CITED

Harris, Marvin (1968). The Rise of Anthropological Theory. New York: Thomas Y. Crowell.
Heider, Karl G. (1976). Ethnographic Film. Austin: University of Texas Press.
Macklin, B.J. (1974). Belief, Ritual, and Healing: New England Spiritualism and Mexican-American Spiritism Compared. IN Religious Move-ments in Contemporary America., Irving Zaretsky and Mark Leon (eds.). Princeton, New Jersey: Princeton University Press, pp. 383-417.
Macklin, B.J. and N.R. Crumrine (1973). Three North Mexican folk Saint Movements. Comparative Studies in Society and History 15(1) 89-105.
Macklin, B.J. and N.R. Crumrine (1974). Saints, Cults and General Ceremo-nialism. IN The Unconscious in Culture, Ino Rossi (ed.). New York: Dutton.
Olson, Jon L. (1977). Women and Social Change in a Mexican Town. Journal of Anthropological Research 33(1) 73-88.
Worth, Sol and John Adair (1972). Through Navaho Eyes: An Exploration in Film Communication and Anthropology. Bloomington: Indiana University Press.

FILMS CITED

DEAD BIRDS (1963). Robert Gardner. Color, 83 minutes. Distributor: Phoenix.
THE FEAST (1968). Timothy Asch and Napoleon Chagnon. Color, 29 minutes. Distributor: DER (Documentary Educational Resources).
THE HUNTERS (1956). John Marshall. Color, 73 minutes. Distributor: McGraw-Hill Contemporary Films Inc.
NANOOK OF THE NORTH (1922). Robert Flaherty. Black and white, 55 minutes. Distributor: McGraw-Hill Contemporary Films.
NAVAHOS FILM THEMSELVES Series (1966). Sol Worth and John Adair. Black and white, 7 films. Distributor: New York University Film Library.
THE NUER (1970). Hilary Harris and George Breidenbach, with assistance of Robert Gardner. Color, 75 minutes. Distributor: McGraw-Hill Con-

temporary Films.
RIVERS OF SAND (1974). Robert Gardner. Color, 85 minutes. Distributor: Phoenix.
THE TURTLE PEOPLE (1973). Brian Weiss and James Ward. Color, 26 minutes. Distributor: B and C Films.
WE BELIEVE IN NI^NO FIDENCIO (1973). Jon and Natalie Olson. Color, 45 minutes. Distributor: Jon and Natalie Olson.
YANOMAMO: A MULTI-DISCIPLINARY STUDY (1971). Timothy Asch and Napoleon Chagnon. Color, 45 minutes. Distributor: National Audiovisual Center, and Documentary Educational Resources.

THE MAJOR FILMS OF JON AND NATALIE OLSON

WE BELIEVE IN NIÑO FIDENCIO. 1973. A film by Jon and Natalie Olson. 43 minutes, color, sound. Distributor: Jon and Natalie Olson, P.O. Box 14914, Long Beach, California 90814.

European Visual Anthropology: Filming In A Greek Village

Colette Piault
Structures Sociales et Familiales en Grece
Centre National de la Recherche Scientifique

ABSTRACT: The aim of this short article is to relate my own experience of filming in Europe, in a Greek mountain village working simultaneously as anthropologist and filmmaker. The problem that I have studied for ten years is village desertion as a consequence of migrations, from the point of view of the village, gathering all possible data, observing year after year and making diversified films.

The article is an attempt to communicate through reflections and anecdotes the making, in 1979, of my first Greek film on Greece, "Everyday is not a Feast Day", in which the "hero" had to be the whole village. I tried to talk about relationships with villagers, and technicians but also about film structure itself, choices, treatment of words, cultural translation. The conclusion is an attempt to point out the problems that we'll have to discuss and solve in the future and that I discovered through my new collaboration with the National Film and Television School (Beaconsfield, G.B.).

This article is a short story presenting two main characters: Ano Ravenia, a Greek mountain village in Epirus, on one hand, and a French female anthropologist/filmmaker, on the other hand.

These two characters naturally do not exclude the implication of many others dependent on them. Let's first introduce these two independently before coming to their initial meeting and subsequent personal evolution in time and space. The center of this relationship is for both characters to know the effects of migration on the village and the desire to transmit this knowledge to the outside world, mainly through a film.

I. The Village

Ano Ravenia is a mountain village like many others found in Greece and in other Mediterranean areas. There is nothing exceptional about it apart from the complete banality of its situation. In 1974, the village had 240 inhabitants. By 1984, there were at most 170 permanent residents, now generally older than before. They live from livestock herding, some subsistence farming and retirement pensions. The population is composed of three ethnic groups: one autochthonous group and two stock herding nomad groups (the Vlachs and Sarakatsanis), who are now settled.

If the village seems on the surface to be independent and self-sufficient, careful observation will reveal that its economic, social and family life as well as the thoughts and feelings of its inhabitants are closely tied to the outside world, in which all who have left have found their livelihood.

Daily life is spent waiting for the two or three annual occasions, Easter, the patronal feast in May, and the summer, when young and middle-aged relatives who work and live away in towns or abroad, make a temporary return visit.

The life of those of the outside world forms the main part of the villagers' conversation both before and after these events. When one event has past, the villagers wait for the next.

This seems to be a widespread phenomenon and unexceptional, an expression of the relationship between town and countryside in areas affected by very strong migration.

Ano Ravenia is well situated, a few miles off the main road connecting Ioannina to Konitsa, located at an altitude of 1,800 feet with a wide plain at its feet, now much too large for the few inhabitants left, dominated by an imposing classical building, the primary school, where nowadays depending on years, only seven to nine children attend. The school was built at the end of the XIX century when the village had probably more than 500 inhabitants. A second church, now abandoned and only opened once a year for the patronal feast, was also constructed in these times at the top of the village. Except during the few annual occasions when the village is temporarily packed with people, it looks rather quiet and empty.

II. Our Meeting

I first came to Ano Ravenia in March 1974 when Greece was still under dictatorship. I was looking for a village of this size still alive with working activities, children at a school, with no police station, and without any contact with tourists nor touristic activities but submitted already for a long period of time to migrations. It was my first working stay in Greece and I took a Greek student, a girl, as interpreter, as my knowledge of Greek was not sufficient yet; but it was my only stay with an interpreter. It was still winter and in the cold and rainy weather we visited about eight or ten villages in the area. If we stayed into Ano Ravenia, it was because its situation coincided with my demands, there was an empty house that we could rent and there was no police station in the village. In the winter, since people in the village have just one room heated and therefore they could not take both of us in, it was necessary for us to have our own house.

So partly by choice, partly by chance, I landed in Ano Ravenia and studied carefully, year after year, the effects of migration from the point of view of the village, as well as the processes of change.

My research was different from studies which imply first a long stay and one or two visits a few years later. Some of the studies could present an aspect "change" to the infrequent visitor, which becomes perceptible only after the event and therefore its "nature," imperceptible. I therefore came to the village for one or two months each year from 1974 onwards to perceive change in action, or at least recently past. Its perceptibility to me meant I could understand "how and why" in terms of the present more than from the standpoint of the past only.

In fact, staying one or two months a year corresponds to the local Greek rhythm too. They did not actually expect me to stay longer than their own children coming from Athens or abroad. Moreover, when we arrived last winter to film they all asked why I came when it was so cold and empty instead of enjoying summertime! So my own rhythm was adapted to local habits, if not to traditional anthropological rules, i.e, one long stay covering all seasons.

Although the villagers were rather surprised by these two women arriving in early Spring to study their life and their village, as soon as I returned alone the second time, I became a friend and without any clear understanding of my aims or work, slowly year after year, they accepted me, as a foreigner of course, and liked me more and more. If being liked is a minimum condition to come into contact with a community and understand it, at the same time it can raise a lot of demands from the villagers and it can sometimes be difficult to respond without being stifled. What is now so clear to me is that you can tell people a thousand times that you are making a film or writing a book about their village, you can show the film to them or have it programmed on television but what is essential for them is you as a person. They said it to me quite clearly: "We agree to collaborate with you on your film through the friendship that we developed with you." Being warm, smiling, and generous will (at least in Greece) always be more important than to be stiff, cold, important, and write a thick book or make a famous film about a village.

However, I introduced myself as an anthropologist, a title which in Greek (because it is a Greek word) can be roughly understood without knowing at all which activities it covers, and I told the villagers that I would write about the village, take pictures and make films. Although they saw my first film about them on television, and later saw it projected in the village, many of them still do not know exactly when we are filming and when I was taking still photographs. Strange, but true!

III. Making a Film, EVERYDAY IS NOT A FEAST DAY

Before 1974, I had already made two films, one in the North of France, and the other one in Africa, shooting on both occasions myself with a spring wound camera, a Beaulieu. I arrived in Ano Ravenia with the same equipment except that this time I had an electric Beaulieu. For the sound I had a Uher tape recorder and my friend and interpreter operated it in 1974. Skipping the details, I must say that although I have about one hour of rushes and some sound from my first three years of filming, because of technical problems (the camera was out of order each time after two days shooting), and because of the unreliability of the young male villagers[1] whom I tried to train as sound recordists, I never managed to make a film under these conditions. Then I tried to obtain from the CNRS in France, a sound recordist with a Nagra and a good camera for myself. The only possible way to do this because of administrative reasons (very determining in my country) was to have a crew of two technicians with more sophisticated equipment (an Arriflex BL and a Nagra) or nothing! It was a long flight to get that crew. Finally, I managed it in 1978, although I had presented the project and was accepted by the Sociology Committee of the CNRS in 1974! If I find it necessary to give these details, it is because anthropologists abroad believe wrongly that it is easy to obtain financial support to make anthropological films through our CNRS (Centre National de la Recherche Scientifique) and they envy us. In the sixties, films were cheaper, equipment simpler and the administrative weight lighter. But since 1972-1974, to raise the money and organize a project is a daily fight for months or even years.

For EVERY DAY IS NOT A FEAST DAY, I had the crew with their expenses, equipment and part of the editing paid by the CNRS, but my own expenses, travel and accommodation, film stock, processing and dubbing costs were financed by other sources, mainly by myself. That is why it took more than 5 years from the project's inception to its completion.

III. 1 - The First Shoot, May 1978

Having given some account of the difficulty of actually raising the money for a film, let us return to a discussion of the village.

I went to Ano Ravenia in 1978 with a cameraman and a sound recordist, (the cameraman's girlfriend). My intention, as it was my first attempt of bringing strangers to the village, was to start shooting the patronal feast. It was easier to insert the presence of new people when the village welcomes its own outside crowd. So we started by filming what is now the second part of the film. There was no problem. The crew could not speak a word of Greek but the villagers liked them. However we had to tell the vil-

lagers that they were already married otherwise they could not have been together all the time, going for walks alone at night and sharing the same
room. Their private behaviour was considered as strange to villagers because
married couples are not expected to show tenderness or love in public in the
Greek cultural context. A couple is supposed to have a baby in its first year
of marriage and to be concerned by "serious" problems such as work, building and settling a new house, etc. I stayed a month myself but the shoot and
the crew's stay lasted 12 days. I had decided that the film would be shot over
at least two periods. It is an important point to me: a look on the first
rushes and some distance seems necessary to me before completing a film.[2]
That was the first.

Back in Paris, I assembled the material and managed to bring the working copy in double system to Athens and showed it in a small room at TV
(ERT 1). I invited people of the village who lived in Athens to this projection and who were in many occasions in the film since they had been in
Epirus for the feast. Such a step was very important for the next shoot because they enjoyed the film very much and told the rest of the village that
they could trust me and collaborate fully with me.

Although this first part was not bad at all, I felt that having known the
village and its inhabitants for so many years I would like intimacy to show
in the footage in addition to the main aspects of daily village life and the
important problem of desertion.

III. 2 - The Second Shoot, April 1979 - Easter

My aim was to put more emphasis on family life and if possible, relationships, and not to be attracted by what was going on during public occasions, nor what the village wanted to show first as more "traditional" or
spectacular. The couple, Philippe Lavalette and Manon Barbeau, who had
fulfilled the first shoot, under the Greek influence maybe, got married and in
April 1979, they already had a baby girl. Although people of the village
were disappointed they had not made a son as was preferred, they were relieved to know that they were a couple like the couples they had around
them. Since Manon was feeding the baby, the CNRS proposed another
sound recordist, Francois Didio. I had to convince people, mainly the
woman who cooked for us, that he was nice, as nice as Manon. Because
they did not know him, it took him a few days to settle himself with the
village. Fortunately, he was kind and being technically competent he fixed
for the villagers one old TV set and a few lamps and plugs. Therefore he
was a "good person" and they accepted him. This shoot lasted four weeks,
covered many sequences of daily life, working as well as leisure activities,
the preparations for Easter, the arrival of kin from towns or abroad, Easter
itself (but not as a religious ritual, but more as a family gathering including
traditional activities like painting the eggs in red, etc.), and finally the de-

parture of the crowd, leaving the village empty and quiet again.

Although it poured with rain around Easter, although the camera failed us at the end of a baptism necessitating us to rush 600 kms to Athens to rent one, in order to return before the last visitors had left the village, I can say that everything worked fine.

Sometimes, despite the pleasant cooperation of the villagers, I had to confront some power relationships. For example, the school teacher said that he had permission to let us shoot in the classroom but without any lesson taught, and no words. I said "Too bad, but let's do it." When we went into the classroom, he was giving a geography lesson, then the children sang and he did not pay any attention to us. We shot and in the event it made no difference to him whatsoever!

The priest, in order to show that he was the "Master of the Church," told me that we could shoot whatever we wished but without lighting. I explained to him that nothing could be seen on film without lighting, that I had tried already in my previous shootings and that it seemed to me a shame that the priest and the church could be absent from a religious feast. He wanted to be filmed but he also wanted to show us that he had the decisions in his hands and thus replied: "If the Church Council--five people--agree, I do too." So I went to see each of the five, some of them very good friends of mine, and asked them. Each one said "If the others agree, I agree too." I went back to the priest, telling him that they all agreed and he said "All right then!" This manoeuvre took me almost a whole day! I am quoting this anecdote to show how even a film made by an anthropologist very concerned by her relationships with the villagers, and not only by the film itself, can raise problems which have little to do either with scientific work or film technique.

III. 3 - The Basis of the Film

Although we all know that as soon as we introduce a camera into a situation it can never be exactly what it would be without filming or even observing, nothing in EVERYDAY IS NOT A FEAST DAY was acted in the sense of asking people to do certain things, say certain things, or to behave a certain way.

For some sequences however, I had "appointments," for example, to shoot women going to the well, I asked two women whom I knew well when they would go for water and if we could shoot that action. They agreed and told me: "Tomorrow at 4 P.M." Thus, we waited for them on their way to the well, and followed them filming.

A few scenes were shot in this way but most of the film was shot by just being there, wandering around the village and recording spontaneously what was going on as long as it was pertinent according to my former study of the village and the aim of the film. What was satisfying to me was to notice that an action that I had observed before many times was the same while filming, without major alteration. It happened however that some tension that I had observed, for example during the waiting for the postman, for reasons independent from us was not as strong the day we shot it as many other times. Let's say it was an average day. There is nothing we can do to avoid that fact. I thought that shooting the same action many times could allow me to choose the most meaningful or the best but I learned that the interaction between the people filmed and the camera very often cannot be a matter of repetition which kills surprise, spontaneity, and therefore, life.

This point is important because many of the criticisms levelled at the film concerned that aspect. It is a new problem for anthropologist film-makers. This arose when anthropological film began to transcend the obvious limits of "public ritual" and attempt to deal with the private and personal aspects of daily life.

For ten or fifteen years already, there are very interesting films about daily life made by very gifted filmmakers focussed on one single family, two children etc...[3] but not being inserted in a long term study, they could avoid that problem, settling with people just the relationship they needed for their period of filming.

My aim was totally different and I was more concerned with the difficult task of making a comprehensive film about a whole village, where the "hero" is the village itself, than by keeping the spectator interested by all means. Knowing more now about anthropological filmmaking, I know that I could probably have conciliated the two aspects.

For example, in EVERYDAY IS NOT A FEAST DAY I was so determined not to break the atmosphere, to have the spectator watching the film as if he was himself in the village and to have him make up his mind by himself, from the data presented, that I forgot an essential point later made by Colin Young when he carefully analyzed and criticized my film on an editing table, the communicability of the material.

III. 4 - Cultural Translations, Captions

When we subtitle a film, we do so in the knowledge that we pass from one language to another--what is said becomes intelligible, what is however misunderstood is that we pass information from one culture to another, thus we need a "cultural" subtitle sometimes to help the spectator understand the footage by seeing into it, instead of giving him (or her) the task of unravelling it. This can be done by means of "captions" or any technical device. I wanted so much not to break the sensitivity to village life that I did not do it and it appeared that it was obviously a mistake. If (according to Colin Young's expression) I let "the spectator see," I think now that I let him see in darkness or in shadow! A few captions would have been enough...although some television stations did not even want to screen it because of the lack of commentary!

III. 5 - Words and/or Commentary

The absence of commentary in my films is a point that I would like to discuss. From the very beginning of my work as a filmmaker in 1965, I disliked and was shocked by commentaries, didactic, descriptive or poetical. In the sixties, when speech was the most important element in films shot without sync sound and with a spring wound camera, it was really a challenge to avoid a commentary. In these times, my solution was to give the minimum necessary explanations using as "voice over" people who took part in the film, belonging to culture presented.

For example, I shot a film in the North of France[4] in collaboration with a group of young fenlanders. We wrote a short introductory commentary together giving the necessary information at the beginning and recorded one of them saying it. But the main explanations were from discussions that they had together, very often controversial discussions, that I recorded along a few evenings and inserted as voices over. I am very concerned about keeping the homogeneity of a culture and not introducing what I call roughly a "colonial voice." So many films for a long time were only images chosen to illustrate an argument that an anthropologist (or an explorer) wanted to communicate to his public.

For me, the visual continuity is very important and I am careful not to break the homogeneity of the atmosphere by an outside "studio" voice, although I am perfectly aware of the fact that my films are my own views on people or actions.

Nowadays, with the possibility of sync sound, the use of a commentary can be optional or only part of the words said. I remember the shock and the satisfaction I felt in the Venice Anthropological Film Festival in 1972 when I saw (and for me it was the first time) a film on Africa subtitled. It was a MacDougall's film, TO LIVE WITH HERDS.[5] The fact that we could suddenly understand some of the daily conversations of the Jie instead of being wrapped in an intellectual westerner commentary was a real event. And if for me it was a positive shock, for some filmmakers used for so many years to participate to their films or to keep the control on it through their own voice, it was also a shock, but a hard one...

How did I face the problem of explanations and words in general in EVERYDAY IS NOT A FEAST DAY? The film opens with a shepherd pasturing his sheep. He explains the village's life and problems. Some spectators[6] thought he was either acting to a script or answering questions which had been erased. This was not so. This man is highly educated, a former agronomist and civil servant, fired from his position for political reasons during the Greek civil war. I asked him to introduce the village as he wished, warning him that too personal interpretation of his politics would be unfair to a general view of the village. He talked non-stop for ten minutes; we changed the magazine and he talked again for ten more minutes. We kept the six more meaningful minutes as an introduction. In the case of others, I told them before filming, "Just talk about your life as you want and stop whenever you feel like it." So they talked to the camera, for the film, to a future public but not to me. They knew that I knew what they had to say already. They were talking to a horizon beyond me! For example, there is a sequence at the end of the film where a young man explains why he loves to stay in the village, how he enjoys this quiet life. His father disagreed with his idyllic presentation of village life so I gave him the opportunity to express himself and he refuted in front of the camera what his son had just said, emphasizing the difficulties of life, money problems, etc...

Everything said in the film has been recounted by the villagers to the camera, i.e to an imaginary public to whom they wanted to introduce the village and themselves.

Therefore, the film is the image that I and the villagers through their explanations wished to give of Ano Ravenia to the outside world. In this context, it is not surprising that, for example, although women can be seen, and heard talking between themselves, they can never be seen (with one exception) explaining something nor talking to the camera about their life or their problems: In Greek village culture, it is not, generally speaking, a woman's role to talk to the outside world. But this fact does not mean that I had any problem collaborating with them in filming.

By contrast, most Greek people (mainly men) in Athens were surprised that I had been able to shoot inside houses and kitchens with male assistants. That was not a problem at all. The technicians were considered as my "extension." Where I could be, they could be too. [7]

III. 6 - Collaboration with *Stricto Sensu* Technicians

Shooting EVERYDAY IS NOT A FEAST DAY was for me the first opportunity to collaborate with qualified but *stricto sensu* technicians. Paradoxically, we have to know more about filmmaking technique when we direct a cameraman than when we are our own cameraman. In short, the cameraman knew too much for me on a technical level and sometimes used "fiction" devices that I could not detect while we were filming. On the other hand, the film benefited from his competence and some shots are visually very attractive. Because he wanted to be a good cameraman and no more, he was not so involved in the film project itself but only concerned by the quality of his camera work. He took great care of frame, light, focus and when he was ready to shoot, I sometimes had to tell him sadly (because he was so concentrated on his preparations that he had not even noticed it) that there was no more action. The situation had changed, people had left!

For example, he also convinced me (and at that time, I had not much experience in editing) that without a "reverse angle shot" I would not be able to edit the sequence. So the film language became a mixture of different languages. I discovered this with Colin Young when he pointed out "inconsistencies" in style in some sequences.

The sound recordist did not raise so many problems. He was experienced and, what is very important, used to work for a long time with this cameraman. He also had the right temper to be a sound recordist. He was independent, having no need to be taken care of and was interested by sounds.

But I must say that technicians who switch non-stop from one shoot to another cannot be concerned by the film project, its content, its aims, its whole making. After our return to Paris, the cameraman took care of processing the rushes, he saw them before synchronization and his technical role was over, he lost contact with the film that he saw one year after it was completed.[8]

From that type of collaboration, I did not conclude that I had to be my own cameraman and sound recordist to make my own film. Quite the opposite. I understood how important is the technical process in the making of an anthropological film and how the type of training and the personal involvement of our collaborators plays an important role.

IV. By Way of Conclusion...

It seems to me that I have described throughout this paper different aspects which occur while making a film and also pointed out some difficulties. But I have not said enough about how important the film project is and the preparation of its making.

There is a widespread idea according to which you can use a camera as a fountain pen and, being an anthropologist who is supposed to know a culture, you can just shoot images the way you gather data. In a certain way, we can say so if we do not forget how long we learned and experienced before to be able to gather systematic and proper data which was usable and transmittable.

A film, anthropological or not, is an autonomous enterprise which should be understood without sending the spectator to written works. We can notice that many--if not most--anthropological films of a good quality have been shot not by anthropologists themselves but by those that Tim Asch calls "Ethnographic filmmakers," which means filmmakers specialized in anthropological matters or/and, far away populations. This shows how the filmmaking is dominant in an anthropological film.

What then is an anthropological film? From my very personal point of view, the only difference would be that there is an underlying period of study which supports the film and which has sometimes to be considered for many years. But I must confess that the best observational documentaries which deal with daily life (which is my main point of interest) are works of filmmakers who are non-academic anthropologists, and who have not worked for years on their subject. These remarks could lead to an interesting discussion about what is finally the specificity (if there is any) of an anthropological film compared to a very fair, sensitive and well made documentary. But the aim of my paper is only to relate my own experience and some consequent remarks about it.

As an anthropologist, I feel that our films imply a precise and sometimes sophisticated methodology. In a book, we usually dedicate one chapter to explain the methodological aspects of our work. In a film, we cannot do the same but maybe we can try, at least, to let the spectator know where we are and what is our relationship with the people involved in the film. What is the most satisfying way is to present the film ourselves in order to answer all questions concerning the making and the methodology. That step is necessary because images are ambiguous and we cannot avoid the spectators watching our films as they watch any other. Maybe, in the future, a solution will be found to this problem. Already we are no more afraid to talk with the people filmed, to give them a camera and incorporate their images in our film, nor to appear in the frame.

Related to that methodological aspect, I feel very strongly that each film project demands its specific approach. Let's give an example. From my point of view, a film should be more than an opportunity to write a dissertation supported by images. Some film subjects, of course, are difficult to be treated with images only, but we need to work on this problem and find some solutions. We have also to show things actually happening instead of trying to convince the spectator with words that they happened that way. Nowadays, because of the relative easiness of recording sync sound, in anthropological films or social documentaries the filmmaker (instead of really making a film on a subject or a problem by showing what should be shown--which is sometimes in practice difficult), asks people filmed to talk about it in front of the camera. He shoots and records them. Then we have a film about something else: the speech of people involved in their problem, or whatever the subject may be.

I have no objection against such films, and I made two like these myself: first, a conversation between young girls, THREAD OF THE NEEDLE[9] and also the life story of an old woman A HARD LIFE.[10] They are what I would call "talky films," expressing mentality, sometimes much more, but they cannot be shot the same way as observational films which try to follow actions and events. For example, these "talky" films in which the subtitling will be important cannot accept too many camera movements. In some films like CELSO AND CORA,[11] spoken parts and actions alternate, but Gary Kildea was aware of these problems and he modified his shooting style according to the content. So everything is possible, if we take the means of our aims and before that, if we make these aims clear and precise. These last remarks are, of course, the product of a new way of shooting and editing that I started to experience through the making of three films in 1983 in Greece. I had the privilege of benefitting by a very stimulating collaboration with Graham Johnston, a student film maker of the National Film and Television School (Beaconsfield, Great Britain). While I am finishing writing down this short and modest paper, I am also at the end of these three films and I need some distance to discuss properly these new orientations and discoveries. I will keep these matters for a next article.

NOTES

[1] Girls, of course, were not allowed to wander around in the village.

[2] In 1983, we shot three films. One was a sort of reportage on a wedding day and had no reason to have more than one shooting but the two others were shot over 2 or 3 periods of shooting.

[3] Let's just quote NAïM AND JABAR (Hancock and Di Gioia), KENYA BORAN (Blue and MacDougall) and more recently, CELSO AND CORA (Gary Kildea).

[4] LE BROUCK (cf. filmography)

[5] TO LIVE WITH HERDS, David and Judith MacDougall, filmed with the Jie.

[6] As well as Peter S. Allen in his review of the film in the American Anthropologist.

[7] Last summer, we shot a wedding, the cameraman and the sound recordist were the only men in the bride's room during the preparations, without any problem.

[8] For the sound recordist, his work was completed after having written down the sound report and made the transfer in 16mm tapes.

[9] THREAD OF THE NEEDLE (cf. filmography)

[10] A HARD LIFE (cf. filmography)

[11] CELSO AND CORA, Gary Kildea, 110', 16mm, color, 1983.

REFERENCES CITED

Allen, Peter S. (1982). Review of EVERY DAY IS NOT A FEAST DAY. American Anthropologist 84: 754-756.
Allen, Peter S. (1984). Review of THREAD OF THE NEEDLE. American Anthropologist 86(2): 510-511.

FILMS CITED

ALBERTINE et DORCAS (1972). A film by Colette Piault, 25 minutes, colour, optical sound, not sync. Short commentary in French. Distributor: Les Films du Quotidien, 5 rue des Saints Peres 75006 Paris, France. tel (1)260 25 76

LE BROUCK (1972). A film by Colette Piault. 45 minutes, black and white, optical sound, not sync, text and commentary in French. Distributor: Les Films du Quotidien (cf. supra).

EVERYDAY IS NOT A FEAST DAY (1980). A film by Colette Piault, (G.R.E.C., and CNRS audiovisuel) 110 minutes (possible to divide into two 55' segments) color, optical sync sound, Greek original version, English or French subtitles. Distributor: Les Films du Quotidien, (cf. supra) or in the USA: B.R.F. Jean-Claude Dubost, 777 Fourteenth Street N.W., suite 747, Washington, DC   20005, telephone: (202) 638-1789..

THREAD OF THE NEEDLE (1982). A film by Colette Piault, (Ministry of Foreign Affairs and CNRS audiovisuel) 22 minutes, color, optical sync sound, Greek original version, English (or French) subtitles. Distributor: Les Films du Quotidien (cf. supra) or in the USA: Maliotis Cultural Center (cf. supra).

A HARD LIFE (1987). A film by Colette Piault with the collaboration of Graham Johnston (NFTS, Beaconsfield, G.B.), 55', color, optical sync sound, Greek original version, English subtitles. Distributor: Les Films du Quotidien (cf. supra).

LET'S GET MARRIED! (1985). A film by Colette Piault with the collaboration of Graham Johnston (NFTS, Beaconsfield, G.B.) 35', color, optical sync sound, Greek and American original version, English subtitles. Distributor: Les Films du Quotidien (cf. supra).

MY FAMILY AND ME (1986). A film by Colette Piault with the collaboration of Graham Johnston (NFTS, Beaconsfield, G.B.), about 90', color, optical sync sound, Greek original version, English subtitles. Distributor: Les Films du Quotidien (cf. supra).

The Role of Anthropological Theory in "Ethnographic" Filmmaking[1]

Jack R. Rollwagen
Department of Anthropology
SUNY College at Brockport

ABSTRACT: The writings on "ethnographic" filmmaking for audience viewing are dominated by filmmakers who are not professional anthropologists. As a result, these writings avoid the very questions that must be explored if "ethnographic" films are to become anthropologically informed and theoretically significant from an anthropological point of view. This article explores the concept of "ethnographic" filmmaking, suggests that the term "anthropological filmmaking" is a more appropriate one for anthropological filmmaking, and provides a model for anthropological filmmaking based on anthropological theory.

Introduction

The role of anthropological theory in "ethnographic" filmmaking has received scant attention in the literature. This is particularly the case in respect to those films that are produced for classroom and/or general audiences (as opposed to the filmmaking which results in footage for research purposes). There are two major reasons why this is so: (1) a high percentage of the most visible writers on "ethnographic" filmmaking are not anthropologists by training and cannot be expected to deal in their writings with anthropological theory in any sophisticated manner; and (2) a high percentage of the anthropologists who write on "ethnographic" filmmaking for classroom and/or general audience use reflect a position common in anthropology in general that the primary task for anthropologists is the collection of data (through ethnography or, in this case, through "ethnographic" filmmaking) and that the collection of this data should be based on the nature of that which is observed, not on theory. Theory is thus viewed as one product of data collection rather than a framework within which ethnography proceeds. As a result, the literature on anthropological filmmaking is, for the most part in terms of anthropological theory, sterile. This paper will discuss the use of anthropological theory in what will be termed "anthropological filmmaking" and will suggest a perspective that incorporates anthropological theory into anthropological filmmaking.

The Meanings Implied in the Current Usages of the Terms "Ethnography" and "Ethnographic"

An initial focus of attention in any re-evaluation of anthropological filmmaking must be the very terms that are used since they both reflect and shape the perspectives of their users. The ways in which the terms "ethnography" and "ethnographic" are often used in anthropology in general and in writings about "ethnographic" filmmaking in particular point to a philosophical perspective that has persisted throughout the rise of Western social science. This position, which appears to represent the perspective of the majority of "ethnographic" filmmakers, anthropologists and non-anthropologists alike, suggests that the goal of science is to describe the "true" nature of "reality" by the "objective" recording of "facts" about that "reality." In this perspective, "theory" is (and should be) subordinate to the collection of "facts." The rise of film as an "objective" media has simply provided the proponents of this position with a new means by which to more easily record the "facts" that they seek. By contrast, there is a second perspective in which the position taken is that whatever "reality" exists is only known through the medium of individual observers. In this perspective, the nature of the cognitive framework (particularly the reasoned theoretical framework) used by the observer is of central importance in observing "reality" and in the recording of those observations whether by written or cinematic means. The literature of ethnography and of "ethnographic" filmmaking is dominated by those who, in the final judgement, are proponents of the first perspective. "Theory" is held to be "important, " but secondary to "facts." The "objective" role of the camera in the "ethnographic" filmmaking variety of this perspective supports the basic premise of this position, which may be stated as: "That ethnography and that 'ethnographic' filmmaking is most 'scientific' ('best') which is least (anthropologically) theoretical (i.e., which describes or depicts 'reality' 'as it really is')." Theory thus becomes peripheral to ethnography and to "ethnographic" filmmaking in this perspective. The implicit definition of "ethnographic" filmmaking that dominates the literature is thus "the filming of a socially constructed reality as it really is"; this definition reduces the necessity for anthropological sophistication and places the emphasis on cinematic technique rather than on anthropological theory.[2] The "objectiveness" of film has relieved both the non-anthropologist filmmaker and the anthropologists who accept this perspective of the need to deal with theory.

This paper takes a different view of the role of theory in anthropological filmmaking. The first section below explores more fully the written statements of some of the more prominent spokesmen of the "ethnographic filming of reality" position and will suggest that the term "anthropological filmmaking" may be more appropriate and less troublesome (although a simple change in terms is not meaningful in and of itself if those same people who now call themselves "ethnographic" filmmakers begin to call themselves "anthropological" filmmakers because they are, after all, filming people). The second section deals with the "emic" and "etic" approaches in anthropology and discusses how their use as theoretical concepts structure observation and recording whether by cinematic or written means. The third section illustrates an approach to anthropological filmmaking which utilizes anthropological theory to produce a range of films applicable for a variety of purposes and audiences, ranging from research footage through classroom and general audience films. The fourth section illustrates a strategy for anthropological filmmaking that encourages a multifaceted approach to anthropological filmmaking for a variety of audiences.

(1) "Ethnographic" Filmmaking and "the Filming of Reality As It Really Is"

There are two distinct connotations in the use of the term "ethnographic" in the phrase "ethnographic filmmaking." The first connotation of the term "ethnographic" is that the *subject matter* of the film (or the writings on filmmaking) is, in and of itself, important to "record" on film (regardless of the cinematic approach that is used). It is in this sense that Flaherty's NANOOK OF THE NORTH, Adair's HOLY GHOST PEOPLE, and Harris and Breidenback's THE NUER are "ethnographic" films. It is within this same context that MacDougall's (e.g., 1975, 1978) and Asch, Marshall, and Spier's (1975) writings on "ethnographic" filmmaking are insightful analyses by cinematographers who have photographed "exotic" cultures.

The second connotation of the term "ethnographic" is that there is a sophisticated *disciplinary framework* within which the subject matter of the film (or writings on film) is treated. Ethnography, as scientific description conducted within a theoretical framework, is primarily associated with the discipline of anthropology (although in recent years sociologists and others have adopted the term in their own disciplines). It is in this sense that Balikci and Mary Rousseliere's Netsilik Eskimo series of films and Ruby's (1975) writings are "ethnographic" and ethnographically sophisticated.

It is apparent that many filmmakers and writers on "ethnographic" filmmaking conceive of their efforts as they do because they have concluded that "ethnographic" filmmaking refers to a kind of subject matter and not to a disciplinary approach to a subject matter. It would be unwise for anthropologists who wish to make films or to write about filmmaking to choose such individuals as models for their own efforts. The strengths that anthropology has to bring to filmmaking and to writing about filmmaking is the framework of the discipline of anthropology itself in all of its manifestations within which the subject matter to be filmed may be treated in an anthropologically sophisticated manner.

"Ethnographic" filmmaking and the writing on "ethnographic" filmmaking are very heavily influenced by documentary cinematographers. The disciplinary framework of documentary cinematography is quite different from that of anthropology, as one might expect. Yet anthropologists have been uncritical in their examinations of the theoretical framework that anthropologically uninformed cinematographers bring to the discussion of "ethnographic" filmmaking. The central theme in documentary cinematography seems to focus on the "recording of reality" rather than upon the question of how that "reality" is to be grasped so that it may be filmed. For example, the definition of documentary film issued by the World Union of Documentary Film-makers in 1948 is: "All methods of recording on celluloid any aspect of reality interpreted either by factual shooting or by sincere and justifiable reconstruction, so as to appeal either to reason or emotion, for the purpose of stimulating the desire for, and the widening of, human knowledge and understanding, and of truthfully posing problems and their solutions in the spheres of economics, culture and human relations" (quoted in Edmonds 1974: 12-13). Edmonds, from whom this quote was taken, concludes that "Documentary is *simply* anthropology on film" (Edmonds 1974: 14; emphasis added). He goes on to say that "We must, therefore, in a documentary seek only for anthropology, for the reality, the actuality, of man's relationship to his work, his environment and his society" (1974: 15). How an anthropologically uninformed cinematographer is to do this (especially in a cultural system very different from his/her own) is never discussed.

That anthropologically uninformed "ethnographic" cinematographers are aware of the disparity between their *desire* to treat subject matters anthropologically and their *ability* to do so is evidenced in their increasing incorporation of terminology into their writings that give them the appearance of anthropological sophistication without changing the basic anthropological unsophistication of the analysis.

The following definition of "ethnographic" film serves to illustrate the increasing use of anthropological terminology without sufficient understanding of the framework necessary to deal with it adequately:

> It is usual to define ethnographic film as film that reveals cultural patterning. From this definition it follows that all films are ethnographic, by reason of their content or form or both. Some films, however, are clearly more revealing than others (De Brigard 1975: 13).

This argument has the obvious implications that since all film that "reveals cultural patterning is "ethnographic" then all those who make those films are "ethnographers"; carried to its logical extreme, this argument results in the reduction of any difference between an anthropologically uninformed filmmaker and an anthropologically informed filmmaker because it is the subject matter in itself and the "objectiveness" of the camera that are central. The products of such a position should be recognized as being of little significance to the creation of an anthropologically sophisticated theory of filmmaking.

The term "anthropological" filmmaking is an attempt to call attention to the problems of "ethnographic" filmmaking and to point to the need to develop an approach that will resolve a number of such problems. The use of the term "anthropological filmmaking" directs the attention away from the framework that implies the "recording of reality as it really is" (or any more elaborate justification based on such a viewpoint) to a framework that requires an understanding of anthropology and anthropological theory in order to treat the subject matter in a sophisticated scientific manner. Judged by the framework of sophisticated anthropological theory, most of the writings about "ethnographic" film (which too frequently serve as the models for anthropologists who are aspiring to be filmmakers) are of little value because they do not reflect sophisticated anthropological understandings. They are anthropologically uninformed not only in what they say but in what they do not or cannot say. They suggest on the one hand that socially constructed ("cultural") reality may be understood in a sophisticated manner by observing (the "reality" of) it carefully (without the help of anthropological training and theory). By contrast, they suggest that "natural" events should be the focus of "ethnographic" filmmaking without indicating what (theoretical) model exists for determining what a "natural" event is in a culture (or cultural system) different from that of the filmmaker nor how the nature of it is to be determined in a scientific manner.

In this approach to "ethnographic" filmmaking, the "reality" which is the subject for the particular filmmaking effort is taken to be a constant. It is a constant in the sense that "ethnographic" filmmakers who take this position assume that "reality" to be "the same" to all perceptive observers. What becomes the filmmaker's task, then, is the photographing of the subject matter in a manner that presents the "true" nature of that reality to an audience. This perspective places the emphasis on the "approach" or methodology used in the cinematic aspect of filmmaking and upon the creativity of the filmmaker in interpreting the "reality" of the subject matter to an audience rather than upon the problem of how the perceptions of the "reality" are to be interpreted and the frame of reference into which they are to be placed to further extend the possibilities of interpretation. The major schools in "ethnographic" filmmaking are thus differentiated one from another over methods of filming and over the relationship between methodology and creativity. The schools of "ethnographic" filmmaking that have the most relevance for this discussion focus their attention primarily upon how the "reality" that is to be filmed may best be recorded, a methodological problem with roots in cinematic and not anthropological theory.

Although this perspective could be illustrated from a number of statements about "ethnographic" filmmaking, the following quotations are two of the most sophisticated examples of that approach and will suffice to exemplify it:

> Over the past few years ethnographic filmmakers have looked for solutions to such problems [of how "reality" could be recorded better (J.R.R.)] and the new approaches to filming within our society have provided most of them. By focussing upon discrete events rather than upon mental constructs or impressions, and by seeking to render faithfully the natural sounds, structure, and duration of events, the filmmaker hopes to provide the viewer with sufficient evidence to judge for himself the film's larger analysis. Films like Marshall's AN ARGUMENT ABOUT A MARRIAGE (1969), Sandall's EMU RITUAL AT RUGURI (1969), and Asch's THE FEAST (1969) are all attempts of this kind. They are "observational" in their manner of filming, placing the viewer in the role of observer, a witness of events. They are essentially revelatory rather than illustrative, for they explore substance before theory. They are, nevertheless, evidence of what the filmmaker finds significant (MacDougall 1975: 110).

And:

> The aim of ethnographic film is to preserve, in the mind of the viewer, the structure of the events it is recording as interpreted by the participants. This is often a very difficult task, and is in many ways determined by the way in which the film is taken and by how it is handled after it is shot. The camera has position in both time and space, and therefore imposes a perspective on any action. Turning a camera on and off is an automatic structuring of events, as determined by the bias of the camera operator. Editing is another selection process and a second restructuring. Skillful editing can lead an audience to almost any desired conclusion. Finally, because each viewer possesses a different background, the significance attached to any particular segment of a film by one person will be different from that attached by another, restructuring the event

for a third time for each viewer. For an ethnographic
filmmaker to be successful he must thoroughly understand
his people, and he must do his best to let the indigenous
structure guide him in his recording efforts (Asch, Marshall, and Spier 1973: 179-180).

The first quotation indicates a methodological solution to what is essentially a theoretical disciplinary problem. It emphasizes the necessity of
dealing with "reality" before (and even instead of) "theory," "constructs," or
"impressions." It suggests that viewers of the completed film may understand events simply by observing them. It suggests that the filmmaker's
analysis will be apparent in the "evidence" presented in the film (although
the basis upon which such evidence is to be gathered and the basis upon
which such analysis of a cultural system other than that of the filmmaker is
to be made are not stated). Although the revelatory method in documentary
filmmaking in general may be an important one, revelatory filming in anthropology implies an understanding of the subject matter that is only possible through knowledge of and experience in the use of sophisticated anthropological theory. Although it is obvious why "ethnographic" filmmakers do not choose to deal with anthropological theory, anthropological theory is the only scientific framework that exists for the study of cultural
systems in human societies throughout the world and in cross-cultural perspective.

The second quotation makes more apparent the complexity involved in
"ethnographic" filmmaking and refers (without attempting any suggestion
of a solution) to the central problem to be discussed in this paper. This
central problem revolves around the question of how, in a socially constructed cultural event, the "reality" of that event (being both what the individual participants understand it to be and what scientific observers understand it to be) is to be known to the filmmaker so that he/she can "...let the
indigenous structure guide him in his recording efforts." The implicit answer suggested by "ethnographic" filmmakers is that the observing is sufficient to reveal the structure of that "reality" to the filmmaker when he/she is
in the field, just as observing the film (as structured by the filmmaker) is
sufficient to reveal to the audience the nature of the events portrayed in the
film. The second answer suggested is that the native informants of that culture form the ultimate measure against which the filmmaker's "capturing of
that reality" is judged.

The major problem with such solutions is that they do not indicate
how a cultural "reality" in one cultural system (that which is photographed)
is to be apprehended by members of another cultural system (the audience
viewing the film). If anthropology has demonstrated anything in its near
century of existence as an academic discipline, it is that the nature of cultural systems is not self-evident to the non-participant, even to the profes-
sionally trained anthropologist except through (and perhaps even after) ex-

tensive fieldwork. How much less so can it be to one not so trained?[3] Anthropology has demonstrated that every human being exists within a culturally constructed reality and perceives a culturally interpreted "reality." Only anthropology provides the cross-cultural framework that is sophisticated enough to deal with the range of variation that exists among human cultural systems.

This perspective also seems to suggest (although never directly) that two anthropologists perceiving the same situation in a particular culture would perceive it the same way because, after all, the nature of the event is the same. This perspective downplays any approach which suggests that "arguments" derived from differing theoretical perspectives (or even differing goals) held by the two observers would significantly effect the observations or the conclusions. Because "arguments" and "perspectives" of the outside observer are inherently subordinate to the perspectives of the natives of the cultural system (all of whom think alike, apparently), the ultimate answer of such "ethnographic" filmmakers to any such inquiry is to say that their film was viewed by the "natives" who completely agreed with the filmmaker.

The meaning of any event is not inherent in "the event" itself but in the various interpretations placed upon that event by the individual participants and by individual observers. Who is so naive as to suggest that all participants in a cultural system perceive the same even in the same way? What anthropology contributes to the interpretation of human behavior is an extensive body of observations ("ethnography") and an extensive body of theory ("ethnology") drawn from the cross-cultural analysis to bring to the interpretation of any observations. Ethnography and ethnology are both necessary if anthropological inquiry is to be of any value. Ethnography provides the data for ethnology. Ethnology provides the framework for ethnography. Together, the two comprise the discipline of cultural anthropology. It is within such a dual framework of disciplinary understandings that anthropologically informed filmmaking must proceed.

Science is an approach to the object of investigation and not that object itself. Although this principle is exceedingly simple and easy to grasp, it is evident that not only have the non-anthropological "ethnographic" filmmakers failed to grasp it but some anthropologists also have failed to grasp the significance of the distinction. The contrast in the ideological frameworks between those who conceptualize "facts" as existing and simply to be "gathered" or "recorded," versus those who conceptualize "theory" as a guide to the selection of "data" is indeed great.

The scientific approach differs from the non-scientific approach not in subject matter but in the nature of the investigation and analysis. The corpus of scientific investigations previously conducted provide a framework within which theory, method, approaches, perspectives, and so forth may be selected and modified for any particular research project. Analysis takes place not only in terms of theory-generated data from a particular cultural system but also analysis takes place in the context of other analyses. Thus, observations have value only in respect to the interpretation of them.[4] Those who claim that they are able to record "reality," or that the meaning of the recordings becomes apparent from the totality of the recordings which comprise the completed film, or who choose to argue that native informants are the ultimate measure against which the examination of a cultural system are judged are simply naive.

An anthropologist who selects a particular research problem and a particular cultural system for study brings to the study of that problem and that cultural system the framework of the *theory* of anthropological investigations and the *product* of those theories in the form of ethnology and particular ethnographic investigations. The theory, the ethnology, and the individual ethnographies are products of nearly a century of continuous disciplinary investigations. Anthropological and ethnographic research, then, is not the recording of what human beings say or do but the interpretation of those observations within the disciplinary framework of anthropology. Likewise, anthropological filmmaking is not simply the recording of what human beings say or do but the interpretation of those recordings within the disciplinary framework of anthropology throughout the *total* filmmaking process from conception to execution. Non-anthropologists cannot make anthropological films because they do not have the conceptual framework necessary to treat the subject matter in a way that is enlightened by anthropological theory, ethnology, or ethnography. Thus, the more that the framework that anthropologists use to examine individual research problems is made apparent to the viewers of anthropological films, the more that they will be able to understand the human beings depicted in an anthropologically sophisticated way. The incorporation of anthropology into anthropological filmmaking as a conscious process is a statement by the anthropological filmmaker that he/she is willing to have his/her ideas and conclusions subjected to the same rigorous evaluations by colleagues as a written work receives. There is no room in such a framework for evasion of responsibility as there is in an approach which suggests that "what is recorded speaks for itself." The individual anthropologists who accept the responsibility of producing anthropologically informed films must bring to those films the same scientific and theoretical rigor that they bring to writing. The model for anthropological filmmaking cannot be those "ethnographic" films produced by non-anthropologists. Nor can the writings of non-anthropologists on "ethnographic" film be used as a guide to the theory or practice of anthropological filmmaking. The theory and practice of anthropological filmmaking must arise out of the theory and practice of anthropology by those who are trained in that discipline.

(2) Emic and Etic Approaches and the Nature of Anthropological Inquiry

Anthropologists have, consciously or unconsciously, rigorously or not so rigorously, followed two general approaches in the collection of their data. The first is embodied in the prescription to depict the cultural system being studied as the natives understand it. The second is to analyze the cultural system being studied using the most appropriate and sophisticated conceptual tools that anthropology has to offer. Very roughly, these two approaches correspond to the "emic" and the "etic" approaches in anthropology. These two approaches will probably be the bases of anthropological approaches to filmmaking in a mix that is comfortable to the individual anthropologist who does the filmmaking.

However, in order to clear up some of the confusion that surrounds the use of these terms and to provide a better understanding of why the "emic" and the "etic" approaches differentiate anthropologically informed filmmaking from that which is not, it is necessary to explore more fully the two quite different conceptualizations of the terms "emic" and "etic." Anthropological filmmaking will probably be conducted within one framework based on an emic approach as defined by Pike (and elaborated by those anthropologists who have come to be called "ethnoscientists" or "cognitive anthropologists") and within a second framework based on an emic/etic approach as defined by Harris (and elaborated by a number of anthropologists who cannot so neatly be labeled).

"Emic" and "etic" are concepts first advanced by the linguist Pike. Pike's analysis of the relationship between the two kinds of approaches deserves attention because so many anthropologists have accepted Pike's definitions and his value judgements about the emic and etic approaches. Pike suggests that:

> The etic viewpoint studies behavior as from outside of a particular system, and as an essential initial approach to an alien system. The emic viewpoint results from studying behavior as from inside the system (1967: 37).

And:

> "...etic data provides access into the system -- the starting point of analysis. They give tentative results, tentative units. The final analysis or presentation, however, would be in emic units. In the total analysis, the initial etic description gradually is refined, and is ultimately -- in principle, but probably never in practice -- replaced by one which is totally emic (1967: 39).

There are two points to be considered in the above quotations: first, that Pike's position values emic data while devaluing etic data; and second, that Pike's position does not differentiate among the kinds of etic viewpoints. Thus, scientific and non-scientific viewpoints are equally devalued because they originate from outside the cultural system under consideration.

Harris' redefinition of "emic" and "etic" permits some insight into the second set of definitions. Harris suggests that:

> Emic statements refer to logico-empirical systems whose phenomenal distinctions or "things" are built up out of contrasts and discriminations significant, meaningful, real, accurate, or in some other fashion regarded as appropriate by the actors themselves. An emic statement can be falsified if it can be shown that it contradicts the cognitive calculus by which relevant actors judge that entities are similar or different, real, meaningful, significant, or in some other sense "appropriate" or "acceptable" (1968: 571).

And:

> Etic statements depend upon phenomenal distinctions judged appropriate by the community of scientific observers. Etic statements cannot be falsified if they do not conform to the actor's notions of what is significant, real, meaningful, or appropriate. Etic statements are verified when independent observers using similar operations agree that a given event has occurred. An ethnography carried out according to etic principles is thus a corpus of predictions about the behavior of classes of people. Predictive failures in that corpus require the reformulation of the probabilities or the description as a whole (1968: 575).

Harris' definitions, then, differ from Pike's in two essentials: first, in the respect that both emic viewpoints and etic viewpoints are accorded high although different value, and second, in the respect that the etic viewpoint refers specifically to the viewpoint of a community of scientific observers and not simply to any viewpoint from outside the cultural system under examination. In this sense, an anthropologically unsophisticated filmmaker viewing human behavior in a cultural system other than his own would, in accordance with Harris' position, be a representative of one emic system evaluating the actions of members of another emic system in an ethnocentric manner through the (emic) perspectives of his/her own system. Anthropologically sophisticated filmmakers, by contrast, would be both theoretically and methodologically prepared to differentiate between the two emic systems involved, to treat each in a culturally relativistic manner, *and to bring the etic system of anthropology to bear on the observations and the research.*

The difference between Pike's and Harris' definitions of emics and etics indicates the probable two thrusts that ethnological filmmaking in anthropology will take since they are in accord with a basic and long-standing division within anthropology. The thrust of anthropological filmmaking that follows the lead indicated by Pike will be toward emphasizing the emic analysis and downplaying the etic analysis (as defined by Pike). The thrust of ethnological filmmaking that follows the lead indicated by Harris will be toward incorporating both emic and etic perspectives (as defined by Harris) into the filmmaking.

Since any anthropologically sophisticated filmmaking effort will undoubtedly take place only after extensive fieldwork in the cultural system(s) involved, the choice of filmmaking approaches will probably reflect the choice of fieldwork approach by the anthropologist in general. Thus, just as fieldwork in anthropology which follows the emic perspective concentrates on the elicitation of the nature of the cultural system as the participants understand it, the selection of material to be presented in film in the emic approach to anthropological filmmaking will be focused on the behavior (including linguistic behavior such as "statements") of the participants in that cultural system. By contrast, just as fieldwork in anthropology which follows the emic/etic perspective indicated by Harris concentrates upon matters deemed meaningful and important both by the participants in the cultural system being studied and by anthropologists because of the disciplinary framework that they bring to the research, the selection of material to be presented in film in the emic/etic approach will involve distinctions deemed meaningful and important by participants in the cultural system that is the subject of the research *and* distinctions deemed meaningful and important by anthropologists.[5]

The concepts of emics and etics applied to the scientific study of human cultural systems is basic to the distinction between that "ethnographic" filmmaking which is an anthropologically uninformed approach and that anthropological filmmaking which is. "Emic" and "etic" are anthropological concepts that symbolize and refer to the extensive anthropological framework in which individual projects of research and analysis in cultural anthropology proceed.[6] If anthropology is to develop "...a way of articulating or organizing images in a manner that is related structurally to anthropological visual symbolic forms which are conventionalized into a code or argot..." [Ruby 1975: 109], it must be on the base provided by anthropology and anthropological filmmaking rather than upon the base provided by cinematography and "ethnographic" filmmaking. It is to a theory of anthropologically informed filmmaking that anthropologists must direct their attention rather than to that provided by anthropologically uninformed cinematography and "ethnographic" filmmaking. It is in this context that Hei-

der's statement "...when the demands of ethnography and film seem to conflict and we choose to fulfill the ethnographic demands in order to have a
more ethnographic film, the results will probably turn out to be a better
film even by cinematographic standards" (1976:x) takes on the entire range
of meanings that it should.

If anthropology is the best framework that is available for the study of
the entire range of human cultural systems, then that framework should be
central to the communication of research results in film as it is in writing.
Anthropological filmmaking must incorporate anthropologically sophisticated perspectives into the very structure of filmmaking since it is only
when the total films is structured by sophisticated anthropological understandings that the subject matter treated in the film can be treated within an
anthropological framework that gives it such extended meanings. The examples of emic and etic approaches to research were introduced in this section to emphasize that there are different theoretical approaches to the study
of a subject matter, that there are extensive literatures on the value of these
different approaches, and that the "recording of a reality" (whether by camera
or by written means) is a complex theoretical problem requiring complex
theoretical solutions. Anthropological filmmaking, if it is to be of any
value, must incorporate sophisticated theoretical understandings into the
production of films since that is one of the most important assets that anthropologists can bring to filmmaking.

(3) A General Anthropological Framework for Anthropologi-
cal Filmmaking

The increasing use of the concept of a cultural "event" in
"ethnographic" filmmaking (see the quotations by both MacDougall, and by
Asch, Marshall, and Spier above) in regard to filming within a cultural system different from that of the filmmaker poses the question that is ultimately of most importance for anthropological filmmaking. This question
is: "Within what framework are the 'cultural events' to be conceptualized for
the filming?" The answer "within the structure of the reality of natural
events" (as suggested in the several quotations cited above) is unacceptable
for the reasons stated above. The implicit assumptions in such a statement
are that the perceptions that guide the filmmaking effort are not based on
anthropological theory or understandings. Although there may be other,
usually highly personal, theoretical frameworks for the interpretation of
cultural "events, " these frameworks usually remain undisclosed in most
presentations that take this position and thus are not as open to the criticism they deserve.

There is some need for a general conceptual framework that may serve
as a basis for anthropological filmmaking. This framework should be based
in anthropological understandings but should permit a wide variety of ap-

proaches to filmmaking in order to allow for a wide variety of filmmakers, purposes, and audiences. Although it may be suggested that anthropology in general is that framework, the application of anthropological understandings to anthropological filmmaking does require some specific discussion.

A general framework for anthropological filmmaking emphasizes those factors that are the basis of contemporary anthropology: the cultural system approach to the study of human beings, the holistic approach to the study of cultural systems, the comparative approach, the case study approach, and the emic/etic approach.[7] This framework will be general enough to allow for a variety of subject matters and approaches but will necessitate sophisticated anthropological understandings and theory for its application to filmmaking. Some of the implications of these factors for anthropological filmmaking are as follows:

The Cultural Systems Approach to the Study of Human Beings: One of the central concepts in anthropology is the concept of cultural patterning. Although the model for the study of human beings in anthropology has traditionally been the isolated small-scale society in which the totality of individuals that comprised it were unified by their participation in one overarching cultural system, recent research has challenged the usefulness of this model as a general model. Human beings wherever they are found appear to participate in a very large number of cultural systems all of which influence their choices in behavior. These systems may be viewed as sets of specific individuals who share and continuously elaborate ideas and behaviors. Cultural systems thus conceived may contain only several individuals or they may contain billions. The world contains an infinite number of such cultural systems of which societies are only a very small percentage. Anthropologists, in conducting research, concentrate upon the nature of individual cultural systems, the relationship of a particular cultural system selected for study to other cultural systems significant to its nature and evolution, and the conditions under which it exists and evolves. The concept of cultural systems allows anthropologists to deal both with group patterning and with variations in behavior between the individuals that comprise that cultural system.[8] (For further discussion of the question of diversity within cultural systems, see Pelto and Pelto 1975. For a further elaboration of the cultural system approach, see Rollwagen 1987.) The concept of adaptive modification through cultural elaboration provides the mechanism for change and evolution.

The Holistic Approach: Anthropology alone among the disciplines that study human beings claims to do so by studying topics within cultural systems taken as a totality. The holistic approach allows any particular behavior in a cultural system to be studied in the context of all other forms of behavior from that cultural system. The focus of attention in studying an event is not simply economic or linguistic, nor is the event interpreted except in the context of the total processual functioning of that cultural system. This approach allows interpretations of an event in ways that are not available when using a more limited frame of investigation. In the context of anthropological filmmaking, it implies that if an audience is to begin to understand the meaning of an event from another cultural system, that event must be presented filmically in such a way that its implications are made apparent to the viewer unaware of the cultural interpretations placed on that event by the participants or by anthropologists. Although it is true that such implications may be discussed in written works that might be available to the viewers of the film, the use of these non-filmic sources of interpretation hinges upon the nature of the audiences toward which the film is directed. In anthropological films for non-classroom audiences, the likelihood that the audience will read materials to supplement the film prior to or following the screening is low. If any degree of understanding is to be achieved, it must be through the film itself. This fact brings us back to the argument already presented, that the filmmaker must be a highly competent anthropologist in order to make anthropologically sophisticated films. Nor can the anthropologist be brought in after the footage for the film has already been exposed in order to edit the footage or add comments that will justify the film being called "anthropological." The basis of an anthropological film lies in the conceptualization of the totality of the behavior recorded in the footage. The anthropological understandings (i.e., the theory, the comparative ethnology, and the ethnographic fieldwork on that particular cultural system) should have been thoroughly explored before the particular behavior that will become the footage for the film is recorded.

Although the concept of the holistic approach is normally used in anthropology to refer to cultural systems at the level of society, the increasing integration of the cultural systems of the world indicates the need for the consideration of holistic approaches in anthropology at all levels including those below the level of society and those above it (see Rollwagen 1987). Anthropological films may have to include some treatment of the effect of cultural systems beyond that selected for central consideration in order to suggest the explanation of behavior in that system. Once having selected a subject of a film, it is the duty of the filmmaker to explain what is being presented within the (holistic) framework that is most appropriate for its understanding. This is one of the major reasons why a combined emic/etic perspective is desirable in anthropology and anthropological filmmaking. Presenting the insider's view of why something is happening when that event or process is caused by forces beyond that cultural system and thus not known to the informant is a necessary complement to the observations of the participants in that cultural system. The cultural system that ultimately serves as the primary context for the world's cultural systems and the study of those systems is the World System (see Rollwagen 1980a and 1987).

The Comparative Approach: A major component of the anthropological perspective is the insight into any one cultural system that arises from insight into the temporal-spatial range of cultural systems. Ethnographic experience in one cultural system is informed by ethnographic understandings that come from the scientific anthropological study of the world's cultural systems. Since the goal of anthropology is to understand humankind in all of its manifestations, the relationship between ethnology and ethnography is more properly that described by conceptualizing ethnology as the discipline that studies humans and their cultural systems, and ethnography as a means of gathering data to be used in ethnology. Restated, ethnology provides the context for the gathering and the interpretation of ethnographic data. The comparative approach is the basis for the etic statements that must inform anthropological film and writings.

The Case Study Approach: There is a continuing tension in anthropology between those anthropologists who conceive of their task as the description of cultural systems so that the totality of descriptions may be used to inductively construct the anthropological generalizations necessary to the development of the discipline, and those anthropologists who conceive of their task as the application of anthropological theory to specific cultural systems in an alternatively deductive/inductive manner so that the efficacy of the anthropological analysis is heightened. Although the perspective in each of these two cases differ, the central importance of the personal examination of a cultural system using the framework provided by ethnography and ethnology is common to both of them. Anthropological fieldwork in individual cultural systems is conducted within the framework provided by the work of anthropologists in other cultural systems. Knowledge of the framework shapes the manner in which the individual research project proceeds.

Anthropological filmmaking in any individual cultural system, then, proceeds within the framework provided by anthropology. The choice of cultural systems, the choice of research perspectives, the choice of theories, the choice of comparative studies for analysis, and the analysis itself are made with reference to what other anthropologists have done. What is filmed cannot be co-extensive with what it is possible to be filmed. Neither can what is filmed be filmed "objectively" and without "prejudgements." Since choice is the fundamental feature of all inquiry, it is necessary to recognize the nature of the framework within which choices are made. Those individuals who do not know the anthropological framework cannot employ it in the observation or analysis of the case study material that they wish to film. Perhaps the area of most importance in the development of a filmmaking that is anthropologically sophisticated is the increasing emphasis upon the explicitness of the framework that provides the context for the choices made in filmmaking and in writing about filmmaking.

The Emic/Etic Approach: The use of the emic/etic approach encourages the anthropological filmmaker to film behavior within what are ethnographically derived meaningful units for the participants in the cultural system being filmed, and to film that behavior within what are meaningful units for anthropologists as well.

(4) Operationalizing Anthropological Filmmaking: The Puerto Rican Spiritist Project

Anthropological filmmaking must follow intensive and sophisticated ethnographic fieldwork that is informed by extensive comparative research including the explicit selection of a theoretical framework within which to treat the subject matter to be filmed. Unlike the scientifically unsophisticated position so often implicitly indicated by "ethnographic" filmmakers which suggests that recording is an empirical exercise, anthropological filmmakers recognize that filmmaking, like anthropological research in general, is conditioned by the anthropologist's ability to conceive of his/her research in terms of anthropological theory. This theory permeates all phases of research including conceptualizing the project, perceiving the subject matter, recording the observations, conducting the analysis, and preparing the research product(s). This position thus stands in fundamental contrast to the position indicated in Asch, Marshall, and Spier (cited above) in that these authors do not indicate how the scientific study of the subject matter *prior to filming* creates a context more significant to the nature of the filmmaking than does the positioning of the camera, turning it off and on, editing, or any of the other cinematic activities (including cinematic theory). What makes anthropological filmmaking superior to "ethnographic" filmmaking (as judged by the discipline of anthropology) is the explicitly scientific framework within which the filmmaking proceeds.

Although anthropological filmmaking is fully integrated into intensive ethnographic fieldwork and is informed by ethnology, its *purpose* is the communication of information to audiences and not simply the recording of subject matter for use in later scientific research. ("Films" are normally differentiated from "footage" in that films are produced fro audience consumption where as footage may be exposed for a variety of purposes of which the completion of a film for audience viewing is only one goal.) The selection of subject matter and its treatment in the film thus must be in terms of its presentation to an audience. In this sense, anthropological filmmaking theory must arise from confronting the problems of how to use emically and etically derived information to explain a chosen subject matter (and the anthropologist's perspective on it) to an audience. Because there are a wide range of audiences and a wide variety of possible films to be made, the approaches to anthropological filmmaking must be correspondingly diverse. Anthropological filmmakers must perceive their filmmaking as integrated into the fieldwork experience in ways that anthropologically unsophisticated filmmakers cannot hope to do. This integration allows and suggests different approaches to recording the footage from which the anthropological films will be made.

In order to illustrate how anthropological research and ethnographic filmmaking interrelate and how this interrelationship provides the basis for a variety of film types for a range of audiences, I will discuss in brief an on-going anthropological fieldwork project which will become (in part) a project in anthropological filmmaking. The subject matter of the research is Puerto Rican spiritism in Rochester, New York. The anthropological (and other related social science) literature on Puerto Ricans, spiritism, and U.S. cities is extensive and provides a range of data and theory as well as a general framework within which the field work and filmmaking will proceed.

Although the anthropological fieldwork will produce both written materials and films (or video tapes), the nature of the audiences towards which the range of films will be directed dictate that some of the films should not rely on audience knowledge of or desire to read the written sources derived from the project (or any other written materials) prior to, in association with, or after viewing those films. Thus, some films (for example those proposed for college audiences) may assume the existence of an available anthropologist ready to provide a variety of frameworks into which the films may be placed. Other films, by contrast, must be produced with the understanding that the film itself must carry whatever information is necessary for the message that the anthropologist wishes to communicate. These considerations affect not only what must be filmed but also the organization of the materials in the final film. Thus, the Puerto Rican spiritist project will have as its goal the production of a number of forms of films usable by a variety of audiences with a wide diversity of prior knowledge of the subject matters involved and the related anthropological literature.

For the purposes of this discussion, I will contrast three kinds of audiences and the kinds of anthropological films that might be produced from the Puerto Rican spiritist project for each audience. These three audiences are: (1) a classroom audience in which an anthropologist is present to interpret and inform the audience prior to, throughout, and after the screening of the film; (2) an anthropologically unsophisticated audience consisting of health professionals interested in knowing more about Puerto Rican folk medicine who are screening the films without an anthropologist present; and (3) a general television audience who will view one of the films on their home television sets.

In order to provide the footage necessary to produce films for all three kinds of audiences, the filmmaking project must be both extensive in the range of subject matter filmed and intensive in the coverage of those that are selected to be central. For the film to be shown in a classroom with an anthropologist present, one approach would be to film a weekly spiritist meeting and explore the range of behaviors and their explanations. Parts of the ritual could be examined in terms of shamanism, magic, curing, world view, and/or group organization. There could be reference in this film to the complexity of the behavior involved and the necessity for some theoretical position from which to interpret it. Reference could be made to various anthropological theories that exist to do this.

For the film to be shown to an audience of health professionals, the central focus might be upon the theories of the causes if illnesses that exist among the world's cultural systems and the logic of curing given those causes (an ethnological approach which would be unfamiliar and possibly not interesting to the Puerto Rican spiritist). The Puerto Rican spiritist example could then be introduced with indications the weekly curing ceremony that is the spiritist meeting exists within a range of other practices and practitioners of curing. Anthropology's holistic approach would demonstrate that curing exists within an integrated matrix of behaviors that support the efficacy of this approach to curing.

The film to be shown to a general television audience would avoid the common assumption that films for general audiences must not approach complex issues. This film might deal with the problems that anthropologists have in conducting their research: in locating a topic and a group for study, in observing and recording, in interpreting the material observed and deciding how it can be related to the interpretations and theories already in existence about similar and different behavior among other peoples of the world, and similar matters. The emphasis in this film might be upon the processes of scientific inquiry. This film could concentrate upon the choices in fieldwork and the implications of such choices.

The value of the anthropological films on Puerto Rican spiritism could be enhanced by the filming of comparable rituals by the same spiritist on different occasions throughout the year or when unusual cures were attempted by the spiritist. Their value could also be enhanced through the filming of contrastive cases of spiritist rituals by other Puerto Rican spiritists in Rochester, and elsewhere. Thus, the principles of comparative cultural research could be introduced either explicitly in the films or implicitly by providing two examples of Puerto Rican spiritism in two different films which differed in cultural context or performance. Other subjects that are also pertinent to the understanding of Puerto Rican spiritism in Rochester (such as the enculturation of individuals to be a spiritist or the explication of the variety of cultural systems that contribute to the dimensionality of Puerto Rican spiritism) might be the subject matter of other films which, together, would expand the range of the set of films on Puerto Rican spiritism in Rochester. Each of the films would be informed by ethnology and by sophisticated ethnographic fieldwork prior to the filming and would incorporate anthropological theory both explicitly (in the case of some films) and implicitly through the filmmaking process. Although these are only a few examples, they provide some insight into the possible approaches and films that would result from an anthropologically sophisticated filmmaking effort.

The concept of a broadly-based, multipurpose approach to anthropological filmmaking runs counter to certain tendencies apparent in other schools of "ethnographic" filmmaking: Young's "observational" filming in which the filmmaker as observer "watches" the "event" as it is being filmed (Young 1975: 69); MacDougall's "participatory" (and "beyond observational" film) in which the filmmaker "...acknowledges his entry upon the world of his subjects and yet asks them to imprint directly upon the film their own culture" (1975:119); or Asch, Marshall and Spier's "reportage" filmmaking in which the subject matter "...is always an event or a complete segment of life" (Asch, Marshall and Spier 1973: 182). Each of the above as representative of an anthropologically uninformed documentary tradition attempts to solve a complex anthropological problem with inappropriate cinematic answers. Their lack of understanding that anthropology is itself a complex and sophisticated system comprised of various perspectives from which many approaches to a variety of research projects (including filmmaking) can proceed is reflected in MacDougall's attempt to depict anthropology as a one-dimensional academic discipline whose primary purpose is to make written scientific statements about culture:

> Anthropologists have sensed these and kindred difficulties which make film so different from words in conveying information and ideas. In anthropological writing, data is held in suspension at the crucial moment to permit abstract expression; in film it is omnipresent. At the same time, film becomes attractive to anthropologists for its contextualization and rendering of data through means other than linguistic signs. This creates ambivalent attitudes toward ethnographic films which aspire to present a theoretical analysis by revelatory means, since that requires a manipulation of the data itself. It may also account for the fact that ethnographic films are more readily accepted by anthropologists when they keep data and analysis clearly separated in visual and verbal domains. But such a separation cannot finally allow ethnographic film to make its most distinctive contribution to the understanding of humanity. It is, after all, an articulation of witnessed human behavior that film can provide but written anthropology cannot. With that as an objective, the invention of new forms that balance the intellectual and informational potentialities of film becomes an urgent necessity for ethnographic film-makers (1978: 420).

MacDougall's statements are replete with misrepresentations and incomplete logics. He somehow assumes that the "theoretical analysis by revelatory means" of the individual filmmaker is somehow more valuable than the insights that arise from the "theoretical" framework brought to the filmmaking by the anthropologist, that "data" are more important than "abstract expression," and that data and analysis can be clearly separated in visual and verbal domains. Furthermore, MacDougall's writings are replete with reification such as when he suggests that film (as opposed to the people who make those films) can make any contribution to the understanding of humanity. His writing evades by stylistic means confronting the implications of what he writes. Film becomes an entity in itself, divorced from the filmmaker and conveniently so, since in this manner the preparation of the filmmaker to deal with his subject matter cannot be a subject for discourse. In the sentence "It is, after all, an articulation of witnessed human behavior that film can provide but written anthropology cannot" (quoted above), the fallacy of MacDougall's revelatory filmmaking becomes obvious. Who is the articulator and witness whose films are superior to written anthropology? From whence arises this power to rise above mere anthropologists who are so limited in what they do and think? MacDougall's comments also suggest a false dichotomy between anthropology and filmmaking.

This argument, which presumes the idea discussed above that the meaning of human behavior in cultural systems different than that of the filmmaker's is apparent to the anthropologically untrained filmmaker by careful observation and to his audience through methodological devices, is, of course, false and misleading; perhaps even a straw-man argument. It fails to deal with the question of the nature of the framework from which the understandings which enlighten the observed behavior proceed. Since it is information which is being communicated and not "reality" no matter how sophisticated the methodology or theory of the cinematic approach, the question remains "How can an anthropologically uninformed 'ethnographic' filmmaker communicate that which he/she does not know?" The failure of the large majority of "ethnographic" films is precisely because the filmmaker does not know how to look at or comprehend the cultural systems which he/she attempts to film or to write about. Nor does he/she know how to deal with the observations within an academic or disciplinary context which provides such enormous enlightenment to what is observed. Proposed solutions to filming cultural systems that disregard emic and etic perspectives because the filmmaker is not so trained can hardly be advanced as superior to ones in which emic and etic perspectives are central to the observations and filmings.

It is in this sense that Ruby (1975) has argued that "ethnographic" films must become more scientific. MacDougall's rejoinder to Ruby fails to deal with the issue that the "science" which anthropology brings to anthropological filmmaking is the theoretical framework such as the emic and etic perspectives which inform the anthropologist/filmmaker and inform the total filmmaking process:

> Ruby considers that the conventions of documentary
> film are altogether inappropriate to the practice of visual
> anthropology and has noted that "anthropologists do not
> regard ethnography in the visual mode with the same or
> analogous scientific expectations with which they regard
> written anthropology." He argues that ethnographic films
> must become more scientific, describing culture from
> clearly defined anthropological perspectives. Ethnographic
> filmmakers must become more conscientious in revealing
> their methods and "employ a distinctive lexicon -- an an-
> thropological argot." In contrast to conceptions of ethno-
> graphic film that would settle for less, such a view asserts
> the primacy of film as a communicative system and holds
> out the hope of a visual anthropology as rigorous as the
> written anthropology that preceded it.
>   Ruby is certainly right in stating that films embody
> theoretical and ideological assumptions in their organiza-
> tion, and that filmmakers should not only become con-
> scious of that coding but make the forms of their work
> consonant with their analysis. But his proposal presup-
> poses a rough semiotic equivalency between written an-
> thropology and potential visual codes that would make a
> similar kind of discourse possible. It raises the question of
> whether a visual medium can express a scientific state-
> ment about culture at all comparable to those that can be
> stated in words. If it cannot, the understandings
> communicated by film may always be radically different
> from those of anthropology and equally unacceptable to
> anthropologists (MacDougall 1978: 421).

The opposition, of course, is not between what a visual medium and a
written medium can express but between the understandings that an anthropologist brings to the observation of a cultural system in order to communicate a variety of information to a variety of audiences through a variety of
forms (including vocal, written and filmic) and the understandings that one
not anthropologically trained brings to the observation of that same cultural
system for the same purposes.[9]

"Solutions" to the problems of anthropological filmmaking must proceed from anthropologically informed filmmakers. Furthermore, anthropological filmmaking must proceed from a more broadly-based, multipurpose
approach to filmmaking for each project undertaken than is apparent at the
present. Anthropologists must be willing to experiment with film in a
variety of ways which are related to a variety of possible audiences for those

films, a variety of possible subject matters, and, equally as important, a variety of anthropological theories, perspectives, and methodologies which explicitly or implicitly inform those films.

Anthropologists, more than other social scientists in my opinion, lack an effective communication with the general public. This is so because (1) anthropologists have always cherished the exoticness of their discipline and the status that the exclusive control of this knowledge gave them; (2) anthropologists have consistently refused to integrate anthropology into the other social sciences, preferring to treat their subject matter as if cultural systems were "isolated" and understandable only in their own terms; and (3) anthropologists have been so uncritical of and so willing to accept the "recording of reality" position that they have permitted anthropologically uninformed individuals to dominate these means of communications that have the greatest access to the general public. If anthropologists feel that what they have to say about humankind is important they must become more actively involved in gaining a greater measure of control over the means of communication to larger audiences than they have at present. Film is the means of communication that is the most important in this regard since through television it reaches the largest and most diverse audience of any means of communication. Since film is such a vital tool, anthropologists must invest their time and energy to make it an anthropologically sophisticated means of communication. One essential step in gaining this control is to accept the fact that the structure of films comes out of the minds of the individuals that make them. The more prepared the individuals are to analyze the subject matter that is to be filmed, the more valuable the film will be to the audiences that views it. Anthropological understandings, based on the disciplinary framework of anthropology (and centrally shaped by anthropological theory) provides the best scientific framework for dealing with humankind as a whole and in all of its variety. "Ethnographic" film and the writings on "ethnographic" film must become anthropologically sophisticated.

ACKNOWLEDGEMENTS

This paper is an extensive revision of a manuscript submitted as a project to fulfill the requirements for a Master of Arts in Humanities degree at SUNY at Buffalo in August of 1979, Gerald O'Grady, director. I would like to extend my appreciation to Marvin Harris, Jay Ruby, and Margaret Blackman for their invaluable comments on earlier drafts of this manuscript. The position taken and the argument pursued, however, are my own.

NOTES

[1] The term "filmmaking" as used in this article refers to the total range of

processes of visual recording including film and/or videotape.

2 Much of the writings in both ethnography and "ethnographic" filmmaking avoid the question of "rules" for the transformation of perceptions into generalizations. It is convenient to indicate that the structure of importance is in that which is observed and to indicate that the role of the observer is simply to record. This paper will suggest, by contrast, that what differentiates a scientific observer from one who is not is the theoretical framework that he/she brings to the observation, in this case the anthropological framework. As Pelto and Pelto state:

> Thus, in addition to the basic tools and instruments of observation and measurement, a scientific researcher must have, at the very least, sets of procedural rules (including concepts and definitions) for transforming sensual evidence into generalizations about phenomena. It is one of the goals of all scientific disciplines to link together low-order generalizations, or propositions, into larger networks of propositions that will make possible the prediction and explanation of phenomena within the given domain. Such networks of propositions are generally called *theories*...
>
> Methodology, then refers to the structure of procedures and transformational rules whereby the scientist shifts information up and down this ladder of abstraction in order to produce and organize increased knowledge. At the point of primary observation, as the bacteriologist peers into the microscope, he must have available some conceptual tools --definitions of things seen and experienced -- for giving form and description to observations. The primary descriptions, in turn, are related to more abstract propositions -- to general theory about microorganisms -- by a progression of logical steps that must be very clearly understood and agreed on by fellow scientists in the profession. This progression through levels of abstraction is not a one-way process, however. The general, theoretical framework is a prime source of ideas and predictions in terms of which particular foci of observations are selected.
>
> Thus defined, "methodology" can be distinguished from "research techniques" in that the latter term is useful for referring to the pragmatics of primary data collection, whereas methodology denotes the "logic-in-use" involved in selecting particular observational techniques, assessing their yield of data, and relating these data to theoretical propositions. In practice, the practical problems of using particular techniques of data gathering cannot be entirely separated from the examination of their logic-in-use. Any methodological discussion, then, must include some reference to techniques (Pelto and Pelto 1978: 2-3; emphasis in the original).

3 As Sapir pointed out more than fifty years ago in an essay entitled "The Unconscious Patterning of Behavior in society":

> It is impossible to say what an individual is doing unless we have tacitly accepted the essentially arbitrary modes of interpretation that social tradition is constantly suggesting to us from the very moment of birth. Let anyone who doubts this try the experiment of making a painstaking report of the actions of a group of natives engaged in some form of activity, say religious, to which he has not the cultural key. If he is a skillful writer, he may succeed in giving a picturesque account of what he sees and hears, or thinks he sees and hears, but the chances of his being able to give a relation of what happens in terms that would be intelligible and acceptable to the natives themselves are practically nil. He will be guilty of all manner of distortion. His emphasis will be constantly askew. He will find interesting what the natives take for granted as a casual kind of behavior worthy of no particular comment, and he will utterly fail to observe the crucial turning points for the course of action that give formal significance to the whole in the minds of those who do not possess the key to its understanding (Sapir, quoted in Mandelbaum 1968: 546-547).

4 A more sophisticated form of the "recording of reality" position is that which suggests that "data" can be generated without reference to theory (or more generally which suggests that "the data are there to be observed and the observation of that data will be of most value when it is done without the prejudgment that theory contains"). Prejudgment is, of course, impossible. The value of science is that the prejudgment is dealt with in a framework that subjects the product to the evaluation of colleagues.

5 My reading of Harris indicates that Harris provides for scientific inquiry both by the emic and by the etic approaches. He says:

> It is clear that the main concern here is to draw a distinction between the entities and processes of social life that are real and important to the participants versus entities and processes which by virtue of their scientific status are capable of efficaciously explaining (and changing) social thoughts and activities, regardless of whether they are real or important from the participant's point of view...But cultural materialism rejects an implication that the thoughts themselves are "unreal" or that matter (whatever that might be) is more real than ideas...The statement of the basic materialist principles of sociocultural determinism rests instead upon the separation of conscious or unconscious autocognitions of actors from the conscious

cogitations of the scientifically informed observer (1976: 330-331).

And:

> Once again, however, let me categorically reject any notion of superior and inferior realities associated with emic and etic epistemological options. Everything that we human beings experience or do is real. But everything we experience or do is not equally effective for explaining why we experience what we experience and do what we do (1976: 331).

6 "Emic" and "etic" are anthropological concepts that provide the framework within which data are collected. They are not those data. This statement is a specific case of the statement made above: "Science is an approach to the object of investigation and not that object itself." An "emic" approach is what the anthropologist uses in approaching the collection of data from a native informant. It is *not* what that native has in his mind. This confusion between science and the subject that it investigates, between anthropology and the subject that it investigates continues to pervade anthropological thinking and to perpetuate the very kind of slipshod thinking that is at the basis of "ethnographic" filmmaking. Hunter and Whitten's perception of the emic/etic contrast in their general textbook (1976) provides an excellent example of the perpetuation of this error: "*Emics* is the set of related categories through which anthropologist's subject perceive the world; in this book we refer to emics by the term *folk perspective*. Etics is the set of related categories used by Western social scientists to explain social phenomena; we refer to etics as the *analytical perspective*" (1976: 18; emphasis in the original). It should be obvious by my above discussion that both emics and etics are anthropological approaches founded in anthropological theory and in that sense analytical.

7 The factors that I have listed are not intended to be exclusive or exhaustive but rather to represent some of the major elements of anthropological inquiry. there are a number of other discussions of the components of anthropology which differ slightly from my own. See, for example, Hoebel and Frost (1976: 4-7), or Hunter and Whitten (1976: 15-18).

It is important to note in reading the material in this section that I have redefined several of the traditional anthropological concepts. Thus "cultural systems" are not equivalent to "cultures"; "the holistic approach" does not automatically mean that the "whole" is a "society"; nor do "the comparative approach" and "the case study approach" imply that the units of comparison are "societies."

8 Leslie White employed the term "cultural system" in his work THE CONCEPT OF CULTURAL SYSTEMS (1975). My use of the concept of "cultural system" derives from the same desire to treat the *causes* of human behavior in terms of cultural *systems* but differs from his (as I understand it) in that he conceives of societies as the level of cultural sys-

tem of greatest importance.

9 MacDougall's reference to "written anthropology" evokes the argument
about the difference between a "linear" language and a "non-linear film."
That argument is not only fatuous but conceptually incorrect, although it
is a splendid example of my argument that anthropologically
unsophisticated individuals contribute more confusion to anthropological
filmmaking than clarity. The supposition that language is linear arises
from a number of incorrect assumptions: (a) that writing and language are
the same; (b) that the processes of reading and writing, conceived as a
whole, are linear; (c) that the models which Euroamericans have for language are universally appropriate; (d) that thought is linear; and so forth.
Writing is only one manifestation of language. The cognitive processes
from which writings emerge is not linear although the orthography is
indeed "straight." The cognitive process of reading is not linear although
in the Euroamerican tradition the eyes do travel from left to right
through a restricted range of space. The argument that the cognitive process from which writing arises, the cognitive process of writing itself,
the cognitive process of reading, and cognition itself are linear, is simply not true. As Hunter (in a basic textbook in anthropology) states:

> American culture strongly emphasizes linear models.
> Because we read from left to right, it is easy to imagine
> ourselves as hearing speech in a linear, "left-to-right"
> manner. Nothing could be farther from the truth.
>
> Let us return again to the word *p i g*. Obviously the
> phoneme *p* consists of a whole bundle of features of articu-
> lation: It is a nonvocalized, bilabial aspirated stop. But
> when we hear the *p*, we do not perceive these individual
> features (unless we are studying linguistics); we perceive
> the whole unit of sound, the phoneme. the same is true of
> the whole word; although we know that *p i g* is a word
> consisting of three phonemes, we perceive it as a whole
> bundle of phonemes unless we are asked to break it down
> into its individual sound units. In fact, our perception that
> the word *pig* is a whole is closer to the truth than the no-
> tion that it is a sequence of phonemes. The signal we hear
> as *pig* cannot be electronically broken down into a succes-
> sion of constituent phonemes: *Physically the three
> phonemes are spread out along the entire length of the
> word...*
>
> Much the same is true of words: We perceive them as
> whole bundles of meaning rather than as a sequence of
> meaningful morphemes. Following the lead of Floyd
> Lounsbury and Ward Goodenough, anthropological lin-
> guists have studied semantics in terms of these bundles of
> meaning. A school of anthropological linguistics known
> as componential analysis has arisen, and the efforts of
> these scholars leave no doubt: The meaning of words is not
> a matter of units but rather, again, of feature bundles. Thus,
> for example, no single unit of meaning exists for *father*.

The word refers to a bundle of features that includes (a) male, (b) first ascending generation, (c) noncollateral (lineal), (d) consanguineal, and (e) relative...

The same is true for phrases and sentences. Although we obviously hear the beginning of a sentence before the end, research is revealing that we understand or decode sentences as whole bundles of features rather than as sequences of morphemes (Hunter 1976: 179-180; emphasis in the original).

REFERENCES CITED

Asch, Timothy, John Marshall, and Peter Spier (1973). Ethnographic Film: Structure and Function. Annual Review of Anthropology 2: 179-187.

De Brigard, Emilie (1975). The History of Ethnographic Film. IN Principles of Visual Anthropology, Paul Hockings (ed.). The Hague: Mouton, pp. 13-43.

Edmonds, Robert (1974). Anthropology on Film: A Philosophy of People and Art. Dayton: Pflaum Publishing Company.

Harris, Marvin (1968). The Rise of Anthropological Theory: A History of Theories of Culture. New York: Thomas Y. Crowell Co.

Harris, Marvin (1976). History and Significance of the Emic/Etic Distinction. Annual Review of Anthropology 5: 329-350.

Heider, Karl G. (1976). Ethnographic Film. Austin: University of Texas Press.

Hoebel, E. Adamson, and Everett L. Frost (1976). Cultural and Social Anthropology. New York. McGraw-Hill.

Hunter, David E. (1976). Communication: Verbal and Nonverbal. IN The Study of Anthropology, David E. Hunter and Phillip Whitten (eds.). New York: Harper and Row, pp. 162-187.

Hunter, David E., and Phillip Whitten (1976). The Study of Anthropology. New York: Harper and Row.

MacDougall, David (1975). Beyond Observational Cinema. IN Principles of Visual Anthropology. Paul Hockings, (ed.). The Hague: Mouton. 109-124.

MacDougall, David (1978). Ethnographic Film: Failure and Promise. Annual Review of Anthropology 7: 405-425.

Mandlebaum, David G. (Ed.) (1968). Selected Writings of Edward Sapir in Language, Culture and Personality. Berkeley: University of California Press.

Pelto, Pertti J. and Gretel H. Pelto (1975). Intra-Cultural Diversity: Some Theoretical Issues. American Ethnologist 2: 1-18.

Pike, Kenneth L. (1967). Language in Relation to a Unified Theory of the Structure of Human Behavior. The Hague: Mouton and Company.

Rollwagen, Jack R. (1980a). Cities and the World System: Toward an Evolutionary Perspective in the Study of Urban Anthropology. IN Cities in a Larger Context, Thomas Collins (ed.). Southern Anthropological Society Proceedings No. 14. Athens: University of Georgia Press, pp. 123-140.

Rollwagen, Jack R. (1980b). New Directions in Urban Anthropology: Building an Ethnography and an Ethnology of the World System. IN Urban Life: Readings in Urban Ethnography, George Gmelch and Walter Zenner (eds.). New York: St. Martin's Press, pp. 370-383.

Rollwagen, Jack R. (1987). Reconsidering Basic Assumptions: A Call for a Reassessment of the General Concept of Culture in Anthropology. Urban Anthropology 15 (1-2): 97-133.

Ruby, Jay (1975). Is an Ethnographic Film a Filmic Ethnography? Studies in the Anthropology of Visual Communication 2 (2): 104-111.

White, Leslie A. (1975). The Concept of Cultural Systems: A Key to Understanding Tribes and Nations. New York: Columbia University Press.

Young, Colin (1975). Observational Cinema. IN Principles of Visual Anthropology. Paul Hockings (ed.). World Anthropology Series. The Hague: Mouton. 65-80.

Imaging Anthropology

Don Rundstrom
Santa Fe, New Mexico

ABSTRACT: "Imaging Anthropology" presents imaging techniques and strategies for unlocking and transforming cultural information into tangible ethnographic results. It proposes a viable means for the advancement of visual ethnography in interpreting the multi-dimensional aspects of culture within a temporal/spatial framework. The anchoring of a visual/verbal dialogue in a visual-spatial/kinesthetic understanding is seen to be critical in mediating the various dimensions of cultural information through the stages of fieldwork to final presentation. By bringing a disciplined somatosensory awareness to the process of ethnographic accountability, a powerful tool can be fashioned to image anthropology. The relevancy of this approach is illustrated by a visual ethnographic project which examines the ritual aesthetics of Japanese traditional art forms, focusing on the practice of tea, and which culminated in the film, THE PATH.

Imaging anthropology requires an ethnographic use of visual techniques and technology to gather, analyze, and present anthropological information. For this, a visual ethnographic frame of reference needs to evolve within the more traditional approaches of participant observation and ethnographic interviewing (Spradley 1979, 1980).

The practice of ethnography is being recognized more and more as an interpretive "making" (Geertz 1973:15) derived from a shared dialogue between the ethnographer as a "native" of his discipline and the "native" participants of the culture being studied.

In traditional ethnography the concern has been, as Geertz (1973:20) has stated, "trying to rescue the 'said' of such a [flow of social] discourse from its perishing occasions and fix it in perusable terms." However, with the incorporation of visual techniques and technology in the ethnographic endeavor, a sensual awareness of the "flow or transformational quality" of a culture can be brought more critically into focus for anthropological inquiry. To achieve this, the visual ethnographer needs to develop a "critical imagistic eye," that is, a disciplined way of interpreting multi-sensual information within a temporal/spatial framework. Such somatosensory involvement with the visual-spatial/kinesthetic modes of processing information offers an important tool for unlocking and transforming cultural information into tangible ethnographic imagery.

Information processed through visual-spatial/kinesthetic modes provides a perceptual baseline to interpret a changing field of reference through time, space, and the relationship of objects to their environment. The visual-spatial/kinesthetic awareness refers to a combination of both physiological and mental information processing of sensory input for the transformation of such information from field data, through an analytic stage, and into a final presentational form. It can thus provide a foundation from which to interpret the transitional aspects of a culture.

By developing a visual-spatial/kinesthetic awareness and consciously incorporating this into analytical strategies, one can record and make direct inferences about cultural flow and rhythmic patterning, as well as perceive how a culture aesthetically and ideologically interprets these patterns. There are two important conceptual frameworks in these analytic strategies regarding the visual-spatial/kinesthetic modes of contextually processing information:

1. As Context: Information as a holistic synthesis;

2. In Context: An inferential reconstruction of the whole through its particle relationships; a transitional process which can be sequenced and/or measured through time.

That is, the synchronic or diachronic approaches of study, respectively. By establishing and confirming meaning through the application of these strategies, a system of "visual evidence" can be developed to transform information from field to presentation. An ethnographer can scan the observational field by comparatively noting differences and/or similarities. Visual tangibles in the objective environment can then be mentally noted or be technically or descriptively recorded to give a visual reference to that field. As patterns emerge through this process, the visual tangible as a visual reference takes on the role of visual evidence. This visual evidence can then be tested to either confirm or reject the theoretical concerns of the ethnographer. Such visual evidence can also be combined with ethnographic description through a system of coding, and this combination of image, description and code presents a framework from which collaborative statements and/or replicative tests can be made. It is from this framework that appropriate presentational forms can be developed.

The process of moving visual information from field data (recorded images or visual tangibles) to the final presentational form may involve one or more of the following visual ethnographic techniques:[1,2]

Techniques for Recording Images:

1. Inventorying: Recording what is there.

2. Contexting: Relating objects, individuals and processes to each other or to the environment.

3. Mapping: Noting orientation and location in space or contexting navigational procedures and protocol (noting such aspects as distance, direction, time, and arrangement, etc.).

4. Tracking: Recording orientation in time or referencing the following:

   a. What goes before
   b. What goes after
   c. Duration (there must be a known time interval)

Techniques for Utilizing Images: (whether still photographs, film, video, graphics, etc.):

1. Interviewing with Images (which allows for agreed-upon visual referents from which observations can be made about an individual's cultural selective perceptions)

2. Using Images as a Mnemonic Device

3. Using Images Gained Through Various Media Approaches for Comparative Feedback

4. Using Visual Images to Reconstruct:
   a. an event
   b. a process or procedure
   c. an object
   d. a technique

5. Using Images to Elicit a Narrative (which ties a visual referent to an interpretive process)

6. Using Images for Illustration

The appropriate techniques, technology, and modes of visual communication should be selected for the task at hand. These may be used separately or in combination, depending on the situation, but should allow for both culturally-determined and anthropologically oriented criteria.

THE PATH Project

The following discussion elaborates on how some of the above techniques were used in a visual ethnographic project that culminated in the presentational film, THE PATH,[3] which was the result of an interdisciplinary effort to articulate culture. My brother Ron and I had lived in Okinawa and Japan and had trained in traditional art forms there before our interest in anthropology. In 1968, at San Francisco State University, we were fortunate enough to take a class on methods in social anthropology from John Collier, Jr., which provided foundations for a disciplined still photographic methodology of recording, analyzing and explicating culture, and which provided a way of "seeing" not only visually but culturally. We brought our experiences in Japanese art forms to this class and they provided a foundation upon which to conduct a systematic photographic analysis of Japanese tea ceremony, which we were studying at the time. The insights and structures gained from both our training in Japanese art forms and still photographic methodology were then expanded and utilized in an interdisciplinary film/anthropology seminar in 1968 taught by anthropologist, John Adair, and animator/filmmaker, David Hilberman. The course, "Explorations in Anthropological Filmmaking," was designed to produce filmically aware ethnographers and to "bring about better communication and better working relations between anthropologists and the filmmakers concerned with the production of this type of documentary."[4] It involved the production of films to explore such an inter-disciplinary process.

The visual ethnographic opportunities offered in these two classes provided an alternative to the limitations of the written tradition in the social sciences in communicating certain elements of Japanese ritual aesthetics. In the case of the film, THE PATH, it was important to emphasize a sensual awareness through a multi-layered portrayal of a cultural context. It was designed for training in cultural sensitivity, to initiate a questioning of the viewers' ethnocentric positioning, through multiple film viewings whereby a viewer initially experiences a form of "culture shock," but through repeated viewings becomes more comfortable with the vicarious cross-cultural experience. In a sub-cultural context, the film was developed for use by the tea teacher as an instructional introduction for new students. THE PATH, therefore, was conceived not merely as a film document of a Japanese early autumn thin tea service, but as a film portraying multiple aspects of the aesthetic underpinnings of the art of tea and Japanese traditional art forms in general. The film's title, THE PATH, reflects this emphasis.

The film additionally represents a sophisticated integration of materials and concepts in which a conscious effort was made to transform culturally-determined research data into the film content and structure through the manipulation of film in the explication of certain aspects of culture.[5] Three main approaches contributed to this visual ethnographic endeavor: I. Non-Native Apprenticeship and Trans-Disciplinary Involvement; II. Visual

Ethnography; III. Imaging Anthropologically.

I. Non-Native Apprenticeship and Trans-Disciplinary Involvement: A distinction is made here between participant observation and non-native apprenticeship. In the former, one may participate in the other culture, but makes observations through the paradigms of one's own culture (i.e., through the discipline of anthropology). It can thus be viewed as a form of ethnocentric participation. In the latter, one apprentices to the paradigm of another culture through transpection.[6] This is done not only intellectually, but through the senses in an attempt to go beyond one's ethnocentric biases and to develop a point of view from the paradigms of the other's perspective. By applying this cross-paradigmatic approach and allowing a dialogue to develop between them, other dimensions may then emerge which may not be initially directly visible.

For this project, non-native apprenticeship was employed and explored in different ways:

A. Non-native apprenticeship of the anthropologists in various traditional Japanese aesthetic systems.[7] During these apprenticeship periods, aspects of the knowledge systems of Japanese traditional culture were learned through a process of "doing." This provided insights not only into specific techniques and protocol, but also into various aesthetic sensibilities and ideologies that metaphorically addressed a traditional idealized essence of Japanese culture.

This concept of "doing" is submerged in a process of learning through observation, repetitive practice, and allowing the total body senses to become involved in the paradigm of a cultural transmission process. A transpective paradigmatic repositioning (Rosaldo 1983) is epistemologically important and was acutely noticed during the apprenticeship to the system of Japanese archery. The importance of this "repositioning" was reinforced many times in various art forms and eventually led to critical metaphorical insights. The archery experience proved valuable not only because the apprenticeship was the most complete, but also because comparative paradigms were more readily available. I had studied Western archery during a major transition of the basic Western bow design from the Norman longbow style to incorporating features of the 3,000 year old Asian composite bow. Despite the Easternization of the Western bow and years of experience shooting various bow styles, I missed the target in my initial attempt to shoot a Japanese bow, even though the target was quite near. This served to reinforce the importance of being aware of how one's body posture, movement, energy control and intellect must change paradigms to accommodate another cultural way.

One learns to respect and to participate in another culture for the value it has within the confines of that tradition. During the archery apprenticeship, the more advanced students would give us advice and instruction while the master would observe our "progress." Only at specific times would the master become directly involved in our learning process. This was generally done non-verbally, not necessarily because of the language barrier, but because the Japanese traditional way of teaching archery is more tactile and kinesthetically oriented. For example, I was consistently missing the target for a period of time; the master quietly stepped behind, observed my shooting stance, and then gently placed his hands on my hips to reposition them slightly just before the moment of release of the arrow. (See photograph number 1.) The distinctive sound of the arrow flying through the air and penetrating the target added to the sensation of the whole body, reinforcing the importance of correct posture in this archery form. If the master had given this "advice" at the beginning of my training, too much would have been wrong for me to have recognized the importance of the instruction. Although the theory of some of the finer aspects of posture was given through instruction, it was only through feeling or practice that the true insight came. It was by "doing" and accumulative corrective positioning that a transpective repositioning took place. The master's observation and instructive timing allowed insights not only regarding the refined techniques of archery and the deeper aesthetic aspects that make this practice an art form, but "how" these are transmitted.

In archery, as in other traditional Japanese art forms, one encounters and is submerged in a process that leads from teaching and practice towards an enlightened awareness. This knowledge, gained through the non-native apprenticeship practice, was incorporated in the film as a structural metaphor to indicate the importance of this traditional epistemological system. Three main sections of THE PATH were structured as follows:

1. Teaching: The first ten shots in the film serve as the teaching or preparation phase whereby the viewer is introduced to cultural metaphors which underlie many of the traditional art forms of Japan. For example, the rhythm and cultural style of the film are introduced by the drawing of the title character and are echoed by the ensuing whisking of tea and shots of the garden. Seasonal atmosphere and cultural sensibilities are presented to the viewer in this section, as well as indicating that the arts reflect a microcosm of nature. Additionally, a pattern is established by contrastively structuring the film to portray the elements of harmony and balance.

PHOTOGRAPH NUMBER 1

2. Practice: The second section of the film portrays the chronology of the tea event, approximating the actual time of the process. It represents the practice phase of the apprenticeship process, while also serving as a "teaching" phase to an uninitiated film audience. In this section the audience is allowed to relate intimately to the process of the tea service with a minimum of narration to allow the viewer to experience various elements presented in the film visually, audially, kinesthetically, as well as intellectually.

3. Enlightened Awareness: The concluding section of the film (represented by a superimposition of various actions) serves to break the linear, chronological awareness of the second section of the film, and tries to visually portray an aspect of the experience of "enlightened awareness" which can only be attained through "proper" training and practice. It synthesizes an expressive idealization of this experience through the use of slow motion, overlapping images, and extreme close-ups to emphasize that learning and knowledge do not involve the intellect alone, but also involve a synthesis through multi-sensual awareness.

B. Transdisciplinary involvement. Not only did we, as ethnographers, study the tea ceremony, but the tea hostess was involved "behind the camera" in framing two shots[8] in the film which were later used to compare her cultural aesthetic criteria with our filmic rendering and to provide her with insights into the requirements and needs of the filmmaking process through the practice of "native transpection." (See Maruyama 1974:191-192.) (See photograph number 2.)This gave her at least a tacit insight into our needs as filmmakers/ethnographers with regard to the portrayal of the atmospheric environment she was creating for the film's ritual.

The filmmakers were brought into contact with and sensitized to Japanese cultural dimensions as much as possible by having them participate in the tea ceremony, experience Japanese cuisine, and view Japanese cinema in addition to reading books and articles about Japan. This gave them an opportunity to become familiar with another culture's sensibilities and perspectives: for example, the filmmakers needed to understand that framing from a "*tatami* mat perspective" was important to contextualize a point of view. This required an unorthodox camera placement (using a high hat mounted on top of a suitcase) to achieve the height at which one would view the tea room from a kneeling position. Because of their sensitization process, this was more readily accepted by the filmmakers as an appropriate filming technique.

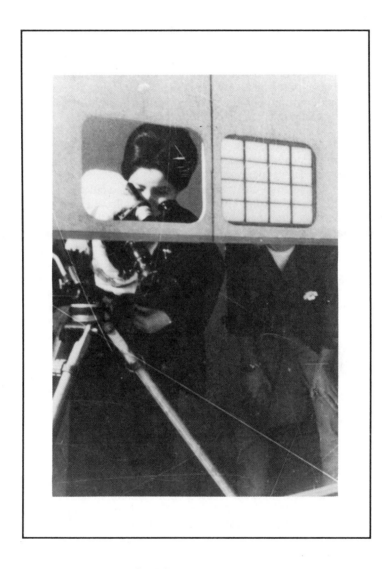

PHOTOGRAPH NUMBER 2

We, as anthropologists/ethnographers, were also urged to view films to learn about editing and techniques of filmmaking, and were eventually drawn into the process of filmmaking in our attempt to translate cultural concepts into a filmic portrayal. We had to learn filmic conventions, language and methodology, and eventually participated in the filmmaking process as part of the crew.

These cross-cultural and cross-disciplinary transpective positionings were extremely important factors in the success of this project. The process contributed to the identification with this project as a genuine team effort. This was not only consistent with the Japanese principle of social organization where the individual and his actions are defined by the group, but also allowed for the exploration of an innovative use of film in presenting cultural information.

II. Visual Ethnography: The second approach consisted of making an ethnographic visual record. At this stage, the non-native apprenticeship experiences in Japanese art forms proved to be particularly valuable. Insights gained from direct involvement in how a culture communicates through a visual-spatial/kinesthetic system allowed us to develop an empathetic and transpective consciousness in a still photographic visual ethnographic process which included image patterning, a photographic interview kit, and projective interviewing.

A. Image patterning. In John Collier's class on methods in social anthropology, tea lessons were documented and analyzed through the use of still photographs. Key concepts and patterns emerged through a process of sharing hundreds of photographs and contact prints with the other members of the tea group, and by studying individual photographs and sequences of photographs from the viewpoint of our experiences in other Japanese art forms. (See photograph number 3.) Certain concepts and ideologies were confirmed and reinforced, while others were introduced through this process. Through such feedback, patterns emerged, photographs were ordered and re-ordered, and then analyzed for cultural information.

Rhoda Metreaux has expressed some of the concerns of this process as follows:

> As in other approaches to a culture, the methods used to analyze imagery are based on the assumption that the details are consistent and form a coherent whole, and it is the aim of any such analysis to organize the details--the images--in such a way that the final delineation is an accurate statement of the configuration of a given culture. To understand and to describe how the world is perceived

PHOTOGRAPH NUMBER 3

and what the people are like who so perceive it through imagery, it is necessary to *learn to know the cultural models on which imagery is based and through this to work out how one image echoes and reinforces and counterpoints another.* For this echoing relationship of images I have chosen the term resonance...(1953:343; emphasis added).[9]

She later elaborates:

> I use *resonance* in imagery to refer to *systematic relationships between images within and among different modalities*--visual, auditory, kinesthetic, tactile, and so on. Resonance is concerned both with the content of discrete images, of clusters of images, and of complexes of images and with the structural properties of images and their relationships to one another in one or in several modalities. I use *image cluster* as it is used by Armstrong (1946) to refer to a series of images that are grouped and associated with each other. By *image complex* I mean images in two or more modalities that together form a unit (1953:351; emphasis added in first sentence).

Some of the visual ethnographic techniques previously enumerated also elicited systematic categorizations of aesthetic symbolism from the transitional nature of process or other areas of focus. For example, knowledge gained as a non-native apprentice in the art of tea established that different bowls of tea were used, depending on set criteria. A photographic "inventory" was then systematically taken of different types of bowls to form a photographic grouping or "image cluster." Similarly, photographs were taken of the *obi* or sash worn by the women. This technique, in combination with the photographic interview process and previous cultural insights, revealed that both image clusters contained references to "season." Thus, this seasonal quality formed a context for the clusters or groups inventoried and established a visual relationship or "image complex." Through such subtle nuances of the interconnectedness of content, context, and process, valuable visual clues were systematically isolated, related, and at times incorporated as elements in the film, THE PATH. The cross-correlation of resonances[10] from the non-native apprenticeship experience, photographic interviews, and the analysis of "image complexes" helped to distill and refine information into a photographic interview kit which eventually evolved into a storyboard for the film.

B. Photographic interview kit. Four areas of focus emerged from the "raw data" to form the basic photographic interview kit:

1. Spatial elements and body movement/posture relationships (e.g., object to object, individual to object, individual to individual, etc.)

2. Status and role orientations

3. Symbolism (e.g., relationships to nature, harmony and balance, season, etc.)

4. Process of an event (chronology, technique, etc.)

C. Projective interviewing. Projective interviews were conducted using this photographic kit to further elicit information from the tea teacher and members of the Japanese community in the San Francisco Bay area. The information was then used to discern the process of the art form, to check for accuracy, and to further elicit cultural meaning, perspective and aesthetic dimensions. This allowed for a more informed aesthetic reconstruction of the tea ceremony and portrayal of Japanese cultural concepts in the resulting film, THE PATH.

The use of photographs in interview situations also enhanced the flow of information by allowing individuals to respond indirectly to their own images, according to their cultural behavioral pattern. For example, when shown photograph number 4 during a photographic interview session, this woman responded to her own image by indicating that the person in the photograph shouldn't be smiling. (See photograph number 4.) Decorum was seemingly broken by her smile due to the particular situation and familiarity with the person behind the camera.[11] Some may point to this and argue that the presence of the camera alters the ethnographic situation. However, such social aspects of photographic recording may be utilized to enhance knowledge regarding a cultural perspective--in this case, the appropriateness of behavior in a given situation.

III. Imaging Anthropologically: The third approach, imaging anthropologically, or relating the specific to the general, consisted of molding selected Japanese cultural aesthetic concepts into a visual format through the use of filmic conventions (e.g., montage, slow motion, editing, camera angles, dissolves, etc.). This served not only to capture certain aesthetic and cultural essences, but also to provide the viewer with a filmic "experience" of the culture or event. The discussion which follows provides a further exploration of this approach in the making of THE PATH.

PHOTOGRAPH NUMBER 4

A. Thematic connections. Photographs number 5, 6, and 7 are examples of tangible visual references obtained through the ethnographic technique of "inventorying." By photographing the sash or *obi* worn by the women, comparisons of color, size, method of tying, or pattern could be made which delineate such categories as social status, role, age, season, or occasion. For instance, unmarried women usually wear intricately tied bows on formal occasions or an informal style of bow as shown in photograph number 5. These are usually brighter and have bolder patterns than those worn by older women. Once married (see photograph number 6), women generally wear the *obi* tied in a simple, square style, and as they age (see photograph number 7), the colors and patterns become more subdued. Each woman in the film chose her *obi* to reflect the early autumn atmosphere of the particular tea ceremony depicted in THE PATH. The *obi* also indicates the women's marital status and "season in life.

PHOTOGRAPH NUMBER 5

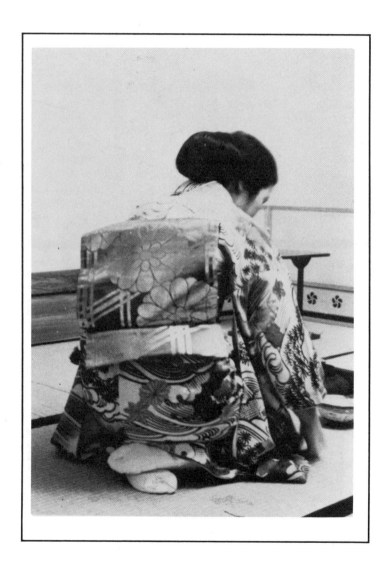

PHOTOGRAPH NUMBER 6

PHOTOGRAPH NUMBER 7

Another example of this seasonal element was consciously incorporated in the structure of the film in specific sequences of shots related to broader Japanese aesthetic and ideological sensibilities which the tea hostess wished to portray. Toward the beginning of THE PATH, the film was edited to juxtapose the following shots: an early autumnal garden; a guest (who is in the autumnal season of life); the *obi* of the guest (which is decorated with plants of autumn); and finally a flower arrangement of a yellow chrysanthemum which naturally blooms during the late summer or early autumn. These seasonal relationships (as indicated by nature, age of individual, article of clothing, or specific object) illustrate how a seasonal element can be coordinated in the tea ritual to create an atmospheric environment. Color and the juxtapositioning of these elements also provide important visual clues.

In keeping with this atmospheric consciousness and the importance of portraying a Japanese color balance, a choice was made to try to achieve this in the film according to the cultural criteria of the color of freshly brewed tea rather than the Hollywood film industry standard of white skin tone. Motion picture technology allows for a certain degree of color modulation through choice of film stock, lighting, filters, and lab "timing." A conscious effort was made to use the most appropriate film stock available at the time. EF Daylight 7241, ASA 160 and Tungsten 7242, ASA 125 were chosen to convey the subdued, cool colors appropriate to Japanese tea aesthetics of *wabi cha*. However, because distribution prints at the time were made on ECO 7255, and because color quality and contrast deteriorate at each stage of printing, subsequent copies of the film were not as true to the original color intent. In an attempt to maintain the color sensibilities originally sought, adjustments were made not only at the time of our initial processing and printing, but also several years later due to the organic nature of film.[12]

An example of cultural color perception was provided when the answer print version of the film was used for feedback. The tea hostess' response to the color of her *obi* was that it was "too red" in the film, indicating that it made her look too young in that context. The actual color of the *obi* was appropriate and coordinated with the thin lines of red texture in the *kimono* material, however, because of the color contrast in the film, the rendering of the red was too saturated and out of balance with the atmosphere which she was creating. Her comment provided not only an opportunity to try to attempt a more accurate rendition during lab processing, but gave further insight into Japanese perceptions of color and aesthetic sensibilities.

B. Thematic contexting. Color preference often reflects the Japanese identification with nature which is also an important aspect of the tea ceremony. Tied to this perception of nature *(shizen)* are the concepts of harmony and balance *(wa)*, respect *(kei)*, purity *(sei)*, and tranquility *(jaku)* which are integrated by balancing the seemingly contrastive elements in nature *(in-yo* in Japanese or *yin-yang* in Chinese). An example of how some of these Japanese aesthetic concepts manifest themselves in the tea room are revealed in photograph number 8, taken during the visual ethnographic process, which shows a "procedural contexting" of the arrangements of objects in time and space. The tea utensils are arranged on the mat in relation to the hot water kettle, and their position indicates a specific time and place during the course of the tea ceremony (when the utensils are presented by the hostess for the guests to appreciate). Furthermore, the placement of the tea kettle in the sunken hearth indicates that the season is late fall or winter (as opposed to spring or summer). The photograph also provides visual "symbolic contexting" of a Japanese aesthetic concept of harmony and balance: "Stillness in motion" and "motion in stillness." The *tatami* mats in the photograph illustrate a symbolic balancing of nature's contrasting forces, with the black lines of the mat representing stillness and the flowing weave indicating motion. In the film this balancing aspect of stillness and motion is also evident: the mats are immobile in contrast to the objects placed on them or the individuals who move across them during the course of the ceremony.

PHOTOGRAPH NUMBER 8

Similarly, photograph number 9 portrays not only a visual asymmetrical symmetry, which is an aspect of thematic repetitiveness in the Japanese art forms, but also a balancing in terms of the sense of taste. During the tea ritual, the sweet confectionary (in the container) is eaten and thereby coats the mouth with sugar. This modifies the bitterness of the tea by creating a balancing of the two tastes within the individual.

PHOTOGRAPH NUMBER 9
The emphasis on nature, harmony, and the balancing of seemingly

contrasting elements in nature was filmically rendered in the THE PATH. For example, in the garden scenes such a balance is not only contained within individual shots, but editing also juxtaposes shots (e.g., the apparent stillness of the foliage in one shot contrasted with a shot of a running brook). The orchestration of behavioral activity is also integral to the practice of Japanese art forms. The relationship of such states of activity and non-activity can be seen in photograph number 10, which was taken during the still photographic research process. In the photograph, one guest's "action" balances the "inaction" of the other guest. In the film, THE PATH, the hostess' action of making tea balances the seeming inaction of the guests as they sit and observe.

PHOTOGRAPH NUMBER 10

Contrasting elements of masculinity and femininity can also be seen in the drawing of a masculine-style character at the beginning of the film (as indicated in photograph number 11), and the still, feminine style character at the end of the film (as seen in photograph number 12). It is also seen in the male hand drawing the title character dissolving into a female hand whisking the tea. This dissolve emphasizes not only the masculine/feminine element, but the relationship between the art forms through the use of a filmic convention. It also alludes to the fact that these contrasting elements are not seen as being distinct opposites, but are contrastive complements with each having the embryonic forces of the other within it. A later dissolve in the film from the tea bowl to rocks and moss in the garden visually symbolizes the art of tea as a microcosm of nature. Such subtle manipulation of filmic convention can thus enhance the dimensional quality of the visual portrayal.

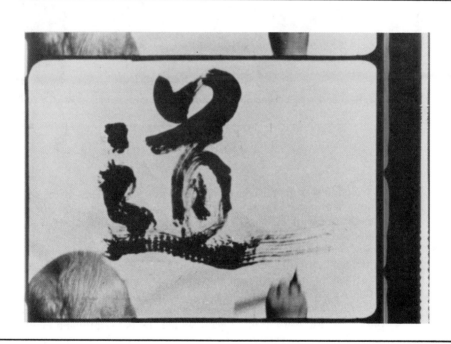

PHOTOGRAPH NUMBER 11

PHOTOGRAPH NUMBER 12

Sound was also used to emphasize this relationship of the tea ceremony with nature by modulating and mixing audio tracks. For example, the sound of the garden brook is merged with the sound of boiling water in the kettle through a sound dissolve, emphasizing how the natural sounds in the garden are linked to atmospheric sounds orchestrated in the tea room.

Such an appreciation of sensual involvement in the tea room also reflects the concept of respect *(kei)*. Photograph number 13, utilizing the visual ethnographic technique of "contexting," shows a guest not only in relationship to the objects which she is visually and tactilely inspecting and appreciating, but to the heat of the hearth and sound of boiling water in the tea kettle, and to the aroma of the tea in the canister. This manner of involving oneself in the practice and atmosphere of tea reflects not only a physical but a sensual way of knowing through "doing."

PHOTOGRAPH NUMBER 13

This process of "doing" can be "tracked" through still photography according to at least three criteria:

1. Shooting to establish referents in time and space according to cultural criteria.
2. Shooting at a set time interval, thus establishing duration.
3. Shooting for the "predominant moment of change"[13] to reference:

> a. the perceived condition that initiates change;
> b. the perceived condition that indicates stability.[14]

(Items 2 and 3 can be used in interview situations to establish item 1.)

In photographs number 14 through 19, the third criteria was used in "tracking the peaks and troughs" of the dynamic rhythmic flow of handling the tea bowl. The visual tangible unit of the tea bowl was photographed in its surrounding context to discern evidence of procedure and protocol. Feedback from consequent photographic interviews revealed a missing step: the act of wiping the bowl after drinking the tea. Thus, a combination of the visual ethnographic practices of "tracking," non-native apprenticeship, projective feedback, and imaging relationally through resonating relevance produced visual evidence that could be refined and developed into a storyboard for the final film production.

PHOTOGRAPH NUMBER 14

PHOTOGRAPH NUMBER 15

PHOTOGRAPH NUMBER 16

PHOTOGRAPH NUMBER 17

PHOTOGRAPH NUMBER 18

PHOTOGRAPH NUMBER 19

C. Metaphorical Imagery. A key photograph emerged as a result of a combination of stages which not only captured aspects of the process, purpose and aesthetics of the tea ceremony, but which unexpectedly became visual evidence at a metaphorical level for what we were trying to develop in the film. Photograph number 20 visually related a specific action to a particular aesthetic practice of the tea ceremony, and further connected these to a broader concept of how the traditional art forms refer to a cosmological view of nature.

During the non-native apprenticeship process it was learned that a certain action in the tea ceremony illustrated a stimulation of the senses. An attempt was made to photograph this with the Japanese cultural criteria of "letting the space define the object and the context define the action." It was hoped that such information would be confirmed in an interview situation. The visual tangible of the steam in the photograph is related to the sound of boiling water and should elicit information about a Japanese aesthetic metaphor of nature: the sound of the wind through the pines, or *matsukaze*. The act of pouring cold water into the hot water also creates steam and moisture which evokes a form of emotional atmospheric quality in the tea ceremony referred to as *wabi-cha*. The photographic feedback, however, went far beyond the original expectations.

Cultural insights in response to photograph number 20, contrary to what was predicted, indicated that there was movement in the hand on the lap, rather than in the "pouring" hand. The hand on the lap was seen as supporting and balancing the activity in relation to the total body posture, which is centered at the lowest point of body mass (represented by the white circle in photograph number 22). A harmonious balance was thus indicated by an effortlessness of action seen in the body posture, in the lack of tension in the facial muscles, and in the non-focused expression of the eyes which reflects a high state of meditative awareness.

PHOTOGRAPH NUMBER 20

PHOTOGRAPH NUMBER 21

To check the agreed-upon visual referents, photograph number 21 was selected to represent the opposite (i.e., non-supportive countenance of the body posture, facial muscle tension, etc.). Thus, through cross-image comparison in interview situations, the visual referents in photograph number 20 were confirmed, indicating proper balance of timing and spatial control *(ma)*, reflecting a state of spiritual forging *(seishin tanren)*, which represented a state of harmony *(wa)*.

All of these elements formed a visual ideographic referent or metaphor of what a tea master might refer to as "the way of a person" or *hito no michi*. Photograph number 22 shows how lines were drawn to code the visual tangible referents in the photograph more clearly. By doing this, it became evident that the photograph could then be "read" as a visual symbolic metaphor. This is similar to the way in which one can interpret a Japanese ideograph or character. Therefore, when the character *Michi* (path or way) was chosen as the title for the film THE PATH, (because it encapsulated metaphorical essences of the idealized traditional aesthetic epistemology of Japanese culture), various renderings of the character were drawn by a master calligrapher and used in an interview with the tea hostess.

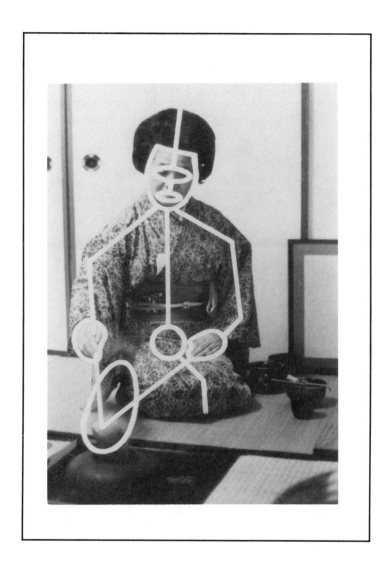

PHOTOGRAPH NUMBER 22

The basic forms of the tea ceremony are said to have been created and defined by borrowing from the vocabulary of calligraphic styles (Fujioka 1973:10):

1. *kaisho*: formal or orthodox, square, block form of Chinese writing (photograph number 23);

2. *gyosho* : semi-cursive form (photograph number 24);

3. *sosho*: informal, cursive, grass-writing form (photographs number 25 through 28).

PHOTOGRAPH NUMBER 23

PHOTOGRAPH NUMBER 24

PHOTOGRAPH NUMBER 25

PHOTOGRAPH NUMBER 26

PHOTOGRAPH NUMBER 27

PHOTOGRAPH NUMBER 28

Each style of writing the character communicates different characteristics (e.g., stability, formality/informality, fluidity, or simplicity). The *sosho* or informal cursive style represented by photograph number 25 was chosen by the tea hostess because it most closely reflected the informal style of tea developed by Sen no Rikyu in the 16th century. This tea style was portrayed in the film through an intimate, yet slightly formal, early autumn thin tea service.

The title character for THE PATH *(Michi)* is also comprised of various other characters: *onozu* (self), *me* (eye), *kubi* (neck), and *shinyu* (movement). Each contributes meaning to the total character and adds different aspects to its meaning. An interpretation sometimes given to the character, *michi* (path), is that it relates to the two aspects of a human journey: an inner and outer path represented by the elements in photographs number 31 and 32 respectively.

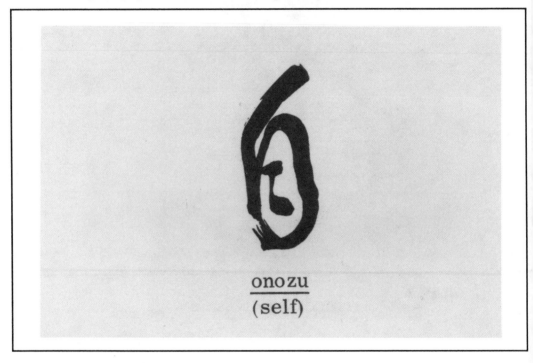

onozu
(self)

PHOTOGRAPH NUMBER 29

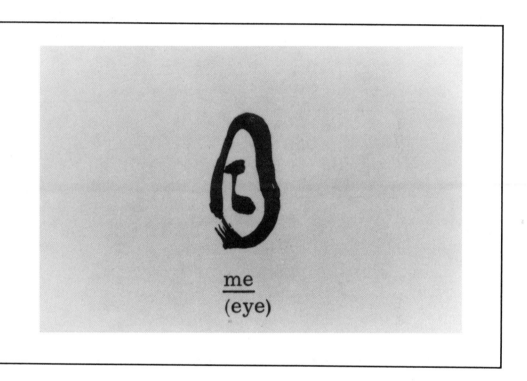

PHOTOGRAPH NUMBER 30

PHOTOGRAPH NUMBER 31

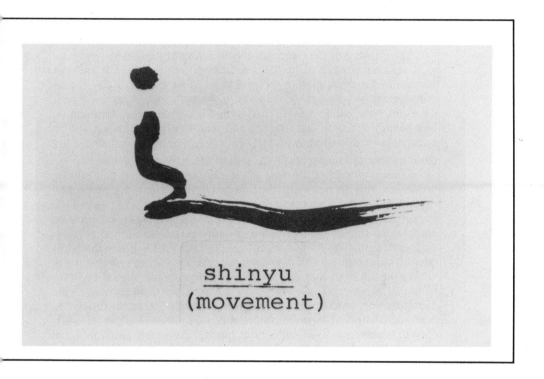

PHOTOGRAPH NUMBER 32

C. Cultural rhythm as metaphorical epistemology. The visual-spatial/kinesthetic element of the drawing of a character is indicated in the dynamics of "how" the ink is laid on the paper by modulating it through time and space. The process of writing a character can be "tracked" through still photography, providing a certain degree of information which can in turn be used to elicit information. The still photographic process, however, lacks the transitional and transformational aspects of a culture's rhythmic flow which can provide meaning at the aesthetic and ideological levels through various somatosensory modes. Therefore, it was decided not to simply use a static character for the title of the film, but to show the character being drawn.

The drawing of the character, the whisking of the tea, and even the reconstructed rhythm of the film reflect and reinforce the traditional essence of Japanese rhythm referred to as *jo-ha-kyu* (*jo* is the slower, introductory or preparatory phase; *ha* is the breaking action, and *kyu* is the rapid, concluding phase). This rhythm is present in the formulation of a cultural dynamic that shapes traditional Japanese behavior, and an awareness of this rhythm in THE PATH can be enhanced through a participatory consciousness on the part of the viewing audience.[15]

Conscious efforts must be made during the filming and editing processes also to maintain the integrity of cultural dynamics and rhythm so that such a participatory consciousness can take place. THE PATH incorporated shots of over 2-minutes in length, contrary to commercial film convention which usually uses shots around 5-7 seconds in length. The longer shots used in THE PATH allow the audience an opportunity to become involved with the pacing and movement within the shots so that a sense of body rhythm and spatial involvement can be conveyed. At a metaphorical level, the three sections of the film (teaching, practice and enlightened awareness) were constructed to echo the traditional Japanese rhythms of *jo, ha, kyu* to allow the audience to become involved not only in specific movement patterning, but also to be submerged in a filmic rendering of a metaphorical epistemology.

Conclusion

Motion picture or electronic imagery provide mediums for the creation of environmental experiences whereby multi-sensual approaches to cultural interpretation can be presented. It thus allows the viewer an opportunity to explore an intimate relationship between his/her own sense of movement and the visual-spatial/kinesthetic portrayal of the cultural movement of the film environment. Multiple dimensions of cultural information may thereby be absorbed and processed in a more holistic manner.

The rhythmic transformational flow of a culture is an extremely important source of cultural knowledge. A disciplined way of interpreting multi-sensual information within a temporal/spatial framework has always been problematic in ethnographic accountability. This is mainly due to the fact that cultural "flow" presents information in a changing field of reference. Abraham Kaplan's remarks can be applied in this regard as a useful frame of reference:

> What we need for knowledge is not permanence but persistence, not the absolutely unchanging but rather changes sufficiently slow or limited for patterns to be recognizable (Kaplan 1964:167).

This is paramount if image accountability is to be brought within the framework of the ethnographic endeavor. Elsewhere Kaplan states:

> ...it is *not repeatability that is called for, but the instituting of controls* ... doing this...takes skill and effort to introspect in a way that is scientifically useful (Kaplan 1964:141-142; emphasis added).

The nature of persistence of vision, coupled with visual-spatial/kinesthetic awareness offers a powerful tool for establishing an interface whereby complex levels of information, which exist simultaneously within the "flow" frame of reference, may be unlocked and transformed into the identifiable tangible evidence of ethnographic imagery. By allowing somatosensory positioning to take place within the ethnographic dialogue, various navigational and diagnostic procedures can evolve. These procedures can thus establish necessary controls to operationalize and interface image recording and image utilizing strategies with the ethnographer's internalized models to provide a broader disciplined foundation from which to image anthropology.

NOTES

[1] These techniques were developed through a direct involvement in "doing" visual ethnography as an independent investigator, as well as through collaboration with Ron Rundstrom and our mentors, John Adair and John Collier.

[2] Jacknis (1984:2-60) suggests that Boas used these techniques except for the "narrative" approach.

[3] 16mm, 34 minute, color, sound film produced by the Sumai Film Company. An accompanying ethnographic written monograph by Don Rundstrom, Ron Rundstrom, and Clinton Bergum was also published, entitled, JAPANESE TEA: THE RITUAL, THE AESTHETICS, THE WAY.

[4] John Adair, personal communication.

[5] Beryl Bellman and Benetta Jules-Rosette, 1977:11, describe the advantages of the innovative ethnographic technique used in this project as follows: "The overall result of this interpretive strategy is a documentable procedure for creating an ethnographer's account of a naturally bounded event that claims to preserve cultural sensitivity and the depth and subjectivity of those who participate in it."

[6] Maruyama 1974a:191 defines transpection: "This process consists in getting into the *head* (not shoes) of another person. One erases as much of his/her own paradigm as possible from his/her own head and gets into and thinks in the paradigm of the other person." In this paper, however, I use the term in a broader sense by relating it not only to the mind, but to somatosensory learning as well.

[7] *Kyudoo* (the way of the bow; archery) and *jodo* (the way of the stick) in Japan; *sado* (the way of tea) both in Japan and the United States.

[8] Shot 6 (48.10 - 54.11) of leaves against the bamboo fence; Shot 65 (1075.15 - 1083.17) of the tea container and spoon on the *tatami* mat.

[9] See also Maruyama 1974a, 1974b where the concept of resonance is developed within the framework of information theory. Especially important to this discussion is his concept of "relevance resonance" where "convergence of purpose" (Maruyama 1974a:181) as a relational technique is vital in handling feedback information during this process.

[10] For important insights into this process, see Bateson (1979: Introduction) on "the pattern which connects."

[11] This reinforces Byers (1966) thesis that "Cameras Don't Take Pictures."

[12] In the final analysis, the color sensibilities sought were too magenta and contained too much contrast in the final prints. However, it is felt that the tea aesthetic color balance can be more closely approximated now because of better technological controls than were available at the time.

[13] Background for this conceptualization can be found in Bateson's (1979:250) definition for information as "any difference that makes a difference."

[14] For a broader discussion of conditions a and b, see Anatol Holt's work in Bateson (1972:Ch. 9-10).

[15] A stylized form of posturing accompanied by a deep, rhythmic breathing technique is important to the Japanese traditional aesthetic epistemology and is therefore important in enhancing the viewing of this film. An awareness of these techniques on the part of the ethnographer during the field analysis stages of inquiry would also be valuable in processing various aspects of cultural information.

REFERENCES CITED

Bateson, Gregory (1979). Mind and Nature. New York: Bantam Books.
Bateson, Mary Catherine (1972). Our Own Metaphor. New York: Alfred A. Knopf.
Bellman, Beryl L., and Benetta Jules-Rosette (1977). A Paradigm for Look-

ing: Cross-Cultural Research with Visual Media. Norwood, New Jersey: Ablex Publishing Corporation.

Byers, Paul (1966). Cameras Don't Take Pictures. The Columbia University Forum 9(1):27-31.

Fujioka, Ryoichi (1973). Tea Ceremony Utensils: Arts of Japan 3. New York: Weatherhill.

Geertz, Clifford (1973). The Interpretation of Cultures. New York: Basic Books, Inc.

Jacknis, Ira (1984). Franz Boas and Photography. Studies in Visual Communication 10(1):2-60.

Kaplan, Abraham (1964). The Conduct of Inquiry: Methodology for Behavioral Science. San Francisco: Chandler Publishing Company.

Maruyama, Magoroh (1972). Non-Classificational Information and Non-Informational Communication. Dialectica 26(1):51-59.

Maruyama, Magoroh (1974a). Paradigmatology and Its Application to Cross-Disciplinary, Cross-Professional and Cross-Cultural Communication. Dialectica 28(3-4):135-196.

Maruyama, Magoroh (1974b). Endogenous Research vs. Delusions of a Relevance and Expertise Among Exogenous Academics. Human Organization 33 (3):318-326.

Metraux, Rhoda (1953). Resonance in Imagery. IN The Study of Culture at a Distance, Margaret Mead and Rhoda Metraux (eds). Chicago: The University of Chicago Press, pp. 343-362.

Rosaldo, Renato (1983/4). Grief and a Headhunter's Rage: On the Cultural Force of the Emotions. SWAA Newsletter 22(4)/23(1):3-8.

Rundstrom, Donald, Ronald Rundstrom, and Clinton Bergum (1973). Japanese Tea: The Ritual, The Aesthetics, The Way. Warner Modular Publications, Module 3. Andover, Massachusetts: Warner Modular Publications.

Spradley, James P. (1979). The Ethnographic Interview. New York: Holt, Rinehart and Winston.

Tedlock, Dennis (1979). The Analogical Tradition and the Emergence of a Dialogical Anthropology. Manuscript of Harvey Lecture delivered at the University of New Mexico, March 20, 1979 and submitted to the Journal of Anthropological Research.

THE MAJOR FILMS OF DON RUNDSTROM

THE PATH. 1971. A film by Don Rundstrom, Ron Rundstrom, and Clinton Bergum. 34 minutes, color, sound, 16mm. Distributor: The Sumai Film Company, 521 East Garcia Street, Santa Fe, New Mexico 87501. (505-982-8872).

UPROOTED: A JAPANESE AMERICAN FAMILY'S EXPERIENCE. 1978. A film by Don Rundstrom and Sue Rundstrom. 29 minutes, black and white, sound, 16mm. Distributor: Don and Sue Rundstrom, 521 East Garcia Street, Santa Fe, New Mexico 87501 (505-982-8872) or The Manzanar Committee, Inc. 1566 Curran Street, Los Angeles, California 90026 (213-662-5102).

VISUAL ETHNOGRAPHIC RECORD OF THE ILAKIA AWA OF THE EASTERN

CENTRAL HIGHLANDS OF NEW GUINEA (unpublished). July-August, 1970. A visual ethnographic record by Don Rundstrom. 17 hours, 46 minutes, color, silent. Distributor: Don Rundstrom, 521 East Garcia Street, Santa Fe, New Mexico 87501 (505-982-8872). (Screening selections must be accompanied by above ethnographer.)

REVIEWS OF THE ABOVE FILMS

Beardsley, Richard (1975). Review of THE PATH. American Anthropologist 77:463-464.

Bellman, Beryl L., and Benetta Jules-Rosette (1977). A discussion of THE PATH. IN A Paradigm for Looking: Cross-Cultural Research with Visual Media. Norwood, NJ: Ablex Publishing Corp. pp. 10, 60-61.

Heider, Karl G. (1976). A discussion of THE PATH. IN Ethnographic Film. Austin and London: University of Texas Press, pp. 8, 44, 55, 56, 62, 65, 83, 93, 100, 102, 103.

Ruby, Jay (1975). Review of THE PATH. American Anthropologist 77: 464-466.

Ruby, Jay (1975). A discussion of THE PATH. Is an Ethnographic Film a Filmic Ethnography? IN Studies in the Anthropology of Visual Communication Vol. 2, No. 2, Fall: 109-110.

Sorenson, E. Richard (1975). A discussion of THE PATH. Visual Evidence: An Emerging Force in Visual Anthropology. National Anthropological Film Center Occasional Papers, No. 1, December: p. 3.

Choices And Constraints In Filming In Central Asia

André Singer
Oxford Ethnographic Films

ABSTRACT: A discussion about the making of seven documentaries for British Network Television on the anthropology of Central Asia. The problems of filming lay as much in the union-management struggles in England as with the differing administrations of Afghanistan, Pakistan and China. The resulting films were aimed at a general public but at the same time were meant as relevant anthropology in their own right.

The author does not believe that the two are mutually exclusive.

Although the general issues being discussed in this paper are relevant to all anthropological filmmakers, the examples are taken from Central Asian projects done over an eight year period between 1975 and 1983 which have resulted in the televising of seven documentaries. The societies in question live or used to live within a 300 mile radius of each other but for various reasons now find themselves subject to the different ideologies and regimes of China, Pakistan, Afghanistan and Turkey, with the past or present influences of Britain and Russia also of great importance. Of the seven resulting films, five were made for Granada Television (a British Independent television company), one was made for Oxford Ethnographic Films and transmitted on Channel 4 (a network outlet for Independent television productions in Britain), and the last was made for the B.B.C. The common denominators are that they were all aimed at a general audience and that they were all produced and directed by myself (with the exception of THE KIRGHIZ OF AFGHANISTAN, which was directed by Charlie Nairn). These last two facts are important only in as much as it makes it possible to discuss production issues knowing that the films in question have similar aims. That they were made for a general audience needs some clarification before the films themselves come under discussion.

The Audience

It is the issue of "audience" that marks the major difference in approach, style and content between anthropological filming in Britain and that in the U.S., Canada, Australia or France. The reasons for British anthropological filming having a longer and generally more successful outlet on television have been discussed in several recent publications (Henley 1984, Singer 1983). Briefly these stem from on the one hand, the importance of factual documentaries as part of British viewing and on the other, the lack of any educational funding for aspiring British anthropologists or filmmakers who desired to use celluloid as a means of presenting their fieldwork rather than just paper. It took the success of television series like DISAPPEARING WORLD or WORLDS APART to break down the barriers of academia that were placed in the way of the specialist filmmaker. Even today, despite the fact that most universities use anthropological films as a part of their teaching course, or at least as an adjunct to the course, there are only a handful of people who would claim the label "anthropological filmmaker." Marshall, Gardner, MacDougall, Rouch or Asch are better known to the British anthropologist than are Moser, Curling or Llewellyn-Davies. The former make films for an audience of anthropologists, the latter make films for the public with the knowledge that the anthropological audience is secondary. It, of course, boils down to finance. The British funders are the television stations; there is no philanthropy involved. What happened in the past was crudely as follows: the major Independent Network Companies (Granada, Yorkshire, Central, Anglia, Thames and London Weekend) had a brief from the Independent Broadcasting Authority, the watchdog that gave or revoked licenses, to produce a proportion of "cultural" material to balance the more commercially viable soap operas, quiz shows, comedies or dramas. A sort of informal gentleman's agreement developed, with Anglia Television taking wildlife and Granada Television developing anthropology. DISAPPEARING WORLD thus became the flagship of Granada Television's cultural output and Brian Moser was able to expand and develop the series between 1969 and 1973 from the occasional programme about South American Indians under threat (LAST OF THE CUIVA, END OF THE ROAD, WAR OF THE GODS etc.), to a major anthropological series with a staff of trained anthropologists and filmmakers working side-by-side. Subtitles and a concentration on narrow relevant themes did nothing to stem the popularity of the series for the public (as measured in viewing figures) and at its peak (probably 1975), it was being shown at peak mid-evening viewing time (9 P.M.), won the most prestigious British documentary series award (BAFTA) and thoroughly justified Granada Television's investment.

The irony of the series' success was that the aspirations of the "amateur" anthropologist filmmaker were held even more in check since the criteria for good film had become the expensive professional productions of the TV stations. Educational institutions were even more reluctant to fund a process that for a TV station cost (at today's prices) around $150,000 for an hours film. Anthropological filmmaking was becoming respectable (by 1980) but financially out of reach for the private individual and eventually even for the TV stations themselves. Union disputes and soaring costs resulted in the collapse of DISAPPEARING WORLD and subsequently its BBC sister programme WORLDS APART. 1984 saw British anthropological filmmaking in chaos: the economic squeeze on education ensures that funding through the universities stays a remote and unlikely option. Since 1985, Granada Television has revived DISAPPEARING WORLD as an "occasional" series but most BBC funding has been switched away from anthropology to more lucrative areas as part of a current battle for ratings and revenue. Central Television invested in a series about the founding fathers of anthropological fieldwork (Spencer, Boas, Rivers, Malinowski, Mead and Evans-Pritchard) called STRANGERS ABROAD. This series, written and presented by Bruce Dakowski and produced and directed by myself are films about anthropology, rather than being in themselves "anthropological" films. The Leverhulme Foundation through the Royal Anthropological Institute has initiated two film fellowships in an attempt to maintain some impetus but I suspect that for some time to come the British public audience will have to be satisfied with a diet of blockbusters in the manner of COSMOS, CIVILIZATION and ASCENT OF MAN. Other recent projects have been studies of China (HEART OF THE DRAGON) and Africa (AFRICA): of psychology (THE INNER EYE) and food (SPICE OF LIFE); of adventure (ASSIGNMENT ADVENTURE and SURVIVAL) and politics (END OF EMPIRE). In the pipeline are series on Oceans (THE BLUE REVOLUTION), and on other regions such as the Soviet Union, Latin America and Asia. The trend has yet to decide that anthropology is fundable, although many producers are knocking at the portals of the financiers' castles.

The Area

The wish to make films in Central Asia began against a backcloth of a personal commitment to the area at a time that DISAPPEARING WORLD was expanding to reach a mass public audience for the first time, i.e. 1974. As a student of Evans-Pritchard and with an anthropological training in one of Britain's most established centres of learning, the move to popular television was traumatic: the cut and thrust of academic in-fighting was nothing compared to the aggressive world of television. Survival was insured by having a "specialist" background. The comfortable and esoteric island that was DISAPPEARING WORLD aroused jealousies but less competition since it was assumed we were not chasing other peoples' roles but were concentrating on our own exotic field. With an anthropological field background in Iran and Afghanistan, it was naturally to that area that I was allowed to turn my attention. The unwritten laws for researching programmes were:

1. Whatever the society chosen, be able to present the material to the television company so that the non-anthropologists among them (100%) would be excited. This was the "tits and spears" philosophy. It boiled down to a matter of packaging the product, since any society can be made to appear exciting if presented in the right way. It was a cynical but pragmatic approach and the anthropologists among us did not rule out any film we deemed important simply because an initial presentation did not immediately sound exciting. Nor could we expect television executives to get excited about matrilineal descent patterns simply because we felt it was interesting from an anthropological viewpoint.

2. Although anyone, particularly an anthropologist, should be aware of the myriad of cultural differences between societies, never assume that those same television executives appreciate the differences in the same way. I was once told to stop pursuing a project among the Bedu of Jordan because the company had "already made a film about Arabs." The "Arabs" in question happened to be Kurds in Western Iran but the stereotype had become entrenched. Packaging therefore included emphasizing the uniqueness of the project in question. To be able to add "the first film team ever to..." was a particular bonus.

3. Present that part of the society in question that is under threat at the beginning of the proposal. Programme makers often forget that anthropological subject matter is dynamic and everything is always under "threat." A series called DISAPPEARING WORLD was under some obligation, it was believed, to live up to its name.

The area in this instance was to be Afghanistan and a short list was easily drawn up that fitted the above criteria. More importantly, the project had a "cultural interpreter" (i.e. an anthropologist who could work alongside the filmmaker). The anthropologists working on the DISAPPEARING WORLD series at the time were regarded by the television management as "middle men." The traumas that often appear between film director and anthropologist were to be overcome by having an intermediary that spoke both languages, that of the film world and that of academia. An interesting principle but one that perhaps underestimated the foibles of human nature. Certainly the anthropologist in television could spot accessible and fruitful subject matter but the problems of interpretation are doubled when in the field and it was only when the anthropologist-researcher became filmmaker in his or her own right that the dividends were properly reaped.

The Subjects

1975 saw the research and successful filming of THE KIRGHIZ OF

AFGHANISTAN. The director was Charlie Nairn with a track record of three previous DISAPPEARING WORLD films. The anthropologist was Nazif Shahrani, an Uzbek with considerable field experience among his neighbours, the Kirghiz and an academic background from Kabul, Hawaii and Washington. The choice of the Kirghiz admirably fitted the criteria listed above. A society in the remote Pamirs of Afghanistan, isolated from their neighbours, difficult of access, gave every opportunity for it to be "presented" on paper as the dramatic and exciting community that it was. We would need a ten day journey, much of it on horse and yak, to reach them among dramatic 15,000 feet peaks. Despite the fact that these people wore clothes, smoked cigarettes and listened to the BBC World Service and the Voice of America, there were sufficient elements to attract the TV executive and to get the project off the ground. On a more serious anthropological level the Kirghiz were fascinating. A community of less than 2000 people living in a region above 11,000 feet bounded in the north by the Soviet Union, in the east, China, in the south the peaks leading to Pakistan and to the west the narrow exit to their own national state, Afghanistan. Their physical isolation enabled them to live apart from the Afghans and their own Turkic language kept them even more isolated. The rest of their society were living a collectivized existence in the USSR or China. This isolated group of sheep, goat and yak herders had opted against both systems under the leadership of their Khan (chief) Rahman Qol. Charlie Nairn's problem thus became the perennial film director's quandary: on what should we be concentrating? With the constraint of only five weeks filming this was not meant to be a definitive film study of the Kirghiz. That would have required years. Nor was it practical to opt for an observational "five weeks in the life of the Kirghiz." Verité has its strengths in anthropological filmmaking but it would be a brave TV executive who would transmit a Jean Rouch style programme for peak-time popular viewing. The final decision was to concentrate upon the influence, character and control exercised by Rahman Qol over his fellow Kirghiz. The film became a study of how a society was organized through the mechanics of control by the chief over the main resource, the herds. The Khan was interviewed extensively and expressed vigorously his anti-communist, anti-Soviet and anti-Chinese views. Also, some of his poorer "subjects" were interviewed to give an implicit criticism of conditions for some of them under his leadership. "I went to Russia," complained one poor herdsman. "I left because I was hungry and I didn't have any kinsmen. They just told me that I could not stay in Russia and they didn't ask any questions. They just told me I wasn't allowed to be there. So they returned me."

The resulting film, transmitted on British Television later in 1975 was judged a success, winning its share of international awards but sadly also arousing some controversy over interpretation and a heated exchange of letters between a reviewer, Nancy Tapper, Shahrani and myself over whether Rahman Qol was portrayed as a benevolent despot or a feudal exploiter, continued into 1976 (RAIN issues 13 and 16, 1976). But what the film demonstrated more clearly than other DISAPPEARING WORLDS before it, was how good television can also be good anthropology.

In 1980 under less favourable circumstances, Rahman Qol again became the focal point for a documentary. This time his circumstances had changed dramatically and tragically. His old enemies the Russians had moved into Afghanistan and he knew his position there in the strategic corridor against their frontier was untenable. After a few exchanges of rifle fire, most of the Kirghiz who were able to, collected their herds and fled to Pakistan. "The journey was difficult," explained Rahman Qol in a subsequent filmed interview, "The water was very high and carried away many of our animals. I had yaks and sheep but sold them all. There was no grazing here so I got a poor price."

Granada Television by this time had put DISAPPEARING WORLD into cold storage because of incessant union/management squabbles over crewing and as a result were left with only one of the original team. Brian Moser went to Central Television, Chris Curling and Melissa Llewellyn-Davies went to the BBC and Pattie Winter became a film editor. I was allowed to follow the story of Rahman Qol, not as a DISAPPEARING WORLD project but as a refugee documentary about the Afghan struggle. The resulting AFGHAN EXODUS became, in anthropological terms, episode two in the story of a society in transition. Rahman Qol's power base in Afghanistan, i.e. his control over herds, had gone and his role had developed as an intermediary between his people, the Pakistan Government and International agencies over the future of the Kirghiz. He was (in 1980) seriously arguing for the possibility of uprooting his people and resettling in Alaska. This scheme that was being investigated on his behalf by anthropologist Professor Louis Dupree, an old Afghan hand and friend of the chief. In 1983 Rahman Qol and 800 of his tribe accepted the offer to settle east of Lake Van in Turkey. They are currently settling into high altitude homes there, and episode three needs to be filmed quite soon.

A second set of films, KHYBER, THE PATHANS, and THE LOST TRIBES similarly demonstrate the compromises that had to be undertaken in order to make them at all, and the value of so doing. During the hiatus in the DISAPPEARING WORLD series, circumstances militated against anyone inside Granada Television successfully proposing an anthropological film; hence Brian Moser's departure to funding elsewhere, and Chris Curling's move to set up a rival unit in the BBC. We all still felt strongly that besides a commitment to making such films, the demand among the British public if not elsewhere, was strong. In 1979, prior to arrival of Soviet troops inside Afghanistan, Granada Television gave the opportunity for me to make a documentary about the history of the North West Frontier. This was also not to be anthropology but a two-sided look at colonial history. What did the Pushtun tribes think and remember about the British, and what did those officers who served on the Frontier remember about the time before independence in 1946? What gave the project an exciting scope beyond normal historical "reconstruction" was the ability to place tribal participants in the Anglo-Afghan upheavals on the screen alongside such venerable Western figures as Field-Marshall Sir Claude Auchinleck or the last British Governor, Sir Olaf Caroe. Pushtun spokesmen put the recent happenings along the Afghan Frontier in some perspective. What the film trip also enabled us to do was to stay longer in Pakistan, recruit the help of anthropologist and Political Officer, Dr. Akbar Ahmed and make a film study of the little known or understood process of Pushtun tribal organization. The resulting film, THE PATHANS, heralded a back-door revival of DISAPPEARING WORLD although the root causes of earlier troubles had by no means been overcome, just temporarily circumnavigated. It was interesting to note that when the film was shown under the DISAPPEARING WORLD title, many of the reviews in the press, after comments about the programme itself, went on to discuss the state of the series. "This film is the first DISAPPEARING WORLD to be seen for three years," wrote the Daily Telegraph on Feb. 21, 1980. "The series has always seemed to me one of the most valuable on television and I only wish THE PATHANS was the start of a new series." The Sunday Times were more explicit: "THE PATHANS might herald the re-emergence of Granada's highly successful DISAPPEARING WORLD series which was killed off by union-management squabbles over crewing." Indeed the Sunday Times proved to be correct and a limited revival began the following year resulting in six new anthropological documentaries, more internecine battles and instead of a real second coming, a further collapse. The current *ad hoc* revival is without any staff anthropologists and no full-time team. What might change matters is the establishment of a new Centre for Visual Anthropology at Manchester University in 1988 with support and finance from Granada. All British anthropological film makers anxiously await the effects of the combination of the University with the commercial TV station. It could only be an improvement. Meanwhile those earlier films about Pushtun society, with the addition of a further film, THE LOST TRIBES made with the help of the United Nations High Commissioner for Refugees and shown on Channel 4 on British Network Television, at least partially succeeded in their main aim: to give the general public insight into societies that were everyday news because of their involvement in the war in Afghanistan, but remained romantic shadowy figures. Between 12-15 million Pushtuns live in Afghanistan and Pakistan with a particularly complex social organization; an understanding of which would give insight into the struggles happening in that part of the world today. Little has been written about it for the public and even less portrayed on film. So to reach millions with a description of the Pushtun political hierarchy in one small village as a backcloth to understanding decision making in today's international turmoils was particularly satisfying.

    The final film under discussion in this paper was made about a tribal society close to both the Kirghiz and the Pushtuns but living inside a very different nation state to both Afghanistan and Pakistan. The Kazakhs of the Sinkiang Province of north-west China have a cultural heritage very similar to their Kirghiz neighbours. They are Moslem, high altitude pastoral herdsmen, speak a Turkic language and have a Turkic-Mongol heritage not only like the Kirghiz but also like the Uzbeks and Tartars. Having "tackled" Central Asian pastoralists under pressure from (a) environmental constraints (Kirghiz in the Afghan Pamirs) and (b) Political upheaval (Pushtuns and Kirghiz as refugees), we were particularly keen to look at how a society similar to the Kirghiz was surviving under the political constraints we imagined must exist inside both the Soviet Union and China. With the political thaw between China and the West during 1981 and with the earlier research "criteria" in mind about what would be most likely to placate management and union, we approached the Chinese and negotiated permission to film among the Kazakh horsemen. Sceptics were convinced that access would be too limited to be able to make anything worthwhile and that the end product would be a propaganda film for the Chinese authorities. We went to Sinkiang armed with two weapons that we hoped would overcome these protestations. The first was a decade of experience in filming relevant anthropological data among Central Asian society under difficult circumstances. The second was the services of an ethno-linguist (Dr. Shirin Akiner) who was to enable us to communicate directly with the Kazakhs whereas our Chinese "protectors" were unable to do the same. The situation developed in our favour. We were given two officials to "help" our project; a Han official from Peking and a Kazakh official from Urumchi, the provincial capital. The former found himself in a social setting where he couldn't speak the language, had to ride horses to move anywhere, had to eat mutton and had to live in a tent. All were anathema and we saw little of him. The Kazakh guide was euphoric at being released from his town desk and allowed up into the mountains. His pride in his own background and society often overcame his caution about reasoning why certain filming sequences were deemed necessary by the film team. Censorship lay not in their presence but in the awareness by the Kazakhs that to be too outspoken against the Chinese authorities could have serious repercussions and so answers to our questions were guarded. The final film, THE KAZAKHS OF CHINA, had one lasting and important impact on the general viewing public: an astonishment that inside China lived a society that were so un-Chinese, a society that were Moslem, that lived in spectacular mountains and who fitted Chinese stereotyping only in the costumes that many of the young wore. Of course, any well-shot documentary could have shown the same. THE KAZAKHS film had the added dimension that it portrayed how, on one level, the Kazakhs abided by communist strategy by having to accept a commune structure and ideology whilst at the same time adapting this new structure to their own resilient traditional tribal organization. The film trod a tight-rope which allowed the Chinese to interpret the material as saying how well the Kazakhs survive beneath a currently benign Chinese regime, and allowed others to view how well the Kazakhs were surviving by manipulating the Chinese regime (perhaps even with Chinese implicit knowledge) to their own ends. The major lesson learnt was that the effort is worthwhile, if the result can provide the viewer with insight into the motivations and workings of other societies whilst breaking away from expected stereotypes.

Oxford Ethnographic Films is currently attempting to add to the Central Asian cycle of films by gaining access in the Soviet Union. Here we are confronted with a nation whose own experience and history of film is profound. The Soviet knowledge of the power of the filmed image was acknowledged and used by Lenin and every subsequent government; and it would be naive to expect to gain the fortuitous access we were given in China. Also, there was an element of calculated opportunism in the Chinese readiness to allow a Western scientific film team among the Kazakhs. There the post-Cultural Revolution policy towards the minorities was to calm these potential trouble spots (they were allowed their own language, were exempt from the one-child national child birth policies and were being placated for the years of oppression under Mao Tse Tung). The Chinese wanted the West to know about these new efforts among the minorities and felt therefore they currently had little to hide. The same may not be true in the Southern Provinces of the Soviet Union, with the tensions of Afghanistan and Iran so pertinent to home policy. On the other hand, initial reactions from Moscow have been positive. It remains to be seen whether the sceptics again would prefer the filmmaker to steer clear of attempting to gather footage for the public under such difficult constraints. It might be that the anthropological filmmaker is the only person whose material can provide real filmed insight into the working of Soviet society by showing how that society deals with its minorities.

THE MAJOR FILMS OF ANDRÉ SINGER

THE KIRGHIZ OF AFGHANISTAN (1976). A film by Charlie Nairn with Nazif Shahrani and André Singer. 52 minutes, colour, sound, English subtitles. Distributor: Granada International, 36 Golden Square, London W.1. 7348080.

KHYBER (1979). A film by André Singer. 53 minutes, colour, sound, English subtitles. Distributor: Granada International.

THE PATHANS (1979). A film by André Singer. 52 minutes, colour, sound, English subtitles. Distributor: Granada International.

AFGHAN EXODUS (1980). A film by André Singer. 52 minutes, colour, sound, English subtitles. Distributor: Granada International.

WITCHCRAFT AMONG THE AZANDE (1982). A film by André Singer. 52 minutes, colour, sound, English subtitles. Distributor: Granada International.

THE KAZAKHS OF CHINA (1983). A film by André Singer. 52 minutes,

colour, sound, English subtitles. Distributor: Granada International.
THE CAMP ON LANTAU ISLAND (1984). A film by André Singer. 52 minutes, colour, sound, English subtitles. Distributor: Oxford Ethnographic Films Ltd., 98 Mortlake Road, Kew, Richmond, Surrey. (01 876 6728).
THE LOST TRIBES (1984). A film by André Singer. 52 minutes, colour, sound, English subtitles. Distributor: Oxford Ethnographic Films.
A MAN WITHOUT A HORSE (1984). A film by André Singer. 52 minutes, colour, sound, English subtitles. Distributor: Oxford Ethnographic Films.
STRANGERS ABROAD (1986). Six films by André Singer. 52 minutes each, color, sound, English subtitles. Distributor: Central Television, International, 46 Charlotte Street, London, W1. 6374602.

REVIEWS OF THE ABOVE FILMS

Beattie, J. (1982). Review of WITCHCRAFT AMONG THE AZANDE. Royal Anthropological Institute Newsletter No. 42
Feuchtwang, S. (1983). Review of THE KAZAKHS OF CHINA. Royal Anthropological Institute Newsletter.
Henley, P. (1984). Recent Development in Ethnographic Film Making in Britain. IN Die Fremden Sehen, M. Friedrich, ed. Ethnologie und Film. Munich: Tricksterverlag, pp. 145-159.
Leis, P. (1985). Review of WITCHCRAFT AMONG THE AZANDE. American Anthropologist 87(4): 1066-1067.
Muecke, M. (1986). Review of THE LOST TRIBES. American Anthropologist 88(3:) 780-781.
Tapper, N. (1978). Review of THE KIRGHIZ OF AFGHANISTAN. Royal Anthropological Institute Newsletter No. 13.
Tapper, N. (1979). Tribal Society and Its Enemies. Royal Anthropological Institute Newsletter No. 34, pp. 6-7.
Tapper, N. (1980). Review of THE PATHANS. Royal Anthropological Institute Newsletter No. 38, pp. 5.

Contributors

CONTRIBUTORS

TIMOTHY ASCH is an anthropologist and ethnographic filmmaker. In 1950-1951, he studied at the California School of Fine Arts and later apprenticed with Edward Weston, Ansel Adams, and Minor White. He received his undergraduate degree in anthropology at Columbia University in 1959, having worked with Margaret Mead, Conrad Arensberg, and Mortin Fried. He studied at the African Studies Program at Boston University and read anthropology from T.O. Beidelman at Harvard University, obtaining his masters degree in anthropology from Boston University in 1964. He has taught anthropology at Brandeis University, New York University, Harvard University and has been a senior research fellow at the Australian National University's Institute for Advanced Studies' Department of Anthropology as well as a Visiting Research Scholar at McQuare University's Department of Anthropology near Sydney, Australia. He is now Professor of Anthropology at the University of Southern California where, with several of his colleagues, he directs the Graduate Program in Visual Anthropology. At present, he is the editor for the American Anthropology Association's Society for Visual Anthropology. He was co-founder, with John Marshall, of Documentary Educational Resources and in 1973-1974 Adjunct Associate Professor of Film and Assistant Director of Brandeis University's Film and Media Communications Program. He has made, or has helped to make, over 70 ethnographic films, several of which have won international awards and he has written extensively on ethnographic filmmaking. His latest work, in collaboration with Linda Connor and Patsy Asch, entitled J E R O TAPAKAN, BALINESE HEALER, has been published by Cambridge University Press. Currently, he is making a film of an Ata Tana Ai, society wide, purification ritual (the island of Flores in Eastern Indonesia) with Douglas Lewis and Patsy Asch, and a film about a Balinese village cremation with Linda Connor and Patsy Asch. He is going back to the Venezuelan jungle to continue his earlier studies of the Yanomamo Indians of southern Venezuela.

ASEN BALIKCI's present position is Professor of Anthropology at the University of Montreal and Chairman of the Commission on Visual Anthropology of the International Union of Anthropological and Ethnographic Sciences. He did his undergraduate studies in Geneva, Switzerland and completed his Ph.D. in Anthropology at Columbia University in 1962. Much of Balikci's field work was done in several Eskimo and Indian communities,

383

and in Afghanistan. This work outlined ethnography and processes of ecological adaptation (1957-1965). A example of one title of such articles to come out of these studies is: "Pakhtun Nomads of Northwestern Afghanistan: Political Leadership and KInship Structure." Asen Balikci has published numerous articles and monographs, including THE NETSILIK ESKIMO (Doubleday, 1970). Notable films include The Netsilik Eskimo film series (10 1/2 hours, distributed by the National Film Board of Canada), SONS OF HAJI OMAR (1 hour long documentary on a Pakhtun nomad family in Afghanistan). Of Balikci's special projects, a notable undertaking was MAN: A COURSE OF STUDY, which was an anthropology curriculum program for the elementary grades (distributed by Curriculum Development Associates, 1211 Connecticut Avenue, N.W., # 414, Washington, DC 20036).

PETER BIELLA received a Ph.D. in cultural anthropology from Temple University in 1984 and an M. A. degree in film production from San Francisco State University in 1975. His dissertation, THEORY AND PRACTICE IN ETHNOGRAPHIC FILM, concerns three films he directed in Tanzania about the pastoral Ilparakuyo Maasai. The thesis emphasizes the Brechtian approach to film style and extends Biella/s earlier essay THE LOGIC OF IRONY: MARY HARTMAN (1979). Recently, Biella completed production for a two-hour videotape, KA TEI: VOICES OF THE LAND (1985) which analyzes the social and economic articulations of a Cabecar Indian community with the dominant capitalist economy of Costa Rica. Biella is head of Contemporary Historians, a non-profit corporation that facilitates production of anthropological media. Anthropological interests independent of media include pastoralism, "development," and theories of ideology. Essays on these topics temper structuralism with political economy. Biella has exhibited his still photography and drawings, and has written a number of short stories, plays and poems.

JOHN COLLIER, JR. was born in Sparkhill, New York in 1913. He was trained in the Fine Arts (painting) and apprenticed to a western muralist, Maynard Dixon. He studied at the California School of Fine Arts and turned to photography to document the Great Depression. He joined the Farm Security Administration, Photographic Section, directed by Roy E. Stryker. Later the section became a branch of the Office of War Information. In 1943, he joined the Merchant Marine, sailing to England and the Mediterranean. In 1945, he joined the photographic section of Standard Oil (NJ), also directed by Stryker. While there, he documented oil exploration and use in the Canadian Arctic and in South America. He completed a photo-ethnographic study of the Otavalo Indians in the Andes of Ecuador which was later published (1949) by the University of Chicago Press as

THE AWAKENING VALLEY, with Anibal Buitron. In 1948, he made a photographic survey of Navajo culture and published an article in THE FARM QUARTERLY.

He worked as a Research Assistant for Cornell University to develop research methodology for photography in anthropological studies. He made a photographic survey of "Stirling County" in the Canadian Maritimes under Dr. Alexander H. Leighton for a social-psychiatric research project on English and Acadian-French adjustments to rapid technological change. He worked with the Cornell Fruitland Project on the Navajo Reservation in an applied anthropology program to encourage development of a pastured sheep economy on irrigated lands. Later, he was involved in fieldwork for a year on the Cornell-Peru Vicos Project, an applied anthropology program to improve agricultural techniques and to develop self-reliance and self-direction among the hacienda peons. He photographed a cultural baseline against which to study the process of change. He completed a 16mm film for Wide Wide World TV series. Some footage from this shooting was later incorporated into a CBS special SO THAT MEN ARE FREE (1962), which documented the final sale of the Hacienda Vicos to the peons.

He received a Guggenheim Fellowship in 1957 to work on photographic methods for anthropology. This work culminated in a teaching career and publication of VISUAL ANTHROPOLOGY: PHOTOGRAPHY AS A RESEARCH METHOD (published by Holt, Rinehart and Winston, 1967).

In 1958, he joined the California School of Fine Arts (later San Francisco Art Institute) as an instructor of photography, and has taught there almost continuously since. He was awarded an Honorary Doctorate in Fine Arts in 1978. In 1961 he started teaching at San Francisco State College in the Anthropology Department and the School of Education, developing courses in Visual Anthropology, Nonverbal Communication, Cross-Cultural Education, and Multi-Cultural Education.

In 1962-1963, he did photographic research on the life style of relocated Indians in San Francisco, part of a project directed by James Hirabayashi at San Francisco State University, on a National Institute of Mental Health grant. In 1968-1969, he participated in research and evaluation of Eskimo education for the National Study of American Indian Education, using Super-8 film. This was published as ALASKAN ESKIMO EDUCATION: A FILM ANALYSIS OF CULTURAL CONFRONTATION IN THE SCHOOLS (Holt, Rinehart and Winston, 1972). Starting in 1972 on a Spencer Foundation grant, he did film research on Navajo-controlled Rough Rock Demonstration School, an ethnography of classrooms. Under the same sponsorship, he also did film research in schools in the San Francisco Bay area, recording and analyzing twenty classrooms on film, culminating in EDUCATION FOR ETHNIC DIVERSITY.

LINDA H. CONNOR is a lecturer in the Sociology Department, University of Newcastle, New South Wales, Australia. She received her Ph.D. in anthropology in 1982, from Sydney University, Australia. Since 1976, she has completed three years fieldwork in Bali, Indonesia, focussing on the relationship between traditional and modern systems of healing, and the impact of wider social changes on rural Balinese society. Her ethnographic film collaboration with Timothy and Patsy Asch began in 1978 and continues to the present. They have completed four films on Balinese healing, and are currently working on a fifth film, about a cremation ceremony in a small Balinese hamlet. Dr. Connor, with Timothy and Patsy Asch, has written an ethnographic film monograph (JERO TAPAKAN: A BALINESE HEALER, published by Cambridge University Press, 1985) to accompany the Balinese healing films, . She also plans to write a monograph to accompany the forthcoming cremation film.

JAMES C. FARIS is professor of anthropology at the University of Connecticut, having taught previously at McGill University and the University of Khartoum. His Ph.D. was received in 1966 from Cambridge University. He has published on Newfoundland fishing communities, on the Nuba Mountains region of Sudan, and on the Navajo of the American Southwest, as well as on theory, political criticism, art, cognition, and cultural knowledges in general.

SOLVEIG FREUDENTHAL is a Research Assistant at the Department of Social Anthropology at the University of Stockholm, Sweden. She is engaged in research on the transmission of culture in bilingual Turkish-Swedish kindergartens. She has also completed training in documentary film production at the Swedish Film Institute and has made several documentaries and anthropological films.

PAUL HOCKINGS (b. 1935, England) studied anthropology at the Universities of Sydney, Toronto, Chicago, Stanford, and California (Berkeley). He has written several articles on the Irish village dealt with in this book, as well as many articles on the tribal and peasant cultures of South India. He has edited several books, among them PRINCIPLES OF VISUAL ANTHROPOLOGY (1975), A BIBLIOGRAPHY FOR THE NILGIRI HILLS OF SOUTHERN INDIA (1978), BLUE MOUNTAINS: THE ETHNOGRAPHY AND BIOGEOGRAPHY OF A REGION IN SOUTH INDIA (in press), and, with Junichi Ushiyama, AEZOJIN-RUIGAKU (1979). He is currently editing a collection of essays on social organization contributed by a wide range of anthropologists, and is also the author of two books, ANCIENT HINDU REFUGEES: BADAGA SOCIAL

HISTORY 1550-1975, and SEX AND DISEASE IN A MOUNTAIN COMMUNITY (both 1980). He has worked as an anthropologist on several documentary films, including THE VILLAGE (1968) and THE MAN HUNTERS (1970). As this book goes to press, he is completing a study of Badaga ethics as expressed in their folk literature.

SUSANNA M. HOFFMAN received her doctorate in anthropology from the University of California at Berkeley specializing in social structure, symbolism, psychological anthropology and European culture. A former associate professor of anthropology at the University of San Francisco, she left the position to become a full time writer. She now writes books, articles and films for both academic and popular audiences. Among her recent works are: MEN WHO ARE GOOD FOR YOU AND MEN WHO ARE BAD (1987, Ten Speed Press); THE EROTIC BOND (forthcoming 1988, Simon and Schuster); GOOD AND PLENTY (forthcoming 1988, Harper and Row); "The Nature of Culture" (an introduction to THE FACES OF CULTURE film series); THE CLASSIFIED MAN (1988, Coward McCann); numerous articles and features appearing in such newspapers and magazines as LONDON EVENING NEWS, LOS ANGELES TIMES, BOSTON HERALD, COSMOPOLITAN, NEW WOMAN, and a column for THE NEW YORK TIMES syndicate on such topics as: "The Wages of Neglect," "Step by Step to Leisure Land," "The Enemy Within," and "We All Grew Up to be Cowboys."

She has appeared on numerous television shows, including the Phil Donahue Show, Hour Magazine, and David Suskind and radio shows nationwide and as far away as Great Britain and Australia.

Dr. Hoffman is currently serving on a national AIDS task force in anthropology and is working on another book. The mother of two teenage children, she writes from her house in Oakland, California.

ALLISON JABLONKO was born in Switzerland in 1936. She travelled widely with her American parents as a child. She attended school in Boston, attended M.I.T. from 1954-1956, and received her B.A. in Religion from Mt. Holyoke in 1958. After two years of study in Austria and Germany, she entered the Department of Anthropology of Columbia University, and in 1963, joined by her husband, she took part in the Columbia University Expedition among the Maring of the Simbai Valley in New Guinea.

After a year of filming in the field, she returned to New York where she studied human movement with Irmgard Bartenieff, who introduced her to Labananalysis. This proved to be a powerful tool for the analysis of the visible movement patterns in the research footage, and led to a Ph.D. dissertation on Maring movement in dance and daily life. The dissertation was the first to include a film as part of the written presentation: MARING IN MOTION (Distributed by The Pennsylvania State University, Audio

Visual Services, Special Services Bldg., University Park, PA 16802).

Returning to New Guinea in 1968, she and her husband continued to make research footage among the Maring, and also made a film record of the fieldwork of French anthropologist, Maurice Godelier, among the Baruya of the Eastern Highlands.

Since 1969 she has lived with her husband and two daughters in Italy, devoting most of her attention to family life until 1979, when it was again possible for her to work with the earlier footage. In cooperation with Italian colleagues, she made an eight episode series on the Maring people, for Italian public television. She then joined Stephen Olsson in making two films on Godelier and the Baruya: "TO FIND THE BARUYA STORY" and "HER NAME CAME ON ARROWS" (distributed by C.E.M., Industrial Center Building, Suite 260, Sausalito, CA 94965).

She is currently exploring low-budget film and video production, hoping to enhance the possibilities of research filming, general presentation, and, especially, access to the footage by people in Papua New Guinea.

SABINE JELL-BAHLSEN (Berlin/Germany, 1950) is self-employed with Ogbuide, Ltd., Film Productions, in New York City, pursuing various independent projects in film and anthropology. She was educated in Berlin, and at the New School for Social Research in New York, where she received her Ph.D. in 1980, and where she is currently pursuing a certificate in filmmaking. She did fieldwork among the Igbo of South Eastern Nigeria in 1978-1979, and produced four ethnographic films in co-operation with Georg Jell.

GEORGE J. KLIMA is an Associate Professor of Anthropology in the State University of New York at Albany, New York. He received his graduate training in Anthropology from Syracuse University and the University of California at Los Angeles. He holds a Ph.D. from the University of California, Los Angeles and has taught at Syracuse University, University of California, Los Angeles and at the University of Southern California.

Fieldwork was conducted among the Barabaig, a cattle-herding society in Tanzania, East Africa, during which he used cinematography and still photography as aids to data-collection and historical record. His interest in photography started as a hobby in his youth and served as a foundation for more serious study of filmmaking in later years. While he had no formal training in photography, his extensive reading, attendance at film lectures, conferences, and occasional auditing of film courses helped to broaden and deepen his understanding of the nature of film and its place in the communication of ideas and concepts in anthropology.

Among his publications are THE BARABAIG: EAST-AFRICAN CATTLE-HERDERS and a book on innovative filmmaking, MULTI-ME-

DIA AND HUMAN PERCEPTION. His film BARABAIG, is distributed by PCR, Pennsylvania State University. He is currently teaching courses that combine ethnography and ethnographic film with various concepts and models developed in cultural anthropology.

JUNE NASH is Professor of Anthropology at the City College of the City University of New York and director of the Masters Program in Applied Urban Anthropology. She began her field work in Bolivia in 1969 following the completion of her field study of the Maya of Chiapas, Mexico. Filming was done in the second year of field work with the assistance of Roy Loe. June Nash is now working on the impact of industry in a New England Industrial Town in Pittsfield, Massachusetts.

JON L. OLSON is professor of anthropology at California State University at Los Angeles, where he teaches the course in anthropological film. He received his Ph.D. in anthropology (1972) from Michigan State University, where his research in Northern Mexico was sponsored by the National Institute of Mental Health. His publications are in the areas of symbolism, political, economic, and medical anthropology. He has been film editor of CALIFORNIA FOLKLORE. He continues to do research in Northern Mexico and the Los Angeles area, and has led various student teaching/research projects to Mexico. His wife, Natalie, who co-produced WE BELIEVE IN NINO FIDENCIO, has a private practice in psychology in the Los Angeles area, and specializes in the treatment of clients from non-western cultural backgrounds.

COLETTE PIAULT, a social anthropologist and filmmaker, is Director of Research at the CNRS (Centre National de la Recherche Scientifique) Paris, France. She received her Ph.D. in Sociology from the University of Paris (Sorbonne, 1963). She was Post-Doctoral Research Fellow at the University of California (1963-1964), studying linguistics and semantics. She did field work in West Africa between 1958 and 1967, in France 1967 to 1973, and now, able to speak Greek, she works in Greece since 1974. She published an article in Dell Hymes (ed) entitled "The Use of Computers in Anthropology" (1965), and a book on daily life of Hausa women of Niger. She was the editor and contributor to PROPHÉTISME ET THÉRAPEUTIQUE, a book on Africa (published by Hermann in 1975).

She was responsible for a Research Team of the CNRS "Social and Familial Structures in Greece" (1977-1986) and editor of a collective international book FAMILY AND PROPERTY IN GREECE AND CYPRUS (published in 1985 by Harmattan in Paris). She learned filmmaking in 1965 at the Musée de l' Homme, Paris and shot three films (camera and sound) before her Greek series. She was associated with the NFTS to make 3 films in the Greek series.

She is co-editor of a special issue of the journal of the Association of French Anthropologists (AFA) dedicated to visual anthropology (May 1984). She is now responsible for an annual film seminar "Regards sur les Sociétés Européennes" dedicated to European anthropological and sociological films, and General Secretary of the French Association for Visual Anthropology (SFAV), the thematic section of the French Association of Anthropologists (AFA)..

Her field work is focussed on the problems of migrations from the point of view of the deserted village. She published an article on that subject in French (National Center for Social Research, EKKE, Athens).

JACK R. ROLLWAGEN is an anthropologist, editor, publisher, and filmmaker. He has edited and published the journal URBAN ANTHROPOLOGY since 1972. Since 1986, the journal is called URBAN ANTHROPOLOGY and STUDIES OF CULTURAL SYSTEMS AND ECONOMIC DEVELOPMENT. He is also editor of a series for SUNY Press, ANTHROPOLOGICAL STUDIES OF CONTEMPORARY ISSUES. He founded the Society for Urban Anthropology, now a component of the American Anthropological Association, and served as its first president. He has also served as co-president of the Society for Latin American Anthropology, another unit of the American Anthropological Association. He served as editor of the NEWSLETTER for the Society for Visual Anthropology for three years, and then served as president of the Society for two years. He received a postdoctoral M.A. degree in Humanities in 1979 with a concentration in film analysis and filmmaking in order to begin the production of anthropological films. His interests in film production are in visually rich and anthropologically insightful films, a combination which he feels possible even with an anthropologist as director of the project.

DON RUNDSTROM is a visual anthropologist/ethnographer living in Santa Fe, New Mexico. As an independent scholar and teacher, he works as a consultant and researcher for educators, museums, and special projects and lectures on various subjects including Japan, cross-cultural and non-verbal communication, and visual, applied and cultural anthropology. He is on the Board of Directors of the Society for Visual Anthropology and has participated in various symposia on visual anthropology. He is currently a Ph.D. candidate in anthropology at UCLA. His M.A. in Interdisciplinary Studies in Social Sciences at San Francisco State University produced a collaborative pioneering visual monograph in the social sciences and provides an interdisciplinary perspective for his work. His projects encompass still photography, motion picture film, video and graphics that utilize both contemporary and historic/archival material. He has conducted fieldwork in various cultures, including an extensive visual ethnographic research project in the Eastern Highlands of New Guinea focusing on the cultural transmission of aggression. His work in visual anthropology includes two films in distribution: THE PATH with Ron Rundstrom and Clinton Bergum (with an accompanying ethnographic monograph, JAPANESE TEA, THE RIT- UAL, THE AESTHETICS, THE WAY); and UPROOTED! A JAPANESE AMERICAN FAMILY'S EXPERIENCE, centering around their World War II concentration camp incarceration. The latter film utilizes both home movies and family album photographs combined with the narrative of a family member. Training in traditional Japanese art forms and experiences in Okinawa, Japan, New Guinea, and with various ethnic groups in the United States have encouraged him to explore communication theory from an anthropological perspective and explore how information is processed at the tacit levels of culture. In particular, his interests lie in how this relates to the use of images to identify and communicate ritual aesthetics, cultural symbolic metaphors, symbolic processes, and the transmission of cultural identity.

ANDRÉ SINGER is adjunct associate professor of anthropology at the University of Southern California. He is Chairman of Oxford Ethnographic Films and a Vice-President of the Royal Society for Asian Affairs. From 1971-73 he was research assistant to Professor Sir Edward Evans-Pritchard under whose supervision he did an Oxford University doctorate on tribal migrations in Eastern Iran. From 1973 to 1983 Dr. Singer researched, pro- duced and directed films for Granada Television's DISAPPEARING WORLD series of which he became the Series Editor after the departure of Brian Moser. He has produced and directed over twenty-five documentaries for Network Television in Britain, and has won several international film awards. Dr. Singer is the author of GUARDIANS OF THE NORTH-WEST FRONTIER: THE PATHANS (1982), and LORDS OF THE KHYBER (1984) and editor of A HISTORY OF ANTHROPOLOGICAL THOUGHT by E.E. Evans-Pritchard (1981).